THE ENCYCLOPEDIA OF
INTERIOR DESIGN
■ & DECORATION ■

NONIE NIESEWAND ■ MIKE LAWRENCE

THE ENCYCLOPEDIA OF
INTERIOR DESIGN
& DECORATION

NONIE NIESEWAND ■ MIKE LAWRENCE

Macdonald Illustrated

A Macdonald Illustrated BOOK

First published in Great Britain in 1988 by
Macdonald & Co (Publishers) Ltd
A member of Maxwell Macmillan Pergamon Publishing
Corporation

First reprint 1991

ISBN 0 356 17242 2

This book was designed and produced by
Quarto Publishing plc
6 Blundell Street
London N7 9BH

Art Editors: Nick Clark, Ann Sharples
Editors: Emma Johnson-Gilbert, Stephen Paul,
Peter Brooke-Ball, Ricki Ostrov
Art Directors: Alastair Campbell, Pete Laws
Editorial Directors: Christopher Fagg, Jim Miles
Photographer: Rose Jones
Illustrators: Sotos Achilleous, David Ashby,
Stephen Gardiner, Simon Roulstone, Dave Weeks
Special thanks to: Phil Chidlon, Judy Crammond,
Mick Hill, Anne Holker, Lucinda Montefiore,
Judy Martin, Deirdre McGarry

Typeset by Dimension Typesetting, Leaper & Gard and
Text Filmsetters Ltd
Manufactured in Hong Kong by
Regent Publishing Services Ltd
Printed by Leefung-Asco Ltd, Hong Kong

Macdonald & Co (Publishers) Ltd
Orbit House
1 New Fetter Lane
London EC4A 1AR

CONTENTS

SECTION ONE: STYLE AND COLOUR

STYLE   8
COLOUR   28

SECTION TWO: ROOM DESIGN

LIVING AREAS   48
MEDIA ROOMS AND WORK AREAS   74
BEDROOMS   82
KITCHENS   110
BATHROOMS   136
AWKWARD SPACES   158

SECTION THREE: HOME DECORATING

MEASUREMENTS AND QUANTITIES   166
PAINLESS PREPARATION   169
THE COMPLETE PAINTER   201
THE COMPLETE PAPERHANGER   229
THE COMPLETE TILER   253
THE COMPLETE PANELLER   271
THE COMPLETE FLOORER   279
CEILING IDEAS   297
FINISHING TOUCHES   303

INDEX   314

SECTION ONE

STYLE   8

COLOUR   28

STYLE

Style: most sought after; most difficult to pin down. You may know someone who possesses that indefinable quality, just as you recognize it in a room or a house. Never confuse style with character. Property agents' endorsements of character — inglenook fireplaces and a collection of horse brasses — carry no pretence of style. Yet humble materials in the same setting — a drag washed apricot wall, rush matting underfoot, a basket for logs, loose covers in a flowery print on a comfortable sofa and basket chairs in all the colours of a pot-pourri — could be stylish.

Style has little to do with good taste either. The apartment of French designer, Olivier Gagnère, could hardly be described as tasteful, yet his bedroom is stylish in a most unusual way. He uses an invalid's steel walking frame as a clothes rail, keeps his television on a skateboard and installs his telephone on an extendable trellised arm at his bedside. As a backdrop for this mobile furnishing he chooses white lacquered walls, white painted floorboards and black Venetian blinds. It is this sense of drama, coupled with a deft use of materials, that creates his particular brand of style.

Stylish interiors constantly change, absorbing new enthusiasms in a timeless setting: pictures are moved about, patterns are transposed, a piece of glass suggests the colour of a piece of silk, a collection builds up on a table-top, and a lamp highlights some new find.

Professional stylists who create live-in interiors, rather than those artificial room-sets for magazines, are loosely grouped as designer/architects, and

interior decorators. The designer will consider the structure of the interior, make the most of space and light and add architectural details if necessary. The decorator chooses the materials and furniture to fit the scheme. Style is ageless: Art Deco stainless steel, chrome and black lacquer is used in an open-plan apartment; high-backed dark wood bedhead, chairs, towel rail and shoe rack sit in a Shaker-inspired, white-washed bedroom of monastic simplicity in New York City; Bauhaus geometrics are reproduced on Liberty cotton for 1980s upholstery, or car paint is sprayed on industrial components to complement the interiors of London architect, Eva Jiricna. All these contemporary interiors and furnishings have an originality that is timeless.

Modern interior design styles are numerous, so in order to provide guidelines for choosing one, this section covers the four major themes. They are grand style, which has its roots in the past, borrowing freely from classicism to Vic-

A witty interpretation of function and purpose is revealed in Marc Chaimowicz's desk and filing cabinet designed for the 'Four Rooms' exhibition (**above**). The 'lying-down' desk symbolises the artist's difficulty with the written word, yet there is real practicality in the filing cabinet design — a column to fill a space. Chaimowicz sees the interior as an ideal room to do nothing in. And there is a contemplative restfulness about the soft blues, the wavy lines of his fabrics, and the coloured glass panel set high in the wall.

The loft apartment of Ger van Elk in Amsterdam (**right**) displays the owner's love for Art Deco. His few handsome pieces, are set against a spacious, restrained background. Notice how the furniture and lamp are anchored by the rug, and only the two handsome tables break out of its confines to become display pieces on the golden floor-boards.

toriana; the country house style that combines simple crafts with down-to-earth materials; modernism which includes post-modernism, minimalism and high-tech; and eclectic — those idiosyncratic styles, such as surrealist, kitsch and retro, that defy conventional grouping.

Inspiration for style
Everyone has a particular room, or style of room, that they like or feel comfortable in. Inspiration for details often come from unexpected sources, so always take notes when you respond favourably to an interior. Designers and decorators do this all the time, scribbling down such details as picture framing colours, lamp shades and wall finishes.

So a lifesize sepia photograph of Charles Darwin's study, used as a backdrop in an exhibition at the Science Museum in London, produces some interesting design ideas based on Victoriana. The workmanlike scene, featuring bookshelves on either side of the fireplace, screened by a small curtain on rails, and the marble mantelpiece surround with a still-life of nature studies suggest the bookish and studious atmosphere suitable for a library or study

room. By contrast, a recent exhibition of the work of Raoul Dufy acted as inspiration for a range of fabrics, based on 1920s designs, showing willow and wheat-sheaf patterns in primary colours on a gigantic scale. Sometimes the work of a designer disappears for a generation and is then re-discovered and restored, or copied in a different setting at a later date. In 1980 the 'Willow' tearooms in Glasgow, Scotland, were renovated using the original designs for furnishings (lamps, rugs, even cutlery) of Scottish-born architect Charles Rennie Mackintosh (1868-1928). The single peacock feather motif and the tall ladder-back chairs — both features of his interiors — were used in the decor.

In the twenties, Irish designer Eileen Gray combined the thoroughness of the Bauhaus tradition with an oriental exoticism, for the interior of her house in Roquebrune, France. She used an interesting juxtaposition of steel, sycamore and glass, padded leather and lacquer for the closets and cabinets, furniture and furnishings, mirrors and light fittings.

Alternatively, it may be from paintings that we get inspiration for interior decorating: those cosy domestic scenes of Edouard Vuillard's, for example, in soft pinks, greys and lilacs, or Claude Monet's home at Giverny with the rush chairs in two tones of yellow, the blue and white china and the terracotta tiles. Van Gogh's bedroom at Arles, simply furnished, yet brightly coloured in sunshine yellow and blue, provides a basis for a stylish decorative scheme. Notice how the colours in these paintings always contrast light and dark, pale and deep. The current enthusiasm for pastels in formless rooms — icecream colours that threaten to melt away — merely emphasizes this point.

Interior designer, Diana Phipps, always adds a smidgeon of black to her colour schemes, off-setting the yellow and white gingham in her bedroom, for example. She uses black canopy supports, or threads a black velvet ribbon through a broderie anglaise bed pillow cover. Colefax and Fowler introduced a striking citric lemon to cut through the softness of pretty pastels in their newest Brook collection of chintzes. Even the minimalists, whose interiors are devoid of positive statements, so that paintings are propped against the wall and seldom hung lest they give an air of permanence to a place, will use a sharp colour on a cornice or skirting board to anchor the neutrals.

Contemporary rooms in houses built after the Second World War, reflect their time in many different ways. The height of the rooms, for example, suits the

Oriental-inspired interiors have an exotic appeal, the magic of the traveller in far countries, though these days the intrepid home decorator need go no further than the local shops to buy the lacquerware and silks, barks, rushes, jute and rugs of the East. Colours are Chinese red, marigold, the blue and white of china, or the vegetable dyes in spicy colours and natural weaves of India. The room (**right**) has the unifying element of an all-wooden floor called 'Random Plank'. It is made by Amtico from vinyl. Such a large expanse in wood would have been expensive and this alternative creates a pleasing painted finish underfoot. An oriental rug on top would look good, adding a splash of bold colour.

scale and shape of furniture which was fashionable at the time. This, in turn, often relates to the clothes people wore. The London home of David Harrison and Jean Barrow, has a distinctive fifties flavour and style. A couple of curvy armchairs, a cocktail cabinet, spiky wire frame chair, formica-topped table and bakelite radio are teamed with the black and white vinyl floor; the walls are flecked and dashed to suit the style of the period.

Discover what period your house was built and how it was meant to look. You can then decide whether to dress it up in authentic style, or change it completely in a way that is sympathetic to the architecture. For example, instead of using wall-to-wall carpeting in an open-plan sixties house, which was designed to house Scandinavian spiky-legged teak furniture, up-date it for the eighties with Japanese futon bedding rolls and bolsters on platforms, low tables for eating and folding screens for providing privacy within the open interior. Coach lamps outside a neo-Georgian house do not signify Georgian style unless you already have slender windows featuring lengthy, narrow panes, high ceilings, authentic mouldings, sanded floor boards, waxed golden from centuries of polish, and a fireplace surround of simple marble or stone. It would be better to remove the lamps and treat the furnishing in the austere English style that favours simplicity of line and purity of form, such as the lined oak furniture of the Ambrose Heal Collection.

Grand style

This is the style of kings and emperors, reborn in provincial fashion with inlaid woodwork, canopied beds, damask, flounced draperies and flocked papers with gilt edges. In scale and ambiance it recalls eighteenth-century paintings of stylish interiors, but all these details can be added to a modern room. So the elaborate patterned cloth that covers a round plywood table also conceals the television on the shelf below and a gilded mirror (an example of do-it-yourself water gilding) hangs on marbled gift-wrap paper, pasted directly onto the wall. David Mlinaric, a leading British interior designer, says that many people no longer want the real thing... 'They want cheap, effective artifice. Having mastered marbling, graining and stippling, they are going on to tackle draped curtains and gilding.'

Clearly, you cannot hope to achieve all the grandeur of an age-old craft, but simple adaptations are perfectly possible. A print room, often the ladies' sewing room in eighteenth-century houses, comes to

Style with simplicity Cotton curtains, floor cushions, a couple of wicker chairs and a palm. These simple objects make the room dance with pattern and light. Pattern upon pattern, colour set against colour are the reasons for this charming effect.

'Putting paint marks on cloth' is how designers Susan Collier and Sarah Campbell describe their distinctive textile designs. At the window *Côte d'Azure* from their 'Six Views' Collection, won the Duke of Edinburgh award in 1904. The inspiration for the design was the unfamiliar light and vegetation seen from a window in the South of France.

Grand Style means window-dressing on a large scale Glamour and artifice replace all that clean, scrubbed country style. The white walls are stippled, marbled and drag-rolled, floorboards are stencilled, not with the folksy patterns of the Mid-West of America but the Neo-Palladian designs from Venetian churches. A boring box spring mattress is draped in layers of fabric, creating a room within a room (**right**).

Four pillars anchored to the bedhead and bedstead with a wire strung up between are strong enough to support a pelmet in this style. Cloak the pillars in drapes tied round with a ribbon. For a more casual four poster, loosely entwine white cheesecloth saris around the pillars, taking up one end of the seven-metre-long fabric to loop over the structure so that it falls in soft swathes.

Designers Peter Sheppard and Keith Day laid these hand-stencilled wooden blocks (**centre**) in their own homes (they manufacture them). The designs on the linoleum were taken from Venetian churches. This one, San Zaccaria, is one of the most baroque designs of all time. In three individual marbles: white marble, black portico and pink fossilstone, the optical effect is stunning, even in a medium-sized room.

Peter Farlow's elegant paint finishes are well suited to the gracious proportions of Caroline and Charles Leveson's London house (**far right**). The soft blue of the drag-rolled walls can be difficult over a large surface which is why they chose the maize and white and turquoise striped chintz for the curtains, and terracotta for the chair seats.

life in a New York City bedroom, designed by Albert Hadley. He has taken a variety of engravings and prints from old books and cut them into ovals, octagons and rectangles to paste on to a lightly dotted wallpaper. Regardless of date or origin, engravings are mixed with different borders, corners and bows cut out to surround the prints, simulating frames and hanging chains. Hadley has used lacquered furniture, an oak veneer bureau and a rope pattern border paper running round the room under the cornice.

Another exponent of the grand style is Jacques Grange, French interior designer, who used the flatboards from a theatre set to evoke ancient Egypt in a Parisian bedroom. He created a four-poster bed frame from the painted columns, using sheets decorated with hieroglyphics from an American department store range. He surrounded the bed with a frieze of sphinxes and ornate borders and completed the theatrical backdrop with striped silk curtains and striped matt carpeting in muted colours of peach, grey-blue and terracotta.

Wall finishes are important with a grand style. Paint can be marbled or rubbed on with rags, varnished with matt finish or drag washed in the Victorian style. For traditional rooms, wall finishes are either marbled in panels, then varnished with a matt finish, or papered with stripes in the ranges popularly called 'Regency'. Fabrics are striped, plain, or chintzes in archive colours of blue, red, sage and amber. Furniture grouping depends on pairs placed symmetrically — two porcelain lamps on a pedestal; two Chinese ginger jars; two sofas set on either side of a central gilt table to support a bust, a clock, a vase. So regular heights are fixed in spacious rooms, and the sense of balance and proportion maintains the formal style.

A window dresser, or stage set designer, will maintain that you need this understanding of space and proportion. A grand window display in a London department store featured the new furniture for 1984 in a setting of drapes and columns, marbled by floating sheets of lining paper over oil paint. The drapes, in the deepest midnight blue, billowing in

folds from the ceiling and falling in flounces to the floor like theatre curtains, formed a neo-Palladian backdrop to the modern Italian electric-blue sofas and chairs and grey lacquered tables from Magistretti.

Laura Ashley takes window dressing ideas from a Victorian upholsterer's book at the Victoria and Albert Museum in London. Fabric is gathered into a swag across a wooden fireplace surround, festoons adorn the window, curtain drapes are tied back with ornate tassels, and cord is used in loops and bows to frame a selection of mahogany pictures.

Country style

Country style heeds the gardeners' maxim to plant, not in pairs but in odd numbers or in an irregular grouping. Vita Sackville-West, who created the Sissinghurst gardens in Kent, England, now a part of the National Trust heritage, believed in exaggeration: 'Big groups, big masses. I am sure it is more effective to plant twelve tulips together than to split them into groups of six.' A profusion of pattern and colour is an integral part of the country style. Vita's tower study has walls washed in soft ochre, hung with a French tapestry in blues, ambers and hunting green. There are rows of books, a large desk, a central table that houses a vase of flowers, and some faded Eastern rugs on a flagstoned floor. Honest materials, handcrafted treasures, a mixture of soft colours sifted together like pot-pourri will produce a country cottage atmosphere even if you have an urban view outside. This is a look that travels, like country mice, to the cities' more modest dwellings. It is a style attained with the irregularity of flagstone or boarded floors, old rugs, patchwork over an occasional table, blue and white china, sofas covered with a splashy cabbage rose printed cotton, a travelling rug or shawl thrown over the side.

The United States is the home of an eclectic country style, which evolved in the eighteenth and nineteenth centuries from the influence of the English, Irish, German, Scandinavian and Dutch communities. The Pennsylvanian Dutch interiors, with their blanket boxes stencilled with flowers and birds, stained floorboards covered with rag rugs, and iron bedsteads covered with a patchwork quilt, are now found far from Pennsylvania.

In a more spartan way, the Shaker interiors of the Mid-West are a source of plagiarism in homesteads which bear no relation to the original concepts of the religious community. The elegant high-backed chairs, the severity of line in the hand-carved dark wooden

objects set against whitewashed walls, and the simplicity of small brass candle holders and lamps, are Shaker elements used in purist new interiors.

The original source of the rustic style, associated with country living, is the hand-built wooden house. In the Catskill Mountains outside New York, home-owners short of cash, and in sympathy with the rolling hills and trees of their surroundings, pieced together some original wooden houses from an assortment of junk, such as old packing cases, discarded chimney pots and iron railings. Most of us could not achieve this idiosyncratic architectural style, even assuming that planning permission was granted. Yet there is plenty of scope for the do-it-yourself enthusiast like fabric designer Stephen Montgomery who colours and designs on white cotton slip covers with a fabric felt pen. He makes rugs in the same way, painting flower designs on to a canvas backing, and putting them on the green painted floorboards of his Connecticut cottage.

A coat of silvery grey paint, with silver embossing on walls, ceiling and woodwork creates this splendid effect (**above**). Recreate it yourself with those ornamental mouldings in lightweight polystyrene that are rather frowned upon by the Grand-Style enthusiasts. They come in myriad shapes and sizes and, once glued to the ceiling and painted over (with an edging of masking tape to stop smudged edges), they look every bit as good as plasterwork from the eighteenth-century masters. In this way you can turn an anonymous bedroom into a magical place. This bedroom is almost medieval with the battlement edging on pelmets, bed drapes in velvet and silver tassels centred on the cut-out motifs.

Country style involves natural textures and handcrafted pieces. Sometimes country style conjures up that rather weary look of the stripped pine, bread crocks, dried flowers and patchwork quilts of the 1970s, now a little over-worked. So these country interiors, all infected with the quirky, original enthusiasms of their owners, offer an idiosyncratic country-cottage style. Two small windows in a Suffolk country cottage (**left**) are given separate treatments by photographer Caroline Arbor. The window on the left has curtains that hang vertically, while the other window has festoon blinds that draw horizontally, a light-hearted attempt to break away from uniformity. Accessories accentuate this: a Victorian wax dummy poses beside the potted geraniums, and Art Nouveau mirrors and light fittings are set against a rural brick and flagstone background.

This folk art, rustic-style living room (**below far left**) portrays a richness of pattern and weave in its rugs and rushes, rocking chair and occasional chair, barrel tables and wood-burning stove — all in contrast to the modern technology of the white laminated kitchen glimpsed in the background.

Like a Somerset Maugham stage set, the bedroom (**below left**) has the style of old colonial rooms, the dress fabric, cheaper than furnishing material and perfectly adequate in plain or stripe, is gathered onto narrow poles and attached to the wall, on hooks. Battens painted the same colour as the drapes anchor them here and there, away from the simple rustic seat.

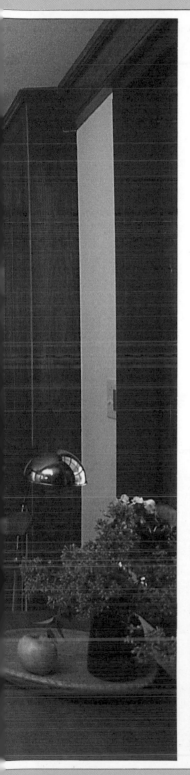

Purity of line and austerity of form make for a traditional style, which is often allied with country style because the pieces have that handcrafted quality.

Shaker furniture (**above and left**) has become classic. The Shaker community fled religious persecution in England in the eighteenth-century to establish a community in New England, USA. Their motto 'Hands to work, hearts to God' possibly inspired them to carve practical household items with such simplicity yet strength. The peg rail that holds chairs (**above**) is a feature of Shaker interiors. Its intention was to clear floor space for the constant cleaning that upheld the other maxim: 'Cleanliness is next to Godliness' Appreciation of simple classical furniture is not confined to antique dealers. Modern pieces of furniture are still designed with this austere, simply yet elegant look in mind.

These pictures are a reversal of all that is handcrafted or pre-packaged good taste — individual, image-conscious, excessive; above all, stylish.

The vivid colours, theatrical effects with inventive lighting and classical furniture shapes used by designer Roger Bazeley for the Skelzo apartment in the USA can be seen in the picture (**right**).

To create an interior like this, you need an understanding of dramatic effect as well as courage. One false move and the style is lost. Three yellow arums set in a floral wire base without a vase, the period street lamp used in a room with neon clouds decorating the ceiling, two shades of purple for the two-seater sofas, linked with a red chair — these moves are the mark of a stylist, whether you feel you could live with the effects or not. Even the flowers are chosen to surprise and startle.

British fashion designer Zandra Rhodes created this extravagant stage set (**above**) which has a gloriously tented ceiling, drapes, festoons, borders, cushions covers in fabrics designed by her. Even the painted floorboards have a squiggle stencilled on them. Notice how this room is anchored in the classical tradition of columns set at different heights but always symmetrical, from the lights backstage to the vases of tulips and the Carol McNichol porcelain vase containing a lily; the irregular form of the satin cactus breaks the uniformity.

homes) links the kitchen with the diner. Just as these crafts are used without adornment to contribute colour and pattern to the rooms, the modern materials used for drapes or upholstery are grandly finished with edgings, braids, borders and pipings as a formal contrast.

Surrealist and kitsch

In this age of self-parody, where everything and anything is sent up with theatrical exaggeration, visual jokes are creating a contemporary decorating style.

In the 1970s, when Christopher Strangeways introduced the walking teaset — teapot, cups and jugs, which stand on striped, stockinged feet — the British Design Council refused to recognize it as fulfilling the design criterion of 'function with purpose'. What could be more useless than a cup with feet? However, the walking teaset was a runaway success and can be found on tables or artificial green turf the world over.

Surrealist interiors also invoke criticism — and impassioned admiration — for their dramatic effects. Designer Antony Redmile creates this kind of startling interior using ostrich eggs to house light bulbs, stag antlers to decorate each dining chair, a turtle shell table, and an elephant foot umbrella stand. In amongst all this shell, skin and hide, stand eighteenth-century carved wooden blackamoors.

French designer Jacques Grange has an understated style which combines late nineteenth- and early twentieth-century excesses with a witty selection of contemporary objects. Wooden carvings of African children, made in Vienna in the nineteenth century, low African ceremonial stools, a very tall pierrot painting (so tall, he extended the mouldings above the door to balance it) and a free-standing bed built like the extinct dodo with a canopy of a beaked bird by François Lalanne — all of this transforms a bed-sitter into a stage set. The background is neutral, with cream sofas and a pair of cubist paintings hung above a cream ceramic tiled fireplace. In the bathroom there is a pink flamingo painted on the wall.

Kitsch style — the gnomes in the garden syndrome — is described by Jocasta Innes as 'the bad taste of one generation, rediscovered with hoots of glee by another.' Contributions to the 'naff' interior, assiduously being assembled by enthusiasts, are the mock leopard and tiger skin fabrics, spangles and sequins stitched on to cushions, mosquito netting bedheads and fake furs in electric colours. Fantastic paint finishes, mottled with metallic car spray, can be

Country style can embrace any country, as anthropologist Joss Graham and his wife Daphne, who trained as a decorator with Colefax and Fowler, illustrate in their Victorian home in London. They have used an artful display of textiles and rugs collected on their travels in Turkey and India, in search of items for their two shops, the Rug Shop and Oriental Textiles. Floorboards stained in earth colours are strewn with Indian dhurries and Caucasian kelims; walls are dappled with glowing Portuguese earth colours, ragged and dragged on with water, as a background to their eclectic collection of embroideries; appliqué work and weaving is hung in panels on the walls. At times these crafts from the East are used to suggest architectural detail: so an African tent band pinned up becomes a cornice, and a Gujarati appliqué work runner with a mango leaf border motif (a sign of welcome in Indian

stippled with a darker colour over a pale tonal base, to make a perfect back-drop as in pop-star Adam Ant's house.

Glamour and artifice replace all the earnest endeavours of the craft movement. To be stylish, the effect must be achieved speedily with staple guns and spray guns, using materials in unconventional ways, such as gift wrap ribbon for cornices and newspaper cut-outs for architraves. As Georgina Howell, journalist and author of 'In Vogue' muses, 'Interior decoration becomes rather theatrical, literally scene painting on a grand style. More important than status is styling, and the decoration of the 1980s is applied like so much stage costuming, with special effects in paint and finish, theatrical additions, classical and rural references so nothing is what it appears to be.'

Modernism and post-modernism

In the last decade fewer houses have been built and, as a result, there has been a positive trend in architectural planning to convert existing buildings — factories, warehouses, workshops, schools, even chapels — into unorthodox living accommodation. Because these buildings were not originally designed as residential homes, the interior design has been adapted to encompass such features as cast-iron girders, timber supports, high ceilings and industrial flooring. As a natural progression the high-tech style has developed to incorporate industrial design features in the modern home.

For high-tech homes you strip away the clutter and add the latest technology for wall and floor finishes, in lighting, labour-saving devices, sound and vision. You use fewer fabrics, have less decoration, fewer ornaments, make more structural changes, and own more equipment, from microwaves to electronics. Background material is often industrial with PVC blinds, rubber matting, steel, chrome, bulkhead lights, garage mechanics' trolleys, catering cups and saucers. A traditional mews in London takes on a new look with this architect's (**above**) house. The front is not out of keeping with the street, and shows how, by restructuring, you can remove guttering and clutter. Inside, the house was gutted and a spiral staircase links two floors with the roof garden (**right**).

An architectural shell, immaculately finished and lit, is the interior of an art historian's house in Utrecht (**left**). There is nothing self-conscious in this sparse, sculptural room. The well-proportioned sections of the hall lead the eye into the rest of the house. The relationship between the architectural details and the objects is established by the positioning of the sculpture (Giacometti), the table, the lights. There is great respect for form in the geometry of this room.

Modern interiors without the architectural details of an earlier, more gracious age, need careful furnishing to introduce style. Fabrics are one way to add interest to a scheme, but the modernist eschews them, preferring to keep the interior background suitably restrained. So colour and pattern are introduced in less conventional ways: with Rietveld furniture in one interior, or with a stained glass window in the other.

The graphic designers, in their house in Amsterdam, have relied on their collection of Rietveld furniture to give this living room (**right**) its distinctive style. Walls are plain white, floors covered in a subdued grey cord, Venetian blinds at the window. So the playful colours and stylish form of the Rietveld furniture gives the room its charm. Wooden boxes are used as seats. The height of the ceilings has been emphasised by the low furniture and the custom built high tower for housing electronic equipment — a lesson in offsetting low and high furniture to emphasise the proportions of a room.

Stained glass windows are currently enjoying a revival in modern buildings. Performance artist Marc Chaimowicz included one in his ideal room for the 'Four Rooms exhibition' produced by the British Arts Council. In this Amsterdam house (**far right**), the angularity of the stairwell and landing and the all white scheme is enlivened by the inset glass panel.

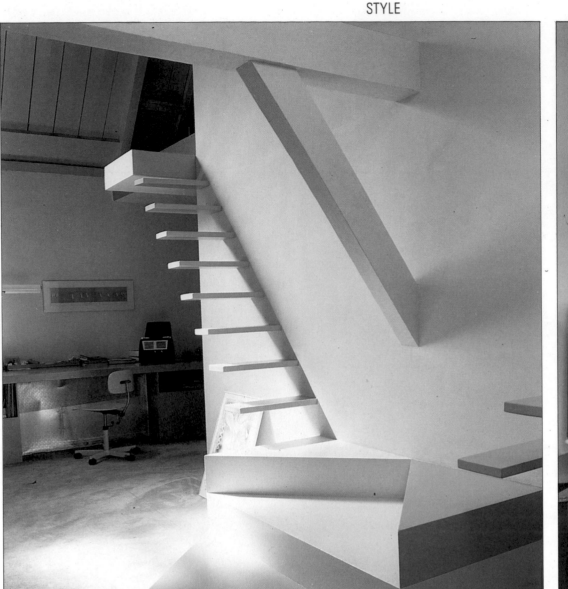

In the high-tech house, furniture is mostly mobile. Hospital trolleys are used to hold bathroom accessories and cosmetics, canteen trolleys display kitchen equipment and the television set is placed, for easy mobility, on a garage mechanic's tool box on wheels or, in the style of French designer Olivier Gagnère, on a skateboard.

Industrial track shelving presents items on view, and folding screens can be used temporarily to divide inner space. Nowadays even conventional middle-income furniture stores have trolleys and track shelving for hi-fi equipment, televisions, videos and home computers.

Italian lighting is favoured for this style of interior — use neon lights at floor level or fluorescent tubes, like street lighting, with a back-up system of photographer's clamp-on lights that can be moved around the room as desired.

Post-modernists (a term first used by historian and architect, Charles Jencks) appreciate classicism in much the same way that architects over the ages have done. When Edwin Lutyens and Herbert Baker made their architectural plans for imperial Delhi in the 1900s, they put forward their intention to 'build with the best elements of East and West', using colonnades, deep portal arches and columns. In his California home, Charles Jencks has used telegraph poles as columns to divide his house into four parts, representing

The period of a building need not determine its furnishing style. One of the skills of an interior designer is not to be intimidated by the age of the building.
Rather than slavishly follow the fashions of nineteenth century designers, this interior in Amsterdam (**above, centre**) retains the original ceiling mouldings, teamed with twentieth century furnishings.

The loft apartment of artist Ger van Elk in Amsterdam (**far left**) uses the pastel colours of the fifties to highlight the idiosyncratic stairs and joists, making a feature of the more

recent architectural structural changes.

Syrie Maugham first introduced the all-white room in the 1920s. This room (**far right**) is a contemporary version, with its industrial flooring and graphics very much a product of the 1980s. Yet the same decorating principle remains to offset one texture against another in a monochromatic scheme.

the four elements. Such iconography is a feature of the new modernist interiors.

Post-modernists hate clutter, shrink from excesses of fabric and resist fitted furniture. Their interiors offer a stripped aestheticism, as in the home of Piers Gough, a London architect, who has combined the sculptural with the functional by anchoring a pedestal basin in the centre of his bedroom.

Minimalism

Minimalists have a less committed approach than modernists. Nothing is anchored in its space, unless it is the fitted cupboard that hides the clutter and the ubiquitous futon. Paintings are propped against the wall lest they make too fixed a statement. Nothing is permanent.

Joe d'Urso, who has inspired a whole school of minimalist decoration in the United States, says that minimalism does not reduce individuality, but enhances it. He calls it a transformation of space. The living area is simplified to produce a clutter-free environment that allows everything to be appreciated individually. In d'Urso's Spanish revival house in Los Angeles, a casement window featuring 96 panes of glass forms the backdrop to a platform seating and sleeping area. Black scatter cushions and a superb Le Corbusier chaise longue give this minimalist decor a touch of class.

COLOUR

Putting colour on to wide open spaces — walls, floors and ceilings — and co-ordinating the furnishings, is the basis for all home decoration. It is also very rewarding. Colour can be matched, contrasted or highlighted with the use of paints, papers and fabrics to create both mood and style, change proportion, lighten space, emphasize good features and disguise bad ones.

So a cold north-facing room can be warmed with apricots and creams, accented with turquoise, or it can be made cosy with all the colours of an antique Kashmiri shawl, soft grey flooring, outlined with a charcoal skirting board, shutters stained a dappled red, and wall colour sponged with layers of lacquer red. Details such as lacquered boxes, a splash of turquoise glass, picture frames painted with gold, then antiqued with a rub-down of wire wool, give the room its accent colours.

Interior decorators define colours in these terms: advancing colours are those warm tones like red, orange or yellow, that bring a surface visually nearer; accent colours are the sharper contrast colours that heighten or lighten, complementary colours are the shades closest together in the spectrum, such as indigo, navy, sea green merging into jade; harmonizing colours are of the same intensity, either mellow as in coral with sand, or sharp like orange with lemon.

Colours have certain characteristics that need to be understood before you can use them to good effect. If you put a yellow square in a white square, it appears smaller than if you put an identical yellow square inside a black square of the same size. It is the juxtaposition of colours that makes them look different. Tone also changes so that yellow will appear lemony in a white surround, but hot and vibrant, like sunflowers, in a black background.

Even a white light is made up of bright colours. When sunlight shines through raindrops, it breaks up into these colours — hence a rainbow allows us to see them separately. If you use a triangular wedge of glass or a prism, to break up a ray of light, you will see the same six colours, always in the order of that childhood chant — red, orange, yellow, green, blue, indigo and violet — that make up the rainbow. The colour wheel is made up of the many tones and shades that range between these basic colours. A scheme that uses one colour in a variety of shades is called monochrome; so yellow schemes encompass lemon, mimosa, sunflower, saffron, mustard or banana. A toning scheme is made up of a combination of the colours that lie closest to each other in the spectrum, while contrast schemes are more vibrant, being made up of those colours which are furthest apart in the spectrum.

In any colour scheme there are subtleties: for example, when you add white to other colours they

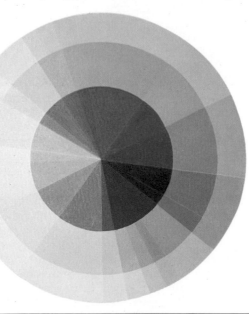

'Colour Wheel' by Bridget Riley (**left**) is not just an artist's impression of the power of colour, but a practical illustration of the tones, values and combinations of colour. Consider the many shades of any one colour from the big six on the wheel: red can be earthy as in terracotta, scarlet in the lacquer colours, palest pink, or coral. Orange, once the favourite colour in the kitchen, with everything orange from cast ironware to electrical gadgets, vibrates with heat and sets schemes aflame. It can also be tempered with neutrals or contained with dark woods. Yellow fills the room with light, and ranges from the warmth of sunflowers to the blandness of buttermilk, sharpened with citrus. Green brings the freshness of outdoors inside, from palest mint through willow green and grass green to the darkened green-like palm fronds. Blue, from turquoise and aquamarine to navy is adaptable, damping down the hot colours, making pales zing. Purple sounds better as the indigo and violet of the colour spectrum, and looks better too. Purple can be the colour of lilacs, lavender, blueberries, heather. Monochrome rooms rely on different textures and colour accents to carry such a great expanse of one colour. Walls carry the colour in this scheme (**right**) planned by Dulux, with woodwork, window blinds, vinyl flooring and upholstery all keeping to the white scheme, emphasised by the Mackintosh chair-back, and the steel grid system for electronics, the scatter cushions and the graphics to add a little accent colour.

Pastels have less immediate impact than brights with their more intense colours. This does not make them any easier to handle in a scheme. Anchoring pastels in a room needs a skilful hand if they are not to melt away in a rather sickly jumble of ice-cream colours.

The room (**left**) is a lesson in restraint, in which the cool and restful colour scheme with its blue-grey background, creamy furniture, rug the colour of bleached sand and palm tree in a wicker basket, give a Mediterranean feel to the room. Recessed downlighters illuminate the soft matt finish of the tongued and grooved boards.

In the room (**right**) the pastels jolt the colour scheme, an unusual role for pales to play, with the lines of the angular modern white rooms emphasised by an unexpected coral and lilac cupboard front. The fireplace becomes the focus of the room with its blue and white grid tiled border.

become light; if you add grey, the colours lose their brightness, and if you add black, the colours will darken and become richer. Nearly every fabric collection has a range of 'neutrals', ranging from white through cream to the colours of clay and peat and it is these tones that provide a simple background colour.

Texture will also affect the tone, so that in a neutral colour scheme the shaggy pile cream rug is complemented by the cream Navajo blanket striped in spicy shades, off-set with a white linen sofa and the pinks, oranges and yellows of the silk scatter cushions.

Response to colour is influenced by fashion and mood. We may become bored with one scheme and switch to another in search of a new stimulus. Fashion colours filter through to furnishings so that fabrics are now launched annually like fashion collections. Most

of these collections include fabrics, paints and papers in both plains and prints to help you co-ordinate an entire colour scheme for the whole house. A total-look colour plan with bed linen, as well as table linen and towels for the bathroom, can carry continuity into every room in the house.

Tricia Guild, the adventurous colourist of furnishing fabrics and wallpapers which sell at Designers' Guild showrooms in Europe, the United States and Japan, pioneers the changing fashions. In the seventies she introduced the pastel look that washed over, and absorbed, the primary colours of the Italian synthetics of the sixties. Now she introduces, for the eighties, the bright new geometrics in spicy shades, and the old design favourites, re-coloured for the 'Natural Classics' collection, based on shades of stone, peat and

clay. 'Colour creates each new look,' says Tricia Guild. 'Using those fresh, lively pastels in the seventies, we mixed patterns in the English country house manner, but nothing too grand, too contrived. It was this soft natural look that brought country colours into urban interiors, setting them off against old pine and fruit wood furniture. The greens were lime, the yellows lemon, the pink a coral to suit the informality of contemporary living in the seventies. Within three years this colour scheme softened again: the limes became pistachio, the lemons changed to cream, the coral bleached to peach. Then the 'Watercolour' collection in the late seventies introduced sharper accents of lavender, old rose and lime sherbet in full blown petal shapes, curved and rounded. All this sharpened into the angular geometrics of the 'New Angles' collec-

tion of the eighties, coloured in indigo, ochre and crimson.

'Colour moods change all the time, says Tricia Guild. 'At present turquoise leads, mixed with blues and greens in Mediterranean style.' This scheme can be seen in Tricia Guild's London office where she has damped down the colour with irregular striped 'Network' wallpaper in charcoal, emphasized with skirting boards painted in grey, the charcoal tumble-twist carpet giving depth to the scheme. Furniture is stippled and marbled with paint finishes, a tub chair covered in a brilliant turquoise glazed cotton to match the window blinds. The sofa is covered in fabric from the 'New Angles' collection in a charcoal and grey abstract pattern and the cushions quilted in glazed cotton pick out the turquoise with green and grey.

Furnishing fabrics and papers are presented annually like fashion collections. Tricia Guild, of Designer's Guild fabrics, sells her collection all over the world. In her living room (**above**) Tricia Guild wears black in emphatic contrast to the restrained white of her room, accented with splashes of vivid colour. 'Accent pale colours with a hint of strong contrast — not too much or you kill it — and damp down fiery colours with charcoal and grey,' she says. She applied this practical advice to her room: witness the finishes to the Roman blinds, piping on the sofa, the striped rug lain over the coconut matting, the hand-marbled paint finishes on the occasional tables. Another view of the living room (**right**) shows a jolt of vibrant colour introduced by the abstract painting which has slabs of the indigo and green reproduced in the glazed cotton 'Moonshine' cushion covers.

Tricia Guild says that there are no right and wrong colours; you should merely choose the colour you like best and complement it with other shades. Think of a single colour, say blue, use it in various tones and accent it all the time. Use tones in conjunction with texture to create effect. On different surfaces — wood, paper, cotton, vinyl and paint — colours will take on different depths of tone. That is why the little swatches shown by colour consultants can never give an idea of a colour scheme on a grand scale. A white surround, or the wood of a desk top can make colour look different. So too can walls in another colour, or a sofa upholstered in other shades. So where do you begin when choosing your colour scheme? Fabrics introduce colour combinations in a professional way, so choose a patterned piece you like and pick out the colours in it. Start with a large area of surface colour (the walls or floor) to harmonize or neutralize the fabric colours then paint accent colour round the cornice or skirting boards. A floral slip-cover in blue and green which concentrates pattern and colour in the centre of the living room can be picked out with a striped wallpaper in blue or grey, then the blue background of that slip-cover can be used for the curtains, edged with a green border. As a finishing touch, add silvery grey shades to the lamps.

Tricia suggests that you replace any large areas of colour you dislike in your new home, or add different shades of the same colour to it so that it becomes the basis of a scheme, rather than the intruder. You may hate the brown carpet, so reduce its prominence with other shades of brown so that it does not dominate the colour scheme. Furniture in different woods, such as walnut, oak, maple and pine, and furnishings in shades of brown, such as mahogany and russet, highlighted with cream and white wall surfaces can smarten up a dull decor.

Try accenting colour in your own room; buy a metre of cord or ribbon to wind around the curtains when drawn or use it as piping around sofa cushions. It is the quantity of colour that is as important as the tone. The more sophisticated the eye, the more risks you can take. Teach yourself more about colour by looking at paintings from the Impressionists onwards — the German Expressionists used bold colour combinations of greens and red. Study Howard Hodgkin's print (see page 54), Frank Auerbach's abstract paintings and learn how the balance of colour creates energy. 'Just one or two stronger tones like cherry red or brilliant blue set against white, cream or grey can look very striking,' advises Tricia Guild.

When you plan your first colour scheme for your home, caution often determines your final choice. To enliven your choice, colour consultants will show you swatches of colours that harmonise or contrast together. You can teach yourself more about the way in which colours work together by looking at paintings.

In the painting 'Saint Tropez, the Customs House Pathway' by Paul Signac (1905), (**above**), colours applied in mosaic-like daubs build up the structure of the painting from the soft blues of the horizon to the intense reds of the foreground. You can translate this in your home by introducing the pastel blues of the background colours, anchored with a warm apricot on the floor, accented with lime to achieve the same sunny aspect.

This colour woodblock print, 'Wisteria Blooms over Water at Kameido' (**centre, top right**), was painted in about 1857 by Japanese artist, Hiroshige. In the print, Hiroshige contrasted the stylised wisteria in cream with the soft blues and greens of the lake and foliage. In your home you can achieve this effect by painting walls in high gloss cream, and introducing green foliage in the form of house plants.

Cézanne, who painted this landscape, 'Mountains seen from l'Estaque' (**below right**) contrasted warm and cool colours like his predecessor Renoir. Translate such skills in your own interiors, using the cool, tonal colours to push out areas, the warmer ones to bring them nearer and into focus.

Edouard Vuillard, post Impressionist painter, imparted a rich glow to the soft pastels in all his paintings of interiors. The soft pinks and creams in 'The Laden Table' (**top, far right**) are anchored by the ochres and umber in his shadows — a simple illustration of how to prevent the pales from melting away in a formless scheme.

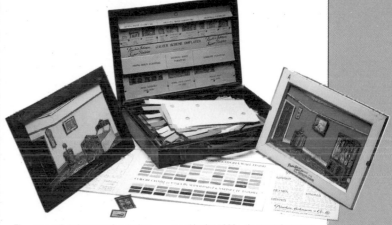

The conventional approach to colour schemes is to combine paint sample cards with fabric swatches as colour consultants do. You can do it yourself by choosing a fabric in many colours that you like, and using it as the base for your scheme, using some of the larger colour areas to reproduce on walls or floors, and the accent colours on small areas. In this travelling salesman's box (**above**) used in the 1930s, the samples were cunningly set against roomset cut-outs, with doors and windows, to give the impression of a room. Such an approach requires some caution, though, since larger areas dominate any colour scheme and the roomset in miniature cannot convey the final effect.

The Lacquer Colours

Red, the symbol of light in the Chinese Han dynasty is a good-luck colour, full of light, heat and energy. From as early as 206BC red has lit up every aspect of Chinese life.

Marigold, or chrysanthemum is the holy Hindu shade for garlands of flowers and the gilding that embosses lacquerware, never too strongly applied, but hinted at for its soft, sunny richness.

Blue and white, the colours of porcelain dates back to the days when the ballast on the ships on the spice route from the East was blue and white. In China, the first blue and white porcelain appeared around the middle of the thirteenth-century. The reds, blues and yellows of the lacquer colours are to be used in rooms with lacquered furniture, with bamboo, or white paper pleated into fan shapes or screened in the Japanese shuji. Walls are painted in high gloss paints or covered with silk; or less expensively, with bamboo or hessians. Floors are adorned with splendid rugs from Tibet or China, or more simply, with the sisal or jute of India. In the patterns, there are the broken tracery lines of the Japanese and Indonesian batiks, with the curious little animals that adorn them, or jungle flowers and foliage.

1. Cole and Son
2. Conran 'Ikat'
3. G.P. & J. Baker 'Hawaii'
4. Conran 'Ikat'
5. G.P. & J. Baker 'Jaipur'
6. G.P. & J. Baker 'Han'
7. Souleiado
8. Osborne and Little
9. John Oliver
10. John Oliver
11. Collier Campbell 'Spice Route'
12. Marvic Textiles
13. J. Pallu & Lake 'Cinnabar'
14. J. Pallu and Lake 'China Zoo'
15. Warner & Sons 'Semeru'
16. Arthur Sanderson & Sons
17. J. Pallu and Lake 'French Blue'
18. Marvic Textiles
19. Marvic Textiles
20. Charles Hammond
21. G.P. & J. Baker 'Chinese Schoolhouse'
22. Habitat Designs 'Nouda'
23. J. Pallu and Lake 'Cinnabar'
24. Laura Ashley
25. Mary Fox Linton
26. John Lewis 'Kitami'

Swatches shown here with turned down edges are wallpapers; other swatches are fabrics.

The tape measure is used as a scale device.

The document colours

Archive prints that are still popularly printed by the big textile designers usually have documented colours accompanying them. These specify that the leaves, if any, will be blue. This dates back to the time when vegetable dyes were used and yellow was overprinted on blue to get the green on leaves. The yellow always faded. Today's blue leaf comes from synthetic dyes but the presence of it means a document colour. Often hand-blocked prints form the collection on backgrounds the shade of pale tea. Some manufacturers still use the original pear wood blocks, now 120 years old.

In the nineteenth-century, William Morris gave this advice 'Have nothing in your house that you do not know to be useful or believe to be beautiful'. Today his patterns are documented. The designs of Owen Jones, a Victorian interior designer are also influential today. Mostly these designs are large, for Victorian buildings were more generously proportioned, but some have been scaled down for contemporary living, and there exists today a line of wallpaper and upholstery fabric with a Gothic pattern and navy, burgundy and colouring that has been named 'Mr Jones'.

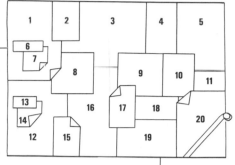

1. Cole and Son
2. Loo/Jofa
3. Tissunique 'Thorpe Hall'
4. G.P. & J. Baker 'Hungarian Point'
5. Liberty 'Honeysuckle'
6. Laura Ashley
7. Laura Ashley
8. G.P. & J. Baker 'Beauchamp'
9. Colefax and Fowler 'Haseley Acorn'
10. Arthur Sanderson and Sons 'Seaweed'
11. Chalon 'Forest Green' from Tissunique
12. Liberty 'Sita'
13. Laura Ashley
14. Laura Ashley
15. Arthur Sanderson & Sons 'Art Nouveau'
16. Liberty 'Hera'
17. Arthur Sanderson & Sons
18. John Oliver
19. Colefax and Fowler 'Passion Flower'
20. John Oliver

Swatches shown here with turned down edges are wallpapers; other swatches are fabrics.

The tape measure is used as a scale device.

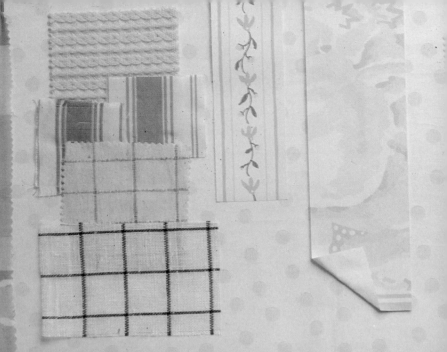

The neutrals

Colouring with neutrals is a matter of balancing the textures on floors and walls, with soft furnishings to off-set one against the other. It needs skill; a dash of magenta or a hint of ice blue can warm up or cool down the scheme and sharpen the mixture. Too much, and you will flatten them. Neutrals can be creamy with the brown tones, or icy with the blue greys. In India the five shades of white are actually specified in the ancient Vedic texts as the white of ivory, jasmine, sandalwood, moon-white (blued) and water-white (reflective).

In her New Delhi home, Pupul Jayakar, India's cultural director and organiser of the Festival of India worldwide has sandalwood tables set upon pale rush matting, walls painted in water-white to reflect a collection of paintings and form a backdrop to her art treasures of ancient stone carvings, terracotta figures, a bronze water vessel from Gujarat. 'In India we are known for our brilliant colours,' she says. 'Saffron, indigo, turmeric and chili red. Yet our skill in decorating lies in the harmony of tone, balance and texture in all the shades of white.'

Neutrals are flexible and easy to revive when you tire of a season's colour. Pep up last year's white and cream with bright accessories, a fresh plant, some contrast colour on the skirting boards or piping round the sofa cushions.

Sir Cecil Beaton wrote of the 1920's passion for all-white rooms: 'The white world made fashionable in the interior decorations of Syrie Maugham invaded the photographic studios. Every texture of white was sought in order to give vitality and interest: glass fibre, sheets of gelatine, cutlet frills, coils of carnival paper streamers, doves, egg boxes, cardboard plates, plaster carvings, driftwood branches.'

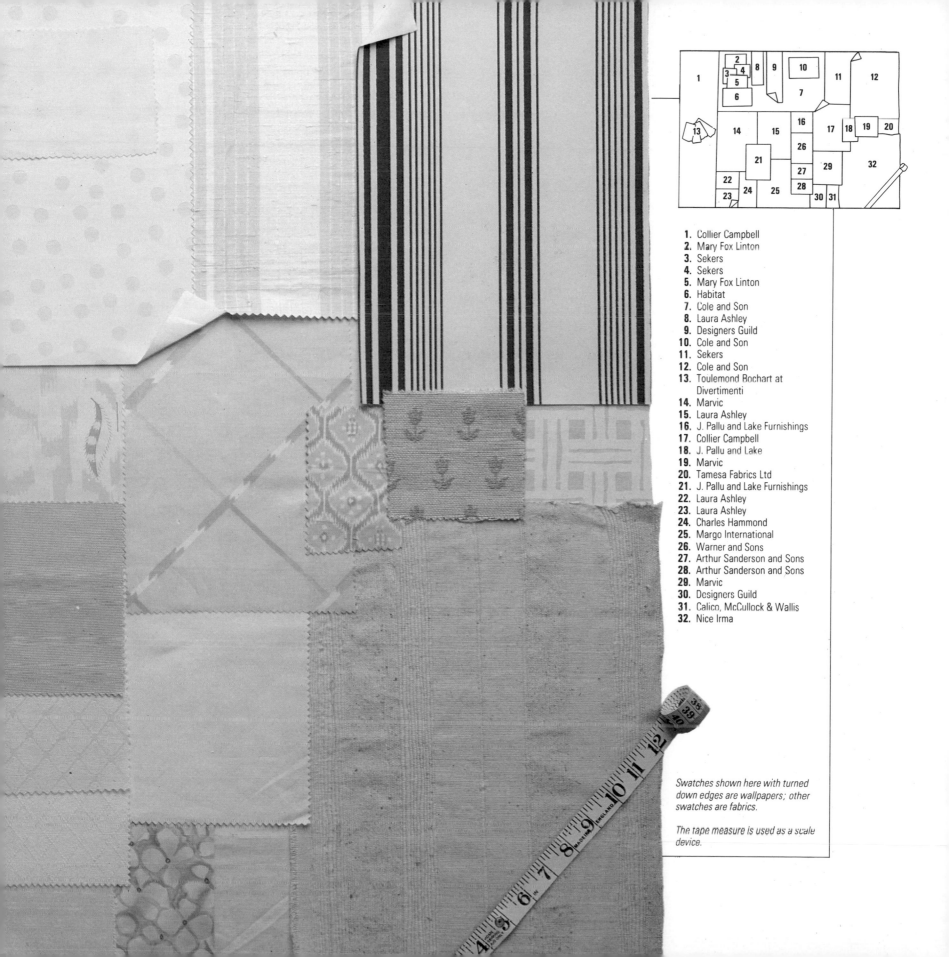

1. Collier Campbell
2. Mary Fox Linton
3. Sekers
4. Sekers
5. Mary Fox Linton
6. Habitat
7. Cole and Son
8. Laura Ashley
9. Designers Guild
10. Cole and Son
11. Sekers
12. Cole and Son
13. Toulemond Bochart at Divertimenti
14. Marvic
15. Laura Ashley
16. J. Pallu and Lake Furnishings
17. Collier Campbell
18. J. Pallu and Lake
19. Marvic
20. Tamesa Fabrics Ltd
21. J. Pallu and Lake Furnishings
22. Laura Ashley
23. Laura Ashley
24. Charles Hammond
25. Margo International
26. Warner and Sons
27. Arthur Sanderson and Sons
28. Arthur Sanderson and Sons
29. Marvic
30. Designers Guild
31. Calico, McCullock & Wallis
32. Nice Irma

Swatches shown here with turned down edges are wallpapers; other swatches are fabrics.

The tape measure is used as a scale device.

The pastels

Allied to the white look and the neutrals is the pale palette. This is the look of the faded chintzes, the soft colours of old rugs, pot pourri and summer gardens, the sort of look that has come to represent English style. Yet this country-house look translates well to the urban interiors in the ice-cream and candy colours of ice blue, soft pink, pale yellow, mint green and lavender. Pastels are mostly used round the room in multicolour combinations accented with deeper or sharper shades. To her 'Watercolour' collection, Tricia Guild of Designer's Guild adds a touch of deepest magneta to the softest colourings, as a piping on the sofa.

The pastels can be muddied a little the way painter Edouard Vuillard saw them in his interiors, with old rose and grey-blue accented with ochre and grey or charcoal.

1. Colefax and Fowler
2. J. Pallu and Lake Furnishings 'Canary'
3. G.P. & J. Baker 'Sierra'
4. G.P. & J. Baker 'Solange'
5. Marvic Textiles
6. Mary Fox Linton
7. Mary Fox Linton
8. J. Pallu and Lake Furnishings
9. Sekers Fabrics 'Brampton'
10. Liberty 'Sweetpea'
11. Toulemond Bochart at Divertimenti
12. Collier Campbell 'Raffia Braid'
13. Collier Campbell 'Okra'
14. Osborne and Little
15. J. Pallu and Lake Furnishings 'Surabaya'
16. J. Pallu and Lake Furnishings
17. Habitat
18. Tissunique
19. Warner & Sons 'Wood Anemone'
20. Marvic Textiles 'Seersucker'
21. Designers Guild
22. Designers Guild
23. Designers Guild
24. Designers Guild
25. Sekers Fabrics 'Arkley
26. Osborne and Little 'Messara'
27. J. Pallu and Lake Furnishings 'Primrose'
28. J. Pallu and Lake Furnishings

Swatches shown here with turned down edges are wallpapers; all other swatches are fabrics.

The tape measure is used as a scale device.

The mediterranean colours
Colours that dance with light, with the blue of the sea, the sky, the jade of the Greek-island sea, the sunny yellows and bleached sands of summer.

Use white for contrast, for coolness, or add the dusty green of olives, and terracotta and melon shades to hold down those vibrant blues. If the fabrics carry the pattern and colour, accent the upholstery.

Use jute matting or white tiles underfoot, paint open brickwork white, add basket-weaves and terracotta pots with plants. Patterns in this range seem to dance with light in the irregular wavy lines of birds on the wing, palm fronds that move, sandy ripples and dancing waves. Reduce their intensity with shade, damping down with the pales and the charcoals.

1. Collier Campbell 'Cote d'Azure'
2. Designers Guild papers and fabrics
3. Jonelle 'Bergen'
4. Mary Fox Linton 'Blue Waves'
5. Nice Irma
6. Tamesa Fabrics
7. Tissunique 'Bleu Ciel'
8. Tissunique 'Poussin'
9. Designers Guild 'Moonshine'
10. Warner & Sons 'Parasol Stripe'
11. Margo International
12. G.P. & J. Baker 'Sierra'
13. G.P. & J. Baker 'Sierra'
14. Habitat 'Pollen Ribbon'
15. Laura Ashley paper border
16. MacCulloch and Wallis ginghams
17. Laura Ashley 'Trellis'
18. J. Pallu and Lake Furnishings 'China Stripe'
19. Laura Ashley
20. J. Pallu and Lake Furnishings
21. J. Pallu and Lake Furnishings 'Nara'
22. Arthur Sanderson & Sons 'Trellis'
23. G.P. and J. Baker 'Lemon'
24. G.P. and J. Baker 'Ice Blue'
25. G.P. and J. Baker 'Mint'
26. G.P. and J. Baker 'Pistachio'

Swatches shown here with turned down edges are wallpaper; other swatches are fabrics.

The tape measure is used as a scale device.

SECTION TWO

LIVING AREAS   48

MEDIA ROOMS AND WORK AREAS   74

BEDROOMS   82

KITCHENS   110

BATHROOMS   136

AWKWARD SPACES   158

LIVING AREAS

At the time of unpacking tea chests after a move, priorities vary in every household, but the living room is usually the first area to receive attention. Few people begin from scratch with no belongings or furniture and it is important to evaluate what you have before you plan the layout of the room.

For some people it is essential to get the sound system working; consideration is given to positioning speakers for the best acoustics, or placing the television where it will get the best reception and be easily accessible for the video and home computer. For others it is the china collection that needs to be displayed, graphics that require lighting, or books that must be cleared from vital floor space and put away in the correct place. Seldom will a library fit into self-assembly storage units and a quantity of larger books cannot be displayed on a single coffee table.

Throughout the house our enthusiasms determine the style of each room. The minimalist, who dislikes clutter, will be preoccupied with the business of storing things behind blinds, or in trunks, and letting the bedding roll serve as a backrest on platform seating by day, to be unfolded on a sleeping mat at night. The traditionalist will be busy stapling lengths of fabric to the walls to match patterns, pasting up a wallpaper border to co-ordinate with paint colours, and dressing the windows. Country lovers in urban dwellings will concentrate on stripping pine furniture, dabbing colour onto mantelpieces and cutting stencils for floorboards.

Assess your living area carefully before you go out and buy metres of expensive fabric or choose wall colours. Consider such questions as who will be using the room, and for what purpose. How much natural daylight does the room have? Study the light and shadow for days before deciding whether it is a bright, average or dull room. North-facing rooms are generally too chilly for blues, for example, unless you choose a bold, bright blue, warmed up with amber; this looks cosy with night lighting.

What kind of lighting is there in the room? You may want to replace ordinary light switches with dimmer circuits so that you will have more control over the intensity of light. Fitting semi-recessed downlighters in the ceiling with low voltage beams can wash the walls with an effective light, but this is not a job for an amateur; for anything complicated, you should consult a lighting expert. Low voltage lights need either a built-in transformer or a separate transformer that can be recessed in the ceiling. A lighting consultant will give you a light show to demonstrate how effectively lighting creates the right atmosphere in a room. Reflectors on spot bulbs can bathe a room in a friendly golden light; a silvery reflector can

An old flat with 'chronic damp' (**above**) was converted into this airy living room of journalist Gilly Love's. Advice from architect friends who had lived in Japan clearly influenced the decor of low seating and restrained colours. Furniture is kept to a minimum so she can move things around to change the look. She prefers to sit on the floor than in a chair, hence her low-level seating with bolstered sofa. Walls are painted soft grey, the Indian flat-weave dhurrie rug is in the pastel colours she favours. Thinned grey paint has been painstakingly rubbed into the grain of the floorboards to silver them before sealing with varnish.

to create a minimalist interior in a mid-Victorian house, but retained the original cornices, and painted the mouldings a startling pink. This is one way of using architectural detail without letting it dominate the room. Often the grace and beauty of a period building dictates its own decoration. In a small box house the choice is greater and almost anything you do will improve it. A simple colour throughout will widen horizons, but make sure the wall finish is good. Pay particular attention to colour in details such as door trims and handles, electrical sockets and window frames, all of which can benefit from a contrasting colour.

List the colours you like or dislike. Dark blue may remind you of a school uniform, but a similar colour, called indigo and peppered with saffron and paprika, may suggest something more exotic. Response to colour is a very personal thing and adjectives used by manufacturers to sell their products, such as 'restful', 'vibrant' or 'exotic', will not make you like better those you react against. Instead use the appropriate adjectives to describe the mood or effect you want to create — spacious or cosy, dramatic or restrained, warm or cool, restful or exciting. Some paint manufacturers sell tiny sample pots of paint so that you can try the effect in your own living room.

Barratt, the biggest house-builders in Britain, made a positive statement about lifestyle in the 1980s when they launched a scheme of apartments for the new generation of house buyers. Despite the stolid name of 'The Dorchester Suite', there is little that is traditional about the concept, either in the floor plans or the decoration of the rooms. The 'Harmony' interior is designed for two singles, jointly purchasing a flat, and it contains two bedrooms, each with a bathroom and dressing room en suite; 'Tempo' is a bedsitter for a single person, with one bedroom recessed from the living area and 'Accord' is a studio apartment for two with a double bedroom.

The designer, Margaret Byrne, chose furnishings for the three schemes that would reflect the different lifestyles of each. The black, grey and white colour scheme of 'Harmony' gives the shared living areas a distinctive unity while allowing an individual colour preference for accessories (she chose red). In the 'Tempo' interior the designer has struck out more boldly with an individual treatment of navy, red and white, using red gloss skirting boards throughout to accent the navy carpet and white piping on the nautical navy sofa. 'Accord' is more subtle, with pastel colours for furnishings, and grey lacquer fur-

make it more mysterious. Filters can be used to create moonlight effects, or make conservatories seem more lush; spots or projectors can specifically light shelves and paintings, while downlighters and uplighters flood a wall with light. Once you have learnt how to control lighting, you can create interesting shadow patterns by filtering light through the leaves of a plant or behind a piece of coral.

Next, work out what surfaces you will repaint or cover. These will include floors, ceilings, walls, cornices and skirting boards, doors and frames, radiators and windows as well as shelving. Take into consideration the kind of house you live in. Is it semi-detached, a bungalow, an apartment, or a period residence? The dimensions of the room — its length, width and height — could influence your choice of colour as much as the style of furnishing. Architect John Pawlson chose

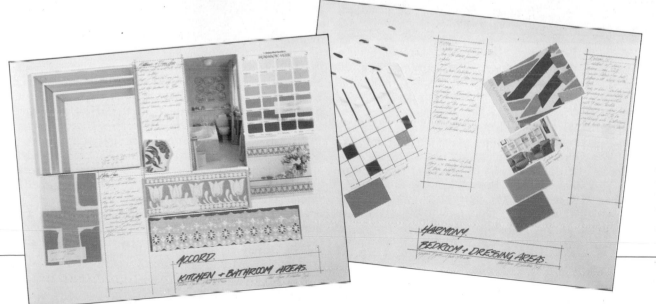

Pages from designer Margaret Byrne's notebook (**left**) illustrate how she drew up schemes for the Barratt's show houses at the 1984 Ideal Home exhibition in London. The dining/living room in the 'Accord' one bedroomed flat (**above**) is unified by the colour scheme. In the pages from her notebook, you can see how Margaret Byrne builds up colour schemes around border patterns, paint colour and fabric swatches. For your own scheme, pick out a multi-coloured fabric you would like to use in the living room for upholstery or curtains and isolate the colours for the walls, ceilings and floors. Then introduce accent colours that you recognize in the fabric design.

Hand-painted finishes can transform a fireplace surround or an architrave, turning such unlikely material into the focal point of the room (**above**).
John Canning's feathery strokes with a fine brush apply veining in a darker paint colour mixed with scumble glaze on top of the eggshell base, to give a hand-marbled finish to this early American fireplace surround (**left**).

Tortoiseshelling the architrave on doors of differing heights draws attention to them (**above**), and the group of pictures hung on the yellow walls gives this potentially awkward corridor area of the living room a grand entrance.

niture set against the natural background tones of wood, cork and tinted glass to anchor the pales. Margaret Byrne's working notebook (page 99) shows how an interior decorator tackles a scheme from scratch.

Flooring covers the largest area in the room, so never underestimate how important it is to get it right. A brown carpet inherited in a dull flat, can deaden the entire scheme. Silky straw blinds, called 'chick' in India, give the flooring throughout the same flat a distinctive texture if laid directly onto the brown carpet. The material itself suggests a few instant decorating ideas — a large wicker tray with shells on it and paper fan shades.

Fabrics on the wall, or pinned to the window, will also give you an idea of the colours you can live with. Invest in a staple gun — the most powerful you can operate — and you can cover a wall temporarily with patterned double sheets. Put up poles above windows for simple drapes, or place simple shades in the window frames. Use narrow dowelling cut to the right length and pinned to plasterwork with map indicator pins. This will be strong enough to hold a length of lace, a swatch of muslin, even an Indian sari in flimsy cheesecloth, knotted in one corner and swagged in loops over the pole. These may only be temporary measures but they will help you to define your style.

This living room (**left**) has a distinctive display of ducks on the walls, not the winged variety that classify kitsch today, but a handsome collection of decoys. They make a graceful setting for the upholstered green sofa. Rough plasterwork here enhances the sense of outdoors, so cleverly introduced with the solid greeen sofa and the dried grasses and flowers that seem part of the ducks' natural habitat. The white floor increases the sense of space in this narrow room as do the spotlights on curved aluminium tracks, freeing the floorspace of table or standard lamps, and illuminating the painting. Collections require a setting where they not only look at home, but can be enjoyed against a low-key background.

Finding a focus

Your living room is an introduction to your home. It is the room that people will be invited into most often. Those fortunate enough to have a fireplace will probably make it the focus of the room, around which chairs and sofa can be grouped. Undistinguished fireplaces can be enlivened with hand marbling; paint the surrounds with a mid-sheen base, then streak on artist's oils, mixed with gloss paint, in marbled shades of grey mixed with umber to darken it, or white to lighten it (see marbling page 23).

Prop a plain mirror above the mantelshelf to reflect the light from the opposite window into the room, and adorn it with a length of fabric draped across the top. Casually tie the fabric in the centre, and at the top left and right corners with silk ribbons. Let the sides tumble down in swags on either side to hide the ugly mirror edges — an idea taken from the Laura Ashley decorators' showroom in London. Place a plaster bust or a porcelain bowl in front of it, with some lacquered boxes or silver frames to give a gracious double image.

In place of a mirror, you could hang a picture. Reproductions of old paintings in the right frame can look charming, as decorator Daphne Graham displayed when she put a print of Van Gogh's camellias in an ornately carved wooden frame that she had

More displays are illustrated here — this time using the traditional sideboard in unconventional forms. Ducks on the wall are set in a humorous application against the blue wall with the cloud-like backdrop of the custom-built furniture (**above**). The lines of the sideboard are geometrically balanced with its angular base following the line of the curved top, an Art Deco device that is followed in the Odeon cinema fronts of the 1930s. Theatrical, amusing, not grand, this showpiece is a talking point.

Restoring furniture can be satisfying and rewarding, but it does involve painstaking work. The most important step is the first one — to properly prepare the surface to be painted or varnished. The old finish should be removed carefully so that you get back to clean, bare wood. Any cracks or scars should be filled to provide an even surface.

The sideboard (**right**) was originally covered with black paint. This was carefully stripped off and the piece was covered with a gloss polyurethane varnish. The result (**far right**) is both pleasing and elegant.

scumbled with white and grey and rubbed down with wire wool to antique it. Make a note of the way pictures are framed so that you can create your own little gallery. A simple engraving, bought as a loose leaf in a book-shop, will look splendid on a grey mount with a bevelled edge. A fine red line painted about a fingertip away from the bevelled edge adds the perfect finishing touch. Put this in a red wooden or light-weight aluminium frame.

Furniture

In the living room it is often the furniture that is the focal point of the room, but just as in a garden, careful pruning is needed to bring out the best in a room. It can be an 'herbaceous border' of pattern and colour, the sort of charming picture that the Continental calls English style — but this requires careful consideration of both scale and proportion.

In a small, cramped room a large unit can house your stereo and television more effectively than a series of small tables. When you have decided on a theme, pick one really fine piece of upholstery to anchor it. Chipboard units and knockdown chairs never really improve with age — in fact they worsen — whereas a soft leather chair or good wood ages very well.

Slip covers create an instant effect with upholstery. Hallie Greer, whose flourishing fabric business, 'Laurie Morrow', is called the 'Laura Ashley' of America, says: 'Slip covers are practical as well as celebratory. They last twice as long as upholstery and transform the mood…the season's change is heralded by changing the slip covers to cooler, more sprightly colours.'

If you don't want to use slip covers, consider hanging 'throws' — a woven blanket, a Kashmiri shawl, or a piece of old patchwork — over the back of a sofa or chair. Never underestimate the value of plenty of cushions, with raw silk patterned embroidery covers, or home-made petit point from a tapestry kit. In a modern household, you could scatter these cushions on the floor, around low tables, and on platforms that are used for eating and seating.

One-room living

Whether you call the space a studio, pied-à-terre or, more graphically, a bed-sit, the one-room apartments of the inner cities are, ironically, the biggest growth area in twentieth-century housing. Entirely a product of the squeeze on inner city space, these one-room apartments that perform as sleeping, sitting, working

Architect Piers Gough's room (**above**) shows the same sense of form in the balanced juxtaposition of an original designer's plan chest with its idiosyncratic collection of china dishes that take the form of the contents they were intended to house — a celery stalk jug, asparagus bunch dish, a bulbous fish for the soup tureen, vegetable and fruit bowls shaped like tomatoes and grapes respectively. Balance and symmetry inform this display with the added jolt of illumination of the peeling wall surfaces and damp.

The proportions of a room can be altered visually with different wall treatments that extend or shorten the run. Clever use of colours, fabrics, papers and furnishing, pictures and distractions can complement the scheme. What you do with a room's background is important because the areas involved on floors, walls, and ceilings are so large. Three ingenious solutions to create impeccable backgrounds are shown here, each using different wall treatments: rough plaster in an all-white room, a documented chintz used to line the walls and curtain the window in a modern townhouse, and a bold display of pictures and masks to occupy an entire wall. The rough plaster finish is painted white (**right**) and all the furnishing kept white to create a room of Mediterranean freshness and light, despite its tiny window. Space beneath the window is cleverly used to house shelves and an upholstered white sofa.

The rooms (**left**) show pattern on the walls in two variations, one created with fabric on the walls, the other with a collage of decorative pieces and pictures.

Interior designer David Mlinaric selected and coloured designs found in old country houses for his National Trust collection made by Tissunique of Lyons. Erdigg, reproduced here in a chintz, was found in a late seventeenth-century house in North Wales, hidden under many layers on a fine set of chairs. Original fragments did not constitute a full repeat so the design has been completed in the same style and used here in a library (**above left**) in a modern town house in Blackheath, South London.

Owner/designer Gil Barber is an American model, actor and agent who collects American sheet music and theatre posters. Each room is treated differently: this one (**bottom left**) is covered in pictures and masks from Bali which Gil rearranges frequently. Junk shop furniture is Gil's other enthusiasm. Her modern electronics and video are housed in an old sideboard. England of the 1930s and 1940s captures Gil's imagination, hence the 1930s standard lamp and Art Nouveau lamp from Milan. The art of hanging pictures together in well-planned groups is illustrated in this view — large Indian painting on cloth with vegetable dyes anchors one end and is hung at exactly the same height as the window at the far end of the collection; smaller pieces are hung near the window to benefit from the light, as the windows are kept bare.

Bedsitters, the result of the urban squeeze on space, can be handled imaginatively as illustrated by these pictures of architects' apartments, one in Holland (**right**) and one in Britain (**far right**). Space can be divided, either structurally with platforms or with innovative furnishings, to make rooms twice as habitable.

High ceilings in this Amsterdam flat at Prinzengracht (**right**) meant that the architect owner could suspend his bed on a platform above the living area. So the bookshelves reach astonishing heights, yet books are at arm's length, depending on the level. Soft colours — a pink alcove, grey and white bed linen, and the cream flooring — keep the room looking spacious.

and cooking areas, demand a pragmatic treatment.

Architects tackle this problem with structural changes, sweeping away partition walls, removing parts of the ceiling, taking out doors to create a space that highlights the austerity of the structure. They will then go on to define the different areas with pits or platforms, panels of white muslin, simple white paper blinds or PVC roller blinds, or the slatted Venetian blinds that have replaced conventional walls to give slight, but significant divisions between areas.

Designers will favour furniture that folds up or folds out to create floor space, like the Murphy bed in America, or the sofa bed, as well as room divider shelving systems that mark off areas within a room and offer valuable storage space.

Both architects and designers will ensure that when space is at a premium, no section of the whole is totally divorced from the rest. American minimalist Joe d'Urso believes that functional items like bath furnishings should be on display too. From one end of the living room that he designed in the famous nineteenth-century Dakota building in New York, the pedestal basin is clearly visible. A sheet of glass screens the shower and lavatory, a half-height partition divides the kitchen and dining areas, and the space behind the stairs that lead to a platform bed is used as a seating area.

One-room living has inspired a whole range of furniture designed specifically to save space. This new approach brought about the demise of the matching three-piece suite, impossible to fit into irregular schemes and gave rise to modular push-together seats and ottomans that give smaller rooms new dimensions. Heavy, space-swallowing furniture is usually replaced by a small-scale, portable sofa that converts into a bed at night; tables that double up as desks and filing cabinets that serve as bedside tables. Spotlight systems can be set into tracks across walls and ceilings, which frees floor space from standard lamps. Even fittings are adaptable, even mobile, in these new schemes. Clip-on shelving, also on tracks, can be adjusted to house various sizes of books and objects.

Anything on wheels — from vacuum cleaners and filing cabinets to clothes rails and TV trolleys — can be contemporary solutions to restricted space, while hooks on the walls, traditionally used as pegs, can support table tops, fold-out chairs, even beds.

Architects Christopher Williamson and Karen Moloney hook their six-foot-square mattress on to the wall and cover it in a lightweight nylon kite material that makes it an abstract wall-hanging by day in their

North London flat. At night, when the sofa is wheeled away, the bed is unhooked from the wall support. Adroit space engineering is essential when one room plays many parts.

Sometimes you will want to make a clear distinction between living and sleeping areas. Either use screens and room dividers that mark off boundaries in the room, or demarcate a sleeping area from a seating area with a simple rug. Beware of using too many different patterns in a small floor area lest the walls seem to close in on you. Concessions to small-scale living should be in the harmonious background colours of walls and floors, unless you are skilled at painting, in

Architects Christopher Williamson and Karen Maloney are in their North London flat, with their storage trolley system that can be moved away when necessary. Inset above shows the mattress covered in nylon kite material designed to make an abstract painting when hooked up on the wall by day, in the blue, grey and yellow colour schemes of the entire flat.

These pictures show two views of the living room in the early Victorian London house of Daphne and Joss Graham. Their travels to Turkey and India to buy textiles, flat weaves and rugs for their London shops produced some beautiful pieces which are used decoratively with antique English furniture.

A desk and chair in the corner of the living room is pictured (**far right**). Cast-iron Punch and Judy figures hold back the shutters that are painted white in a matt eggshell finish to reflect the light. Curtains were never hung because the centrepiece of the room is the eighteenth-century French needlework rug with its autumnal colours that suggested the colour scheme, and conflicting patterns in a small room can become too dominant.

Apricot, russet, coral and a hint of green are the harmonising colours of the living room (**right**). The wall colour was inspired by Portuguese houses that are washed each year with earth colour. Daphne Graham mixed terracotta, umber and yellow powder paint into a little white emulsion with water and dragged it swiftly across the walls. This fast-drying technique gives a dry look which comes alive at night. The new floorboards were stained with earth colours before the rug was laid to give a grain and make the floor lighter.

which case *trompe l'oeil* (the art of deceiving with three dimensional painting) can create magical vistas. In this way you can create a harbour view from your modest apartment, the balustrades of the terrace from which you view it painted in the foreground. Rather than let colour and pattern dominate in one room, choose a tranquil monotone setting that gives the impression of space. Understated backgrounds allow different zones to be highlighted. A white ceiling, white doors and shutters, and a mirrored panel inset behind the sofa, or backing the shelving system, all add to the impression of light and space.

Displaying objects

Unlike the kitchen, where display units are mainly functional, the living room needs space for creative visual displays. Use mantelpieces, window sill, ledges, steps, shelves or any other flat surface for a changing display of objects in your living room. Display items that are sympathetic to your theme, such as brass boxes in an oriental setting, sea shells against stone or carvings placed in front of an open brick chimney breast. John Stefanides, who designed the ballroom at the British Embassy in Washington, favours unaffected, yet elegant interiors. He is particularly fond of baskets in the home, and sets them amongst shelves so that he can enjoy their irregular shape and texture.

Always exercise self-discipline in the display of objects; learn what to leave out, how to avoid clutter and use accessories to add accent colour to the colour scheme. In Joss and Daphne Graham's living room, red lacquered bowls sit upon a green silk Japanese cloth to emphasize the soft glow of apricot, coral and russet. Daphne Graham, who has been responsible for co-ordinating decorating schemes for some of Britain's grandest houses, gives the following advice: 'Weight your colour scheme with a touch of bright solid colour. Just a hint is needed, for it is the balance of colour that counts.'

Shelves

These need not be hefty constructions. More flexible systems and those with a lacquered finish add a soft sheen to the background display. Custom-built shelving uses space most effectively if you vary heights by running book shelves across the tops of doors to create your own library. Vary heights with display shelving that runs around the room, low enough to enable you to look down on the objects displayed on it.

Flexible shelving is easy to dismantle and move with you. Choose a modular system if you intend

An unholstered button-back sofa is casually covered with a quilt (**above**) from Kutch in the Thar desert of North Western India, and scatter cushions are covered with Indian embroideries and Cretan needlecraft. An old chintz chair (**left**) stands beside another chair covered in Chinese yellow with a coral bullion fringe and piping. The tablecloth is an embroidered silk Japanese tea ceremony cloth with a collection of red lacquered bowls from Rajasthan. The red lacquer bowls weight the colour scheme with a hint of stronger colour. The fireplace is screened with a floral cutout found in a stall in the Portobello Road. The mirror is a Regency portrait mirror and the embroidery above it is a Toran from Gujarat in India. Its mango-leaf border motif is a sign of welcome in Indian homes.

SUPPORTS FOR SHELVING

The kind of support you need for shelving depends on the weight of the shelf itself and the load it must carry, whether it is for storage or display. The most popular materials for shelving are plain wood, chipboard and plywood; those with a plastic veneer are stronger and can be very heavy. They are sold in a wide range of thicknesses and widths, so there should be no problem in finding one suitable to your purpose. Supports may be adjustable or fixed; the shelf may simply rest on the support or be screwed down. Adjustable metal fittings with movable brackets fitted to a hollow channel in the uprights (**1**) are convenient. They are sold in lengths up to 2½ft (2.4m) and can be fitted one above the other, or trimmed with a hacksaw to fit a given space. L-brackets (**2**) are widely available; simply screw one side to the wall and one to the shelf. Angle brackets, straight (**3**) or triangular (**4**) screw into the side walls. Improvised shelving for lightweight objects can be supported by the wire or cord (**5**); industrial shelving (**6**) is a useful stand-by. Basic supports can be slotted into uprights (**7**) or fitted to drilled holes (**8**). For glass shelving choose a plastic stud with smooth jaws to accept the width of the glass. Enclosed shelves can be grooved and run into invisible wires (**9**). Joint blocks, screwed together from two interlocking halves (**10**) fit neatly into shelf corners. Removeable brackets in two sections (**11**) plug into drilled holes.

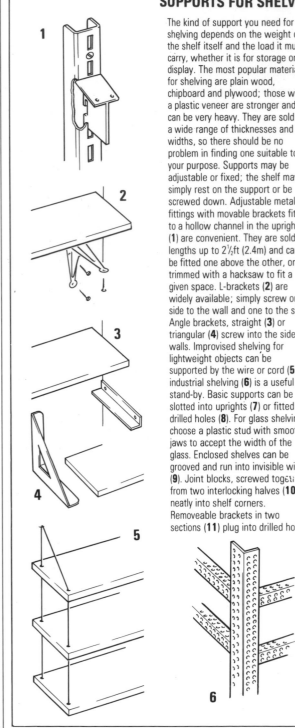

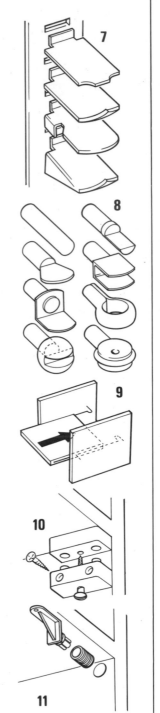

Space-stretching solutions in living rooms are possible without building or moving walls. Shelving takes clutter from the floor, becomes decorative with clever arrangement or effectively partitions off an area. If you wish to separate the dining area from the living room, you can buy a storage system and turn it into a working wall.

Perspex shelving set against white walls with an ice-blue carpet (**above**) shows an eclectic collection of Carol McNichol porcelain pieces. The Scandanavian storage system (**right**), Avanti from Dux, has built-in downlighters and glass shelves wide enough and deep enough to house the audio and video systems.

moving on, or need to re-arrange schemes as you add to your furniture. Bamboo or pine shelves that are light enough to hang on the walls make a good display piece for a collection of special interest, such as carved or clay birds, or glass figures. Heavy duty industrial shelving that clips on to batten strips can be tailored to fit the height of a high-tech room, and clip-on wire baskets or cubed pigeon-holed boxes can be set amongst it. Uprights fixed to solid walls take the slot-in shelf brackets, some of which can be angled up or down like magazine racks.

Glass or clear acrylic shelves make a display base that will not block out the light. Glass-backed shelves will reflect the objects displayed on them and provide a simple way of obtaining the illusion of light and space. Alternatively, use glass topping on a box-frame table to house a collection of things you like. A

cucumber frame from a gardening shop will provide an agreeable box-frame with a glass cover. Screw in four low legs so that you can gaze reflectively upon the objects housed in an unconventional table. For their recent Italian furniture collection, Conran's in London used rather more sophisticated versions of these display tables, filling the tray tops under the glass with Amaretti macaroons sold in twists of pale tissue in nougat colours. Butterflies, paper fans or small carved animals make an attractive display.

Shelf lighting
The most professional way to light shelves is to use low-voltage tungsten lights, housed in slender filament tubes. Although they are expensive, tube batten lights can be specially designed to highlight prized objects. Cheaper alternatives are focussing spotlights

mounted on a track directly onto the shelves, or small uplighters set on the floor below the shelves to bathe the wall with light.

Heating
Anyone fortunate enough to have a fireplace in their living room knows the pleasure of drawing up a chair around its warming glow on a wintry evening. Even in summer when the fire is not lit, the fireplace still draws you with its decorative overmantel, surround and firedogs, a picture or mirror set above it.

When the housing boom began in earnest in the 1960s in Britain, fireplaces went out of fashion. At this time no house was built with a chimney, unless commissioned from an architect. Fireplaces in older houses were boarded up and regulations were published to state the required number of ventilation holes to

To prevent shelves from sagging it is a good idea to fit a strip of wood or aluminium to the length of the front edge. A facing strip also hides a gap where the shelf butts up to an uneven wall. A plain wood strip can be fitted flush to the front edge (**1**) or underneath (**3**); a slight variation in the effect is provided by a grooved batten (**2**). Narrow wood mouldings are more elaborate. Two triangular section mouldings glued together form a concave (**4**) or convex (**5**) edging to soften hard lines. Different types of aluminium strip give a clean effect; T-section aluminium extends the depth (**7**) while right-angled section can be fitted neatly over the front edge (**6**) or recessed underneath (**8**).

If your modern house does not have a fireplace, you can install a free-standing type or decorative stove connected to a chimney-flue system on an exterior wall. You can build these systems yourself. Most older houses have fireplaces although smokeless zones in inner cities can mean they have been blocked up. Decorative treatments can turn them into a focal point once again.

Designer Ulf Mortiz made a feature of the burnished steel fireplace in dress designers Puck and Hans' house in Amsterdam (**right**). Fiery-red satin Art Deco chairs set on either side complete the scheme.

Mint green paint, fresh flowers, ingenious side cupboards and a lectern are all designed to distract attention from the fact that this was a fireplace, yet it is still the focal point of the room (**top left**).

The picture (**above left**) shows another fireplace, blocked up yet used decoratively, with a careful grouping of graphics to anchor the diagonal chimney breast painted a pale yellow. The clay-tiled hearth is an upraised platform.

Buttermilk colours in a dairy-style kitchen complement this old cast-iron range (**above right**) restored to its former good looks by its owner, journalist Maureen Walker. A cast-iron stove is set within a large fireplace surrounded by exposed brickwork (**top right**).

stop damp in a sealed chimney. The soaring cost of fuel contributed as much as aesthetic appeal to the return to fashion of the traditional fireplace. It was in 1976 that the National Consumer Council recommended that no house be built with only one fuel supply: all new homes should have flues.

If you are living in a modern house without a flue, take comfort from the fact that an external chimney can be built on, using the fire-resistant concrete interlocking units that manufacturers claim take less than six hours to assemble. Such pre-fabricated chimneys are equally suitable for brick-built and timber-frame houses. Quick installation of a fireplace opening follows with a fire chamber that can take a room heater, stove or even an open fire.

If you do have a boarded-up fireplace which you want to re-activate, prise away the covering to see what lies beneath. Hold a lit taper near the opening: if the flame is not drawn towards the vent, the chimney may be blocked and will need clearing by a professional. If it is not blocked, clear away the loose materials in and above the fireplace opening and check the hearth. It will either be a concrete or masonry hearth, with a back hearth below the fireback (which should not be cracked). Old-fashioned chimneys sent most of the heat up the flue, but if you install a throat restrictor you will increase the amount of heat directed into the room. In most countries there is an Advisory Board which will offer practical advice on this matter, and on relining the flue if necessary. However this is a task for a professional.

The first thing to decide if you are unboarding a fireplace is whether to make a solid fuel system self-supporting and run room heaters as well as domestic hot water, or merely to use the fireplaces as a back-up heating system. Many homes today use a fire to take the load off a more expensive system. Choose the method that fits the size and needs of your family. A fireplace is cheaper than other forms of heating, but you do have to keep a fire burning in summer to heat the water. In a mansion this is no problem, but in a 12-foot-square living room it can be insufferable. To minimize the problem, well-designed modern equipment is finely regulated by air control. You can set the fire on minimum so that it is hardly burning, or you can get a blaze going by turning the underfloor draught, or fan, onto the coals. The latest appliances have incorporated a new system to keep running costs low, burning the cheap household coal and retaining the smoke they produce. This smoke is re-burned before emission, entering into the atmosphere as

American architect Dennis Davey favours natural materials in this solar envelope house. The honeyed tones of the open-brick fireplace harmonize with the quarry-tiled floor and are accented with the natural weave of grey tweed upholstery. Sharp accent colours in the woven wall-hangings and scatter cushions draw attention to the furniture grouping, for once not clustered around the fire but angled in the corner for maximum impact.

vapour, and in this way it complies with strict clean-air regulations.

Designs of fireplaces

The design of your fireplace can be planned round an open fire inset into the wall, or housed in a freestanding unit with a ready-made chimney stand set away from the wall. Roomheaters and stoves, designed to be inset into the living room fireplace or to stand before it, keep the fire glowing safely behind glass.

You can build your own stone fireplace with DIY kits that offer the ready-cut stone which fits together, following a numbered diagram and assembly instructions. Richard le Droff is a master chimney mason; his 'Magali' design has wood logs stacked on the floor in an arched section, the hearth at cooking level above them fitting into a space of 16in x 8in (40cm x 20cm).

With an inset fireplace, the more expensive models need little adornment. Cheaper, plainer models can be face-lifted with an ingenious wall treatment, such as the stainless steel model set into a plain white plastered wall, edged with wood timber and a panel of open face brickwork. Ornate surrounds, or a firehood embossed with carved swags and urns, will transform a plain fireplace. To this elegant period piece add a grate and surrounds, embossed with mouldings or small flowers and shells in waxed pine. The fireback, the metal that rests against the back wall of the fireplace to prevent scorching of the brickwork, and radiates the heat from the fire, comes in cast-iron designs. To this add firedogs, pillars on either side of the grate, and coal scuttles or chestnut roasters.

Gas fires

Most modern houses have a gas heating system with a boiler that operates wall-mounted panel radiators. However a gas heating system can create a flickering fire in a modern house, without a flue, with the in-

A beautifully proportioned window with dramatic arched outline offers the backdrop to the flue of an original cast-iron wood-burning stove in this design by Paul Pugliese. Adding a white tiled hearth which is practical as well as good-looking, and the free-standing stove, he separates the area from the brown carpeted living room. Window seats on either side pull together the seating arrangement around the central fireplace.

stallation of a fake fire that runs on gas. These fires are more expensive to run than a room radiator, but they are easy to install and pleasant to gaze at. The 'logs' are clay bricks mocked up to look like timber, and you can even buy an aerosol spray with the scent of pine cones burning to complete the effect. For this type of heating you will need a specialist fitting from a gas outlet pipe near the proposed fireplace. Gas fires also give out radiant or convected heat. These cost more to buy and install initially, but less to maintain.

Electric Fires

Once you have fitted a plug to the electric fire, no specialist fitting is needed. Well-designed period pieces give the appearance of a blazing fire, but they are expensive to run and should only be used for background heat in a centrally heated room. You can place the electric fire in the fireplace and black the wall behind with boot polish to add the illusion of soot.

INSULATION

As heating costs soar, insulation becomes essential to keep the warmth inside. Cunning ways to cut heat loss include some unconventional schemes like padding walls with quilting and fabrics (see page 154) or lining the walls with a paperback collection. A chilling thought is that heat loss through the walls is estimated at 35 percent. Modern houses with cavity walls have a gap between walls to prevent outer brickwork reaching the inner walls. This gap can be filled with an injection of foamed plastic or loose mineral fibres, without any reconstruction work. The best way to put a ceiling on heating bills is to insulate the roof. It is estimated that 25 percent of all heat is lost through the roof. Egg boxes, old blankets or cardboard packing cartons flattened out after the move are some of the eccentric but efficient linings devised by DIY enthusiasts, but the thickest roll of glass fibre or mineral wool unrolled the length and breadth of the roof is the most efficient way to prevent heat loss.

Draughts also creep in through windows and under doors. Draught excluders can be fitted to the doors and double glazing to cover the windows. The capital cost on double glazing is high compared with other savings that can be made in insulation, but it is particularly worthwhile if noise is a problem as well, as it will cut down noise drastically.

The logical step to reducing heating bills after insulation, is to control the actual heat output of your heating system. Install radiator thermostat controls that switch on heat when needed and are so sensitive that they switch down automatically when another heat source is turned on, like the cooker in the kitchen, or when a fire is lit. Timed switches ensure that the system only switches on between the hours set on the clock to suit your individual schedule.

If you have a small hearth, buy a big log basket to place on it.

Wintry Rooms Made Warm
Furnish your room in warm shades of coral, old rose, peach or apricot to give north-facing walls and windows a cosy glow. Citric yellows, accented with white will add a certain summery brightness to cool rooms, or darker document colours in claret, amber or hunting green on backgrounds the colour of pale tea, will give a small cold room a richer hue. Remember that traditional patterns were designed to provide warmth and comfort in grand old houses long before the days of central heating.

If you favour a smart grey-and-white scheme, or blues and greens in Mediterranean shades, spice the scheme with bold scatter cushions, tie-backs for curtains, or picture frames and rugs in warmer tones of paprika, saffron or turmeric. Or casually drape sofas with soft, woven rugs or shawls to introduce pattern and texture to a room that can revert back to its summer colours when the weather improves. Full-length curtains with heavy interlinings will shield the wintry view, and you can tie them back in loops for a lighter

effect when spring comes. Slubbed cotton covers, stencilled with fabric paints in bold patterns, are attractive and practical, and they can be used to cover cheap basket-weave chairs when the seasons change.

In winter you will need carpet underfoot, or rugs laid on a base of coconut matting to provide extra warmth. Ceramic tiles and bare boards are cheerless unless they are heated with underfloor heating, blown through ventilation grids — a system that is unobtrusive, but expensive. Painted garden trellis, built in a box frame to conceal the radiator, is an inexpensive alternative to the custom-built grilles with diamond panes, or fretwork taken from Islamic tile patterns. High-tech enthusiasts will paint the radiator a bold colour, varying the bands of colour along the ridges of the panel. Radiator grilles can come in all shapes and sizes so choosing one to blend in with your decorative scheme is an easy task.

Dining Areas
Social changes earlier this century have resulted in the almost total disappearance of domestic staff and, to some extent, of formal dining rooms. Gone are the days when each room had a specific function —

Colour schemes can make north-facing, cooler rooms seem warmer and more cosy. Spice colours of paprika, chili, nutmeg and cinnamon (**far right**) set against yellow walls give a sunny aspect to this room. It has an oriental feel with a central ceiling fan reflected in the giant mirror and wicker baskets, chair and lampshades. No curtains block the daylight and a giant mirror, with a painting hanging on it bounces back the light.
Water lilies bloom on this linen and cushions are plumped into the lilypad shape on the window seat (**right**). Cushions are a comfortingly cosy asset in any room if they are large enough or banked together. It would be fun to stencil out this textile design along the floorboards as a lily-pond edging.

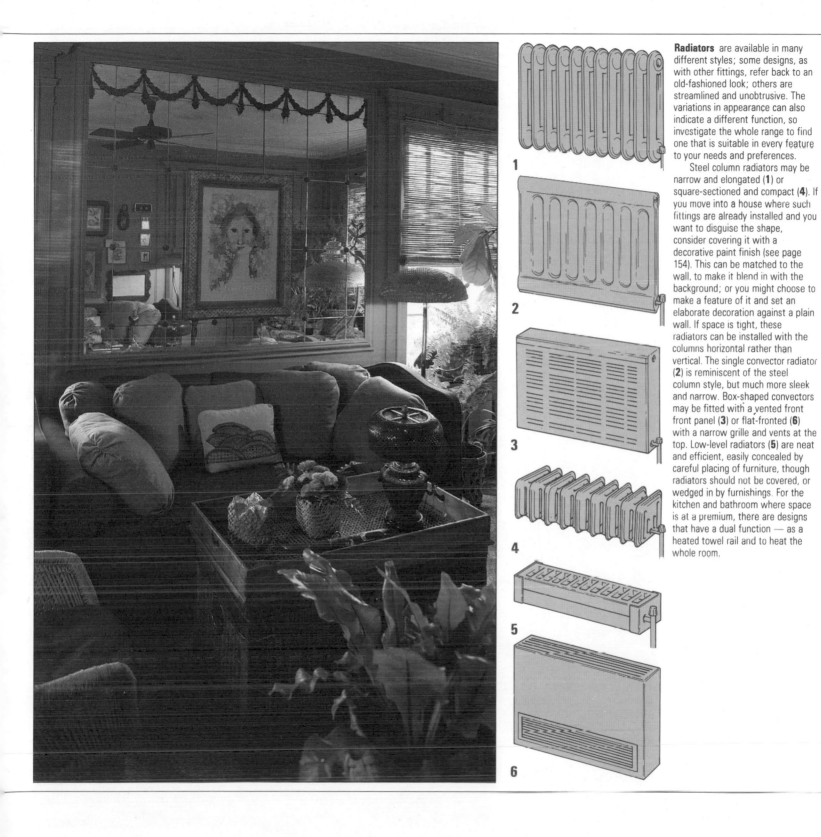

Radiators are available in many different styles; some designs, as with other fittings, refer back to an old-fashioned look; others are streamlined and unobtrusive. The variations in appearance can also indicate a different function, so investigate the whole range to find one that is suitable in every feature to your needs and preferences.

Steel column radiators may be narrow and elongated (**1**) or square-sectioned and compact (**4**). If you move into a house where such fittings are already installed and you want to disguise the shape, consider covering it with a decorative paint finish (see page 154). This can be matched to the wall, to make it blend in with the background; or you might choose to make a feature of it and set an elaborate decoration against a plain wall. If space is tight, these radiators can be installed with the columns horizontal rather than vertical. The single convector radiator (**2**) is reminiscent of the steel column style, but much more sleek and narrow. Box-shaped convectors may be fitted with a vented front front panel (**3**) or flat-fronted (**6**) with a narrow grille and vents at the top. Low-level radiators (**5**) are neat and efficient, easily concealed by careful placing of furniture, though radiators should not be covered, or wedged in by furnishings. For the kitchen and bathroom where space is at a premium, there are designs that have a dual function — as a heated towel rail and to heat the whole room.

The dining room was an important feature of older houses. Only the contemporary squeeze on space has forced it to become part of the living room. 'Country French updated' is the description designer Abi Babcock gives the furnishing style in her home, a 1916 slate, stucco and wood house in Hartford, Connecticut. Preferring to restore rather than to replace, she had walls, floors and ceilings cleaned and treated before tackling paint finishes. The spacious coral dining room has its moulding banded in a deeper coral with white. The original floorboards have been stencilled by John Canning in a geometric design, with an overall pattern and a central motif banded in blue to anchor the refectory-style table and chairs.

The honeyed tones of the original floorboards emphasize the white and green stencil pattern produced by John Canning (**above**).

Since floor surface areas are so great, the stencil pattern chosen needs to be on a large scale, like this one, to cover large expanses quickly and effectively.

First, the diamond shapes were ruled out and masking tape applied to the edges. Then heavy duty yachting paint was applied to the floor to give the diamond panels their sunbleached, white base.

Transparent scumble glaze was then applied and combed through with a giant comb cut from cardboard to reveal the base coat in wavy strokes. For a finer effect, you can comb through with a hair comb. A different angle was used to achieve the wavy border pattern for the duck-egg blue frame.

Dining tables take up a lot of space unless you favour the fold-up variety. In the living room you can disguise the dining table by covering it with flowers and magazines or photographs in frames, but in the kitchen you will want to divide the space decoratively to prevent your dining table becoming just another work-surface. The single girl who lives in this London house has built up the floor for her narrow corridor kitchen (**right**) so that the units and sink are on a platform with a vinyl covering for easy cleaning and to distinguish them from the wooden dining area.

whether it was for sitting, eating or sleeping — and dual-purpose rooms have become the blueprint for modern living.

Although the dining area has shrunk in size to become part of the kitchen or living room, it should not be less decorative or practical. In some homes the dining room has doubled up as a library or study room, while many households have no separate dining room, only a dining area incorporated in the living area. Often the only clue that the dining room is part of the living room is a pretty table placed near the fireplace or a window seat covered with a floor-length cloth and seats to match.

In an open-plan room, space under the stairs can house a round table, with a pretty curtain drape as a backdrop. A small balcony will provide enough room for a barbecue for two while a card table, topped with plywood, will provide an instant dining table for four.

By removing the formal structure of a dining room,

the table setting and lighting will be the most important factors in creating the right atmosphere. Cover the table with a brightly coloured cloth, pull up some painted chairs, and place a jug of flowers, or pannier baskets brimming over with fresh fruit and vegetables in the centre of the table. A low brass-topped table from India, set about with floor cushions, will create the right mood for an authentic Indian meal, with fragrant rose heads floating in bowls and a small wicker lamp to light the scene.

Remember that the dining area should be fairly well lit as you must be able to see what you are eating. However, the lighting on this area should never be so bright that it destroys the atmosphere. Colour is also instrumental in creating the right atmosphere in a dining room. Dark and russet colours give a warm effect, while bold colours and pastels present a bright fresh look. If you have dimmer switches you can adjust the lighting for lamps and overhead lights.

The difficulty of dining in a living area is knowing what to do speedily with the plates and glasses. The easiest solution is a trolley but often floor space is at a premium. Two sensible solutions are offered here: one involving a structural change with a central unit screening off the living area and offering space to hide clutter (**above left**), the other pure window dressing. *Al fresco* dining with architect Jan Kaplichy means high-tech, high styling that looks good enough to leave out on display (**above right**).

MEDIA ROOMS AND WORK AREAS

The post-Gutenberg age, as Professor Marshall McLuhan termed it, has given rise in the last 20 years to a generation closely in tune with electronic learning. Gore Vidal has pronounced it 'an age that marks the time that linear type, for centuries a shaper of our thoughts, has been superseded by electronic devices.'

Certainly, computers in schoolrooms worldwide have raised a generation quick to learn through sight and sound. Even our language is evolving as words, which a decade ago were unknown, have been introduced into our everyday vocabulary — micro processors, VDU units, programmers, sound and envelope statements, processors, chips, discs, print-out. For us they are symbols of the new electronic revolution.

The milestone of technological advance has been the mass-market micro computer at prices that take them into millions of homes, making computer power no longer the preserve of the large organisations. At present, home computers tend to take a backseat in the living room or a corner in the study; in the future micro computing will move into the kitchen also. At the last *Salon des Arts Ménagers* in Paris, Brandt showed 'L'Extra Cuisine', a computer linked to a screen, sending out orders to a number of machines linked to the central command system. In a time warp at the 1984 Ideal Home Exhibition in London, an electronics centre connected to the data banks world-wide was built under the picturesque thatched

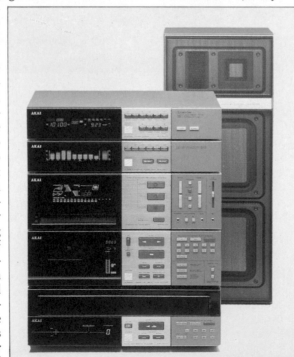

eaves of the Architectural Services show house. A glimpse through the leaded panes (relevant to Gutenberg man) revealed a power house of electronics designed by Roger Coombes for the executive working at home. He has chosen to display the equipment openly on a beechwood office system because he felt the wood suited a home study as well as an office.

Before buying your own computer system, you should know exactly what you expect from the use of the micro computer. A basic micro computer on its own is worthless, engagingly described by Yann Le Galès in an interview with the French magazine, *La Maison de Marie Claire*, as 'like buying a camera without a film.' Your micro computer should have an extensive memory enabling it to run programmes while you type in information, operating with any host computer, using simple commands: micro computers on the market operate with fundamental items like disc drives, VDU, and software.

The word-processor has the facility to create, edit, print and store any form of typed documents, accepts text or graphics of any other package supplied and needs

Home computers, video and audio systems have introduced a new furnishing style to the home that cannot be classified as purely high-tech. There are more than six million home-computer owners in the United Kingdom alone. According to Sir Terence Conran of the Conran, Habitat and Mothercare retail outlets, this is set to be the biggest growth area in furnishing. Some systems (**left**) are styled to stand alone as a decorative asset in the home.

In the picture (**right**) the TO 7 from Thomson, a family computer offering many educational possibilities as well as games, stands on an Italian Casakit chrome-legged table, its trellis-patterned top designed to match the fun tower trolley. The Philips television has an optical crayon for drawing or working directly onto the screen. A clamp-on light with the new low-voltage, high-intensity bulbs directs light onto the task in hand. Of all the equipment displayed, only the clock has a reassuringly familiar face, ideal for the child who is learning to tell the time.

Novel ways of housing electric equipment include French designer Olivier Gagnère's idea of keeping a television on a skateboard. More practical for ease of viewing yet every bit as speedy to wheel around unstructured houses is the television stand that Patty and Michael Hopkins introduced to their London home (**right**). Prefab steel and Venetian blinds divide the inner space so flexibility is the key to their approach.

a print-out machine. Buy a computer magazine to get the real comparison of performance and price. Talk to your children about the skills they have learnt at school. They will introduce you to the progressive world of the micro computer and its basic language. If you are a keen learner, you will want a computer with a better than average memory that has expanded to let you write your own programmes. The more expensive computers can programme and make calculations, offer print-out and word-processing facilities and do the accounts and budgeting. Software support is important so buy the system that has the required discs (mostly games) you like. There are unending lists of games from the idle science fiction blitz ones to the more skilful chess games. It was games that gave personal micro computers a rather futile start, conjuring up images of those video arcades that gobble up

money in a mindless way. If you are one of those who find video games uninteresting you can be certain that today a micro computer at home offers a great deal more.

Storage and Display

Once you have understood your home computer and how it links with other services (telephone, television, cassette recorder or disc drive) you will need to consider how to store it in the home. It is early days for furniture manufacturers and, as models slim down in size, furniture is quickly outdated. More importantly, you need to consider whether your room has a sufficient number of sockets. This chapter considers choosing the equipment, and housing the hardware and software so that it is practical, accessible and decorative.

Housing your hi-fi, home computer and video so they work together in harmony, and yet look good, can be a real problem. Equipment needs to be kept perfectly still and level, yet easily accessible, and visible. It is often heavy and bulky and tends to spread across cabinet tops and bookshelves in a tangle of wires. Furniture manufacturers worldwide have been slow to catch up with the requirements of home computer owners. Only recently has merchandise designed specifically for home computers appeared in the shops and mail order catalogues.

You will need a main desk surface, which provides space for your keyboard, the disc drives and the accompanying print-out if you have a word processor. The Visual Display Unit (VDU) can stand on top of the keyboard, but the desk systems that have a panel that pivots for the VDU are the most useful. Do not under-estimate the amount of software that accompanies this hardware — you will have to house cassettes and discs, boxes of paper which are 7in (17.5cm) deep, as well as documents and manuals.

Television

Your micro computer can be plugged into your television on the aerial socket, or by-passed on that circuit with an audio/video input socket, which gives a sharper image. If you want a socket for a particular job, to connect a specific computer to the television, for example, check that the two will work in tandem. Avoid buying a set that is too large for a small room. A 14in (35.5cm) screen should be viewed from a distance of 4ft (1.2m), while a 26in (66cm) set needs 9ft (2.7m) viewing distance.

The television of tomorrow is the numeric screen

This media room (**above**) was designed by consultant Roger Coombes as an office at home. The computer is linked to Prestel (the British Telecommunications service centre) and databanks worldwide. Also housed is a facsimile copier and the portable battery computer which links with the head office and main home computer to relay, store and receive messages.
Roger Coombes chose the equipment in the smallest sizes he could find for maximum memory capacity, and asked Kinnarps, the Swedish office-furniture makers, to install their desk system which combines streamlined office design with the pleasing appearance of beechwood.

One of the problems confronting sight and sound enthusiasts is how to get the best picture and sound from their system and to house it so that it looks good. Tape deck, amplifier, turntable, speakers and a TV with video take up a lot of floor space yet stacking without the benefit of custom-built furniture is impossible. High intensity sound systems present other problems which involve separating the speakers to cut the bass.

Dutch dress designers Puck and Hans had a special sight and sound system designed for their Prinzengracht flat by Ulf Moritz (**right**).

that is being developed by the Japanese. With this set you will be able to stop the image, freeze it, write on it, and switch to another channel without erasing the image of the one you are viewing.

Telecommunications

On your screen at home you can obtain information on sporting fixtures, travel, updated news, or financial situations. Teletext services from rival centres are broadcast as part of the normal television signal, while Prestel in Britain offers a computerized filing system that contains hundreds of pages of information. To use Prestel, you need an acoustic coupler to link your computer to external computers via the telephone line.

Telephones

Second extensions need not be expensive if you invest in another telephone with extra long cords, a volume control on the call tone, carefully designed dials and key pads, and a memory to store your most frequently dialled numbers. Some telephone systems have digital clocks that tell you what time it is or inform you at a glance that you are dialling incorrectly. Those who have an office at home need an answering service that will play messages back when they telephone in.

Video, Television and Stereo

People who prefer to hide their latest electronic equipment in Louise Quinze armoires, stripped pine linenpresses or rosewood cabinets will need to measure the depth of the television, with aerial, as well as the height required for raising the lid of the record deck to change a record. Shelves will have to be set at the right height and the furniture width must be at least 4ft 10in (147.32cm) for a colour television. Unless you invest in a custom-built piece, you will have to drill holes at the back for the wires. Hilary Green, presenter/designer for a British TV network, keeps her video, turntable and amplifier, and television in a French Provencal cabinet, a reproduction of an original design built by cabinet makers William Maclean. By contrast the modernist takes up the challenge of stor-

Ever since Sony began making transistor radios, the electronics industry worldwide has been getting bigger by building smaller. The picture (**above left**) shows their new miniature FH 9 stereo system. The cool black and grey pieces of sight and sound equipment that match the black lacquer table and chairs are given a warming glow of buttermilk light from the walls lit with wall-mounted chrome Art Deco-inspired lights in this sophisticated interior (**above right**), designed by architects Peter Wadley and Michael Robertson Smith.

This space (**above**) has all the elements for an efficient home office: bookshelves, filing space, telephone, wide desk-top, comfortable chair and lamp. Even better, it has a view which can be removed simply by turning your back on it if it proves too much of a distraction. With full-length glass panels to the garden, it was a sympathetic choice to have a glass-topped work desk in keeping with the neutral naturals used to furnish this unobtrusive study corner.

ing all the audio visual equipment on display and sets a low shelf around the room to keep everything at the right height, including the speakers. Speakers that double up as pedestals for lamps or plants are an unhappy compromise in any situation, and if you have large speakers try not to camouflage them.

Alternative display systems include rotating plinths, modular cubes, trolleys on castors, or swivel shelves in units with sliding doors. The German Interlübke system offers lacquered wood shelving on a pivot base so that the television can be turned to face the wall when not in use. Tubular steel trolleys allow the television to be wheeled away or transported to another room and a most flamboyant idea for a TV on wheels is Olivier Gagnère's skateboard trolley.

Work Areas
Rooms of long-standing in the house, such as the nursery or pantry, have gradually been reorganised

into work space for the home business. Often work areas have emerged in unexpected places — from corners under the stairs to garages (see Awkward Spaces, pages 206-211), or they have developed into the powerhouse for the home computer. For those whose office requirements are less high-powered, desk space can be part of another room, or a spare room can be converted.

The studio has long been the domain of the painter or sculptor, but today they seldom harbour artists. More often they are offices for designers, interior decorators, commercial artists, photographers, architects or writers — people who either work on a freelance basis or take work home. Such studios usually house a drawing board, work table, filing cabinet, bookshelves and reference materials. A light box for viewing transparencies may be included, or an improvised one can be put together with a perspex frame over a tube light.

Whatever the solution, the real need is for work space that is set apart from other living areas. However, because the home worker spends the majority of time in this environment, the office or studio can be integrated with the rest of the house by way of decoration or made more private with the use of screens.

Seclusion and storage space can be combined. Wall units that act as a screen offer library space, magazine racks, shelves for telephone and typewriter; desks can incorporate slide-out filing cabinets beneath the worktop. By their very nature, desks are untidy: they spill over with papers, files, typewriters and correspondence. The best solution to this problem is to keep the working desk out of sight by using an alcove as an office. Run storage shelves on a track system along the far wall, with one shelf wider than the rest, and at the right height to make a desk top. Christopher Vane Percy designed an office like this for a London publisher with fitted shelves in the recess of a deep cup-

board, and pegboard lining the inside, neatly edged with picture frame moulding. Useful for reminders, pegboard also muffles the sound of typing and looks good covered with fabric or felt in a bold colour. Allowing about ¾in (2cm) surplus all round, (plus the depth of the board), slash the corners to mitre, turn it over and staple the fabric onto it. Pegboard panels also offer a firm support for a tool kit, if you back the panel with a spacer bolt and hang the tools from the hooks. Spring clips that screw into this will hold cans for storing nails and other items for the home carpenter. Canvas wall tidies with pockets can be hung on a flat surface and filled with photographic film, paintbrushes, papers and office clutter.

Lighting in studies should be soft focus, backed up by desk lamps for the work area. Studios and workrooms require an even amount of light all over, with task lighting for close work. For further information on the various types of lighting, see pages 52-53.

A bedroom is a sensible place to have a study if there is space, since it is usually the one room in a house that provides privacy and quiet. In a bedroom which has every line on the horizontal plane (**above left**), with a low platform bed, stacking drawers and a distanced white wall space between wooden tongued and grooved panelling and wooden beams, the maple work-top acts as a natural break between sleeping and living areas.

TV presenter Hilary Green houses her stereo and video in an eighteenth-century style Provençal cabinet (**above**). Holes have been drilled on the back of the cabinet for wiring.

BEDROOMS

Interior designers are often asked the question: 'How do I create a scheme for a room?' The answer is usually: 'What are you going to keep in it?' In the living room or kitchen, furniture and fittings can be complex and expensive, but in the bedroom the task is straightforward because the bed is the only essential piece of furniture.

The bed occupies the largest amount of space and is, after all, the purpose for the room. Even if it is not the four poster of your dreams, it is the easiest item in the house to disguise with clever dressing. It may be that the simplicity of white sheets, a white blanket cover and plain quilted counterpane has an aesthetic appeal for you, but if you want a more practical bedcover, use a duvet with a patterned cover slip over a fitted base sheet. The irregular stripes and deep colours of a Kelim carpet make a striking pattern on sheets and covers, as do the dotted leopard spots and fake tiger stripes that American designer Perry Ellis has used to great effect. An iron bedstead will look good covered with a quilt in all the pastels of soft faded prints. Jane Austen's quilt, made for her Hampshire home, Chawton, inspired a whole range of G.P. Baker cottons and chintzes. However, you may prefer the simplicity of a Japanese futon that unfolds like a sleeping bag on a low platform at night, and doubles up as daytime seating with a few bolsters.

It was in the eighteenth century that beds were most grand, with embroidered hangings caught on carved canopies and topped with

ostrich feathers. You may consider this style too extravagant for a modern bedroom, but you can use it effectively to disguise the smallness of the room. If you try stapling fabrics to the cornices of a Georgian bedroom you, and the fabric, will come unstuck, but you can create festoons, flounces, swags and drapes in a box-like bedroom with the minimum of fuss, using a staple gun and scissors.

The centre piece of this 'boudoir' room is the bed, but very often bedrooms have to double up as a study, sewing room, nursery or, as in the studio apartment or bedsitter, the sleeping area may be part of the eating and seating area. Mani Mann, fashion designer for 'Monsoon', based in India, uses her bedroom for entertaining. The high-ceilinged flat was built in 1947, after Independence, in New Delhi, and it is divided into different areas by *jalis*, or screens, created from the concrete blocks that are used to build garden walls. Furniture is set at a low level to suit the informal Indian seating of rugs, floor cushions and low-legged hexagonal Rajasthani tables. The bed is a low platform covered with a hand-blocked print in shades of aubergine and indigo, ac-

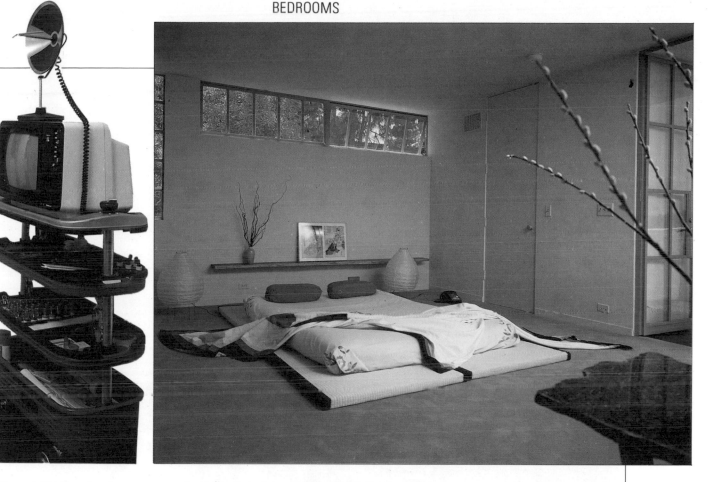

The minimal bedroom with its lack of clutter and distractions suits modern tastes. Here the sparse look is interpreted in two different ways. Architects Patty and Michael Hopkins have created a bed-sitting room (**left**) with extraordinary flexibility. Venetian blinds demarcate various areas and shield storage and hanging space. Primary colours are the obvious choice for a house which is the very essence of 'high-tech': there are no interior walls, just the venetian blind partitions which create an exciting feel of impermanence within the rigid metal steel and glass construction of the house. Everywhere moveable open shelving can be attached to the pre-fabricated metal ridged walls and a glass elevation affords plenty of natural light which is filtered quite dramatically through the blinds.

In Ruth and Jon Elliott's bedroom, high-tech is again employed as the minimalist style; a garage mechanic's tool box trolley (**right**) has been cunningly transformed into the ideal bedside TV table.

cented with terracotta and Indian pink. Sequined embroideries from Gujarat are stitched on to scatter cushions and bolsters to make the bed less like a bed. Eighteenth-century court paintings on glass, and Persian miniatures set at bed-height, add a distinctive formality to the room.

Architect John Pawson approaches the one-room living area in a completely different way in his London apartment. The discipline of eating and sleeping in one room has become an intrinsic part of the design. The room is left empty, the only furniture being a Le Corbusier table and chairs, and the occasional painting, propped against the wall to suggest impermanence. Futons are laid in front of the fireplace at night and hidden away in white lacquered cupboards during the day. This style of modernism, called minimalism, is not designed to deter company, rather to create a stage on which guests play the supporting cast.

It was once said that all the modernist needed to achieve instant radical chic was to use Charles Jencks' coffee-table book, *Post Modernism* as a coffee table, a pane of glass protecting its authoritative cover. Among architects of the eighties the modernist move-

ment includes London architects Michael and Patty Hopkins, who have created interchangeable room space within their steel and glass modular frame house by using industrial sliding tracks and Venetian blinds. Industrial components, like the garage mechanic's tool box trolley which Ruth and Jon Elliott use to house their television, are frequently used for style and mobility.

The pressures of living space in the Far East have produced design solutions that have been copied in the West. Architect Peter Anders took his inspiration for a New York loft conversion from a Sukiyu tea house in Japan. He painted the walls with several coats of white paint and lacquered them to produce a shiny reflection from spotlights on ceiling tracks. Light is critical for the lacquered look, which is why windows are often left unadorned, or simply screened with paper or linoleum blinds. Floor-level bedding is covered with a white slub weave bedspread, and the bedhead is a grey lacquered chest that holds drawing plans.

A bedroom can be made to look exotic with Chinese red lacquered walls, mirrored panels and

The bedroom (**above**) gains its inspiration from the spare, cool lines of Japanese design. The windows are bare of curtains or blinds and the walls are as white as white can be. A simple Futon mattress on a shallow platform suffices, and the effect, although austere, does not compromise on beauty or comfort.

Futon is actually Japanese for mattress, and a London company have borrowed the name to manufacture authentic Oriental mattresses, made with three layers of cotton wadding, encased in a pure cotton cover which has been tufted so that the cotton will not break up while you sleep on it. As the Japanese have known for thousands of years, pure cotton is the best fabric to sleep next to as it is sensitive to skin temperature. Cotton 'breathes' and absorbs up to 30 per cent of its own weight in body moisture.

A dramatic yet simply furnished New York bedroom (**below**) gets all its thrills from a superb view over the city. Designer Tom Foederer has cleverly incorporated a sofa at the foot of the bed from which to fully experience the panorama. Note the bank of down-lighters trained onto the sofa, the shelves carefully inset into the sides of the right-hand window, and the bright blue bedspread to match the brilliant expanse of city sky.

painted screens, fantastic with metallic thread tented to the ceiling in fine pleats in the style of British designer Zandra Rhodes, or restrained, using a bedding roll on a low platform, stripped of clutter. Called functionalism, minimalism or high tech, these very modern interiors are perhaps the hardest to achieve.

Furnishings

Once you have an idea of the style in which you want to decorate your room, consider what furniture you can fit into the space available. Bedrooms in modern houses are seldom larger than 12ft x 10ft (3.7m x 3m). In addition to this, the bedroom houses the bulkiest items — double bed, twin beds, cupboards, wardrobes, chests of drawers, and you may also have a dressing table, bookshelves and even a desk to fit in. The best plan is to mark out spaces for these items and place them at different angles to make sure that you

get corridor space around opening doors. Small, uniform windows can be made to appear larger with window drapes hung from ceiling to floor with a window blind set at the same pelmet height as the drapes so that it covers the wall for at least 3ft (1m) before it reaches the window pane. You need never pull the blinds down, yet the windows will look larger. Another trick that decorators use to compensate for small rooms, is to paste wallpaper borders around the cornice and skirting boards. Nancy Lancaster, a former director of Colefax and Fowler, has an all-white bedroom with carpets faded to a non-colour, a white frilled dressing table and white counterpanes, matching Colefax wallpaper and curtain drapes with a border paper edging the cornice. These strips of colour suggest architectural details that are not original. By hanging watercolours and porcelain plates on the wall above the pelmet, she effectively takes the eye up and

Bedrooms can be as convivial as living rooms if you are canny. A decorative bamboo bedstead (**above**) makes this bed more like a day bed, and brightly coloured cushions encourage day-time lounging. Note the warm coral walls which are such a fine background for delicate pencil drawings. An attractive bedspread and banks of gaily coloured cushions will always transform the most utilitarian bed into a glamorous day-time sofa. Fashion and fabric designer Mani Mann's New Delhi bedroom (**right**) is a room in which one can hold court in an informal yet stylish manner. The low bed is covered with Gujarati embroidered cushions, and the furniture made in the style of the Raj. Raj furniture was produced by local Indian craftsmen for rich patrons. Contemporary nineteenth-century European furniture designs were copied and adapted. On the walls is a fascinating collection of Mughal miniatures and Indian glass paintings.

PUTTING FABRIC ON WALLS

Before you start, make a sketch of your room showing doors, windows and power points in place. Take one wall at a time, work out how many panels of fabric you will need and the measurements of each one (allow about 2in/5cm for a hem at the top and bottom, and a small overlap in the wall angle).

Fabric can be stapled onto the wall, backed with an underlay. Alternatively, you can construct a frame of wooden battens, put padding between them and fasten the fabric to the frame.

Tools You will need a heavy-duty staple gun (hand staplers fit flush into the corners of the room, electric ones do not); scissors; contact adhesive; spray adhesive (from art shops); a sewing machine for fabric seams; needle and thread, including a curved upholstery needle; upholsterer's tacks, and a hammer.

Fabric Cotton or polyester padding in rolls up to 6ft 8in (2m) wide; fabric to cover the wadding (flimsy fabric stretches a great deal so settle for a better quality dress fabric if furnishing weights are too expensive in the quantities required); braid or tape to cover the staples.

Working order Always start in the centre (**A**) and work out, cutting separate pieces of fabric to go above or below doors and

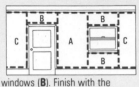

windows (**B**). Finish with the corner sections (**C**).

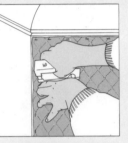

1. Staple the underlay straight from the roll, just under the cornice (see above). No seams are needed when butting lengths together — just a small overlap. Cut off flush to the top of the skirting board. Leave the padding ½in (1cm) clear of the edges of the door to allow it to shut properly.
2. When measuring a length of fabric, cut enough to leave a small hem at the top and bottom. If you seam the lengths of fabric together, three at a time, you can cover a large area of wall more quickly.
3. Finish the fabric off in a corner each time, even if you have

enough to reach further as this will ensure better stretch.

4. Lay the roll of fabric on the floor, face down, and start attaching it from the bottom (see above). Turn up ½-1in (1-2cm) of fabric and put a strip of card over it. Staple along the base, through the card, so that when you lift the fabric up the wall you have an inbuilt hem.
5. Put staples, 6in (15cm) apart, along one edge. Work from bottom to top as this makes it easier to get the hang of the fabric right. When you have stapled the bottom edge and one side of the fabric to the underlay, you can smooth out the tension across the width.
6. When three sides are fixed, give the fabric a good pull upwards to smooth out the creases, and staple the top edge of fabric below the cornice.
7. To hide the staples and cover the edge of the fabric, glue

contact tape along the top.
8. For light switches (see below), cut the padding generously away from the fitting, but make the hole

in the material just large enough to slip the fitting through.
9. Staples, or rough edges of fabric, can be covered with decorative braid that either matches or contrasts with the pattern of the fabric. Braid can also be used as a border for fabric panels on doors.
Safety Be very careful when covering walls with fabric as the operation involves working around electrical fittings.

away from the horizontal.

The great restriction to any decorative scheme is space, but fortunately modern houses offer scope for the enthusiastic do-it-yourselfer who can abandon restraint for a more flamboyant style. Fabrics stapled to the walls, swathed over pelmets, or made up into flounced curtains with a ruffled edge, contribute to the overall effect. Simple supports added to the four corners of a bed can be hung with crackly taffeta curtains, fastened to a central coronet on the ceiling. To this design, add curtains in a watered or marbled silk, generously hung so that they flounce on the floor like the gowns of the period. A striped wallpaper, usually called 'Regency' in contemporary wallpaper collections, is a good base for silver framed photographs

hung from a velvet ribbon, and pictures in gilt frames mounted on a background board of lavender or old rose.

Fabric and colour

It is important to consider pattern in the bedroom, although happily the overall co-ordinated bedroom with everything 'mixed 'n' matched' is a fad of the past. Many different patterns can be used in one room, pulled together with plain colour, or one pattern can be used single-mindedly.

It used to be a decorating maxim that small rooms could not take large patterns. However, David Mlinaric, Britain's leading interior designer, has exploded that particular myth by taking the Chinoiserie

Bedroom fabrics To give a bedroom a luxurious feel, hang the walls with fabric and use fabric to cover an old screen for extra privacy. It is quite simple to staple fabric onto the walls, as in the bedroom (**left**) with 'Havana', a vibrant design from the Collier Campbell Martex collection of American bedlinen, which co-ordinates so well with the comforter and pillowslips in 'Nomad' design, from the same collection.

The cabbage-rose colouring of the Romany cotton furnishings from Collier Campbell (**below**) brings country freshness to this urban bedroom. You can copy this simple screen with the minimum of sewing skills. Hem several widths of fabric quite narrowly and thread elastic through top and bottom hems. Then stretch it over an empty frame, which you can make yourself with pieces of 4in × 3in (10cm × 5cm) softwood. The chair, a junk shop find, is painted white and the chest of drawers is enlivened with a hand-painted motif. This attractive look has been achieved very simply, and quite inexpensively, with paints and fabrics.

Scale is of great importance when designing a bedroom or any other room. David Mlinaric, leading British designer, was commissioned by the National Trust to restore and re-decorate several grand houses in Britain. In the process, he chose some exquisite old chintz patterns to be reproduced by Tissunique, the French fabric company. To re-scale and in some cases re-colour these classic designs took great skill and taste.

The original Oak Bedroom (**right**) at Dunham Massey in Cheshire, was wholly furnished and decorated in 1810 by Henry Grey, 6th Earl of Stamford and his wife Henrietta. From this beautiful room overlooking the ancient deer part at Dunham David Mlinaric copied the charming 'umbrella' pattern of printed cotton, re-scaled it for modern consumption and called it 'Stamford'. He also copied the bold Vitruvian scroll border which co-ordinates with 'Stamford'. In the original Regency bedroom the window pelmets which match the bed valances, and the perfectly upholstered 'curricle' chair are particularly fine.

drapes at Castle Coole (a neo-classical mansion in Northern Ireland) as inspiration for his 'Castle Coole' fabric design (see page 174). To promote it outside the world of grand country houses, he used the fabric for festooned blinds in an all-white London apartment. In doing this he illustrated the point that you need never use pattern in a mean way — be generous with a bold print and allow the pattern to take over; this is exactly what is needed in a small room.

Always settle the issue of scale before deciding on your colour scheme. There are many different pattern colourways to choose from — ranging from pretty pastels in minty greens and pinks, lavenders, old rose, the limes and greys of Vuillard paintings, to the deep earth colours of old dhurrie rugs and the fresh country colours of porcelain. Designers and decorators talk of

'document' colours which means burgundy, bottle green, blue and mustard on backgrounds coloured like spilt tea. Documented colours, taken from printers' archives, always show blue leaves because, in the days of vegetable dyes the yellow, overprinted on blue to give green, always faded. Contemporary colourways faithfully follow that blueprint.

Take another blueprint from the past with a print bedroom. These were once the sewing rooms of eighteenth- and nineteeth-century houses and they adapt well to the scale of modern houses. Black and white engravings of the period, sold by antique dealers as loose leaves from damaged books, are pasted directly on to the walls and framed by cut-out paper swags, garlands, bows and cupids. To complete the print bedroom run a wallpaper border the circumference of

The positive and careful use of colour can dictate the entire character of a room, and where is that more essential than in the bedroom — place of dreams, rest, relaxation and creative thinking. Use pastels by all means, but not to create a sickly sweet confection. White spiced with lemon can be sharp, fresh and bright; blues and greys more demure and elegant. Pink does not need to be irresistably linked to the colour of little girl's hair ribbons. Try the subtle shades of salmon, apricot and coral, and match them with pale lavender and mauves.

In this bedroom (**top left**) the steel blue/grey walls are thrown into relief by the pale cord carpet. A superb gilded chair adds a touch of classical restraint to a bedroom that can easily transform itself into a day room. Note the bolsters which give it the air of a Regency day-bed.

An all white bedroom (**below left**) is particularly fresh and bright. The almost imperceptible addition of pinky-apricot warms the white to a soft glow. The delightful sloping ceiling is accentuated, cleverly, by its whiteness, as is the pretty fireplace, and the LLoyd Loom chair. A gleaming brass bedstead gives the bedroom the air of a Victorian maid's attic retreat. In any room where natural light is scarce, in a basement, or attic for example, white is a natural choice, as it reflects what light there is far more effectively than a darker shade.

In this bedroom (**below right**) light blue is used as an overall colour scheme, with a splash of primary red for dramatic effect. Notice the light-hearted yet practical way in which the dado rail has been used for hanging clothes.

Journalist Gilly Love 'hangs for health' American-style from the rafters of her airy loft bedroom (**left**). Gilly Love works for the British Sunday Express paper. She eschews chairs preferring a low profile cushion on the floor, and in the same vein, has chosen a low-level sleeping arrangement, Japanese-style. Caberboard panels (thin chipboard which can be moulded at the edges) line the walls and ceiling and have been painted a soft grey, outlined with a deeper grey. The floor is simply standard chipboard, stained a dark grey and sealed.

Bedrooms are also the perfect place to meditate and work. All you need is a little desk/dressing table, like the bamboo table in the bedroom (**above**). Place your desk by the window for maximum light, but beware of distractions if you have an enticing view!

The sunny little bedroom has been painted in the Dulux Yellow Collection. The colour Morning Sun has been used on the walls and ceiling, and teamed with Lily White on the cornice and woodwork. For the doorway, the deeper gold of Bamboo matches the bamboo bedstead and table. The bedroom of this 1920s London house (**right**) has been re-vamped by designer Chester Jones and is loosely based on a 1925 Parisian scheme by Atelier Martine. The walls are stipple glazed off-white, and the fabrics have been specially designed. There are two outstanding points of interest: the Graham Sutherland picture over the bed which dictates the golden colours of the room; and the artificial blossom tree which so effectively breaks up the rather hard line of fitted cupboards. Artificial trees and flowers, made from fabric are in vogue: use them in places where sun light does not reach.

STYLES OF BEDS

It is far easier to turn the bed into the most important feature of the room rather than attempt to conceal and minimize its bulk. Today you can choose from a wide range of styles, such as antique four-poster beds, beds in oak, brass or painted iron and Japanese style beds.

If you wish to create an elaborate style of bedroom, perhaps with a four-poster bed, and yet cannot afford to buy one, then it is possible to achieve the same effect with fabric alone. Side drapes, coverings and drapes can be hung from poles, tracks or decorative pieces attached to ceilings or walls. The coronet with sheer drapes (**above far left**) is a good example.

Another effective alternative to a four-poster bed is the half canopy or tester (**above centre left**). This is supported by two posts at the head of the bed. It is about a third of the size as the fabric-covered ceiling used on a full four-poster bed. Tied-back drapes hang down either side of the bed and a back drape completes the effect.

Nowadays you can buy excellent reproductions of classic four-poster beds. You can give the bed the full traditional treatment by adding all round drapes (**above centre right**).

A canopied effect can also be achieved by bringing a long length of material up from behind the pillows, looping it over a rod suspended from the ceiling, then down to another rod attached at the base of the bed, and finally dropped to the floor (**above far right**).

the room, at dado rail height, to serve as a marker for real framed pictures and gilt mirrors. If this bedroom seems too frivolous, take a leaf from the bookish earnestness and simplicity of a later age. Poet Lionel Johnson lined his study in the early 1900s with brown paper; in the same way you can paste sheets of plain brown wrapping paper directly on to the walls to give groundcover for a collection of sepia photographs in silver frames. In your room, add a mahogany towel rail and shoe rack, a wash-stand with a blue and white tiled splashback and a simple iron bedstead. This bedroom, part study, part dressing room, can house a day bed. British interior designer Mary Fox Linton has one made of bird's eye maple with bolstered sides which can be dressed up in Thai silks from Jim Thompson's silk collection, or dressed down in the Indian calico colours of bleached blue, sand, coral and pistachio.

Soft pastel colours evoke a rural bedroom — a soothing retreat for urban dwellers. The country house style is achieved in a modern house by sanding and sealing floorboards, or painting them white, throwing down a rag rug, and drag washing walls in duck-egg blue or primrose yellow. Hand-crafted fur-niture, such as a rocker, or a Windsor loop-back chair, or dowry chest for keeping bed linen, will create the right atmosphere. Add the finishing touches with a patchwork quilt, a sampler or tapestry cushions. This is the home for a four poster with white linen sheets and an eiderdown, or a wooden carved bed and Scot-tish mohair rug. You can add small items to the room to make it welcoming — lavender bunches picked in late summer, drying in bunches on the clothing rails, sprigged cotton laundry and shoe bags hung on hooks, cakes of fragrant soap set inside pinewood drawers to scent them and pot pourri in a porcelain bowl on the mantelshelf.

Actress Shirpa Lane has chosen lace borders as wallcovering to create a nostalgic bedroom in her Paris apartment. Kilometres of lace, found in antique markets, overlap each other in a line along the walls, dappled in colour to suit their antiquity. A filmy gauze, like mosquito netting, frames the bed, and screens the window set in a niche behind. The bed cover is an original 'broderie anglaise' and the pine-wood chest of drawers was a junk shop discovery. Often the furniture you have acquired from junk shops will set the style for you. The French call this

Creative people love designing bedrooms because here you can be as frivolous or as home-spun as you want. Experiment freely with paint finishes and fabric treatments. This gloriously fin-de-siècle bedroom (**left**) is more boudoir than staid sleeping place. Actor Ralph Bates and his wife Virginia run an antique shop in London's Notting Hill area, and theatrical set designers regularly purloin the shop for props. Everywhere lace is used creatively: as borders, fireplace 'fringes', decorative cornices, and valances. Far less voluptuous is this country cottage bedroom (**above**), designed by Norma Bradbury, with its four-poster bed, patchwork cushions and pine chest. Although patchwork is now popular, old pieces can still be bought in sale rooms or junk shops, and stitched onto cushions, thrown over a bed, or pinned to the wall.

respect for tradition 'retro', a term encompassing any aspect from the grandeur of Louis Quinze (a little exaggerated for contemporary living) to the tubular steel furniture of the 1950s. From this era come wire stacking chairs, low-legged teak tables and beds in the Scandinavian style. Abstract geometric patterns on fabric, and a dressing table, swirled in a stiffened skirt of fabric like the dress fashions of the period, complete the decor.

If you prefer not to sit back and rest in a beige bedroom, consider with the curiosity of a voyeur the more unusual bedrooms pictured and mentioned in this chapter. Adapt the ideas you like to fit your own

Children's rooms should be practical but they can be fun and flexible, too. A child likes to feel that his room is his territory, to which he can retreat to read or play. Thus adequate storage, well positioned play areas, and tough work surfaces are a must. Never impose your decorative ideas on children. As soon as they are old enough, discuss with them how they would like the room to look.

There are basically three types of child's room: the baby's room with its cot, changing area and brightly coloured mobiles; the under-fives room, with plenty of provision for quite boisterous play; and the older child's room with a sturdy desk for homework, some book shelves, and enough space for TV, stereo, or home computer. The room (**right**) is for a child in the latter category. It belongs to architect Alan Tye and his wife who live in Herefordshire, England. The room that Alan Tye has designed for his son has had to grow with the child's needs; thus the workdesk was once a perfectly servicable changing platform for a baby. The quarry tiled floor is easy to keep clean, and is an excellent surface for running toy cars over.

A blackboard for early morning scribbling (**above left**) has been thoughtfully set into the tongue-and-grooved pine walls and is just the right height for the child. Try to scale children's rooms sensibly, placing mirrors where they can get a good view of themselves, and storing books and toys within arm's reach. A child-sized chair is always popular and most children's shops and department stores stock them.

The problem of sharing a bedroom has been solved by dividing a room (**above right**) into two separate sleeping areas with the help of this brightly coloured storage system.

space and impose your own scheme of proportion, scale and colour into your bedroom.

Children's bedrooms

You should resist the temptation to use a theme in your child's nursery — he or she may outgrow it faster than your inclination to redecorate. The wise parent will leave the decor relatively simple so that the child can develop an individual character for the room as he or she grows up with it. This does not mean that the bedroom should be unadorned; always be aware of your child's interests. The athletic child with the good fortune to inhabit a high-ceilinged bedroom could enjoy a bed built on scaffolding like a climbing frame with ladders. However, the gentle dreamer who enjoys reading might prefer sprigged wallpaper in pastel colours, an iron bedstead painted white and a small

pine dresser or wash-stand.

Furnishings in the child's room need to be durable, and technological advances in design and printing over the past decade can be used to advantage in this respect. Use modern floor coverings, like foam back vinyl, or sealed cork, rather than a carpet or Indian jute, which scratches young knees and has an uneven surface for playing or building. Small children spend much of their time on the floor and therefore you should consider a surface that is easy to clean and smooth for revving up cars and standing up paper dolls. Some of the French vinyl flooring has games printed on it, but your 11 year old will probably prefer a plainer surface.

Walls should be treated in a matter of fact way as small children have a tendency to unpeel wallpaper. Emulsion paints that sponge off and are long-lasting

If your child is athletic he or she will appreciate sleeping arrangements that can be climbed up to, on to, and swung from. However, bunks or platform beds must be tough to withstand such treatment, as is the tubular steel platform structure (**below**) from the design, manufacturing and retail company, One Off, in London's Covent Garden. One Off make various standard platform beds but will re-design to suit particular needs and colour schemes. With growing children versatility is all-important, and what can be a climbing frame which incorporates a comfortable bed for a tear-away six-year-old, can easily be transformed into bed plus study area for a serious-minded teenager.

are the answer and these are good for stick-on glow stars or posters. Magazine design editor Jocasta Innes stencilled holly leaves and berries in scarlet and glossy green along the walls of her daughters' shared bedroom, taking the stencil cut pattern from the American Museum in England. A painted wooden chest to house toys and patchwork quilts in this bedroom added to the folk art freshness.

Hardboard tacked to the walls in giant squares offers good insulation and reinforces the flimsy walls to cut down on noise. You could add a blackboard to the wall, or a tin baking sheet for magnetic fruits and alphabet letters.

Beds and bedding for children

A child's bed needs careful consideration. Bunk beds are a good investment, even for the single child who

will ask friends to stay the night. Always check the bases because manufacturers tend to use an inadequate plywood base to keep the weight down for stacking. This type of base will warp when you turn on the heating for the winter, and the lightweight slats that fit into the wooden frame will snap under the weight of an active bouncer. Equally unsuitable for young backs are those curved cradle bases that you find on carved wooden frame beds. A firm, flat base and a good mattress that can withstand the occasional bed-wetting is ideal. The most suitable bedding for a child is a duvet and fitted sheets — just a shake-up every day and the bed is made. Polyester-filled duvets are best as they are easy to wash and will not cause discomfort to the allergic child, as feather-filled ones can.

Play areas

Children's bedrooms are inevitably playrooms. They can contain such items as work easels and drawing boards which can be folded away when not in use. Fold-up tubular steel chairs that hang on the wall at a height of 4ft (1.2m) will clear the floor space for complicated games, and you could perhaps erect a long horizontal work surface. At pre-school age it can house drawing books and pens and at a later stage it can become a desk for homework, models that need to be left untouched while they are drying, or electronic games.

Light

Lighting for work areas is crucial. The most useful are the angled clip-on photographers' lights that can be found in most lighting shops, sold in bright coloured plastics. They can be moved around the room, clipped on to work surfaces and set at the right angle to focus on the work in hand.

Try to ensure that light switches are at a lower level so that children nervous of the dark, or anxious to reach a bathroom at night, can find their way around. Alternatively you can leave a low-voltage light on or place a night-light (safety candle) in the room. You should always have wall sockets with safety shields for lights and gadgets in a child's room — toddlers and young children are inclined to stick fingers and objects into exposed sockets. Track-mounted spotlights above a pinboard, or round a mirror in a teenage bedroom, provide light where it is most needed. Mirrors can be hung at a height manageable for a child and moved up the wall as he or she grows.

The light source from a window is worth preserving. Blinds usually lose their spring mechanism as

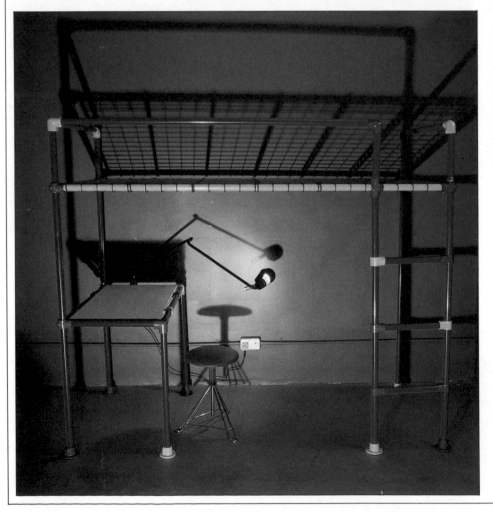

Some houses do not suit the high-tech vocabulary of tubular steel, and in this child's room (**left and below**) a gentler approach has been used. A little attic room can be an ideal hide-out for the very young; children love the atmosphere of these loft rooms with their sloping ceilings and bird's-eye views. The American artist John Canning has quaintly stencilled the floors and painted the little chest of drawers, adding a further element of make-believe. The painted chest (**left**) probably started life as a pretty dull piece of furniture, but it has been given a new lease of life by John Canning. When painting furniture, oil-based paint is best for the background colour, and an artist's oils effective for the decoration.

Stencilling floors is very much like stencilling walls (for technique see page 203). Use graph paper to make a scale model, and adjust patterns accordingly.

your child plays with it, but they are good for daytime resting. Safety sash windows are toddler-proof, but most modern houses with windows that open outwards need screening during the early years of your child's life. Vertical bars set across the window look ugly, but are more practical than the horizontal variety that can be used as steps. Later, when your child is older, you can decorate panes of glass with stencil cutouts on transparent paper and they can be coloured with felt pens so that they look like stained glass windows.

Space

Modular furniture systems for children, incorporating desks, toy boxes, cupboards and drawers, can provide an interesting island unit to section space in a generously sized bedroom. These units are often expensive to buy, but if you are good at carpentry you could try constructing one yourself.

Hanging space for children's clothes is largely wasted. Jeans, T-shirts, jumpers, socks and underclothing can be stored in a small chest of drawers. Colour matched wire-coated baskets (bought from stores) are excellent for storing items of clothing needed for speedy dressing. Suspend the baskets on low plastic shelves on metal tracks and bracket the shelves firmly to the wall so that they are adjustable. Leave some shelf space clear to display items or collections, whether they are glass animals or

Don't crowd a child's room with too much clutter and extraneous objets d'art, which have no relevance. Leave enough space for an older child's interests to develop: accessible shelves for treasured collections and spacious cupboards for games. The younger child's room needs to be geared to physical activity, so use only simple, durable and washable floor and wall coverings. Chipboard/cork tiles have been painted with wide bold stripes (**far left**) to make excellent railway tracks for these younger children. The walls have been felted for posters and alphabet sheets, and a high gloss door ensures that sticky finger marks can be quickly erased.

An awkward-shaped room (**left**) has been turned into a no-fuss teenage retreat. The slatted wood blind allows maximum light from the tall, narrow window, and a pale coloured carpet further lightens what could be a dark room: unwelcoming for quiet study and reading. Under the bed are large box shelves for clothes and games, and an office filing cabinet has been used as the base for a sturdy bedside table which holds a clock and the all-important stereo/tape deck.

SAFETY IN CHILDREN'S ROOMS

Potential dangers to a child alter with each stage of growth and you cannot anticipate every aspect of behaviour that may introduce an unforeseen hazard. The important thing is to deal with obvious and major risk areas before any damage occurs; minor problems can be solved by common sense as and when they emerge.

● Sash windows are generally safe for young children; if the bottom is kept closed it should be too heavy for a child to lift alone. Any window that opens outwards (**left**), whether hinged or pivoted on the frame, is a definite risk, the more so if the child has to climb to reach the catch. Install vertical bars if necessary, sturdy but easy to remove later when the risky age is past.

● Children of all ages use the floor as a play area. Fit smooth, washable flooring and make sure play areas are well-lit. Choose robust furniture in scale with the child and make sure tall units are built-in or bracketed so they cannot be pulled over.

● Keep light fittings out of reach, but place switches where the child can reach them. Any type of fire must be closed off by a child-proof fire-guard. Electrical sockets with safety shutters ensure that a child will not poke fingers into the socket holes while exploring.

● Remove an inside bolt or key from the door of a child's room, as it may cause panic to you both if a child locks the door from inside and then cannot unlock it.

● Toddlers need special care, since they cannot be watched every second. Invest in a stair-gate (**below**), with an adjustable bar so you can fence off stairs at top or bottom. Do not leave a crawling or toddling child unattended in a room with unstable or sharp-edged furniture.

This child's bedroom (**above left**) makes a splendid playroom with its notice board for school paintings and brightly coloured cupboards for toys and books. Even the track lighting is colourful, with red and yellow lights. Children love bright colours, and do not necessarily appreciate 'tasteful' pastels. Their own exuberant paintings make wonderful wallcoverings: attach a pin board the length of one wall, walls, and pin up paintings with brightly coloured drawing pins. Murals have been used in a witty fashion in this child's room (**above**). Large comfy cushions make adequate and flexible seating, and a country pine dresser, enlivened with a Batman poster, houses the TV and toys.

Painting murals on the walls of children's rooms is a good way of pre-empting their own efforts. All children harbour ambitions to scribble on nice clean paintwork. Don't paint your mural upon a porous or flaky wall, however. If possible, apply a base coat of durable, non-absorbant paint. On a base of good emulsion use emulsion tinted with gouache, or artists acrylic paints, for the decoration.

A bank of sleek and faceless fitted cupboards is not everyone's idea of beauty, and the much-maligned free standing wardrobe is making a comeback. Even the ugliest can be redeemed by paint or pretty stencilling. Remember that the free-standing wardrobe, adorned or unadorned, can move when you do. An awkwardly shaped room, such as this one (**right**), might not take a free-standing wardrobe, and so wooden cupboards, a bed alcove and shelving have been sympathetically incorporated into the rafters. The rafters also make a splendid frame for a bedroom swing. There is plenty of storage space under the bed and the white melamine shelf alongside is both a useful bedside table and a support for more pine shelves. The use of red (on the blinds, the alcove and the light) warms up a predominantly pine and white colour scheme. Artist Fiona Skrine stencilled this charming wooden wardrobe (**far right**). In its original state, the wardrobe was undoubtedly no beauty, but it was at least sound and servicable. Don't waste your time adorning pieces of furniture which are rickety or wobbly. Pine, deal or teak make good backgrounds for artistic licence, and you can always 'antique' white laminate by sanding it down and dabbing on paint with rags.

dried seed pods, fish tanks or models. Plastic waste bins stacked beneath shelves can hold bricks, Lego and cars while fabric storage pockets that hang on the wall house soft toys in pouches.

Storage

Many houses are now built with fitted, floor-to-ceiling cupboards in the bedroom and other parts of the house. Although this is a useful, space-saving design feature, it presents a row of doors, against which no furniture can conveniently be placed. However, if you do have to live with built-in cupboards, you can use a variety of tricks to make them part of the decor. Paper the doors in the same paper as the walls or paste on wallpaper borders that edge the cornice and skirting boards around the cupboards. To distract the eye from so much frontage, add window

shutters (they don't have to work) and draw them back against the wall on either side of the window. Paint them the same colour as the cupboards and panel a section on both the doors and the shutters with a fabric to match the bed linen. You can then frame these panels with mouldings.

Louvred doors can be painted so that each slat is a different colour, like an open box of crayons. Venetian blinds coloured in the same shades will have the effect of widening the room with bands of colour. Use an abstract geometric print for the fabric in the room (rather than another stripe) as this will break up the lines, yet preserve the geometry of the whole. Advertisements for fitted cupboards show items stored overhead like airline cargo. Streamline articles for storage behind closed doors, keep as much as possible in the open to add character to the room.

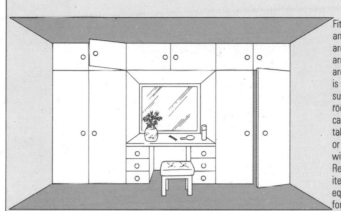

Fitted wardrobes are the obvious answer to storage problems if you are as tidy-minded about the arrangement of furniture as you are about personal belongings. It is an economical use of space, suitable in all but the tiniest rooms, if carefully planned. You can fit wardrobes and a dressing table along the width of one wall, or fill recesses and broad alcoves with specially designed units. Remember to make space for items such as luggage or equipment for hobbies, as well as for shoes and clothes.

Free-standing units offer more variety and are easily moved or replaced. The range is immense, from old-fashioned frippery to high-tech austerity. Clothes can be stashed out of sight in a wardrobe or hung on a wheeled aluminium rack. This kind of informal storage is good if you like to be able to see what you own. If you prefer to conceal bits and pieces, single stacking drawers are a nice variation on the chest of drawers. Aluminium lockers are functional and hardwearing, and can be bought in bright colours or painted to match other furnishings. If the bedroom is also a study, sitting room or work area, investigate different types of bookshelves, cupboards and honeycomb-style units.

Improvised storage space needs doubly careful planning, though whatever type of storage you choose it is wise to make a careful list of what must be fitted inside it. In a small room with deep alcoves, a simple but effective solution is to install shelving and hanging racks and cover the alcoves with curtaining. In this way you can construct different levels of storage exactly as you need them, and use the curtains to bring a touch of extra colour.

If you think of your bed as the centre of operations, then storage should radiate from it. Night time insomniacs should be able to reach out for books or the all-night radio station and the bedside light should be solidly based and not liable to topple over.

The compact sleeping system (**above left**) is from a range of made-to-measure tubular steel designs from One Off in London. Under the bed platform there is plenty of room for hanging clothes, and an alcove space for books and stereo.

Hats, musical instruments and anything else that looks decorative, can be hung on the walls; rackets, umbrellas and walking sticks can be stored in a stand in a corner or hallway.

Another idea for utilizing storage space is to convert a small, spare bedroom into a walk-in dressing room for storing clothes and a dressing table. Alternatively remove the cupboard door in the main bedroom and create an alcove for a dressing table, or place a wardrobe or chest of drawers in the space. Free-standing wardrobes and chests of drawers are still relatively inexpensive because many people do not have room to house them. These could be the only two pieces of furniture in the bedroom, and the chest of drawers can always double up as a bedside table. Trunks and chests can be used as low bedside tables, as well as for storing blankets, linen or ironing. A

cheap pinewood chest of drawers, stripped of varnish, sanded and filled with plastic wood adhesive, could be a decorative item in the bedroom. It will look better painted, but paints need to be rubbed in, wiped off, shaded and scratched to 'age' them. Antique the colour with streaks of burnt umber, mixed into an oil-based paint for a dappled parchment base, then stipple on colour through stencil cuts.

Matching tables on either side of the bed are a nuisance; they usually hold nothing more than a lamp and a bottle of pills. Instead, keep the chest of drawers at arm's length for switching on and off the bedside lamp, or buy a low, wide table. Pillars that support garden statues can also be used to hold a lamp, and these take up far less space. Tables are also useful for housing the television and the lamp, as well as personal items such as photographs and a diary. The

simplest way to store a television is on a shelf below a round table top, cut from hardboard. An old quilt covering this and falling to the floor will hide the television when it is not in use. In a modernist home, this would be looked upon as a disguise almost as bizarre as the Victorian practice of covering the legs of a piano. In a modern interior, the television would be on display on open shelving with adjustable brackets to allow the shelves to be moved up and down for items of different sizes.

Heating

For the bedroom, it is worth keeping any heating system that you inherit which is still functioning. Even cumbersome night storage heaters on off-peak timings can have a purpose in a room that is not lived in during the day. Aesthetics have to be tempered by cost, which is why bedrooms are often the coolest rooms in

the house.

Warm air electric heating, pumped from ducts at floor level, is the best-looking system, but it is also the most expensive and it would be rare to find this in the bedroom. Gas is the most common form of heating in the modern house, with radiators that vary from flat convectors to ribbed or modern steel ones. These are flatter and less obtrusive than the electric storage heaters that house clay bricks to hold the heat; however, with gas heating you will need a boiler. Try not to make the error of installing either electric or gas radiators beneath a window. This not only causes condensation on the glass as heat rises, but prevents floor length curtains from hanging properly when drawn.

Apart from a duck-down duvet, and carpeting which makes the bedroom a warmer and more com-

The ideal temperature for a bedroom is warm for the mornings, yet not too stuffy for sleeping. You can afford to keep the bedroom temperature fairly cool, as long as you are cosy under the bed clothes.

If you have a radiator in the room, position it so that it is not too close to the bed, nor abutting wood furniture, or under a window, as this will cause condensation. Peter Farlow has made this simple radiator (**below left**) a work of art by hand-marbling it with paints. If you are not up to hand marbling, you can always smarten up your radiators by painting them the same colour as the walls, or even a contrasting colour. In this bedroom (**below right**) London architect Piers Gough uses an old-fashioned but functional radiator for a dual purpose. Not only does it warm the room, it also screens the bath from the bed.

fortable place, there is a heating system exclusive to the bedroom. This is the electric blanket — cheap to buy and to install. An electric underblanket that pre-warms the bed an hour or so before it is needed, has to be switched off when you get into bed. Some blankets have an extra warm section at the bottom for cold feet, and the more expensive models have simulated sheep-skin covers. Use tapes to keep the blanket flat on the mattress and make sure that you buy the right size so that there is no overhang, as this can be dangerous. The overblanket is designed to tuck in and be left on all night, if desired. Not much heavier than a conventional blanket, it only needs one other light covering.

Insulation

Two unconventional ways of insulating and sound-proofing a bedroom are either to line the walls with padded underfelt, covered with fabric, or with books. Filled bookshelves create a random pattern that is both decorative and warm and a library of paperbacks is a good deal more soundproof than acoustic tiles. The average-sized book requires shelves about 8in (20cm) deep, but since height varies so much, adjust-able shelves are a sensible investment. Built-in shelves look best in a clearly defined area that will also house

objects like lamps and ornaments. The wall behind can be painted a bold colour or mirror panels can be useful for dressing, as well as reflecting part of the room to give the illusion of space.

There are several different styles of bookshelves to consider: you could have custom-built fitted shelves reaching to the ceiling, above enclosed cupboards, with a ladder to reach them as in a real library. Another idea is to line an end wall around a central window with tracks and adjustable shelving systems, so that the light from the window illuminates the book titles. A more conventional, but attractive, idea is to have white shelves backed with a sprigged motif paper to keep a country bedroom light and bright. The books can be kept in small groups with uprights to divide them. An awkward corner can be made more inviting with two ceiling-high stacks, stocked with books, and a chaise longue or big upholstered arm-chair next to a table and lamp to encourage curling up with a good book.

Use dress fabric for covering the walls as it is the cheapest to buy. It will last for about five years before it looks tatty and needs to be taken down for washing. Back the fabric with cotton or polyester thickening, bought in rolls up to 6ft 8in (2m) wide, and stapled

A four-poster bed creates a sense of timelessness and grace — as well as providing excellent insulation. The bed in the main picture (**left**) has been hung with drapes which are lined with a co-ordinating fabric. Lined and interlined curtains drastically reduce heat loss. The co-ordinated fabric has also been used to line the walls, which is another excellent and inexpensive way to insulate your bedroom. Dress fabric is fine for wall-hanging, but to give it more body, and further improve its insulating qualities, line it with polyester or cotton, stapled directly onto the walls. Book shelves bristling with the latest paperbacks make superb heat and sound insulation at a low cost.

Inside the bed, invest in a good electric blanket, either an under-blanket which has to be switched off before you get into bed, or an over-blanket which can be left on with perfect safety all night. Make sure that any kind of blanket is regularly serviced.

Duvets, either feather and down, or all down, have transformed many people's night-time blues. The light feathers (especially the expensive duck feathers) create marvellous insulation without the weight and bother of traditional blankets. If you have an old eiderdown, it is always possible to convert it into a brand new duvet, using the precious down feathers. Comforters, either feather-filled or polyester, are cosy too, and double up as smart bedspreads.

If you are hard pressed for space it is impractical to keep the 'spare bedroom' unoccupied. It is possible to make your spare room earn its keep by giving it another function.

Convert it into a study room, music room, or child's playroom, but site desks, work benches and train sets as far away as possible from the bed so as not to intrude too much on your guests. A bed can double up as a sofa or a storage system and, with care, it will not look too contrived. The Futon Company's sofa becomes a comfortable bed by night with the minimum of fuss (**above and right**). The stylish, low level sofa base comes in single and double sizes and in a natural or black finish.

when the room is unoccupied.

In a very small bedroom, either build in all the furniture so that it resembles a ship's cabin, or try to site hanging space outside the room. In many modern flats and apartments, the corridor outside the bedroom area is lined on either side with cupboards, and this leaves more floor space in adjacent bedrooms. A folding screen in the room will provide a changing space and hide a dress rail for guest's clothes. A small basin can be fitted, with plumbing connections on an outside wall, for guests staying in a one-bathroom household. This is also a satisfactory way of using up corner space. Make the room as friendly as you can with a jug full of flowers, book-ends that hold a carefully chosen assortment of books, a towel rail with fluffy towels, a bar of scented soap to make the room fragrant.

If you decide to use the spare room as a study, make it business-like and organize the desk and seating so that visitors know exactly where to be seated when they enter. Hide-away sofa beds with storage space underneath for extra bedding are very useful, as are the Murphy beds that fold down from the wall. If budget permits, use sliding panels on industrial tracks to hide a wall of built-in desk space and filing cabinets. Alternatively, buy a range of filing cabinets in primrose yellow, rose pink or primula green — these are excellent occasional tables and can house all the papers and documents in concertina files.

In a more casual set-up, the spare room could serve a dual purpose as a guest room and sewing room, or provide space for model making or jigsaw puzzles — all these pastimes involve patient construction and bits that have to be left lying about until the final assembly. A large trestle table, covered with a PVC lining makes a good cutting place and work area, with a small separate table and chair for machining and gluing. A full-length mirror can be useful for viewing fashion creations, as well as for guests who want to check their appearance. Site the table near the source of daylight and, as hobbies are often done after nightfall, place an anglepoise lamp on the side to illuminate the subject.

Frequently the spare room is used as a television room and consequently seating is required — anything from floor cushions to sofa beds. If you don't have storage drawers beneath the bed, you will have to house the bedding somewhere else — use a wicker basket with a hinged lid. This can also be used as a table surface for the television, the lamp and any books.

in overlapping pieces directly on to the wall. The average-sized room will take approximately two days to line with material if you have cupboards doors to cover.

Spare rooms

The spare room, as its name suggests, will usually be the smallest of the main rooms in the house. Few people can afford the luxury of an unused room for at least part of the year and it is an unfortunate fact that the guest room tends to become the repository for last year's hobbies and enthusiasms. Plan the spare room as an adjunct to housing friends for a short stay and for giving someone in the family a space to work in

A tiny bedroom (**left**) has been cleverly designed so that there is not an inch of space wasted. There is plenty of room for storage underneath the platform bed, which is screened off from the rest of the room with a nifty wood blind, creating a slightly nautical effect. A fluffy sheepskin rug transforms the bed to a window seat/sofa by day.

The two pictures (**below**) show a bedsit which is not ashamed of its dual identity. It manages to look good as a bedroom and elegant as a sitting room. If you are squeemish about leaving your bed without a disguise in a one-room flat, then throw over a rug, cushions, or a patchwork bedspread. Alternatively, invest in a really good sofa bed that is as comfortable to sit on as it is to sleep on.

Some beds flap up against a wall and can be concealed by cupboard doors. But perhaps the easiest and cheapest spare bed can be made yourself. Buy two pieces of foam, join them together, and cover with a furnishing fabric. Fold them on top of one another for a sofa, and lie them flat for a double bed.

KITCHENS

Most people have an idea of their dream kitchen. It might be country-style, with a pine dresser, displaying blue and white china; an Aga oven giving comforting warmth to a flag-stoned floor; a large oak table and chairs, papery onions and garden-fresh vegetables on the chopping block — a look that can be achieved in an urban house as well as a farmhouse.

Alternatively, it could be a narrow kitchen, fitted like a ship's galley, with a line-up of white laminated units that conceal ironing boards, slide-away larders and supermarket shelving for utensils. On the stainless-steel draining board lie some frozen prawns and packets of Chinese stir-fried vegetables ready to go into the microwave oven, the digital clock giving a count-down for the meal in minutes. In short, whatever your taste in food, and the amount of time you spend preparing and cooking it, there are kitchens designed to accommodate your dream.

It was in the 1930s that the concept of the small-scale workable kitchen was introduced, with the utility or galley kitchen being built in semi-detached houses and apartments. Later, in the 1960s, when open-plan living came into fashion, the kitchen was opened out to incorporate a diner. Previously the kitchen had been the sole preserve of the household staff, presided over by the cook and the scullery maids, their only connection with the household being the internal telephone and the 'dumb waiter', the pulley system that transported dishes under silver salvers up to the dining room.

In modern houses the kitchen is the hub of the house. It is the place where friends gather, where homework is done, food is cooked and often eaten straight from the oven. It is no surprise therefore that people devote more time to kitchens than any other room or space in the house.

The prime consideration for any kitchen is function. A good kitchen designer will always ask you how many meals you prepare daily, what kind of food you like eating, the amount of storage space you require and if you intend to use the kitchen as an eating or sitting area. These considerations determine the choice of fittings and appliances that will furnish the room. Most kitchen manufacturers make fully-fitted kitchens to suit any taste. Units in a coloured, laminated finish can house all the equipment you need, but for a grander style these can be trimmed with mouldings, Gothic arches or cathedral-style doors. You generally get what you pay for in terms of fitments for spice jars, trays, pots and pans, or a larder. Similarly you can choose solid wood or veneered doors and work surfaces of marble, wood, or slate. If you cannot afford a fitted kitchen, consider

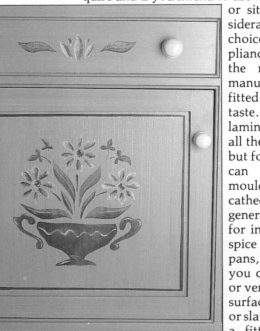

In the last 20 years the kitchen has really come into its own. No longer the 'woman's domain' at the back of the house, the modern kitchen can be a comfortable living room, sophisticated dining area or sleek convenient 'culinary laboratory', in the words of cookery writer and restaurant owner Robert Carrier. The kitchen units (**left**) epitomize the popularity of home-spun kitchen style, which cunningly connives with the most up-to-date modern appliances. The English company Smallbone of Devizes make custom-built kitchen units with a difference. Well-known for hand crafting units in kiln dried old pine, they now offer a hand painting service. Extra variety is provided by three types of finishes, popular in Victorian times: dragging, stippling and sponging. The units have been exquisitely stencilled.

The Allmilmö kitchen (**right**) however, is pure modern kitchen style with no 'period touches'. Called Fineline Edelweiss it is streamlined for speed with a new modular ceramic system which helped it to win a top German award for good industrial design. The door fronts are covered in continuous pieces of high-quality matt laminate.

Anthropologists will look back upon twentieth-century urban living and proclaim it schizophrenic. Half in love with brilliant kitchen gadgets for fast-freezing, fast-chopping and fast-cooking, we long hungrily for an era when kitchens were cosy, food was fresh not fast, and one dined at a stately pace and not at a gobbling gallop.

This beautiful Connecticut kitchen (**right**), belonging to Bill Norton, owner of the Eighteenth Century Company looks at first glance like a faithful reconstruction of that far away and long ago time. But behind the facade of copper pans and wicker baskets, there beats a twentieth-century heart of stainless steel. The most up-to-date appliances blend surreptitiously with the more traditional components of a 'country kitchen', and they ensure that the cook has time to relax in a room which is as much a living room as a kitchen. The warm glow from polished wood and copper pans draws the whole family into its cosy orbit. Hanging baskets from the rafters provide an endlessly versatile storage system, as functional as any high-tech design. The wood block floor is only slightly more irksome to wipe down than cushioned vinyl, but it is certainly more sympathetic to this expression of solidarity with a bygone age. Everything seems so fresh and airy, so brightly painted that it makes you hungry for home-baked bread, just looking at it.

The German firm Neff have decided to cater for kitchen nostalgia by introducing a luxury electric cooker which manages to disguise itself as a Victorian range. This attractive cooker (**left**) is appropriately named the 'nostalgic oven'. Its old fashioned styling positively encourages you to bake home-made cakes and scones. With the superb 'Circotherm' system you would probably bake at least as well as grandma used to! The brass handle, the clock with Roman numerals and black enamel front disguise the sophistication of the machine: the 'Circotherm' system ensures that hot air is circulated evenly throughout the interior; there is a plug-in variable grill element and the oven door can be removed for easy cleaning

open pine shelving for your basic collection of cooking utensils. You can put up shelves for storage jars, stock a dresser with plates, a larder with food and, with a free-standing four-ring cooker and a sink, you will have the basic essentials for building your dream kitchen.

Choosing equipment

When you plan a kitchen begin with the oven — you can choose from a microwave oven, hot air oven, conventional convection oven with built-in grill and burners, or the hob, which today can fit into a worktop only 1¼in (3cm) deep. For urban flat-dwellers a gas hob allows you to experiment with any cuisine that takes your fancy. It is ideal for puffing out golden *chapatis*, held with tongs over the naked flame, or for blistering the skin of fresh aubergines so that they impart a smoky flavour when crushed into a spicy North Indian vegetarian dish. In the country an Aga can be a constant source of heat for the copper kettle, scones warming in the bottom drawer and a stock pot for soups, the top plates large enough to hold great preserving pans for pickling and preserving the farm produce of summer. Thus needs, and cooking styles, change.

Modern technology is not incompatible with a

Aga (**above**) lends its re-assuring authority to a country-style kitchen. Agas have been around for almost 60 years, yet their popularity has not waned. Indeed, for people wanting to re-create an old fashioned kitchen atmosphere, the presence of an Aga is an instant stamp of approval. Agas can be gas or oil fired, or fuelled by coal, coke, wood (and virtually anything else which is combustible). An Aga comprises several ovens of different sizes and a large hob area. If kept alight 24 hours a day, it successfully uses stored heat to cook; the hob is always hot enough to boil water in a trice and it keeps the kitchen snug and warm.

SAFETY IN THE KITCHEN

A kitchen contains many potential hazards and some degree of risk is inevitable owing to the nature of necessary kitchen tools and appliances. But attention to detail in planning the fixtures and appliances you will need can greatly reduce the risks.

● The cooker is the primary danger. Look for child-proof controls, a guard rail around the burners (**see right**) or burners only at the back of the hob, so that pans cannot be easily knocked over or pulled down.

● Keep a small fire extinguisher to hand, specially equipped to deal with kitchen fires. It only increases the danger to douse burning fat or electrical elements with water.

● Place electrical appliances on a stable surface out of reach of children. Keep wires and plugs well away from the water supply.

● Fit electrical sockets with safety shutters. Don't overload sockets by running several appliances into an adapter unit.

● Install adequate storage space so that worktops do not become cluttered. Keep sharp and pointed kitchen tools separate in specially designed racks or drawer divisions.

● Provide good lighting over the main work surface.

● Fit well-finished shelves and cupboards, with no jutting corners or rough edges, at a convenient level for safe and easy use. Fit efficient catches to cupboard doors.

Neff's 'Circotherm' (**centre left**) is a single oven with microwave set into the unit space above. Microwaves are a marvellous invention for fast cooking and, used in conjunction with a well-stocked freezer can save a busy cook hours of preparation and cooking time.

Microwaves can be set into the unit display, as shown in our picture, or they can stand like a medium-sized TV on the work surface. The Neff microwave 6006 has a triple safety door interlock system, special 'stirrers' for turning the food and a meat temperature probe.

The kitchen (**left**) has a split-level oven and hob system with a fume extractor. The advantages of split-level cooking are not necessarily space saving, indeed in a small kitchen a conventional cooker is probably your best bet. However cooks like the ease with which they can prepare food around the hob unit. Split-level hobs are also versatile. it is possible to have a combination of gas burner and electric plates. You can also have a gas/electric mix or deep fryers and plate warmers set into the hob unit. Some models have covers; others have a special ceramic finish which is so hard you can use it as a chopping board when the heat is off.

country-style kitchen: an agreeably rustic exterior can disguise an up-to-date oven. The German company Neff, for example, produces the Nostalgia range of electric hot-air ovens with a dark enamelled front and small oval glass panel, brass towel rail to hold the tea towels and roman numerals on the timer. Cooker hoods in wood, with recessed shelves on either side for the display of pretty china jugs or plates can fit into awkward corners over built-in ovens (like old ovens built into the chimney breast) and this will add to the illusion of the up-to-date country kitchen.

The most advanced cooker is the microwave. These cause the molecules in food to jostle each other and create instant heat, so that it cooks in one-quarter of the conventional time. One minute on defrost thaws out deep-frozen food. Jargon such as 'computing your programme' for the oven in reality means setting the timer according to the recipe in a special cookbook that accompanies the microwave. Some microwaves have revolving turntables to set the food turning round inside, but the real revolution, universal to every microwave, is in the cooking utensils. Paper dishes go into the microwave oven; so do polythene bags, roasting bags and glass. Anything metal overheats and spoils the food, so all those cast-iron pans are relegated to the hob. Sauces can be made in an instant without stirring over a double boiler. The ingredients tipped raw into a glass measuring jug, will set to perfection in the microwave — just one whisk as it cools down and the sauce is ready. Unfortunately microwaves will not brown food, although they roast, braise and bake. Even with the special browning tray that you buy with the ovens, most recipes for microwaves use paprika to colour, as well as flavour, chicken dishes.

Hot-air ovens also cook faster than the more conventional oven, at lower temperatures. An element at the back heats the air inside the oven instantly and a fan circulates the hot air through ducts. The same effect is achieved by baking or roasting in a microwave as spit-turning in medieval kitchens.

Hobs with multicoloured tops, or in stainless steel,

may be set into worktops. They can be gas or electric, or a combination of both. Two other gadgets — the barbecue grill and the deep frier — also fit into the worktop and enable the cook to try more adventurous menus than fish and chips. Beignets and batters, Brie in breadcrumbs, scotch eggs and jam doughnuts are just some of the recipes contained in the booklets that accompany these appliances.

Planning a kitchen

Ergonomics, the wonderword that came into its own in the 1960s, about the same time as open-plan kitchens, made a great issue of labour-saving planning in the kitchen. The easy formula to remember, without a tape measure, and involving only common-sense, is to place plumbed-in items like sinks and washers against the outside wall if possible, and keep the work area compact. Every kitchen has to be equipped to cover various functions: storing food and utensils, preparing and cooking meals, and sometimes space for dining. The cooking area should be close to the cooking pots, and the refrigerator and work surfaces should be

nearby. Kitchen planners who draw up plans of a kitchen for you, should provide an estimate and make suggestions that will fit into your budget. They will install the kitchen units, but they do not necessarily make connections for the essential appliances. Always check whether plumbing and electrical work is included in the estimate as it can be very expensive. You should specify whether a pantry and laundry is to be included in the fitted kitchen area, as well as listing all the things you need — from hideaway ironing boards, fold-out tables, sliding cabinets for saucepans, tall cupboards for ladders and vacuum cleaners, or space for gadgets, such as mixer, coffee-grinder or pasta machine. Different room layouts open up the possibility of planning your own space. Perhaps you already have units fitted, in which case you could consider the addition of a butcher's chopping block, or a marble pastry slab; a central island unit to house a hob, or a breakfast table and chairs.

Individuality in the kitchen

If you are remodelling your present kitchen or instal-

A three sided square of units has been built into a large studio space (**right**), creating a room within a room. The sink, with a narrow drainer, has been positioned opposite the hob and oven. In order to save space they stacked one on top of the other. There is plenty of surface space for preparing food and ample storage space in the deep units is created with room dividers.

The cookery writer Prue Leith has a totally original round work-table part chopping board, part storage cupboard in the middle of her large kitchen (**far right**). This is the centre of operations with cupboards, shelves and drawers recessed into the base of the work table. In the centre is a tiered structure of revolving shelves for herbs, oils, knives and wooden cooking utensils.

KITCHEN PLANNING

THE KITCHEN TRIANGLE
When you are planning your kitchen, remember that there are three essential fittings — the sink, the cooker and the refrigerator. Ideally these should form a work triangle with the sink along one wall and fridge and cooker in the two corners opposite. Lack of space and other irregularities sometimes make this arrangement impossible, but try to place these items at an equal distance apart (but not too far apart) so that there is enough room within which to work.

The following schemes show how the work triangle can be organized in different kitchen layouts.

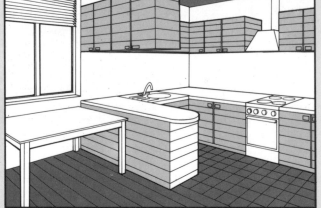

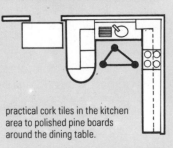

Scheme 1 This plan is for an 'E'-shaped room with the window on the long wall. To make the most of daylight, place a dining table in front of the window and separate it from the kitchen area with a low counter projecting across the room. Behind this counter, line up units to house the sink and cooker. You could emphasize the dining area with a change of flooring — from practical cork tiles in the kitchen area to polished pine boards around the dining table.

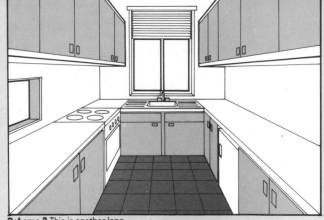
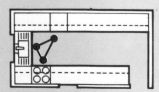

Scheme 2 This is another long, narrow room, with the window at the end of the tunnel in front of which it is wise to place the sink as there is not enough space to push out chairs. Line up units, along both long walls, to house appliances and foodstuffs. On the side with the cooker, put a hatch through into the next room to let in more light and 'unbox' the space.

Scheme 3 In a small square room, the 'L' layout is an easy one, using one wall for a line-up of units and part of the next for a round-up of cooking units and storage space for pans. The dining table can off-set the 'L' shape if placed on the opposite side of the room, and the tip of the 'L' can be made into a feature with a barbecue grill, or snack bar.

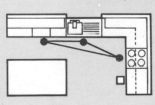

Scheme 4 In another square room, more generously proportioned, consider a central island to house the hob and the sink. Set ceramic tiles over the worktop, or use slate, or a non-porous marble-like material called corian. Add architectural distinction to a featureless room with a handsome cooker hood and display the cook's utensils alongside — a length of copper piping or a rafter will do, bordering the hood at its base. This circular or square hood brought down from the ceiling can have the extract pipe inserted between the ceiling joists and taken to the outside.

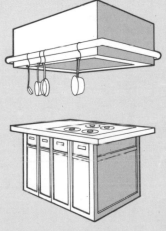

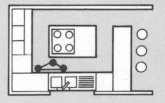

Scheme 5 Make a feature of an awkward corner without losing cupboard space in the angle by placing the cooker into a corner display unit. Overhead cooker hoods, like funnels, will create the impression that it is built into a chimney breast.

The kitchen (**near right**) was specially designed for Robert Carrier's London home by Smallbone of Devizes. The elegant units with their dragged blue finish, co-ordinated with terracotta interiors, would not look wrong in a living room. This is exactly the effect Robert Carrier wanted to achieve — a kitchen that is at once functional and beautiful. The cupboards can store his extensive 'batterie de cuisine' as well as display his lovely collection of old Spode china. Friends can sit on the comfortable and prettily upholstered window seat nearby and watch their host prepare a gourmet meal. A central peninsula work area incorporates a double sized hob and two separate double sink units. An original butcher's block alongside is the best possible chopping board, leaving the white Corian worktops free for stirring, grating and whisking, as well as for displaying the decorative kitchen items Robert Carrier treasures for their looks as well as for their practicality. The floor has been painted a deep Delft blue (to match the cupboards), and the border is trompe l'oeil. The kitchen (**far right, top**) has a more electric feel with its traditional free standing cooker and attractive mélange of old and new styles and ideas.

The kitchen (**far right, bottom**) however is deeply rooted in the 1950s style.

ling a new one, you may have to remove old appliances, tiled surfaces, even walls. If you plan to update your kitchen on a piecemeal basis, the best course of action is to plan it thoroughly around the colours already present and add a few free-standing items, such as a dresser.

A quaint style can be introduced to a dull kitchen by painting simple and cheap units a duck-egg blue. Dab a matt yellow onto the walls, varnish them with matt varnish to bring up a patina and hang up some still-life prints. Bentwood chairs stained a deeper blue, with perhaps a patchwork cushion tied to the cane seat and a maple table will give the room a distinctive air. Robert Carrier's kitchen is personalized with light blue painted units, dragged with coats of a deeper blue to match his blue and white Spode porcelain collection. The walls and the backs of the open shelves are painted terracotta, which suits the earthy shade of the cast-iron ware he uses for cooking. The floor is painted a deep Delft blue to match the cupboards.

Many manufacturers nowadays offer services that add individuality to the fitted kitchen. The units are usually delivered to your home with just a base coat; once installed, they may be stencilled or hand-painted with Victorian finishes such as stippling or dragging. The introduction of an unexpected texture or pattern will break up a conventional line of units. Alternate units of varying heights, an idea borrowed from designer Max Clendenning, can look more interesting than standard ones. In a custom-built kitchen, he staggered the heights of units from floor to ceiling-height to worktop-height, painting the ceiling a glossy red, the units matt grey. If you get a brochure from your kitchen unit manufacturer you can see how to introduce different units or door fronts in bold colours to break the existing line-up.

Described as the maverick of kitchen design, British kitchen planner Johnny Grey says: 'Fitted kitchens have so little pedigree that clichés are foisted upon products to provide them with an image. Timeless wonder, space-age fantasy, streamlined efficiency are just some of them.' His answer is to design individual items of furniture around each of the main kitchen functions: a sink unit, a storage dresser, a chopping block, open shelves, a suspended ceiling around which cooking utensils are hung, a central counter, even a special stove, all drawn together by some original architectural feature, such as a chimney breast or cornice.

Other enlightened kitchen manufacturers offer kitchen furniture that avoids the identikit moulding of a row of units. Pieces include court cupboards, end-grain chopping blocks, white ceramic sink cabinets in the Edwardian tradition, plate racks, wall-mounted storage units for china, or open shelves with ornate brackets to house tea caddies or spice jars.

Nick Ashley, a designer for the successful fabric house of Laura Ashley and son of the same, keeps all his kitchenware — and a great deal besides — on long shelves firmly bracketed to the wall of his London kitchen. Such a system demands a good-looking array of objects, but most cooks are keen to keep the equipment they use out in the open. A softer approach to open shelving is to paint the walls plum red, and just within the perimeter of the shelves, pin a paper-cut along each shelf-border to emphasize a country-kitchen store of preserves in glass jars and homemade fruit butters and jellies.

The last word on kitchen preferences comes from cookery writer, Jane Grigson, whose choice of fully fitted units is from the Wrighton range — a Delft blue-grey laminate with wooden door, painted white, that conceals a spectacular larder. Jane Grigson would add a conservatory next door to this kitchen, as well as tracked doors that slide across the sink area .

Sinks and washing machines

Kitchen planners claim that, ideally, 3ft (1m) should be left at the side of the sink for piling up dirty pots and pans, and 2½ft (76cm) for draining the clean crockery. The oven and hob should be no further than 6ft (1.8m) from the sink. However the ideal juxtaposition is hard to find, especially when one considers the importance of siting the washing machine and the sink on an outer wall for easy plumbing. Often this is impossible.

Those smart, pastel-coloured, oval sinks become irrelevant when you find you cannot fit a turkey roasting tray inside one. A double sink is a good idea, if there is room. Once the preparation is over, one sink can be used for rinsing, one for washing up. Between times, you can cover one sink with a wooden chopping board to stop things toppling in, and to provide extra work space if you need it. A handsome version of the double sink is the old-fashioned butler's sink, until recently, a prize find on demolition sites. Today, they are manufactured along with reproductions of claw-footed baths covered in the same white enamel. As with the baths, no pretence is made of hiding the plumbing pipes, which become an intrinsic part of the design, but with all the advantages of contemporary plumbing.

Underneath the sink a unit can house the bin and

Cookery writer Jane Grigson chooses Wrighton's Delft range (**above**) for a fresh bright kitchen decor. The white painted wood frames and pale grey laminate cupboard panels may look heavenly but they conceal a fiendishly ingenious system of pull-out racks and down-to-earth shelving ideas. A special pull-out larder activates at the touch of a finger tip and, as seen in the picture, it is conveniently placed for both the working and dining parts of the kitchen. Extra panelling has been used to make a free hanging chimney hood to keep the kitchen smelling as fresh and clean as it looks. A central 'island' unit combines a hob and preparation area, and is placed near the dining table for conviviality.

An old fashioned earthenware sink (**above left**) has been preserved not just for nostalgic reasons, but because its size makes it supremely functional.

The rectangular double sink unit (**above right**) incorporates a waste disposal system between the two sinks. Expert dish-washers love double sinks, because they can soak dirty dishes in soapy water in one, and rinse them off in the other. Put a chopping board over one of the sinks and you have the most practical system for washing and peeling vegetables.

The white single sink/drainer (**left**) has a large 14 × 15in (35.5 × 39cm) bowl with handy crockery basket (used here for washing and draining vegetables). Other accessories available include a teak chopping board and Luran draining board. Between sink and drainer is a handily positioned waste disposal unit.

Enthusiastic cooks like nothing more than to display treasured gadgets, pots and pans. An industrial shelving system (**above**) makes a splendid open cupboard.

A well stocked and ventilated larder with produce clearly visible is sadly a thing of the past. Refrigerators have usurped the place of the larder in the modern kitchen, but the very low temperatures of refrigerators can ruin things like creamy bries, eggs, and crisp lettuces. In response to a real need, the German firm of Bulthaup has developed this food cupboard (**above right**), with versatile shelving on a grid system on the doors, and masses of interior space for vegetables and wine.

the indispensable plastic bucket. Somewhere near the sink (if you do not have a separate laundry) you should plumb in the washing machine and tumble dryer, either combined in one machine, standing side by side, or one on top of the other. Buy the best machine you can afford; during the full cycle of rinsing and spinning, machines develop a whine and can walk across an uneven floor — only precision engineering will ensure the calm, smooth performance you expect from such a bulky machine.

Storage

There are many items to be stored in a kitchen, from appliances to chinaware, glassware, cutlery and cooking utensils, so that plenty of storage space is essential. Decorative pieces, such as china cups and plates, look good on open shelving, either on a dresser or in wall cupboards with glass fronts, or leaded diamond pan lights. A huge dresser piled with an assortment of plates, including porcelain and junk shop buys, is the idiosyncratic storage piece used by designer Susan Collier of the Collier Campbell fabric-design team. A cook's equipment should always be close at hand. Keep the mixer, coffee grinder and sandwich snack-grill on the worktop. If you have a pasta machine, clamp it onto a work surface near the pastry slab. The ice cream maker can hibernate in a cupboard during the winter and spend the summer whirring away in the fridge, but few items are so agreeably seasonal.

It is the collection of small items that clutters up a kitchen. Josceline Dimbleby, author of the Sainsbury's supermarket cook-book series, finds Habitat's plastic-coated wire grid, hung alongside the splash back above the worktops, very useful. On this

Diana Phipps has solved the 'should it all be on view or not' kitchen storage dilemma in the wittiest fashion. In her magnificent old kitchen (**left**) she has painted still-life portraits on her cupboards of tempting delicacies, and elegant kitchen paraphernalia. Copper pans, bowls of fruit, bunches of herbs and a collection of books hide, perhaps, more mundane articles such as the lemon squeezer or food processor. If you are not artistically gifted enough to execute such elaborate trompe l'oeil effects, simple stencilling on plain wood or laminate units is surprisingly easy to do. Or just paint your units an outrageously un-kitcheny colour such as pale pink, dark lavender or black. Pretty posters of fruit and flowers are often unit sized. Stick them onto the front of your cupboards, and protect them with a polyurethane varnish. Remember to use a water resistant adhesive.

can be hooked ladles, and baskets to house spoons, whisks, bean peelers and garlic presses. A knife rack for stainless steel and carbonated steel knives is also useful in the food preparation area or you will end up using the same knife for every task.

Neat ways of hiding all those tiresome mops, dusters and vacuum cleaners are provided for in kitchen units. These range from ceiling-height broom cupboards to a skirting-board pull-out panel for the shoe-cleaning kit. An excellent solution to storage in the small modern kitchen is the practical wall-grid system — a series of criss-cross wire frames attached to the wall with baskets and shelves attached to them. The various containers are fixed to the grid with clip screws and plugs, fitted vertically or horizontally, to house a variety of items including bottles, tins, mugs and jars, tools and utensils, even cookery books.

These unusual, yet entirely practical systems come in a range of colours to tie in with your kitchen scheme.

The refrigerator is the conventional place for storing food. It can be concealed behind a unit front that matches the rest of the kitchen, decorated with enamelled magnets, or painted decoratively using enamelled paints. Decorator Diana Phipps has painted an attractive still life of copper utensils, fruit and wine on the glass panel of her oven and the white refrigerator door in her Cotswold country kitchen.

Changing-room lockers, generally sold to schools and games clubs, offer an unusual yet practical pantry. Track doors fit into each other in sections, which saves corridor space, and the clothing rail provides hanging space for pots and pans, colanders and sieves. Bolt-on metal shelving, covered in red PVC, which can be sponged down, can hold the foodstuffs and china. Each locker has its own combination of straight shelves and rods, arranged so that every inch of space is used without stacking.

More conventional, ventilated larder units, marketed as mini-markets in kitchen books, have crates for cold drinks at the base, a cold shelf for dairy produce, wire baskets to house foodstuffs, and carousel shelving that hangs from the central hinge of the folding doors.

Gadgets of limited usefulness, such as electric can-openers, which hint at processed foods containing artificial flavourings and unhealthy preservatives, have given way in many kitchens to mushrooms in a plastic bucket, bean sprouts in muslin, or parsley in a pot — examples of the modern trend towards more fresh food. Pots of peppery basil, fragrant thyme and sage are set on window sills, cress grows on a flannel, runner beans trail their scarlet flowers round the kitchen window in late summer and city-dwellers see the value of a constant supply of red salsify and bright green corn salad grown in window boxes in rotation.

Anton Mosiman, head chef at the Dorchester Hotel, London, keeps a trout tank in his kitchen at home, stocked ready for cooking and eating. He also likes to make his own fresh pasta. John Lewis of Hungerford, who built Anton Mosiman's kitchen, made a pasta table on top of a trellis store of wine bottles so it acts as his wine cellar as well. The pasta machine is clamped next to the corian (fake marble) worktop and churns out strips of tagliatelle and fettucine or flat boards of lasagne.

Work surfaces and wallcoverings

Cupboard ranges can be pulled together with a solid wooden worktop, custom-built to fit your kitchen. Wood makes an excellent chopping surface and ages well. Ceramic tiles are also popular for work surfaces, although they must be grouted with a heavy-duty, non-porous tile grout — you could use a bold colour. You could tile your own melamine tops, but ensure that you have a plumb line with a spirit level before you begin. Then all that needs to be done is to rub down the surface with glass paper, stick down the tiles with adhesive, and grout in between. Sealed cork flooring tiles can sometimes be used to cover work surfaces but they are not heat or water resistant.

Pastry-making or rolling requires a cool surface. A marble board with a cork base will do, though it is seldom big enough for rolling out, so a separate section for pastry- and pasta-making is essential for the enthusiastic cook. Corian is a new material that looks

There is nothing more aggravating than hunting out that bottle of special vinegar, that jar of dried beans, or the one egg cup in the house, when you are in mid-cooking bustle. Worse still is having to search in dark cramped cupboards — with your head wedged inside and your arms flailing about knocking over sticky sauce bottles, you may well feel that your storage system is ready for a rethink. What could be simpler than Bulthaup's white shelving (**top far left**) that can be shifted and adjusted on the panelled wall, as desired. Place on the shelves the things you use regularly and therefore wash every day. Occasional crockery will only get dusty and grease-streaked and have to be washed off before use. Metal industrial shelving (**bottom far left**) makes open shelving a really practical consideration. Team it with plastic containers, usually used for storing screws and nails in the workroom.

A lovely old pine dresser (**bottom centre left**) provides a mellow and sympathetic background to a collection of old china. The deep cupboards at the base can be used for tins, bottles, freshly laundered table linen, or even children's toys. Kitchen drawers are rarely the right size. Either they are so big that the tiny biscuit cutter is irredeemably lost, or they are so meanly dimensioned that big items have to be wedged in. Bulthaup's Vario cupboard (**near left and below**) should solve most people's problems. The cupboard has drawers and shelves in a variety of shapes and sizes. Some drawers are capacious enough for packets of tea or biscuits, others small enough for candles, scissors or napkin rings. Made of either beech or oak, the Vario cupboard looks as much at home in the living room as it does in the kitchen.

In this small studio kitchen (**right**), the fabric used for tablecloth, napkins and blinds is Castle Coole, one of a selection of fabrics in the National Trust Collection, chosen by David Mlinaric and sold through Tissunique Ltd., and Prelle et Cie of Lyons. The elaborate chinoiserie design is an exact replica of glazed chintz used for the window curtains in the Bow Room at Castle Coole, Northern Ireland. Too grand for a humble little kitchen? Rescaled and in a crisp blue and white colour way, Castle Coole is charming. Note, too, the smart black and white tiles for walls and splashback, and the original Victorian tiled floor.

like marble but is stain-proof, reasonably heat-resistant and non-porous. Consider topping a single unit or free-standing island unit with a corian surface.

Wallcoverings and paint surfaces should be easy to clean too. Use a silk emulsion, given greater character by sponging stronger colour over the top, and rubbing on the paint with a piece of material so the base coat shows through. Alternatively try brightening up wooden units with paint and stencils. Oil-based paints are the most durable, but emulsion is easier to use. For stencils use acrylic paint thinned with water, or a silk emulsion. Matt lacquer will protect them. In a laboratory-like kitchen with stainless steel drainers, caterers' utensils and microwaves, paint the walls a high gloss white and then varnish. This sort of kitchen will suit Letraset lettering on the unit doors, spelling out the contents — 'Tea', 'Pasta' or 'Bread'. Vinyl-like brick does not look good over a large surface, but it does add a country look, if used as a backdrop to a collection of cooking utensils on wooden shelves. Laminated cupboard fronts can be resprayed with car paint if you inherit a second-hand kitchen, and window woodwork painted a bold colour will brighten up the room, especially with café curtains in a fresh gingham on a brass rod.

Floors

As kitchen floors are subject to scuffing and tarnishing, they need to be durable and easy to clean. In addition to this they should be waterproof, stain-resistant and durable — an exacting requirement but one which is easily met. Nowadays there is a whole range of practical floor covering available from the traditional flagstone floor to the high-tech style of industrial flooring. The cheapest floor covering is vinyl, bought by the square metre. Available in sheet and tile form, vinyl suits a kitchen with awkward shapes as it is easy to lay and to cut to the right measurement. A smart way to evoke eighteenth-century houses, using contemporary technology, is the bold, diamond pattern on vinyl sheeting. Black diamonds cornering white octagonals, or a chequered brown and yellow tessellate pattern reproduce exactly the marble flooring in the halls of grand houses, which was considered too smart for the kitchen.

The most expensive flooring is ceramic tiles. If you live in a small house or apartment it makes sense to buy vinyl, but if you are staying put, ceramic tiles are stylish and will give an age-old permanence to the place. Use them also for the walls behind the worktops and sink splashbacks. The tiles come in a wide range

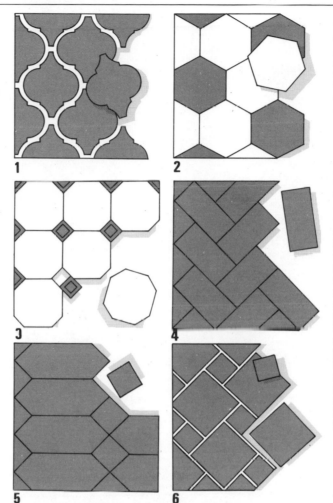

1   **2**

3   **4**

5   **6**

Styles of floor tiling
Floor tiles are available in a wide variety of materials — both natural and man-made, sizes, shapes, colours and patterns. Choose tiles that will suit the style of your room. Warm-toned terracotta and quarry tiles will look good in a rustic kitchen and come in more unusual Provençal (**1**) and hexagonal (**2**) shapes. Italian ceramic tiles, which come in many different sizes and colours, can be pieced together to make a patterned floor (**3**). A herringbone pattern is suitable for wood block flooring or brick pavers — both these materials are useful for linking the kitchen to an outdoor area (**4**). Create interesting effects by using different shapes together for a more intricate pattern, such as narrow hexagons and squares (**5**) or different sizes, small and large squares (**6**). Even plain tiles can be used more imaginatively — use grouting in a contrasting colour to liven up conventionally laid plain ceramic tiles, for example, or lay square tiles diagonally to create an illusion of more space in a small room. Remember that the effects created by all these different textures, designs and patterns can be faked by using good-looking vinyl flooring in sheets or tiles.

of colours and designs, from the witty Italian ones that you piece together to make patterns, to plain earthenware tiles in red or brown clay, fired at a lower temperature.

Expensive brick flooring, whether biscuit-fired or the more common red brick, looks marvellous too, especially laid in a herringbone pattern. Smoky grey slate, the colour of Scottish crofter kitchens, is also a good base. You can pick out the paint colour on the walls, the perfect background for a collection of blue and white china. Cork, in warm colours, and warm underfoot, has great resilience and, as it is flecked does not show the dirt. The cheaper cork tiles are unsealed and need coats of polyurethane to make them kitchen-proof, but you can use them on the wall to create an instant noticeboard.

The three kitchens on these pages represent three approaches to the modern kitchen. For designers enamoured of high-tech or minimalist modernity, the kitchen is the best place to try out schemes. All the most up-to-date, technologically tried and tested materials are perfect for a room which suffers from more than its fair share of thrills and spills. Plastic, laminates, glass, chrome and metal are all ideal for the use and abuse suffered by the average family kitchen. Vinyl flooring can be wiped down in seconds, melamine shelving, likewise. Toughened shatter proof glass is a good front for easy-visability cupboards; PVC coated fabric the best and brightest table cloth when entertaining the under fives.

The bright modern kitchen (**above**) belongs to the fashion designers Puck and Hans. The American architect Fielding Bowman has used wood laminate (**near right**) for custom built 'St. Charles' units which are easy to keep spotlessly clean, yet have the sympathetic appeal of good old wood. The centre work-table is on castors to provide a moveable feast.

The kitchen (**far right**) is in architect Kroen Van Velsen's own house. It is right at the top of the house and is very light. The whole room has been gutted to reveal metal struts on which versatile shelving can be moved where needed. An Expresso machine provides both instant refreshment, and an object of elegant, even sculptural, interest.

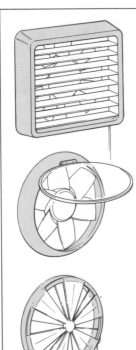

Ventilation
Kitchens and bathrooms both need to be well-ventilated so that they do not become full of steam from cookers or running hot water. Moisture will condense on cold walls and windows and will ruin furnishings and decoration, as well as causing more serious damage to the fabric of the building. An electric extractor fan fitted to the outside wall of the kitchen or bathroom is the best answer. Fans fitted to windows are cheaper and easier to install but are noisier and less effective. Three common extractor fans are shown above: an electric fan which can be fitted to a wall or window (**top**); an electric window fan (**middle**); and a non-electric window ventilator (**bottom**).

Eating in the kitchen

Before you plan the space for the table and seating, consider the ventilation. A badly ventilated kitchen is not only steamy to work in, but distasteful to eat in. An overhead cooker hood with a fan extractor linked to a hidden duct in an overhead cupboard, is the best way to remove vapour. A bright idea is to put the hob unit into a worktop above the tumble dryer, so you can combine the ventilation duct for both items. Ultra-slim cooker hoods from Gaggenau are only 1¼in (3cm) deep and slide out from under the worktop on a wall-mounted cupboard. In the country house kitchen you can make a feature of the cooker hood by installing a giant funnel that looks like a chimney breast (the style is usually called 'rustic' in manufacturers' showrooms).

Lights on a separate switch circuit are essential for the dining area. Take a few tips from restaurants on how to highlight the food yet dim the surroundings. Whatever the shape of your kitchen, you will need an overhead light for the table and specific task lighting. A small kitchen/diner needs four or five overhead spotlights, on horizontal or vertical tracks, that can be moved to focus on areas where they are needed. The only hazard is the bulb replacement, but long-life bulbs do not need to be changed more than four times a year.

A room more than 12ft (3.6m) square will not be entirely illuminated by spotlighting and will need downlighters, in round or square metal casts. They can be ceiling-mounted, semi-recessed or fully-recessed and are even more taxing for bulb replacement than their counterparts on tracks.

Task lighting of the sink or worktop is usually located on the wall under the storage units. Ensure that they are on a separate switch circuit to keep the focus away from pots and pans while you eat. Strip lighting usually fulfils the task; fluorescent is robust but flickers to life and gives a bluish tinge. Tungsten gives a warm glow to food, but it is more fragile and expensive. The output of a 30-watt tungsten strip is roughly equivalent to a 10-12-watt fluorescent tube.

In a U-shaped kitchen, you can achieve an instant effect of two separate rooms, without losing any space, with a peninsular unit at right angles to the main units. It will look less like a unit structure if you dress the table for meals in the French style with flowers, fruit and cheeseboard. The French are particularly good at creating an easy kitchen still life, with seasonal fruits in a wooden bowl, a winter orangerie with all the colours of a Cézanne painting in

Spot lighting is quite adequate for a small kitchen, such as the one in the picture (**left**). Two spots illuminate the sink area, and a moveable spot on a track lights up the high ceiling and the opposite wall. Track lighting is useful for a kitchen because you can add more spots should you need them. Three good sized downlighters are sufficient to light this medium sized kitchen (**above**). They have been fixed onto the metal struts of the ceiling and, unlike recessed downlighters, the light casings are clearly on view.

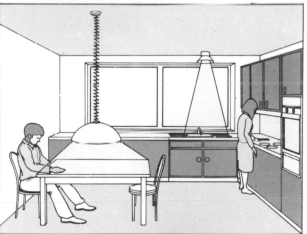

A kitchen needs good lighting for work areas. A central ceiling light which is the only source of light will cast shadows over work surfaces. Instead fix strip or spot lighting on the underside of cupboards over work counters and to the ceiling over the sink. If you use the kitchen for dining fix a pendant lamp with an opaque shade to provide a pool of light over the table. If the light is on dimmer switches you will be able to adjust the lighting to create the right atmosphere. Ovens are fitted with interior lights so that you can see what is going on.

The simplest dining arrangements can be made in a space saving kitchen, using ingenuity and the latest in pull out/flap back/fold away units. Wrighton's Tana design incorporates a useful little pull-out table (**above**): big enough for two to breakfast at; and when no-one is eating, useful as an extra work surface. Tana units and table are trimmed in oak framing and the laminate cupboard fronts come in beige or blue/grey.

Fabric designer Tricia Guild's kitchen/diner (**right**) is large enough for eight or more people to comfortably dine. This is a room for cooking, entertaining and working, and therefore there are two tables. Notice the comfortable bench scattered with brightly coloured cushions. At the far end of the room is the table reserved for more serious eating.

a cluster of citrus fruits, spring tulips in glass jugs, or little peat pots filled with crocuses. Behind the table, hang vegetable panniers on the wall for extra storage, or paint the edges of open shelves with the border pattern of your chinaware. Give the dining area its own flavour, with a natural arrangement of things, such as strings of herbs, onions, dried flowers hung from their stems, plaits of garlic, even sausages and hams strung up as they are in Italian delicatessens. Wooden butter moulds, biscuit cutters or cake tins in your initials can all give character to the walls in your kitchen.

A round table breaks up the framework of units in a kitchen. Emphasize it by changing the floor colour or pattern to encompass the ring of chairs. If tiles are laid across the kitchen area, lay them the opposite way under the table. On a tiled ceramic floor, change the colour or add a border pattern to break the continuity. Alternatively, you could stencil a pattern on a wooden floor.

A certain intimacy can be added to a dining area by pulling around a screen — perhaps a panelled screen found in a junk shop or made from a length of Liberty 'Near East' chintzes with giant peonies and dragons, tacked into a fold-up wooden frame. The glossy blacks and lacquer reds, with a touch of grey and white, will demand some appropriate table dressing to

accompany them. Perhaps a scarlet PVC table cover, set about with little porcelain tempura bowls and chopsticks, the centrepiece a bowl of cherries in a flat basket.

The dining table makes a statement about your approach to entertaining and style. Remember that no amount of kitchen technology in the planning of appliances and work space can compose your kitchen as well as your own judgement and skill. Remind yourself of some of the impromptu meals that have tasted so delicious without too much planning — kebabs grilled on skewers set between two stones on a picnic, or a red mullet flamed over a dry branch of fen-

nel — and make your kitchen reflect the way you like to live.

Utility Areas

It is a great asset to have additional space in a house or apartment for performing such routine tasks as washing and ironing clothes. A laundry or utility room requires space for a sink or washing machine (both of which need to be plumbed into water outlets) and other equipment, perhaps a tumble dryer, ironing board and baskets of washing. You will also need well-positioned sockets for other appliances.

A sealed-off passageway, if it is wide enough, can

Joss and Daphne Graham's relaxed kitchen/diner (**above**) has been decorated quite simply with white walls, Indian fabrics, a well chosen painting and pretty baskets fastened to the wall. An old pine dresser holds an earthenware ceramics collection. A dhurrie rug upon the terracotta coloured vinyl flooring and the Gujarati Toran appliqué work with the mango leaf border motif visually link the dining section with the kitchen.

be transformed into the laundry area, using the space beneath the stairs as the ironing section, and plumbing machines to the outside wall. In older houses the scullery converts into a utility room, providing a sink for soaking. Add a counter for sorting clothes and a wall cupboard for detergents, bleaches, bowls and pegs.

Most people fit the laundry equipment into the kitchen area and manufacturers have been quick to see the potential of making appliances on the same scale as the fittings. These are specially designed and coloured to match the regular kitchen units and they take advantage of the latest technology for programmes and memory recall, without resorting to a laboratory-like decor. If your washing machine does not match the line-up of units in the kitchen, remember that white goods, such as the 'fridge and washer, need not be left white. Use a spray car paint to respray them, perhaps in a dazzling metallic finish or in bold stripes with lines of masking tape to keep the edges straight. Alternatively, you could spray on a stencilled motif and put up a splashback of plain white tiles, grouted with a colour, that matches the background stencil pattern.

Appliances

The needs of your household, as much as the size of your kitchen or utility room, will determine what equipment you buy. A single person in a small flat will find a cylindrical drum spinner that can be housed in a cupboard space beneath the sink the most suitable machine, whereas a family with active sports enthusiasts will need a washing machine with soaking programmes, as well as a separate clothes dryer. The size and layout of the kitchen will also determine whether you have a top-loading machine, a front-loading one that will fit under the worktop or a washer with a tumble dryer stacked on top. Machine programmes vary enormously: they include mixed fabric cool wash cycles with lower spin speed for delicates, hot water soak programmes for whites, and economy buttons that switch on to off-peak electricity and reduce the washing time and temperature. Most machines take a wash load of up to 10lb (5kg).

Tumble dryers are either direct vent or condenser dryers. They get rid of dampness by blowing warm air through clothes in the drum. As direct vent machines need to be plumbed into the outer wall, this will determine the site for the dryer; condenser dryers are for use when direct venting is unsuitable. The most sophisticated version is the electronic sensor which

Utility rooms are considered by many to be as vital as a second bathroom. They certainly remove the less attractive appliances such as washing machine, dishwasher or freezer from the kitchen and leave more leeway to create a pleasing kitchen design.
Photographer Michael Dunne has a laundry room in his London home (**above**). Appliances are tucked away under a useful work surface, above which there is plenty of room for clothes to hang dry. Folding louvred doors pull out to cut the whole area off from the rest of the kitchen.
Space in a hallway has been cleverly used to make this laundry area (**right**). A narrow cupboard has also been built in, for storing such unsightly objects as washing powder and fabric conditioner.

A small laundry room and a downstairs lavatory lead off from this kitchen/diner (**left**). Many people dislike mixing laundering with cooking and eating for more than aesthetic reasons. They rightly feel that the grease in the air of most kitchens will adher to freshly washed clothes. In that case, turn your utility room into a laundry, and send the dishwasher and freezer back to the kitchen. If you don't have a utility room, then it is always possible to partition off a section of the kitchen with folding doors, or even venetian blinds. In the picture (**left**), a sense of unity prevails by tiling throughout with the same colour ceramic tiles.

dries clothes to the exact point required, depending on the fabric and the load. Other appliances that can be kept in the utility room are the deep freeze and the dishwasher. Once considered a luxury, the dishwasher has justified itself as an essential cost-cutter in the home, taking less hot water to wash the plates and glasses stacked inside it than the constant running of hot water to rinse a few items. Dishwashers also relieve the kitchen of clutter as you can stack the washing-up straight into the unit. Choose a good-sized model that takes dishes for three meals a day.

Flooring
Laundry and utility room floors are subject to much rough treatment, so they must be both durable and resilient. The cheapest flooring is probably the vinyl you lay yourself in a colour or pattern which links up with the kitchen floor. Buy the best quality you can afford as you do not want vinyl that tears or splits. Cushion backing will help to deaden the noise of machinery and acoustic tiles on the back of the door will help cut out the whirr of the dishwasher after a dinner party.

Keep bowls and buckets, as well as a peg bag and simple pull-out line for drying off damp clothes, in the space above the washing machine. Some of the new kitchen unit ranges have pull-down ironing boards with a support strut beneath which you can use to divide space between the laundry area and the cooking area in a combined kitchen/laundry. Clean clothes and cooking smells do not go well together so try to keep these areas as separate as possible.

BATHROOMS

Only three major items — basin, bath and lavatory — need to be considered when planning the basic bathroom. Yet it is the most awkward room to decorate imaginatively. The bathroom interior needs careful consideration: remember that once plumbed, your fittings become fixtures.

Manufacturers claim that soft, light colours create a feeling of spaciousness, whereas dark, rich colours are warmer. Before ordering everything in peach or avocado green, visit builders' merchants to look at basins, baths and lavatories in their showrooms. You will be astonished at how much solid colour fittings contribute to a room. That small sample shade in the bathroom catalogue is much more powerful in three bold ceramic shapes and the impact on the bathroom — often the smallest room in the house — can be profound. Take along a tape measure so that you can see how dealers manage to display fittings in small spaces. Their shop floor has to carry a lot of stock and it is a useful exercise in ergonomics to see how they combine all these features in restricted areas.

According to Robert Sallick, president of 'Waterworks', a company in Connecticut, it was the housing boom after World War II that led to the economic design formula that makes the bathroom the 'meanest sized room in the house', at a standard 5ft x 7ft (1.5m x 2m). Builders wedged a standard 5ft (1.5m) bath tub

along one wall and this automatically became the standard measurement for two of the facing walls. Because the tub was 2½ft (76cm) wide, they squeezed the basin and lavatory into the remaining 4½ft (1.37m) on the wall at right angles to the tub. Ideally the lavatory would be in a separate area, but if this is not possible at least partially enclose it.

Grouping fixtures like the bath and shower together makes sense, or you could just combine the bath and shower head attachment. The good bathroom designer will install a pump booster with a shower so that you get a strong jet of water — some are so sophisticated that the water is aerated, giving a similar effect to pouring champagne over the head.

Apart from the main fixtures — bath, basin and lavatory — you will need somewhere to keep soap and toothbrushes, a place for shaving or putting on make-up, a dressing area, perhaps enough room to store towels or put in an airing cupboard. Bigger rooms could have space for exercising, a whirlpool jet tub, and a sofa or window seat as well as pictures and books, reminis-

The bathroom is often left out in the cold when people design their homes. It is enough for all the plumbing to work and bath, lavatory and basin to fit into the one tiny space. But what is functional can also be fun, and your bathroom can adopt many styles, from simple to sybaritic. In the two pictures, left and right, the same scene has been set in very different ways.

A mosaic of Victorian tiles has been used for an unusual splash back (**left**). Although each tile has a different pattern, they are all the same size. If you would like to copy this idea with a collection of old tiles, make sure they are more or less the same size, or you will have some unsightly gaps in the mosaic. The marbled oval basin with walnut surround is Edwardian, as is the idea to panel the walls in wood. Edwardian bathrooms looked wonderfully luxurious with their glowing wood bath surrounds and panelled walls.

Copy this idea with chipboard on the walls stained a walnut colour, and decorated with picture frame moulding. The lights are copies of Edwardian gas lights. The ferns on the edge of the bath and the pretty pitcher above the basin, add the final decorative flourishes.

Mirror glass has been set into wood surrounds (**right**) to create the maximum amount of light in this rather theatrical American bathroom. Note the light bulbs going down the side of the mirror over the oval sink: the idea was filched from theatre dressing-rooms. Position the bulbs on either side of the mirror, as harsh light from above can 'bleach out' the reflection. Plain white tiles across the vanitory unit are an ideal background for treasured silver-topped scent bottles.

This loft bathroom (**left**), home of Dutch artist Ger Van Elk, explores the clinical style very successfully. Red and black border tiles and a turquoise tiled floor draw the eye to the pure architectural features. Note the dormer window which allows light to fall where it is most needed; over the corner bath.
Designer Adam Tihany has used mirror panelling to create an optical illusion of space in this tiny New York Furnetti apartment bathroom (**above left**). The handsome dark blue basins and bath are set into varnished wood surrounds.
White has been used everywhere in this bathroom-cum-dressing-room (**above right**), yet the effect is far from clinical. If the whole process of bathing proves too exhausting, then there's the Chevron quilted day-bed to recover on. The bath is actually hidden behind the white screen.

cent of David Hicks' designer bathrooms. However, larger bathrooms are not necessarily more luxurious than smaller ones. Often they are draughty, ill-lit, badly-carpeted, or sport acres of tiles that are cold underfoot. Heating and flooring are particular problems in large bathrooms.

Style

David Hockney's bathroom, featured in the film *A Bigger Splash*, can hardly be said to mark the turning point at which sanitaryware became high art, yet the bathroom was central to the theme, as in Hitchcock's *Psycho*. Tchaik Chassay, who designed the bathroom for David Hockney, is an architect who dislikes the fancy shapes and glittering finishes of fantasy bathrooms. He believes that fittings should be white, streamlined and classically shaped. He favours oval baths and semi-circular basins set into a custom-built top, with walls and floors covered with small square matt finish tiles in watery blues, greys and whites, to create a mosaic effect. He likes to put mirrors on the walls, and to cover double-fronted doors. He uses chrome fittings for cross-head taps and shower fit-

tings, and wall-mounted chrome Art Deco lights.

Bathroom designer Max Pike, who features a scarlet, roll-top, cast-iron bath in the window of his London showroom, says you can create an illusion of luxury with eye-catching fixtures, but nothing disguises the lack of well-designed fittings. Ideally, he likes white, or the creamy colour, called 'Champagne'. Max Pike enjoys working on exacting floor plans. He suggests grouping bath and basin to separate an area for the lavatory if you have a limited amount of space. Disguising the basin plumbing in a custom-built vanity unit offers extra storage space, as well as an opportunity for a paint finish such as dragging. Light greys, blues, white and minor finishes all add to the illusion of space.

An alternative to light colours and mirrored walls in a tiny, dark bathroom has been inspired by the grand, early twentieth-century cloakrooms with mahogany surrounds on white, cast-iron bath tubs and basins. The lavatory would be enclosed in a chair or box, like a commode, a design now manufactured commercially for smart washrooms. Chipboard panelling, stained mahogany, could cover the sides of

Why relegate your bathroom to a tiny space, when it can perform so many useful functions. A bathroom can be the ideal dressing-room, laundry-room, exercise-room, quiet reading-room, or extended children's play area. Install speakers, and you can get the benefit of your stereo system while you soak. Line the walls with books, and soak up some good literature. A bathroom also makes a good photographic dark room, or even an excellent place for painting. Have a sofa or easy chairs instead of uncomfortable standard bathroom furniture, and members of the family can talk to you while you snuggle under the suds.

The bathroom (**left and inset**) is certainly spacious, and commands an excellent view of the London street below, yet is in no danger of being overlooked by curious neighbours. Superficially, it is a bathroom-cum-dressing-room, but if you look hard at the dressing table by the window, you realise that it is in fact a solid mahogany desk. Just clear away the mirror, hair brushes and make-up, and you have the pefect spot for letter writing, novel writing, or crossword puzzle solving. Books jostle with after shave on the pine dresser (inset picture), and a special swivel mirror is exactly the right height for hair brushing. It is lit by a well-positioned downlighter. The elegance of the bath tub is left unadorned for all to admire, exposed plumbing and all, but when your plumbing is as handsome as this, there is no need to be bashful. Less attractive pipe-work can always be painted in bright primary colours. The elegance of the bath tub is pure Edwardiana. these superb taps (**right**), made in brass from original Edwardian moulds come from the London firm of Czech and Speake. Mahogany panelling is used for the bath surround, and interior decorator Peter Farlow ragged the wall in an authentic dark clover colour.

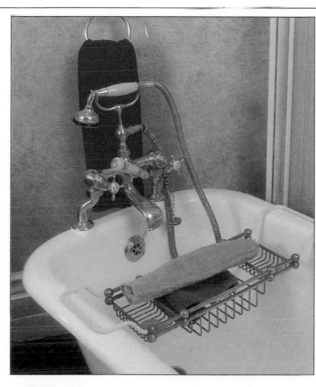

the bath and the walls to dado height, with smoky-brown tinted mirrors above. Cross-head brass taps and shower attachments, and a heated towel rail in brass would complete the setting.

Bath fittings assiduously ripped out of terrace houses and mansion blocks in the sixties, to be replaced with coloured fibre glass, are now much sought after. Some specialist shops sell nothing but authentic and reproduction Victorian bath fittings — cast-iron baths, large square-topped pedestal basins, brass taps and mixers, wooden lavatory seats and 'finds' such as the four-poster bath with elaborate and lofty shower attachments on four corner pillars, similar to those in Manhattan hotels in the early twentieth century.

Rusty and stained old baths inherited with a house sometimes turn out to be beautiful Victorian porcelain enamelled cast-iron baths. You can clean up the outside with a power drill fitted with a special wire brush attachment. When it is clean, paint it with rust inhibitor, primer and then a final coat of white gloss. The inside can be re-enamelled by a professional re-surfacing company, and rusty taps replaced with new ones to match the originals. One problem with free-standing cast-iron baths is that the plumbing always shows, for the shape prevents boxing in. To modern-

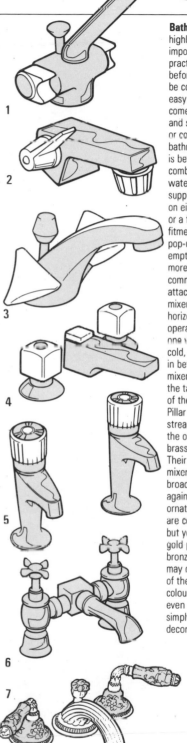

Bath and basin fittings can be highly decorative, but it is obviously important that they are chosen for practicality and you should check before you buy them that they can be comfortably turned and will be easy to clean when in place. Taps come in a huge variety of shapes and styles, to suit the most austere or cosy, stylized or luxurious bathroom scheme. The basic choice is between mixer taps providing a combined flow of hot and cold water or pillar taps giving separate supplies. Mixers may have two taps on either side of a swivel spout (**1**) or a fixed position spout (**3**). The fitments shown here also have a pop-up waste lever that controls emptying of the basin, perhaps a more elegant arrangement than the commonly seen chain-and-plug attachment. The single control basin mixer shown here (**2**) has a thickset, horizontal spout. This model operates by a lever control, turned one way for hot water, the other for cold, with graduating temperatures in between. A three-piece basin mixer (**4**) is similarly stoutly built, but the taps are mounted on either side of the spout and detached from it. Pillar taps (**5**) now have a streamlined, economical shape, but the old-fashioned types, originally of brass, are enjoying a new vogue. Their style has been adapted to a mixer design for a bath (**6**) with a broad central spout. New ideas again borrow from antique styling in ornate ceramic fitments (**7**). Taps are commonly finished in chrome, but you can choose more expensive gold plated or antiqued silver or bronze finishes. Tap control knobs may or may not be an integral part of the unit; they range from clear or coloured acrylic to polished onyx, or even the luxury of white marble, in simply sculptured or elaborately decorative designs.

The bathrooms on these pages make the most of limited space. There may not be extra room for installing an exercise bike or shelves of books, but the effect achieved by both designs is cool and uncluttered, almost aesthetic.

The Nordic influence has proved extraordinarily popular all over the world for bathroom schemes. The very sight of tongue-and-grooved pine clad walls is refreshing. English designer Alan Brown, who planned this bathroom (**left**) has used the Nordic style particularly expressively. The colour scheme is basic, yet always successful: white pine and red. Bath and basin are plain white, as is the ceramic tiled floor and one wall. The other walls are pine clad, with large pieces of mirror glass inserted to double the apparant size of the room. Red is used for the 'extras': towels, mirror, lighting, and big plastic waste bin. The bathroom (**right**) shows how you can make an all white bathroom breathtakingly beautiful , and not at all clinical. Architect Bill Herman has an architect's preference for white sanitary ware, and he has built upon this scheme in a Manhattan apartment to create an exercise in purity and balance. Bits and pieces are carefully placed in a simple wicker basket, or hidden from view entirely in the pale maple cupboards beneath the double basin. Recessed spotlights in the ceiling, and a neon strip under the mirror in the basin alcove provide adequate and un-fussy lighting.

ists, this presents few problems, as they like to feature the plumbing as an integral part of the design, but those seeking a pretty bathroom will have to be inventive.

Designers Joan Barstow and Sandra Shaw canopied an old cast-iron claw-footed tub with fabric for the Philadelphia Vassar Club show-house. The high shower attachment inspired the chintz tent, which was draped around the bath and canopied into a shirred valance that hid the shower rod. Elastic in the hem tucked the edges neatly under the roll-top. The outside of the tub was then hand-painted with a vine and flower design to repeat the pattern on the chintz.

The Nordic spa look is achieved very simply with white fittings, a corner bath or round tub, tongue-and-groove pine boarding on the ceiling and built around pipes to conceal them. An exercise mat and bar on the walls for aerobics, and a touch of red on the taps, door handles and bath accessories will complete the healthy, energetic look.

A spectacular fantasy bathroom on the top floor of a New York residential block has an entire wall of reinforced glass, uncurtained because it is not overlooked, and commanding an unrivalled view of Manhattan as you step out of the wooden tub. This style of bathroom is dependent upon the site for its effect, yet more down-to-earth bathrooms can indulge flights of fancy with unusual fittings. Fantasists who wish to emerge Botticelli-like from a shell-shaped sunken bath can buy exotic fittings from Porcelaine de Paris, for example, or Bonsack. Hexagonal or shell-shaped baths can be sprigged with anemones, and

painted wisteria can adorn the bathtub, toilet, towelling, shower curtains and soap dishes. Tap heads can be decorated with a single flower, or you may prefer dolphin taps and turtle water spouts. American designer Sherle Wagner creates fantasy bathrooms with a water-lily set upon a pedestal stem, or a round basin lined with burnished pewter. Her speciality is painting flowers on basins with gloss paint, sealed with a watertight varnish: 'Chinese Cherry' or 'Wisteria' sprays in palest lilac blossom on white porcelain. The designer for the *James Bond* films actually borrows set pieces for bathrooms from 'West One', the bathroom shop in London. Finished in glittering gun-metal or black fox metallics and sunken into marble surrounds, with bolstered foam-filled head rests, these bathtubs are big enough to hold two or three bathers. However this range is not for anyone with limited space or funds.

Fabrics and paints in soft colours contribute to the pretty cottage freshness. Sue Leigh, former home editor on *Brides and Setting Up Home* magazine wanted a bathroom that had a light and airy country cottage style. When she bought her Victorian terrace house in London, the bath was in a small lean-to that also served as a kitchen. She decided to convert the bedroom above the kitchen, for easy water outlets, into a bathroom. The old cast-iron bath was renewed with professional enamelling and set in the centre of the room; a square pedestal basin from a demolition yard and a modern white toilet (the most expensive item) completed the fittings. The floorboards were sanded to a pale honey colour and sealed, pale rugs in mint, white and rose were scattered on the floor, and the small fireplace — 'too pretty to rip out' — was painted inside with stove black and filled with ferns. Mint green and white wallpaper and matching tiles for the splash-back and hearth reinforced the colour scheme, with ceiling, window frames and skirting-boards painted white. A fine chest of drawers housed towels, cotton wool, tissues, toilet rolls, spare soaps and hot water bottles, and a set of open wicker shelves by the basin held toothbrushes, shaving gear, lotions, oils and shampoos. A bamboo bathrack accommodated flannels, sponges, soap and a nail brush. 'Careful accessorising contributes a lot to the final effect,' says Sue Leigh. 'Hang prints and paintings, framed mirrors — not just a functional one over the basin — and put out a collection of sea shells and pebbles and a bowl of scented pot pourri.'

Repairing chipped basins with filler and painting designs with waterproof artists' oils is a good idea if

If you move into an old house and inherit sanitaryware dating back to the time of Queen Victoria, don't even think about replacing it with acrylic modernity. The shapes of Victorian, Edwardian, even 1930s baths and sinks are enchanting, and they were constructed with pretty hard-wearing materials: glazed ceramic and cast-iron. You may even be lucky enough to inherit a decorated lavatory: all the rage one hundred years ago. Some such lavatory bowls are so intricately decorated, they are veritable works of art, attracting frantic bidding at auctions. By all means decorate an existing lavatory or basin, as has been skillfully done in this bathroom (**right**). Make sure first that the surface is properly enamelled. Enamel can be renewed, either by yourself or by professionals. The pattern on this basin has been stencilled on and copied onto surrounding tiles.

The bathroom (**far left**) should satisfy the most glamorous bather. It has echoes of Edwardian decadence with its chandelier and flounced net curtains, and even earlier classical features, such as the marble floor and round sunken bath with Greek Key design, gold taps, and a finely decorated washbasin add the flourishes to a bathroom which may be a trifle excessive, but certainly fun.

The sunken bath (**left**) has a certain distinction. High above the American valleys a bather can watch the play of sunset or sunrise as the light filters through a delicate arrangement of windows and skylights. The tub can easily spring into life and become a jacuzzi and, for withstanding the sustained bliss of a scenic whirl, the tub has been specially contoured into seats and reclining positions. All in all, an idea to be treated carefully if you inhabit the northern hemisphere.

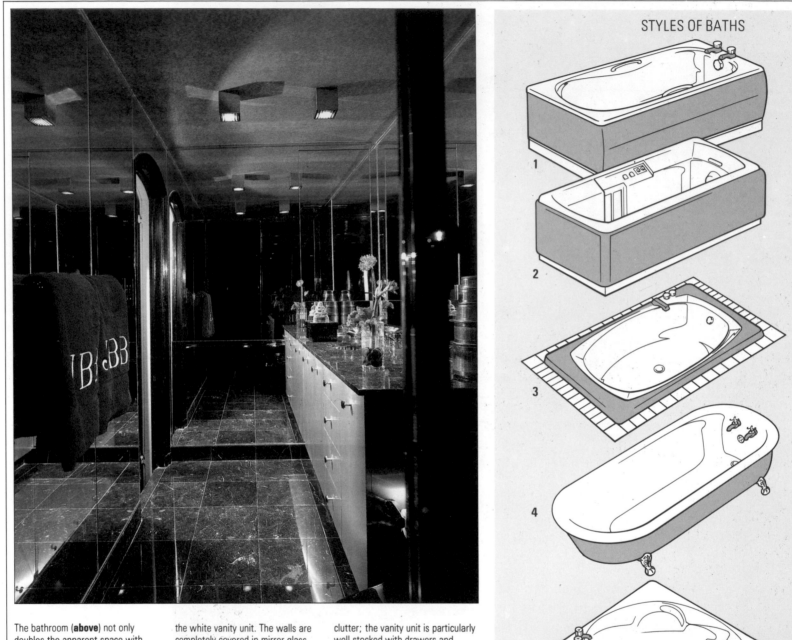

STYLES OF BATHS

1

2

3

4

5

The bathroom (**above**) not only doubles the apparent space with mirrors — but actually increases it ad infinitum. The Blumert residence in New York, designed by architects Ohrbach and Jacobson fairly glistens with reflected light, made dramatic by the chrome and black colour scheme. The floor is constructed with black marble tiles and the same black marble has been laid across the white vanity unit. The walls are completely covered in mirror glass. The ceiling is metallic grey and the lighting consists of four grey downlighters, reflected forever in this dream world of mirrors. To anchor the colour scheme, touches of scarlet have been used: on the monogrammed towels, and the black and scarlet lacquered wicker containers. Notice the absence of clutter; the vanity unit is particularly well stocked with drawers and everything can be hidden from view.

Whether your bathroom is cramped or generous, the bath can hardly go unnoticed, but with the range of fittings now available, you can choose whether to make it a dominant visual feature, or one that is simply functional, attractive but unobtrusive. Old-style, heavyweight baths were made from cast-iron with porcelain enamelled finish. Modern baths are more likely to be pressed steel beneath the enamelling; lightweight baths are formed from plastics. Plastics introduced an explosion of colour to the cheaper ranges of bathroom fittings. White is still the least expensive choice, but delicate pastels are popular and higher priced designs include a range of vivid hues and rich, dark tones. To conceal awkward spaces or unsightly plumbing, you can buy preformed and coordinated panels; some are designed to include storage units within this otherwise wasted space. Standard baths now routinely incorporate features such as hand grips set in the sides and internal contouring designed to support the reclining body (1). Similar in design but different in effect is the bath that includes a whirlpool fitment (2). The system can be attached to any bath or you can select a specially designed model with this as its primary facility. A sunken bath (3) is often considered the height of luxury, but arrangements to fit and plumb it in must be carefully planned and costed. The old Victorian model of the free-standing bath is very much back in fashion (4). It need not be pressed against the wall; set it with the short side to the wall and allow it to protrude into the room, if you can successfully use the surrounding space. A corner bath (5) is space-saving; loss of length may be compensated by depth and comfort. Corner baths frequently include a recessed seat and can be adapted as shower units.

As a complete contrast to the picture on the opposite page, this charming vanity unit (**left**), has been built into an old pine dresser. Plumbing was no more difficult than plumbing a basin into a standard vanity/storage unit. If you like the look of old wood lovingly restored, polished and sealed, don't feel that you have to live without it in the bathroom and put up with shiny plastic. Hunt round junk shops for useful cupboards (old oak office furniture can be especially sturdy). As long as the wood is properly sealed, these pieces will make serviceable and attractive bathroom units.

you inherit old fittings in classic shapes. Designer Janet Allen of the Boston Junior League of Decorators spruced up a chipped basin with Renubath filler and then painted camellias over the basin base. When the oils had dried, she sealed the design with polyurethane to make it water resistant. Pipes situated below were concealed with the floral print fabric that inspired the camellia painting, and this was gathered into a shirred smocking top.

Plumbing

Few things are as irritating as showers that trickle, and baths that drain slowly. Good plumbing (and that means easy access to both inlet and outlet pipes) is essential. Make a plan of where the water supply and waste pipes enter, and make a layout that uses existing plumbing. Mandatory regulations concern waste water, which must flow into the down pipe on the ex-

terior wall. If fittings are positioned at a distance from this pipe, you may need to raise the floor area to get a good angle for swift drainage.

Baths

The standard British bath is rectangular, measuring about 67in x 30in (170cm x 76cm). Slightly narrower baths are available, but they are rarely less than 26½in (67cm) wide. Cast-iron tubs from the Continent are sometimes 47in (120cm) long and slightly deeper for soaking; the 'Sitty' from Italy measures 47in x 29½in (120cm x 75cm) and has deep sides and a shaped base for comfort.

Corner baths make better use of floor space than rectangular models, but make sure they will fit through door and stair space if you install them upstairs. The corner bath or shower is even deeper and supplied with a curved shower rail. Oriental soaking

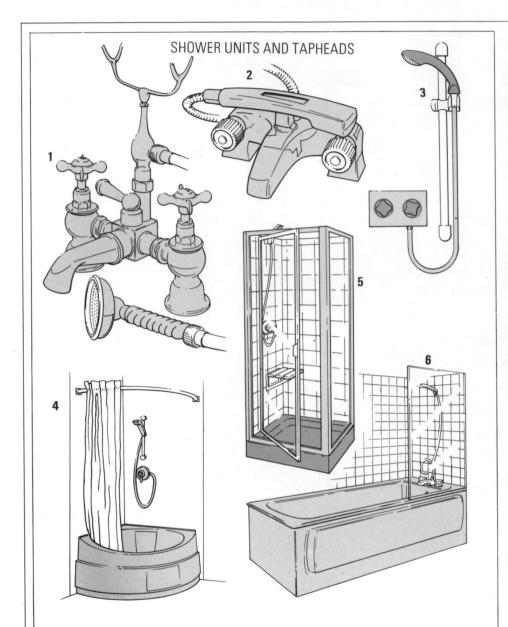

SHOWER UNITS AND TAPHEADS

A shower spray fitted to bath taps is handy for hair-washing or a quick all-over wash. Such fittings come in a variety of styles — imitating the old Edwardian brass taps (1) or from streamlined modern ranges of chrome and acrylic fittings (2). A neat and economical wall unit (3) can be installed above the bath or in a separate space with shower tray

and curtains. Showers spread steam and condensation, so be sure to check damp-proofing of walls. A corner bath can be adapted to include a shower (4), closed off with a curtain on a specially designed curving rail. For luxury and complete privacy, erect a self-contained shower cubicle (5), with rigid plastic walls and a plastic or enamelled-metal shower

tray. Such units can be placed outside the bathroom — in a hall or bedroom alcove, for example — if plumbing arrangements permit. Alternatively, for a spray attachment wall-mounted above the bath, use plastic panels to enclose the space (6). If the side flap is hinged, it can be pushed back against the wall when not in use.

tubs combine the sit-down bath with a shower in a space not much larger than a shower tray. Lowering the bath effectively increases the apparent size of the bathroom, though it is a job for the professionals. A sunken bath can make even the smallest bathroom look luxurious and the best bathroom shops feature several.

Some baths also provide room for storage, like the Armitage Shanks bath with a side panel that can be let down to reveal space for bottles, cleaning fluids and more practical bathroom accessories. American designer Patricia Drummond placed a simple but solid wooden frame over a functional bath tub, topped it with a platform and added upholstered cushions, pillows and a curtain to turn it into a seating alcove by day.

Whirlpool baths make bathing a health spa exercise; they are invigorating and increasingly recognized as beneficial to stress. The first model was invented by Senor Jacuzzi for his arthritic son. Today whirlpool baths have many different names, but they all operate on the same principle: strategically placed jets regulate the pummelling or swirling effect of the water. Some maternity homes install Jacuzzis to help in the first stages of labour. As long as your ceiling joists can support the weight of a Jacuzzi it is a feasible alternative to several weeks on a health farm where they are used to help break down excessive cellulite.

Showers

Manufactured shower cubicles that separate the shower from the bath area are complete units made of metal, plastic sheet or glass fibre, with all the fittings and attachments. They are completely waterproof and need only to be connected to the water supply and waste pipes. Thermostatically-controlled fittings for the shower ensure that the water is at the correct temperature. The head of the shower has to be at least 3ft (91cm) below the bottom of the cold water tank for adequate water pressure, though electric pumps can give booster pressure.

Basins

Usually rather wide and deep, the smallest basin measures 20in x 16in (51cm x 40.5cm). In a single-bathroom house it is worth installing the largest basin you can buy. Decorator Diana Phipps recommends fitting kitchen-sink faucets as they have a longer spout than the standard bathroom version, and make hair washing more pleasant. A wall-mounted basin means exposed plumbing, so build in a narrow shelf to par-

The bathroom (**left**) belongs to Frans Molenaar, the dress designer, and was designed by Mark Sutton-Vane. White is the dominant theme, and it has been used for the sanitary ware, for the tiles, paint work and curtains. Floor, walls, and bath and basin surrounds are tiled, yet strangely, the effect is not clinical and austere, but very pretty, and the little round basin looks quite endearing.

TYPES OF BASINS

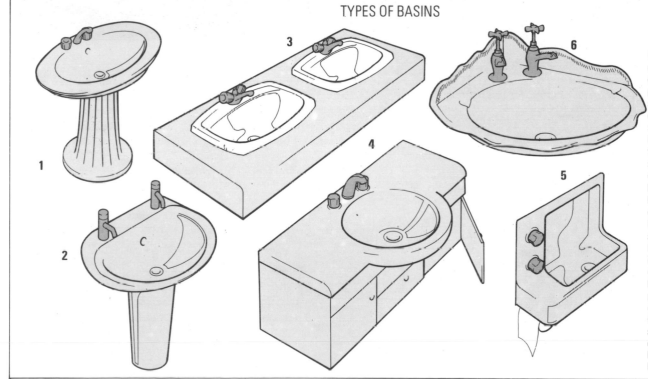

Basins are made from a variety of materials, including vitreous china, enamelled steel or lightweight plastics. Pedestal designs include a sturdy, old-style basin with fluted column (**1**) or a simple, modern shape with clean lines, a generous bowl and a flat back to fit snugly to the wall (**2**). More lavish with space are built-in basins — the double vanity unit (**3**) sunk into a laminated counter top, which can be backed with a sweep of mirrors, or a moulded fitment with a built-in base which provides extra storage space (**4**). An advantage of built-in basins is that they conceal plumbing completely. An economical design that can be suitably fitted beside the toilet is a shallow basin partly recessed into the wall (**5**). A corner basin can save space in the bathroom, even if it is elaborately styled with shell-like edges and old-fashioned taps (**6**). A wall hung basin should be fixed securely to a load-bearing wall.

PLANNING A BATHROOM

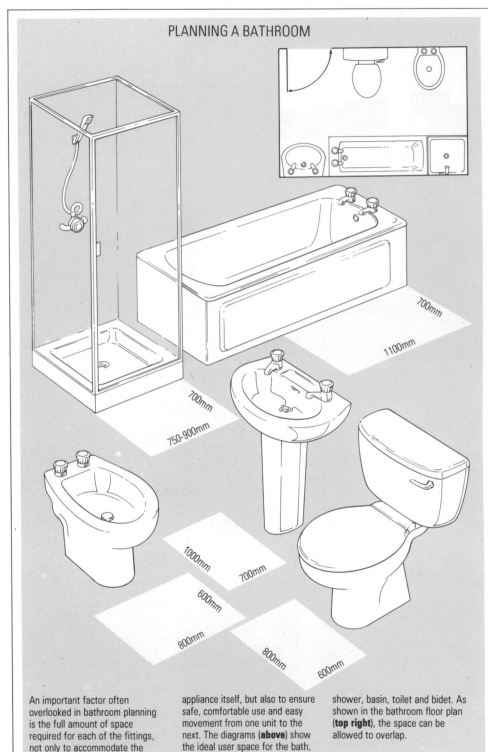

700mm

1100mm

700mm

750-900mm

1000mm

700mm

600mm

800mm

800mm

600mm

An important factor often overlooked in bathroom planning is the full amount of space required for each of the fittings, not only to accommodate the appliance itself, but also to ensure safe, comfortable use and easy movement from one unit to the next. The diagrams (**above**) show the ideal user space for the bath, shower, basin, toilet and bidet. As shown in the bathroom floor plan (**top right**), the space can be allowed to overlap.

tially conceal pipes, or cover with tongue-and-groove boarding on battens. A dual-purpose solution to this problem is to build a cupboard under a wall-mounted basin to hide the pipes and provide storage space. If you are panelling the wall to cover the basin plumbing and house the lavatory cistern as well, make sure the height of the cistern lines up with the height of the basin. You can always consider a pedestal basin instead of a wall-mounted one as it will leave more floor space.

Bathroom accessories

Most people associate yards of mirror with luxurious bathrooms. Mirrors certainly create the illusion of space, but they need a lot of cleaning and can throw back reflections that are not visually appealing. If you do favour mirrors, consider the slightly tinted ones in bronze tones for a healthy glow. If your walls are plasterboard, buy featherlight mirrors made of plastic film on polythene sheets, coated with aluminium, which need no structural support and are less inclined to steam up.

Put up open shelving to hold your prettier bottles

What in America is called the 'master bath' and in England the main or the ensuite bathroom, is more and more being geared to relaxation, and not just to puritan cleansing and unenjoyable showering down.

The bathroom (**above**), located in a French château, is just such a relaxing spot. It is a very elegant, pannelled, ensuite bathroom with its tie-back curtains and period furniture. In fact it can be used just as well as a dressing room, as it can a bathroom; the large bay window, an unusual feature in a bathroom, allows plenty of natural light for applying make-up.

The bathroom (**right**) is a neat ensuite, making good use of a space created by an alcove. A simple foot tub doubles as a shower, and the white tiles are nicely decorated with splashes of red.

and jars. Pick a good background colour for the shelves and place a few items on them, such as coral or shells, or buy boldly coloured towels to accent it. Thus a deep blue shelf can be emphasized with lavender and turquoise towels in a white bathroom.

Heated brass or chrome towel rails that are timed to warm up an hour before bath-time are cost effective and provide cosiness in winter. Hang hooks for towels at lower levels for small children, as it is easier for them to hang towels on pegs than over bars.

Windows
Blinds make the most practical window dressing in the bathroom, unless you have a large bathroom that will take drapes. You can improve split bamboo blinds with yellow-ochre paint, thinned down with white spirit, and a coat of French polish.

Walls
If you inherit large, square glazed tiles in a rather sludgy colour, take off the top third and paint the wall surface a matching colour in gloss paint for shine, putting on several coats for a deeper tone. Then stencil a border pattern along the wall-to-ceiling edge, and paint a simple pattern on the tiles. You could paint a ribbon design, threaded through each tile with mock eyelets. Shade the bottom for emphasis and on every sixth tile, paint a bow in the middle. A pastel striped cotton dhurrie rug on the floor will link the colours beautifully.

Floors
Foam-backed tumbletwist, used to cover bedroom

Both the bathrooms on these pages are typically small in size, yet the treatment is radically different. The bathroom and small picture inset (**left**) is fresh and pretty, Mediterranean-fashion, in crunchy blues and sweet pinks. The bathroom (**right**) has a kind of outrageous adolescent charm which harks back to the confident swinging sixties. Neither high-tech, nor minimalist, it is quite simply rebellious with its white vinyl padded walls, black painted shelving unit, and black door. The architect is Jan Kapilchy who wanted a tiny bathroom in a tiny London flat to look that bit different.

Joss and Daphne Graham designed the bathroom (**left**) for their London home. They were clever enough to match blue and white tiles from Portugal, with crisp wallpaper and matching border from Osborne and Little and with Colefax and Fowler chintz for the festoon blind. Daphne Graham maintains that ordinary curtains are a nuisance in a bathroom, yet a festoon blind, especially in chintz, and with a pleated taffeta edging adds a touch of flamboyance. Notice how the wallpaper border starts at the top of the window, and not where the ceiling meets the walls. This is quite deliberate. As Daphne explains: 'The idea of a border at this level was to visually take the ceiling downwards as the room is taller than it is wide.'. Above the bath is a rather lovely Japanese painting of a fish on silk. The rag rug is Swedish, and the custom built unit around the basin has been dragged with cream over white, and the moulded edge scumbled with blue.

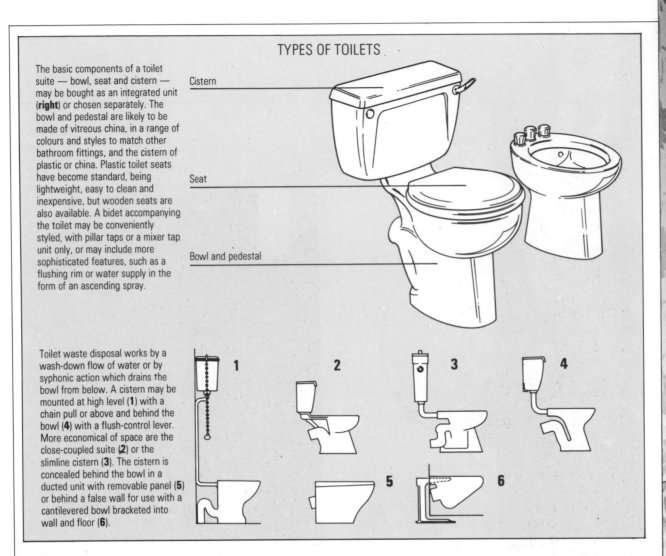

TYPES OF TOILETS

The basic components of a toilet suite — bowl, seat and cistern — may be bought as an integrated unit (**right**) or chosen separately. The bowl and pedestal are likely to be made of vitreous china, in a range of colours and styles to match other bathroom fittings, and the cistern of plastic or china. Plastic toilet seats have become standard, being lightweight, easy to clean and inexpensive, but wooden seats are also available. A bidet accompanying the toilet may be conveniently styled, with pillar taps or a mixer tap unit only, or may include more sophisticated features, such as a flushing rim or water supply in the form of an ascending spray.

Cistern

Seat

Bowl and pedestal

Toilet waste disposal works by a wash-down flow of water or by syphonic action which drains the bowl from below. A cistern may be mounted at high level (**1**) with a chain pull or above and behind the bowl (**4**) with a flush-control lever. More economical of space are the close-coupled suite (**2**) or the slimline cistern (**3**). The cistern is concealed behind the bowl in a ducted unit with removable panel (**5**) or behind a false wall for use with a cantilevered bowl bracketed into wall and floor (**6**).

1 2 3 4

5 6

floors, is also practical for the bathroom, although it is rather bulky. Smoother foam-backed vinyls and ceramic tiles are preferred for the eighties bathroom. Chipboard floor tiles that are sealed with polyurethane make a warm base underfoot and are the cheapest solution for a large area. The most expensive floor covering is wall-to-wall carpeting, preferably in nylon or acrylic, as these materials dry out more quickly than wool.

Lighting
Electricity and water don't mix, but fortunately safety regulations governing the placing of electrical sockets in bathrooms make wearing rubber boots to change a light-bulb merely an unnecessary precaution. Accord-ing to British standards, the only socket allowed in a bathroom is for an electric razor, on a low wattage. Mirror lights often incorporate shaver sockets with an isolating transformer to minimalize any shock. Light switches have to be placed outside the bathroom door, although you can have a pull-cord switch inside the bathroom. Bathroom light fittings are usually fairly restrained, with a ceiling-mounted overhead light and task lighting at the mirror.

To ensure an adequate amount of light, remember that filament lighting needs 20 watts per square metre, and fluorescent lighting needs 10 watts. Thus a bathroom measuring 6½ft x 9¾ft (2m x 3m) requires 120 watts of filament lighting, which could be planned as an overhead light of 60 to 80 watts with additional

Fiona Skrine created the unique, delicate decoration for this small bathroom by the simple stencilling process shown here.

1. Draw out the motifs for the design on tracing paper, using a soft, dark pencil.

2. Transfer the motifs to stencil film and go over them to mark the outlines clearly. Transparent film enables you to see the layout of motifs underneath as you apply the paint.

3. With a fine, sharp scalpel, cut carefully around the outlines.

4. Place the stencil firmly on the surface and fill the shape with colour. Use a flat-ended stencilling brush with stiff bristle and keep the paint to a fairly dry consistency.

5. Repeat the process with different shapes and colours until the design is complete. Then shell the surface with varnish or a solution of PVA, which is white while liquid but dries to a clear, waterproof finish.

1

2

3

4

5

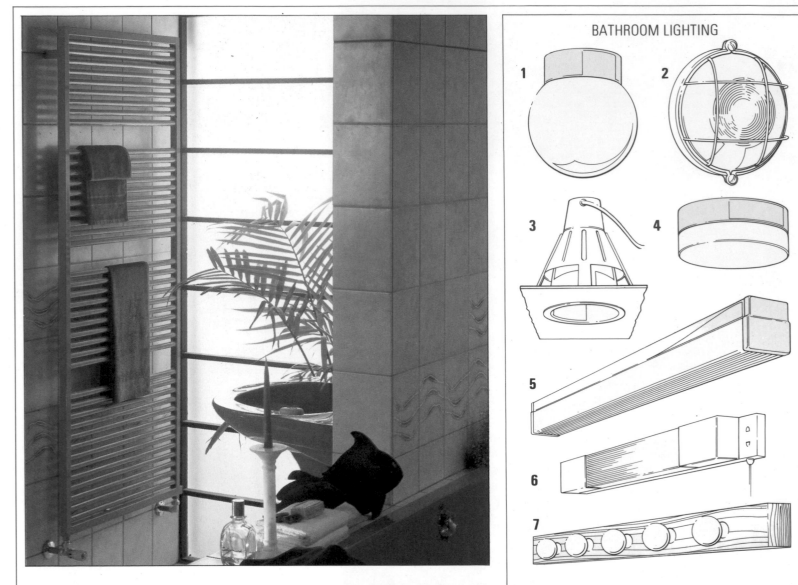

BATHROOM LIGHTING

There is almost nothing more essential to the enjoyment of a decent bath than a properly warmed towel. No such problem arises in the bathroom above. A ceiling high towel rail by the Swiss company Zehnder could keep a newly bathed rugby team happy with dry towels. The sink has been recessed into an alcove, amply lit by a wall of frosted glass, divided by bright green bars.

small wattage above the mirror. Diffused light could be given from wall-mounted fittings. Chrome and white glass Art Deco lights look good in a bathroom with matt finish white and grey tiles, chrome or nickel taps and lots of mirrors.

For shadow-free illumination, make sure the light is directed at the face rather than at the mirror. Actors and actresses fringe their make-up mirrors with a ring of light bulbs, a trick copied by bathroom manufacturers, but regrettably often with bulbs only along the top. This has the same effect on the eyes as badly positioned downlighters, so hang the mirror upside down

Bathroom lighting must combine efficiency and safety, as well as adding something to the mood of a well-designed room. For a general source, enclosed ceiling lights come in a variety of styles: a globe (**1**) or cylinder (**4**) or the bulk head lamp with wire grille which can be ceiling or wall mounted (**2**)or the fully-recessed downlighter (**3**). Fluorescent strip lighting is a powerful source, pleasantly dispersed by a diffuser cover (**5**). A

small striplight (**6**) for a basin mirror is fitted with a shaver socket; the socket has a built-in safety device and is the only type allowed in a bathroom. The theatrical style of a row of bulbs is an attractive idea for task lighting, mounted in a simple pine strip (**7**). All lights must operate by a pull-cord or from a switch outside the bathroom. See also Lighting, pages 50-53.

The bathroom (**left**) is in the Klein apartment, designed by the Space Design Group. Grey is the predominant colour, both on the tiled floor, and the tiled walls. The bath is on a platform, which actually creates more space for lounging, and undressing, than a normal floor level bath. A row of theatrical spotlights illuminates the mirror and sink area, and the shelving and storage systems are all-glass, for easy visability.

The bathroom (**below**), is high-tech at its jolliest, and least serious. Exposed pipework has been painted in child's crayon box colours, contrasting with the clinical white tiling. Jokey lights on mock pipe work stands peer into the room's interior.

so that the light travels upwards. Cheaper everyday bathroom light fittings are bulk-head lights to match wire grid soap dishes and bath accessories. Fun lights for bathrooms include a fluorescent tube captured in a Mickey Mouse gloved hand attached to the wall, and a light bulb in a pickling jar, suspended from a twirly cord.

Heating and ventilation

Bathrooms must be warm. An appliance that creates instant heat is all that is needed, provided it complies with the stringent safety regulations. No socket outlets may be installed, apart from the shaver socket, so electric heaters and towel rails must be permanently fixed and connected directly to the circuit wiring by an electrician. Wall-mounted heaters with safety pull cords are sometimes combined with light fittings for the centre of the ceiling. Other models can be adjusted to beam warmth where it is most needed.

According to building regulations, any internal bathroom (one without access to fresh air), is obliged to have an extractor fan that comes on automatically with the light switch. Extractor fans fitted to the wall (or in the window) will provide the efficient solution to any ventilation problems in the bathroom.

AWKWARD SPACES

The current trend for redesigning space in contemporary houses has resulted in the imaginative transformation of awkward space into extra space for accommodating hobbies, books, work surfaces and equipment. Older houses that have an attic or basement are considered good value as these areas can be readily converted, but even streamlined modern blocks have corridors, landings and space under stairs.

In the past decade the basement has graduated from the junk room to the more functional work centre. An adequate damp-proof course and the installation of a solid fuel or wood-burning stove with a central flue (warmth travels upwards so it will heat the rest of the house), make the area habitable. Use all available sources of natural light and install window seats with hinged lids for storing clutter. In the evening use a back-up system of anglepoise lamps and clamp-on movable lights.

The basement also provides generous floor space for a large table, so essential to the model-maker, train-set enthusiast or seamstress. A trestle table makes a good cutting surface in a basement that converts to a sewing room, with a separate lower table for the machine, cupboards with wide shelves for folded cloth, deep drawers for patterns, shallow drawers for pins, scissors, silks, chalks and tapes, a full-length mirror, a fold-out ironing board and perhaps a small sink for damp pressing. Practical vinyl flooring is best for a work area as it can be cleaned easily.

The basement, attic or hall will invariably have stairs leading to it. Convert the space under the stairs into a cupboard by putting panels over the meter and fuse boxes and adding a strip light ('cool' lighting that will not overheat). Here you can store cleaning equipment — fluids, mops and brooms — on shelving, clips and hooks. For electrical equipment such as vacuum cleaners, run the basement or hall flooring surface into the cupboard so that you can manoeuvre the appliances on an even surface. A more unusual yet practical idea for storing household tools is to fit a pull-out box on castors under the first tread of the staircase. Turn the area below stairs into a more interesting arrangement than merely a site for cleaning materials, by filling the space with a bed covered in a striped weave that complements the stair carpet and painting the bannisters in alternating colours.

Open-tread stairs make very good shelves if extended along the wall. Continue the line of the first tread into a narrow shelf that runs along the wall, providing space for an ar-

LOFT CONVERSIONS

There is no doubt that it is less expensive and in many instances preferable, to utilize space in your home rather than move to a larger place. If you are lucky enough to have a good-sized loft or attic room, investigate the possibility of using it or converting it to give you an extra area. This could prove to be the most pleasant and popular room in the house.

There are endless possibilities: you could have an open-plan scheme or divide the space into a work area (lofts make wonderful studios), space room, bedroom or play room. You could even open the attic to the floor below to make a high-ceilinged room with rafters. By adding a platform for bedding or seating, you would be making good use·of the existing loft.

Before you proceed with your plan for conversion, consider such things as structural alterations; stair access and the laws governing this; weather-proofing; adequate light from windows and skylights; flooring and storage. Remember also that a loft will be very warm in summer so you will need some protection from solar heat. You can use blinds inside or weatherproofed pinoleum blinds fixed on the outside, but operated from the inside.

Insulation As long as the roof is adequately insulated there should be no problem keeping the loft warm in winter as heat will rise from the rest of the house. Consult an expert on the type of roof insulation to use. If the water tank is above the roof you will have to box it separately.

Flooring Most loft and attic floors were originally considered as ceilings for the floor below, so make quite sure that they are strong enough to take additional weight. Floorboards can be stripped and polished, or painted and covered with rugs or carpeted to provide extra soundproofing.

Storage Traditionally used for storing junk, lofts have many nooks and crannies that can be utilized in a functional room. Sloping roofs provide excellent storage space in a loft and are often good places to put the bed, chest, cupboards or shelves. From the preceding page we have followed the spiral staircase up to the loft of this tiny London mews flat. It is in fact not a loft in the conventional sense at all, because the roof flips open to reveal a roof garden.

Squares of astro-turf line the floor and a bright red frame covered with canvas provides shade, and variable shelter should it rain. Glass side walls ensure that the rest of the house benefits fully from the light and sense of aerial space.

rangement of objects, or extend one tread width to make a desk, using the treads above the desk as bookshelves.

For the wine collector, this area could be an ideal place to set up a cellar. You should be able to stack a dozen bottles of wine to rib height (approximately six treads deep) with nine bottles across the width of the staircase. Above the wine rack, add a narrow shelf for jars of olives, nuts and other accompaniments.

Spiral staircases in small townhouses take up less space than a conventional staircase and can be enlivened with paint, in a bold colour. Use a wallpaper with a vertical stripe to accentuate the curvy height of the staircase. Landings mid-way along a conventional staircase need not be wasted space. Obviously the size of the landing dictates how you use it, but on a large landing you can set up a desk below a window to create a simple study.

Stair carpet

Wall-to-wall carpeting that is suitable in weight and texture for the stairs is very expensive, although it has the advantage of sound-proofing the treads. The cheapest heavy-duty carpets are haircords and needle-looms: rush matting is also cheap but more difficult to lay. Try painting the stairs and running a heavy-duty sisal matting up the centre. Traditional carpet strips are only 27in (68.5cm) so the border trims on either side of the carpet must be sanded and sealed.

Many staircases are made of hardwood which can be sealed and polished. Sanded floorboards can be stained with a white emulsion, watered down thinly to take the dappled grey/white paint wash. Or paint stairs with four coats of a matt black varnish after sanding, applying a final coat of varnish before you leave for your vacation, as it takes some time to dry.

Halls

The first impression of your house is given by the hall. Sadly it is often the area that is most neglected because it has no specific function, other than to serve as the reception area for letters and visitors.

The size and shape of the hall usually makes it an awkward place to decorate. Often it houses the pipes

This American family home (**above**) has a multi-functional loft area. Arranged on various levels, the loft areas are either fully open to the skies, partially covered, or proper enclosed room. In this loft the bedroom leads out to a semi-enclosed patio and a bathroom. Further on a wide and sunny balcony houses a round warm tub for outdoor bathing.

The tiny kitchen (**right**) is cleverly tucked away behind louvred doors that can fold across in a flash to hide the clutter.

and the meter points, in addition to being the darkest place in the whole house. One advantage is that you can decorate it as dramatically as you like, introducing decorating ideas that you might be reluctant to try in a larger area. In a large hallway, use the black and white diamond-patterned flooring made of cushion-backed vinyl which imitates a grand tiled entrance.

The hall is a perfect place for displaying your enthusiasms. So Wellington boots and oilskins suggest the great outdoors, while sun hats and pannier baskets, together with botanical prints, indicate a keen interest in gardening. If you are a winter sport enthusiast you could decorate the hallway with photographs of snowy peaks and hang skis on the sloping wall of the stairwell. A perch mounted in a glass case, a green net on the wall, some rods and a picnic hamper make a decorative set-piece at the same time as accommodating the angler's equipment.

In a modern town house that has few architectural features, a dado rail running around the hall area and up the stairs, can suggest an alternative paint colour. Either hand-marble or use marbled wallpaper below the dado line, with a lighter colour taking the eye upwards. A group of pictures, a table set with some flowers and an elegant mirror will make this a gracious reception area. In a nineteenth-century house you can make full use of a generously proportioned entrance hall by decorating it with flocked wallpaper in an elaborate floral pattern, painting the door in high gloss, and using curtains on rails to conceal adjoining doors.

If you have used patterned wallpaper in the living room, decorate the hall with a sympathetic scheme. An oriental woven carpet, for example, is complemented by a hall in red lacquer paint with a pair of blue and white ginger jars forming the umbrella stand. For a style that contrasts textures, linking exterior finish to interior simplicity, make a feature of unplastered walls, a wooden tongue and groove ceiling, tiled flooring in cork or vinyl, and an array of plants chosen for their foliage.

Since the hall is usually a small area, you can try out an elaborate wallcovering which would be too expensive to use over a larger surface area. This makes it the ideal place to experiment with fabric on walls. A lightweight dress fabric, such as striped shirting, can be glued directly on to the wall; polyester wadding underneath will make it more luxurious. Border it with a woven webbing strip or ribbon to hide ragged edges at the top and bottom. Hang a central light, add

a console table (with flowers), a few formal pictures.

Wallpaper panelling can create a wonderful landscape in an entrance hall. Open up a romantic vista with instant *trompe l'oeil* on a grand scale, showing balustrades and urns on a terrace by the sea, mysterious castles or follies, or a naïve jungle painting.

In a long corridor hallway, make use of the corridor aspect by turning the space into a library. Bookshelves give the peaceful feeling of browsing in a library. Take the shelves up as high as possible and add a tortoiseshell or bamboo ladder to heighten the effect. Mirror panelling can also look good, set opposite fanlights or doorways so that light bounces back into the dark hallway, but place them discreetly as it can be disconcerting for guests to see mirror images of themselves as they enter unfamiliar surroundings. Another idea is to create a little gallery for drawings, prints or miniatures. Avoid hanging a large painting in a small hallway as you need to be about 12ft (3.6m) away in order to view it properly. Ceiling spots or downlighters that bathe the walls in light are good in halls, and deep, vibrant colours such as red, brown, peach or coral will make a draughty hall warmer and more intimate without reducing its size. A highly glazed ceiling that reflects light on its surfaces will give a feeling of space.

A built in wardrobe has been converted into a dressing table alcove simply by removing the wardrobe doors (**far left**). The door frames have been painted brilliant red, and the interior of the alcove has been papered in a pretty pink design to match the pink walls of the rest of the room. Dried flowers hang from the original top shelf of the wardrobe, and a simple Victorian mahogany mirror sits on the lower shelf.

A high-tech steel mesh trolley on castors serves as a drinks table and magazine rack and can be moved to anywhere in the room.

A space-age cubicle (coveniently marked with a K) is the kitchen in this living room come kitchen/diner (**left**). Inside the aircraft like step over door is a fully fitted kitchen with enough storage space and appliances squeezed into a tiny space to keep anybody happy and well fed.

SECTION THREE

MEASUREMENTS AND QUANTITIES   166
PAINLESS PREPARATION   169
THE COMPLETE PAINTER   201
THE COMPLETE PAPERHANGER   229
THE COMPLETE TILER   253
THE COMPLETE PANELLER   271
THE COMPLETE FLOORER   279
CEILING IDEAS   297
FINISHING TOUCHES   303

INDEX   314

MEASUREMENTS AND QUANTITIES

Careful planning is the key to decorating success; prepare a checklist of all stages in the work, such as applying sealer, undercoat or lining paper, as well as the work involved in putting on the final surface. It is important to calculate quantities as accurately as possible before buying paint, wallpaper, fabric or tiles, but it is best to err on the generous side, as it can be difficult to match a precise shade or pattern. Make sure you have items such as adhesives, dilutents and solvents suited to the task and the materials.

Paint Different types of paint have different covering power, and this is further affected by the condition of the surface being painted — rough or porous walls use up more paint. Multiply height by width of the walls to find the basic area to be covered and refer to the paint chart (right). If mixing your own tint, work out the proportions of each colour using small sample cans and then translate the ratio into larger quantities. Remember to calculate the ceiling area also, if necessary, or make a separate estimate.

Wallpapers The width and length of a roll of wallpaper depends upon its origin. American and European papers are usually 18in (0.46m) wide, but in length are 8yds (7.35m) and 9yds (8.25m) respectively. Standard English sizing is 21in (0.53m) width by 11yds (10.05m) length. The charts (far right) show how to calculate the number of rolls, based on these measurements, according to the height of the walls and the measurement right around the room. To match a large repeat pattern accurately at the seams, you will need to allow for wastage.

Fabrics For a wall-covering, it is easiest to use paper-backed fabrics which behave like wallpaper. Unbacked fabrics are difficult unless specially treated and must be overlapped when hung, meaning wastage on each width. To calculate fabric for curtains, multiply the length of curtain track by the fullness recommended for the heading tape, divide it by the fabric width to find the number of widths needed, and multiply this figure by the drop, allowing for hems and matching patterns at the seams.

Tiles Tiles are available in an increasing variety of shapes and sizes and again it is better to overestimate slightly (see chart far right). It is almost impossible to fit tiles precisely to a given area, so arrange them to have cut sections at the bottom of the wall or tucked away in a corner.

Adhesives There are a number of specialized brand-name adhesives for particular decorating jobs. These may be recommended by the manufacturer or supplier of tiles, wallpaper and wall fabrics, but there are also three basic types of adhesive that cover different needs. It is easier to bond two materials of basically similar composition than to join two quite different substances. The strongest bond is provided by epoxy resin adhesives; these are two-part components that must be mixed freshly for each time of using. The resin takes about six hours to set. Less tough, but also useful for decorating are contact adhesives; the glue is spread on both surfaces and allowed to become tacky before they are pressed together. Clear household adhesives are valuable for small repairs. Other types are increasingly in use — PVA for wood and plastics or rubber latex for carpet and fabric repairs. If in doubt about the adhesive needed for your job, take advice from a reliable DIY supplier.

PAINT: AMOUNTS

Quantity	Emulsion		Gloss	
	sq yds	(sq m)	sq yds	(sq m)
1 pint (0.568 litres)	12	(10)	10	(8½)
1 quart (1.135 litres)	24	(20)	20	(17)
1 gallon (4.54 litres)	96	(80)	80	(67)

PAINT: INTERIOR USES

Ceilings and Walls

Water paint:	flat finish (2 coats), not washable, thin with water
*Oil-bound distemper:	Flat finish (2 coats), not washable, thin with water
Emulsion paint:	flat or semi-gloss finish (2 coats), washable, cheap, but use in high condensation areas not recommended
Oil paint:	high gloss, semi-gloss or flat finish (2 coats), washable, thin with turpentine

Woodwork

Emulsion paint:	flat or semi-gloss finish (2 coats), thin with water, do not use as an undercoat for oil paints
Oil paint:	high gloss, semi-gloss or flat finish (2 coats), easily cleaned
Plastic paints:	high gloss finish (1 or 2 coats), do not thin, quick-drying, non-drip

Iron or Steel

Oil paint:	gloss or semi-gloss finish (2 coats), use alkali-resistant primer, thin with turpentine
Plastic paints:	high gloss finish (1 or 2 coats), do not thin, quick-drying, non-drip

Lead, copper, zinc

Oil Paint:	gloss or semi-gloss finish (2 coats), use wire wool and white spirit to clean the surface, use special primer, thin with turpentine

AMERICAN WALLPAPERS

Ft/m around room	Height of wall (ft/m) 8ft (2.4m)	9ft (2.7m)	10ft (3.0m)
28 (8.5)	7	8	9
32 (9.6)	8	9	10
36 (11)	9	10	11
40 (12.2)	10	11	12
44 (13.4)	11	12	14
48 (14.6)	12	13	15
52 (15.8)	13	15	16
56 (17.0)	14	16	17
60 (18.3)	15	17	19
64 (19.5)	16	18	20
68 (20.7)	17	19	21
72 (21.9)	18	20	22
76 (23.2)	19	21	24
80 (24.4)	20	22	25
84 (25.6)	21	23	26
88 (26.8)	22	24	27

ENGLISH WALLPAPERS

Ft/m around room	Height of wall (ft/m) 8ft (2.4m)	9ft (2.7m)	10ft (3.0m)
28 (8.5)	4	5	6
32 (9.6)	5	6	7
36 (11)	6	6	7
40 (12.2)	7	7	8
44 (13.4)	7	8	8
48 (14.6)	8	8	9
52 (15.8)	8	9	10
56 (17.0)	9	9	10
60 (18:3)	9	10	11
64 (19.5)	10	10	12
68 (20.7)	10	11	13
72 (21.9)	11	12	13
76 (23.2)	12	12	14
80 (24.4)	12	13	15
84 (25.6)	13	14	16
88 (26.8)	14	14	16

The charts on this page will help you to estimate the number of rolls/tiles you need. The larger the pattern, the more paper you need to allow for matching. You also need to allow for more tiles if they are not square. Always ask your retailer's advice.

To calculate the number of rolls required for ceilings using imperial measurements, work out the square area in yards and divide by four. To calculate the number of rolls with metric measurements, work out the square area in metres and divide by five.

CONTINENTAL WALLPAPERS

Ft/m around room	Height of wall (ft/m) 8ft (2.4m)	9ft (2.7m)	10ft (3.0m)
28 (8.5)	6	7	7
32 (9.6)	7	8	8
36 (11)	8	8	9
40 (12.2)	8	9	10
44 (13.4)	9	10	11
48 (14.6)	10	11	12
52 (15.8)	11	12	13
56 (17.0)	12	13	14
60 (18.3)	12	14	15
64 (19.5)	13	15	16
68 (20.7)	14	16	17
72 (21.9)	15	16	18
76 (23.2)	16	18	20
80 (24.4)	17	19	21
84 (25.6)	18	20	22
88 (26.8)	19	21	23

TILES

Sq. ft. (sq m)	4in × 4in (10cm × 10cm)	6in × 6in (15cm × 15cm)	8in × 8in (20cm × 20cm)
2 (.19)	18	8	5
4 (.37)	36	16	9
6 (.56)	54	24	14
8 (.74)	72	32	18
10 (.93)	90	40	23
12 (1.11)	108	48	27
14 (1.30)	126	56	32
16 (1.49)	144	64	36
18 (1.67)	162	72	41
20 (1.86)	180	80	45
22 (2.04)	198	88	50
24 (2.23)	216	96	54

PAINLESS PREPARATION

PREPARING WALLS   170

FILLING CRACKS *172* ◆ REPAIRING CORNERS   *173* ◆ STRIPPING WALLPAPER *174*
STRIPPING WASHABLE WALLPAPER *175* ◆ REMOVING FABRICS *176*
REMOVING TEXTURED FINISHES *177* ◆ REMOVING CLADDING *178*
REPLACING BROKEN TILES *179*

PREPARING CEILINGS   180

MOVING LIGHTS *180* ◆ FILLING CRACKS   *181* ◆ FILLING JOINS IN PLASTERBOARD   *182*

PREPARING WOODWORK   183

WASHING AND SANDING WOODWORK *183* ◆ TOUCHING IN CHIPS   *184*
STRIPPING PAINTWORK   *185* ◆ USING A LIQUID STRIPPER   *136*
USING A PASTE STRIPPER   *186* ◆ FILLING KNOT HOLES   *187* ◆ BLEACHING STAINS   *188*
REPAIRING WOODWORM AND ROT DAMAGE   *189*

PREPARING FLOORS   190

LIFTING CARPETS   *191* ◆ LIFTING RESILIENT VINYL   *191* ◆ LIFTING WOOD MOSAICS   *191*
LIFTING CERAMIC TILES   *191* ◆ FIXING LOOSE BOARDS   *192*
PATCHING SOLID FLOORS   *193* ◆ SANDING FLOORS   *194*

PREPARING DETAILS   196

STRIPPING AND REPAIRING CORNICES   *196* ◆ PREPARING METALWORK   *197*
REPLACING GLASS   *198* ◆ REPAIRING STAINED GLASS   *199*

TOOLS CHECKLIST

1 *Steam stripper*
2 *Belt sander*
3 *Orbital sander*
4 *Dusting brush*
5 *Abrasive paper*
6 *Sanding block*
7 *Scrubbing brush*
8 *Clean absorbent cloths*
9 *Sponge*
10 *Wire brush*
11 *Steel wool*
12 *Sharp knife*
13 *Broad filling knife*
14 *Pointing trowel*
15 *Protective gloves*

Ask anybody what they least like about decorating, and they will almost certainly tell you that it's the preparation. It can certainly be a hard, messy, and boring job, but it is important to do it thoroughly: skimp, and you run the risk of new decorations looking shabby. Thankfully modern materials, techniques and tools simplify the task and, although the traditional craftsman may frown on them they do make the job both quicker and easier.

So, where should you start? To begin with, you need room to work, and traditionally that means clearing the room of everything movable — ornaments, furniture and even carpets. In practice though, it is rarely necessary to go that far. A lot depends on the scale of the redecoration work, the materials you intend to use, and the amount of messy preparation required. Unless you are tackling a floor, you should be able to get away with merely protecting carpets and large items of furniture, in situ, using dustsheets or polythene sheeting (cotton sheets are better because plastic sheeting is slippery underfoot). Stack furniture in the centre of the room so you can work round it most of the time, thus minimizing the need to move it again. Remove wall lights, light shades, and similar minor obstacles, too, if you can; protect exposed electrical wiring with insulation tape (be sure to turn off the electricity supply at the mains before you remove light fittings). Strictly speaking, door and window furniture (knobs, latches and so on) that isn't to be painted should also be taken off at this stage, but for convenience and security you may prefer to leave this until the last minute and replace everything as soon as the paint has dried.

Preparing walls

Perhaps the simplest situation you are likely to face is an existing wall painted with emulsion. Generally all that is needed is to wash the surface down with detergent to remove dirt and grease, and then to fill obvious defects with a proprietary interior filler — sold either ready-mixed or, less expensively, as a powder to which you add water. Most cracks are easy enough to fill. Enlarge them slightly with the corner of a filling knife (this looks like a scraper, but is more flexible), aiming to undercut slightly the surrounding plaster, and press the filler into place, smoothing it off with the filling knife's blade. It's best to leave the filler just proud of the surrounding surface to allow for shrinkage during drying. The excess can be removed when hard using medium and fine grade glasspaper to leave a smooth finish — an orbital sander is a boon here. Incidentally, don't bother with hairline cracks. These will not show through the decorative finish.

Small holes can be treated in exactly the same way, but larger ones need a different approach. Those in solid walls

are best tackled in stages to stop the wet filler 'slumping' under its own weight. With large holes (more than 50mm/ 2in across), use ordinary plaster for the initial filling — it's cheaper than filler when bought in 'handy packs' — but finish off with proprietary filler for a smooth finish. Level off the plaster infill by 'sawing' a timber batten across the surface, keeping it pressed against the adjacent plaster to leave the repair flush with the wall.

As for large holes in stud partition walls, the only satisfactory way to make a repair is to remove the damaged plasterboard, cutting it back until half the width of the adjacent supporting timber studs are exposed. Nail new horizontal timbers between the exposed studs, and use these, together with the studs themselves, to support a piece of new plasterboard cut to fit as a patch. The cracks around the edges can be made good by covering them with plasterboard joint filler and tape, but for a small repair, it is simpler to use just filler, having first chamfered the edges of the old and new boards with a sharp knife or file.

The only cracks and holes that may not respond to any of the above repairs, are those between masonry and woodwork such as door and window frames. Ordinary plaster-type filler simply falls out as the wood expands and contracts. The solution is to use a permanently flexible filler such as acrylic based caulk. Sold ready for use in cartridges, caulk is extruded into the gap, rather like toothpaste, with the aid of a special gun.

Cracks apart, there are just two other common faults you are likely to find in an emulsion painted wall. One is efflorescence — salts that have leached from the plaster. Scrape these off before washing down. The other is where the existing paint has begun to bubble or flake. Scrape off as much loose material as you can, and feather out the sharp edges of the remaining paintwork using wet and dry abrasive paper (used wet). The resulting shallow depressions in the surface can be 'filled' by retouching with two or three coats of emulsion before repainting in earnest. To complete the wall's preparation, if you intend hanging a wall covering, brush on a coat of size, or wallpaper paste diluted according to the manufacturer's instructions.

Gloss painted walls are treated in much the same way as emulsion painted ones; the only big difference being that you must take off the shine to provide a key for new decorations — most stick better to matt surfaces than to glossy ones. Do this by rubbing down with damp wet and dry paper — another job for an orbital sander — before washing the wall. Even so, you can still run into trouble if you don't repaint with gloss or some other resin/oil based paint. Emulsion tends not to adhere very well to non-porous surfaces, especially where there is a lot of moisture about, as in, say, a kitchen or bathroom. Similarly, if you plan to put up a

16 *Stripping knife*
17 *Club hammer*
18 *Overalls*
19 *Crowbar*
20 *Plasterer's float*
21 *Cold chisel*
22 *Brick bolster*

23 *Combination shavehook*
24 *Wallpaper scraper*
25 *Claw hammer*
26 *Disc sander*
27 *Electric drill*
28 *Mastic gun*

wall covering, it is best to cross-line the wall first. The resulting smooth, slightly porous surface helps the new wallcovering to stick.

And if you are dealing with a wall that has been papered over? The textbook method is to strip off the old paper and start again from scratch. To be on the safe side, this is still the best policy. Washables and vinyls must certainly be removed — in the case of 'easy strip' vinyls, all you have to do is remove the vinyl surface. With ordinary paper (and the backing paper of 'easy-strip' vinyls), so long as it is reasonably clean, in good condition, and still firmly stuck to the wall you may well get away with leaving it in place and decorating over the top. Try to arrange for the vertical joins in the old and new paper not to coincide, or the finish may be weakened. If this isn't possible, cross-line the wall before hanging the new wallcovering.

Painting over old wallpaper is another matter, especially if you intend using a water-based paint such as emulsion. Unless it has already been successfully painted (thus sealing the surface), there is a risk that the water in the paint will soften the wallpaper paste and cause the old paper to peel off. The older the paste, the greater the chances of this happening, which is why you can hang woodchip, or something similar, and safely paint over it straight away. There is also a risk of the inks in the old paper bleeding through the new paint — you can end up with the ghostly images of the original design dotted unevenly across the wall. Metallic inks are especially bad in this respect, though treatment with shellac knotting compound does help. There is also the possibility of dirt and grease embedded in the paper's surface stopping the paint sticking.

Assuming you have decided to remove the old paper, the first step is to soak it thoroughly with plenty of water in order to soften the paste holding it in place. It's best to use a wall brush or a sponge to slap the water on. Adding a proprietary wallpaper stripper to the water will also help speed things up by helping the water to penetrate, as will adding a few drops of washing up liquid. You must now allow the water time to do its work — say, for ten or fifteen minutes. If the paper is still difficult to peel off, repeat the soaking process and try again later. Since all this is rather time consuming, if you have a lot of paper to strip, it may be worth renting a steam stripper from a local tool hire shop. Rather like a giant steam iron, it brings the paper to a strippable state very quickly indeed.

Obviously, neither soaking nor steaming will have much effect on washable wallcoverings — the surface is designed to keep water out. With many, therefore, you have to score through the surface with either a special serrated scraper (called a Skarsten scraper), or a makeshift 'comb' made by driving panel pins through a piece of scrap timber until the points just protrude — with either tool, take care not to scratch the plaster while scoring. Fortunately, many modern vinyls offer a simpler way around the problem. If you pick at a corner, you should find that the vinyl surface simply peels off, leaving ordinary paper on the wall. This can usually be left as a lining for new decoration. Novamura

FILLING CRACKS

1 *Use a narrow-bladed scraper to rake out any unsound material from the crack, and undercut the edges slightly at each side so the filler can make a more positive bond.*

2 *Wet the crack before applying the filler, to help cut down on the suction; if this isn't done, the filler may dry out too quickly and could crack. You can use a small hand spray unit as shown, or simly brush water along the crack.*

3 *Mix up the filler to a firm, workable consistency (if it's too wet, it will slump out of the crack) and press it into the crack. Draw the blade across the crack line first, then remove excess material by drawing it along the crack.*

4 *Leave the filler slightly proud of the surrounding wall surface. When it has dried hard, remove the excess using abrasive paper wrapped round a sanding block or a softwood offcut to leave a perfectly smooth surface ready for redecoration.*

wallcovering is still easier to remove because it contains no paper and is hung with a special adhesive: you merely work a corner free and pull the whole lot off the wall.

But back to ordinary paper. When the paste is soft enough, choose an easy starting point — there is usually one bit that is obviously liftable — and use a stiff, broad-bladed scraper to strip off the softened paper. Take care not to let the scraper blade dig into the wall, and don't worry about islands of paper that refuse to budge at this stage – further soaking will lift them off in time. You can ignore completely the little flecks of paper that inevitably cling to the wall. These will disappear during the preparation of the newly revealed bare plaster, which you should tackle in exactly the same way as the emulsion painted wall described earlier. There is just one additional point to watch. If the surface of the plaster leaves a chalky deposit on your hand when you brush over it, be sure to seal the surface with a stabilizing primer.

Of course, all this rather assumes that the surface of the wall is in reasonably good condition. If, when filling cracks and holes, you find you are virtually replastering, you need to think again. Cross-lining (or even double lining in extreme cases) should produce a sufficiently smooth surface for papering. You can also paint over lining paper, though a woodchip, or a more heavily embossed paintable wallcovering such as Anaglypta, tends to be more attractive and covers defects rather better. Or you could actually replaster.

Applying a skim coat of traditional finishing plaster to produce the necessary smooth, flat surface is, however, a rather skilled job, so consider using a synthetic plastering system designed for the amateur. This is a cross between very thick emulsion paint and filler. Once brushed on, you can take your time to smooth it out with a plasterer's float or with the special tool that is usually provided in the pack. Unfortunately, it is also rather expensive, and therefore best reserved for relatively small areas — those too small to make it worthwhile hiring a professional plasterer.

And what about preparing surfaces prior to redecoration with something other than paint and paper? For most the preparation is no different, though clearly, with something like cladding there is no need to be too fussy — it will happily cover quite major defects. If you are putting up ceramic tiles, though, make sure that the surface is not only smooth and clean, but also reasonably flat. Level off very bumpy walls by cladding them with plasterboard or tempered hardboard.

Preparing such miscellaneous finishes themselves for redecoration is a little more complicated. Cork tiles are so difficult to remove they are normally best left in place. Cross-line the walls if you want to paper; cover the tiles with lining paper, woodchip, or something similar if you want to paint. In both cases, apply plenty of size (or diluted wallpaper paste) to the tiles first, and if they have been sealed with a high gloss finish, rub down with wet and dry abrasive paper or wire wool to remove the shine.

Ceramic tiles are also usually worth leaving in place, so

REPAIRING CORNERS

1 *Where an external corner has been chipped or broken away, use a timber batten as a guide to replastering. Pin it to one face of the corner, flush with the other face. Leave the pins partly driven.*

2 *Press fairly dry filler into the gap between the batten and the edge of the damaged area using a filling knife or a small pointing trowel. If the gap is deeper than about 6mm ($\frac{1}{4}$ in), apply the filler in stages until it's just proud of the surface.*

3 *When the patch on one side of the corner has dried hard, prise the batten away carefully by pulling out the partly-driven fixing nails. Don't worry if a little of the patch is pulled away as the batten is removed; it can be filled afterwards.*

4 *Reposition the batten on the patched side of the corner so it's flush with the other face of the wall. Then repeat the filling process. Remove the batten, touch in any defects in the repaired area with more filler and finally sand it smooth.*

STRIPPING WALLPAPER

1 *Strip ordinary wallpaper by the soak-and-scrape method. Start by saturating the surface of the wallpaper with water from a sponge or a small garden sprayer.*

2 *Start scraping at a seam, keeping the blade of the scraper at a low angle to avoid gouging out the plaster surface.*

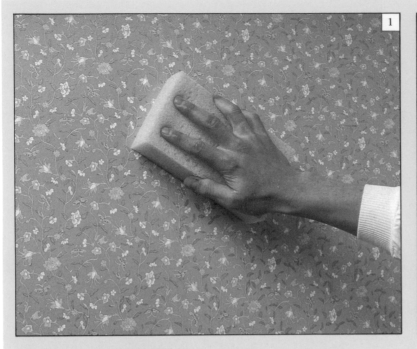

3 *Repeat the soaking as necessary to soften the paper and the paste holding it in place.*

4 *Continue scraping until the wall surface is bare, then wash down thoroughly to remove the remaining scraps and nibs and leave the surface clean, ready for redecoration.*

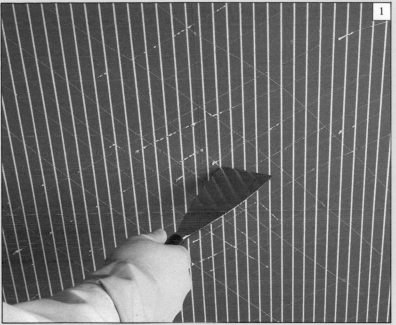

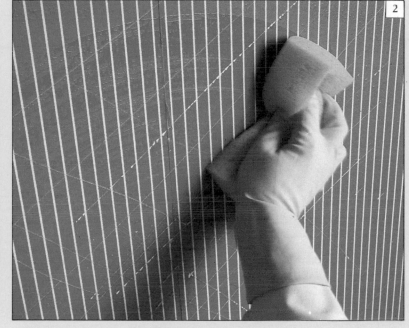

STRIPPING WASHABLE WALLPAPER

1 *Washable wallpapers are extremely difficult to strip because the water cannot penetrate and soften the paste.*

2 *The traditional method of removing them is to score the surface with the edge of a scraper (or with a special serrated tool), then to soak,* *scrape, soak and scrape until the paper is removed.*

3 *However, this can be very long and tedious process, and quicker results will be obtained by hiring a steam stripping machine.*

4 *This has a hand-held plate which forces steam into the paper, softening the paste and allowing it to be scraped off more easily.*

REMOVING FABRICS

1 *Some paper-backed fabrics can be removed by soaking the fabric thoroughly with water using a sponge or garden sprayer, then lifting a corner and peeling the material off the wall.*

2 *Other types stuck direct to the wall with adhesive can generally be peeled off in continuous lengths. Start at a bottom corner seam, peel the full width away at skirting-board level and then pull the length steadily away from the wall.*

long as they are in good condition and firmly fixed to the wall — potentially loose ones have a hollow sound when tapped. Removing them involves hacking away with a club hammer and bolster chisel and you will almost certainly have to replaster the exposed wall. So, consider a cover-up instead. New ceramic tiles can be stuck directly on top of the old ones, or you can apply a resin-based paint. If you decide to paint, give them a good wash, degrease with white spirit, and wait for a warm, very dry day — to reduce the risk of painting over condensation — before priming with an all-surface zinc chromate primer ready for the finishing coats. But don't regard painting as a permanent solution: it tends to flake easily, particularly in the humid environment of a kitchen or bathroom. Smartening up old, dirty grouting provides a more permanent facelift, and can be surprisingly effective. Either rake out and replace the old grout, or carefully paint it with emulsion paint. Better still, use a modern, purpose-made grout paint; any that strays on to the glazed surface can be polished off when dry. To complete the renovation, chip out any badly damaged tiles using a club hammer and cold chisel, and replace with a few new contrasting 'feature' tiles.

That just leaves one final aspect of wall preparation to be considered — making sure the surface is dry. This doesn't simply mean waiting for it to dry after a washing down, it means making sure the masonry itself isn't inherently damp, because that sort of dampness will ruin almost any form of decoration and is quite likely to lead to more serious problems such as wood rot.

The condition of old decorations is a good indication of the extent of any problem. Badly flaking paint and peeling wallpaper could be due to poor workmanship, but when accompanied by soft, crumbling plaster, and possibly mould growth, damp is the more likely culprit. Before you do anything else, you must identify the source of the problem, and put it right. There are two main types of damp in walls — rising damp and penetrating damp.

Rising damp is due to masonry soaking up moisture from the ground. All walls do this, but in all modern homes a damp-proof course (dpc), built into the structure about 150mm (6in) above ground level, stops the dampness reaching anything that might be damaged by it. If your home doesn't have a dpc, most of the lower parts of ground floor walls may be damp, and you should have one installed by a specialist contractor whether rising damp is obviously present or not. For cheapness and simplicity, this is normally done by drilling holes into the wall at dpc level, and forcing in a silicone-based solution under pressure to saturate the masonry and render it waterproof. The holes are then made good with mortar.

Where your home has a dpc, rising damp tends to appear in patches near sections that have failed to do their job. This may be due to physical damage (either due to subsidence or old age) in which case you should call in a specialist contractor or a competent local builder to make repairs — a new chemical dpc may be required. It is more likely, though, that dampness has found a way round the dpc, perhaps using a flower-bed or the walls of an extension as a 'bridge'. In the former case, simply remove the offending heap; in the latter, call in a builder to put things right — preferably the one who built the extension because new work should not cause this sort of problem. There is one other way dampness can get past a dpc. If a path or patio finishes less than 150mm (6in) below dpc level, heavy rain can bounce off it on to the wall above.

Penetrating dampness is usually more straightforward, the most common causes being faulty pointing in brickwork, leaking gutters, and things of that sort. Making the necessary repairs should be all that is necessary, though in old houses the bricks themselves can become porous with age. In this case, protect them with paint, rendering, or clear silicone exterior sealant.

If dampness does not appear to be due to either of the above, suspect condensation. This appears independently of wet weather. Choosing a 'warm' finish such as cork for the affected surface may help, but it is better to tackle the problem at source by improving your home's heating and ventilation.

Whatever the cause of dampness, allow plenty of time for the masonry to dry out before decorating in earnest. To complete the cure, scrub off any mould growth and treat the wall with a proprietary fungicide to prevent regrowth.

REMOVING TEXTURED FINISHES

1 *Remove modern textured emulsion paints by brushing on a generous coat of special textured paint remover.*

2 *Traditional powder-based textured finishes such as Artex will not be shifted by the chemical. Instead, use a steam stripper to force steam into the surface and soften it.*

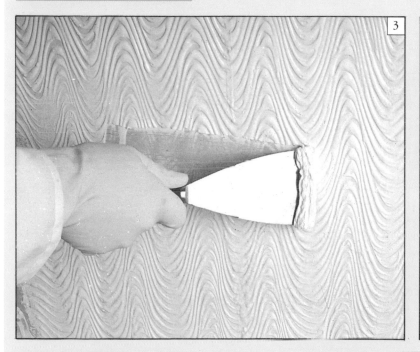

3 *When the solvent stripper has penetrated sufficiently to soften the paint, use a broad-bladed scraper to remove it from the wall. Have a metal container handy to take the scrapings.*

4 *When you have removed the bulk of the finish from the wall surface, use a medium grade abrasive wrapped round a sanding block to remove the remaining nibs.*

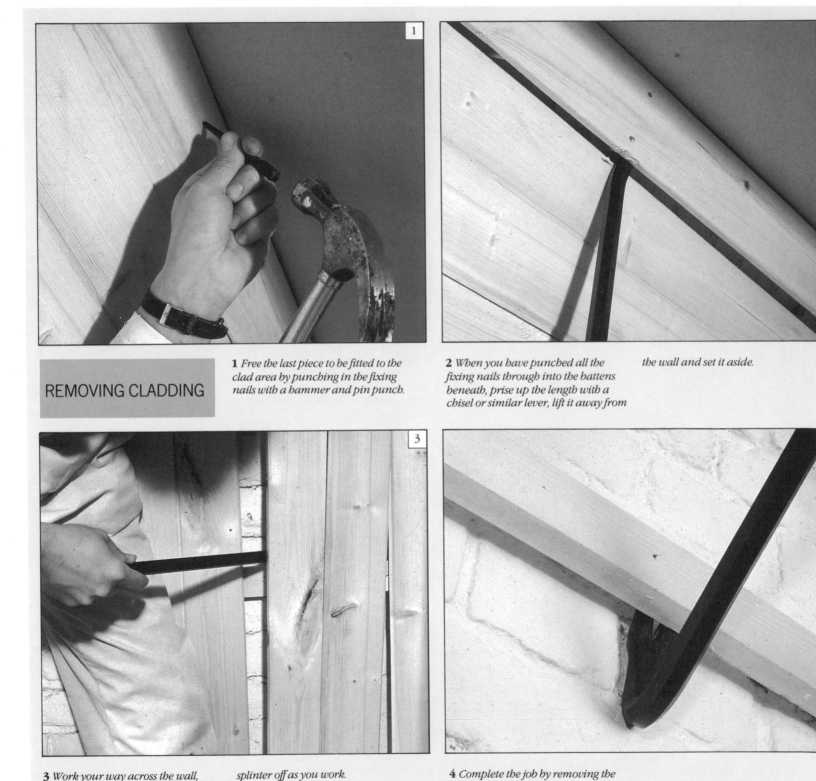

REMOVING CLADDING

1 *Free the last piece to be fitted to the clad area by punching in the fixing nails with a hammer and pin punch.*

2 *When you have punched all the fixing nails through into the battens beneath, prise up the length with a chisel or similar lever, lift it away from the wall and set it aside.*

3 *Work your way across the wall, prising away each length in turn. The fixing nails will have been driven through the tongues on each length; pull away any strips of wood that splinter off as you work.*

4 *Complete the job by removing the wall battens using a crowbar. Insert the end of the bar behind each batten and press down on the other end in a rolling motion.*

REPLACING BROKEN TILES

1 Prise out the pieces of any broken tiles using a small cold chisel. Work from the centre towards the edges.

2 Chip away as much of the old, hard tile adhesive as possible. If you have damaged the plaster underneath, make good with filler. Then spread a thin layer of tile adhesive in the recess

3 Wipe the surrounding tile surfaces with a damp sponge to remove excess filler or adhesive before it has a chance to set hard

4 Press the replacement tile firmly into place, flush with its neighbours, and grout the edges all round it using a squeegee. Polish off excess grout when it has dried using a dry cloth.

Preparing ceilings

Ceilings are prepared in much the same way as walls — the work is just a little more awkward, and you are likely to encounter a few new existing finishes which need special handling.

The most likely of these is the sort of textured finish created using a plaster-like texturing compound. Artex is probably the best known brand name in the UK, but there are others, some of which have slightly different properties. For example, whereas Artex and similar products need the protection of paint, other textured finishes are intrinsically waterproof. Then there are finishes which are essentially thickened emulsion paint — usually recognizable by the low relief of the texturing. Whichever applies in your particular case, so long as you want to do no more than repaint, the preparation is relatively simple. You just give the surface a good wash with warm water and detergent, taking care to flush out any grease and grime that may be trapped in the texturing's detail; then rinse off.

Your problems really begin when you decide that you want a change from a painted, textured ceiling. With the possible exception of a very low relief decoration where cross-lining or double lining may 'soak up' the texturing sufficiently to allow the ceiling to be papered or painted flat, the only sensible options are to have the ceiling replastered (and a DIY plastering system is ideal here), or to install an expensive cover-up such as a suspended ceiling. Stripping off the texturing compound itself is that difficult. With the non-washable types you have to use paint stripper to remove the paint, and then repeatedly soak the exposed texturing compound until it is soft enough to scrape off — both jobs that are far easier said than done. With washable and paint-like finishes, you are likely to have to use a special chemical stripper throughout, softening and scraping off the finish as if it were an extra-thick coat of paint.

Polystyrene ceiling tiles and mouldings form another potentially difficult surface to deal with. The choice is between washing them down in order to give them a new lease of life, or removing them. Never paint them. The paint film negates the effect of the fire-retardant chemicals used in modern tiles, and increases their flammability to the point where a fire can sweep across the room in seconds. In fact, if you are not sure that the tiles have been correctly put up, it is probably worth removing them in any case. The old practice of sticking them up on blobs of adhesive rather than on a continuous adhesive bed makes them especially dangerous in the event of a fire.

Unfortunately, although stripping off the tiles themselves is relatively simple — just prise them off with a scraper — quite a lot of adhesive gets left behind. Removing this is far from easy. Really all you can do is hack at it with a scraper, which, no matter how carefully you work, tends to leave the ceiling in need of a lot of repair. It is therefore best to leave the adhesive where it is and choose a decorative treatment that will cover it — a thickly embossed paper, some form of panelling or even new ceiling tiles. Or you might consider a high-relief textured finish.

MOVING CEILING LIGHTS

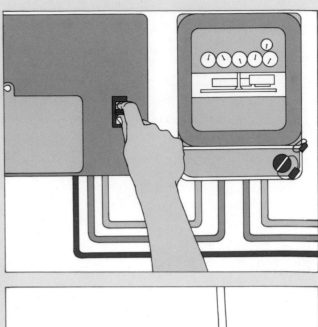

1 *You may need to take down a pendant light fitting to redecorate a ceiling; you may even want to remove it altogether and reposition it somewhere else. Start by turning off the electricity at the house's main on/off switch, and then either remove the appropriate lighting circuit fuse or switch off the miniature circuit breaker (MCB).*

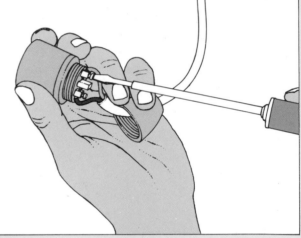

2 *With an ordinary pendant lamp, remove the lampshade. Then unscrew the lampholder cover to gain access to the terminals inside, and use a small screwdriver to disconnect the two flex cores. You can then pull the flex through the cover and set the complete lampholder aside.*

3 *Unscrew the cover on the ceiling rose, and slide it down the pendant flex to remove it. Then disconnect the other end of the pendant flex from the rose terminals and remove it. Replace the rose cover. If you want to remove the rose entirely, disconnect the cables from each terminal bank in turn and connect each group to a small connector block to maintain circuit continuity.*

Old acoustic ceiling tiles are another matter. Having been thoroughly cleaned, these can be painted using either resin-based or emulsion paint, provided you first seal the surface with a coat of stabilizing primer. Don't be tempted to remove them unless they are in very poor condition. Quite apart from the fact that taking them down can prove difficult, the chances are that they were originally put up to disguise an awful ceiling.

Finally, in old houses that haven't been all that well looked after, you may still find ceilings painted with distemper — the standard interior wall and ceiling paint before emulsion paint came along. There are two types — one washable, and one not. The former can be treated in exactly the same way as emulsion paint; the non-washable type — easily recognizable, because if you wipe it with a damp cloth it comes off — must be removed. Even if you succeeded in getting new decorations to stick to a powdery distemper, the material is so unstable that they will almost certainly peel off again in no time. Removal isn't difficult, but it is hard work. You have to scrub it off with a stiff brush and warm water. Once you have got back to clean plaster, treat the surface with a coat of stabilizing primer.

Don't be surprised if the ceiling revealed by the removal of these old finishes is riddled with cracks. Cracks are a problem even in modern plasterboard ceilings, though here they are usually confined to the joins between individual plasterboard sheets. The reason is that ceilings tend to flex in use due to people walking on the floor above, and to the natural movement of the supporting joists. Filling is therefore really something of a temporary solution. Textured finishes offer one way out because they are semi-flexible — hence their popularity for ceilings. But if they are not for you, consider papering instead.

Of course, the real difficulty in preparing a ceiling (and in decorating it, for that matter) is not so much the work itself as the fact that you are doing it off the ground and with your arms above your head, which makes it very tiring. There isn't, unfortunately, a great deal that can be done to alleviate this problem. But good access equipment undoubtedly helps. It's safer, too.

Most people normally work from a step ladder, but while that is certainly better than using chairs and tables, it is far from ideal. To begin with, the average step ladder allows you to reach only fairly low ceilings in comfort. If you find you have to work standing on the step's top platform, you should find some better means of access: on many ladders, the top platform isn't designed to take weight — its primary function is to provide a convenient place to stand paint pots and tools. The other main drawback with steps is that they allow you to work on only a relatively small area of ceiling at one time. This, of course, means that you tend to waste a lot of time and energy climbing up and down and moving the steps from one place to another, which in turn may tempt you to overstretch in order to reach that extra little patch. And that's how accidents happen.

The problem of reach is easiest to overcome. Team the step ladder up with a painter's trestle and span a scaffold

FILLING CRACKS

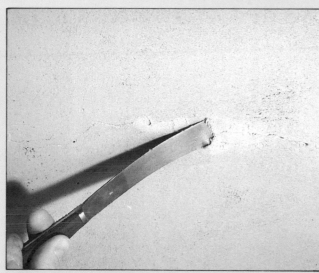

1 *Fill holes and cracks as for walls, drawing the knife across to remove excess filler from the area before leaving it to dry hard. Leave the filler just proud of the surrounding ceiling surface.*

2 *When the filler has set completely, sand over the repaired area with a sanding block to leave a perfectly smooth surface. Avoid standing directly underneath the patch, or you will get plaster dust in your eyes.*

3 *Seal troublesome cracks between sheets of plasterboard or in the angle where the ceiling meets the walls using a flexible decorator's mastic. This comes in a cartridge, and is piped along the cracks like toothpaste. Run over it with a moistened finger for a neat finish.*

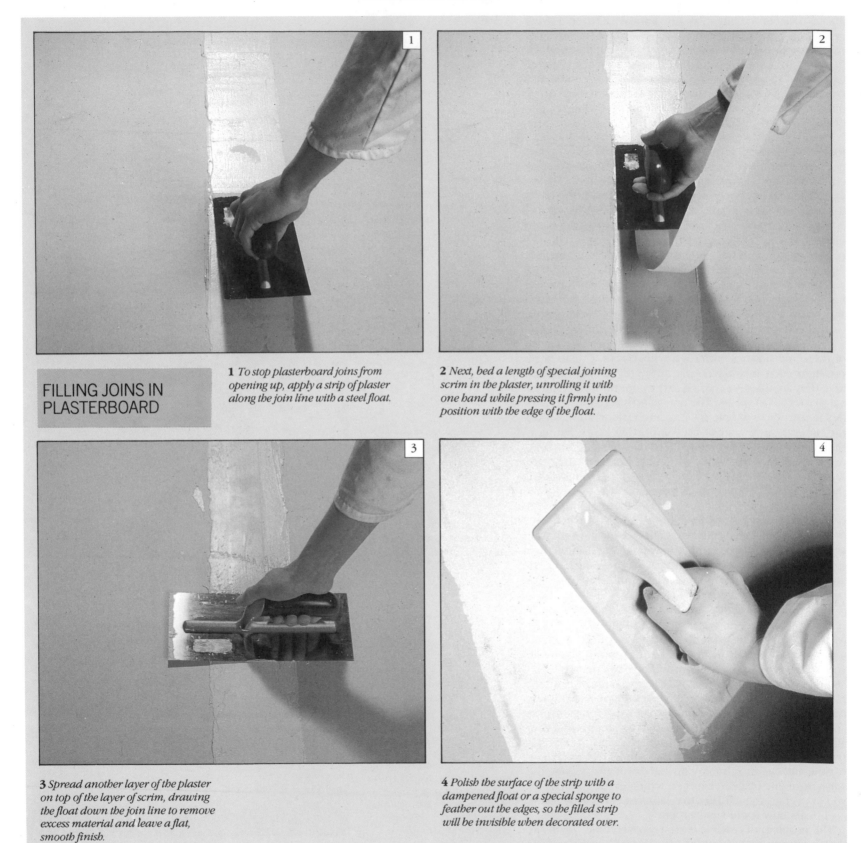

FILLING JOINS IN PLASTERBOARD

1 *To stop plasterboard joins from opening up, apply a strip of plaster along the join line with a steel float.*

2 *Next, bed a length of special joining scrim in the plaster, unrolling it with one hand while pressing it firmly into position with the edge of the float.*

3 *Spread another layer of the plaster on top of the layer of scrim, drawing the float down the join line to remove excess material and leave a flat, smooth finish.*

4 *Polish the surface of the strip with a dampened float or a special sponge to feather out the edges, so the filled strip will be invisible when decorated over.*

board between the two. Both trestle and scaffold board can be rented quite cheaply from a good tool hire shop, and you will find that because you can walk the length of the board in comparative freedom, the work will progress far more quickly. You will certainly appreciate the benefits of the set-up when you come to paper the ceiling, and it is equally useful for cross-lining walls. If you are not very good with heights, tie a rope or long timber batten between trestle and ladder to provide a comforting handrail.

The alternative is to work from a small scaffold tower — undoubtedly the safest option if you have to work a long way off the ground to reach a very high ceiling. Again you can hire one suitable for use indoors quite easily, and they are really very simply to use. You should be given detailed assembly instructions by the hire shop, but basically you just slot the component parts together, tighten up a few bolts, and slide in enough short scaffold boards to provide a safe secure working platform complete with safety rail. The area you can cover from one of these is quite sizeable, and in any case, since most models are fitted with heavy-duty castors, moving the tower is no problem. But, for safety's sake you must remember to lock the wheels with the brake provided before climbing the tower to resume work.

Preparing woodwork

Although new, bare, smoothly planed timber may not look as if it needs much in the way of preparation, there is, in fact, a fair amount to do if you want the best results from a paint or varnish finish.

The first job is to fill any cracks, holes, and dents. Traditionally, ready-mixed stopping compound in a colour that matches the timber is used for this, and it is still best if you intend to give the wood a clear finish. If you plan to stain the wood before varnishing, choose a stopping or wood filler designed to take the stain — not all will. Under paint, however, you can use almost any filler you like. Ordinary plaster-type interior filler is certainly suitable for small cracks and holes. For making good larger defects, a modern, two part epoxy resin based wood filler (usually marketed as part of a wood rot repair system) will give more durable results.

The minute holes formed by the wood grain may also need attention. On some timbers, notably those used to face the plywood cladding on the cheaper flush doors, the grain is so open that no amount of sanding will produce a satisfactory finish. The trick is to fill them with a slurry made from interior filler — the sort that comes as a powder. Mix this with water in the usual way, then keep adding water until the mix has the consistency of thick cream. Pour this on to the wood and then scrape it off again with the edge of a steel rule, scraper blade, or something similar, holding this hard against the surface so that you carry the slurry across the entire surface of the wood at the same time. Given the amount of slurry that comes off, this may seem a pointless exercise, but, in fact, enough filler gets left in the grain pores to to the job.

The next step is to get the surface really smooth, and that

WASHING AND SANDING WOODWORK

1 *Always wash woodwork down before repainting, even if the surface seems to be in perfect condition, to remove dirt, grease and so on from the surface. Use detergent or sugar soap, then rinse down with clean water.*

2 *Next, key the surface of the paintwork with abrasive paper or a proprietary sanding block to ensure that subsequent coats will bond well to it. Silicon carbide abrasive (known as 'wet-and-dry' paper) used wet gives the best results.*

3 *When the grain of the abrasive becomes clogged with a fine slurry of paint, rinse it out in clean water. Use an old scrubbing brush to clean the surface if it won't rinse off easily.*

TOUCHING IN CHIPS

1 *To touch in a damaged area of paintwork, sand the surface round the blemish lightly first of all to provide a good key for the new paint.*

2 *Use a small paintbrush to work paint into the blemish. If bare wood is exposed, wood primer should be used rather than undercoat or gloss. A second application may be necessary to give good coverage.*

3 *When the touched-in paint has dried completely, brush on second and third coats and feather the edges with light brushstrokes away from the blemish onto the surrounding paintwork.*

means sanding. A light hand sanding will do the trick in most cases. Wrap a sheet of medium grade glasspaper (or dry, wet and dry paper) around a cork sanding block, and work it to and fro across the surface, taking care to keep your movements in line with the timber's grain. Working across the grain tends to produce unsightly scratches which can be difficult to remove — that is, unless you are sanding endgrain in which case it is best to work the sanding block in a circular scrubbing motion. Having got the surface as smooth as you can, switch to a fine grade abrasive paper and sand it all over again to leave it smoother still. If sanding complicated mouldings, sand using wire wool instead of abrasive paper to reach right into nooks and crannies.

Obviously, all this requires a fair amount of elbow grease, but over small, often fiddly surfaces there is very little you can do to mechanize the job. There are, of course, a fair number of sanding gadgets that you can fit on to an electric drill, but in this situation the only one likely to produce a finish comparable to that achieved by hand is the sanding drum — basically a foam plastic cylinder wrapped in abrasive paper (normally medium grade garnet paper, a tougher version of glasspaper). Relatively large flat surfaces, however, can be sanded very successfully using an orbital sander — available either as an integral power tool, or as a drill attachment. In theory, given its scrubbing action, there is a risk of scratching the surface, but in practice this shouldn't occur. Disc sanding drill attachments, incidentally, are not to be recommended for this sort of work. They are difficult to control, and will almost certainly scratch the work, if not gouge chunks from it. They are far better reserved for rough shaping.

Having smoothed the wood, you must now seal it. If you are going to varnish it, the usual method of sealing is to dilute a little of the varnish itself using white spirit, and to rub this firmly into the grain using a soft, lint-free cloth. If you will be painting, brush on a thin coat of ordinary wood primer, all-surface primer, or primer-undercoat (which should be thinned enough for the grain to show through). In all cases, once the priming coat has dried, lightly sand the surface once again ready for the finishing coats. This removes any roughness caused by the surface wood fibres absorbing liquid from the primer and swelling up, and gets rid of any dust that may have stuck to the surface while the primer coat was wet.

The primer will stop the wood soaking up too much expensive finish, but it won't stop any resin in the timber from oozing out, and resin will damage paintwork. On ordinary softwoods, this harmful resin is to be found in the timber knots. If you carefully warm a knot with a blowlamp or hot air paint stripper, it will actually seep out in sufficient quantities for you to scrap it off, and this is a worthwhile procedure on very new wood. In most cases, though, it is sufficient merely to seal the knots with shellac knotting compound before priming. The exception is where you are dealing with a particularly resinous wood. Here, a special primer is needed — aluminium wood primer. It is also advis-

STRIPPING PAINTWORK

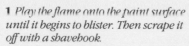

1 *Play the flame onto the paint surface until it begins to blister. Then scrape it off with a shavehook.*

2 *Where there are several layers of paint to be stripped, you may have to go back over the area you've just stripped and burn off the earlier coats.*

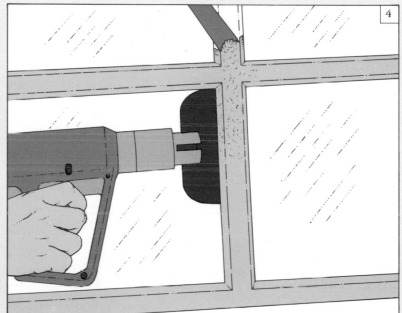

3 *Continue burning and scraping the surface until you are back to bare wood. Don't keep the flame on any one area for too long or you risk charring the wood. Use a combination* shavehook to strip intricate mouldings.

4 *Take care on windows not to crack the glass. A hot air stripper with a deflector shield may be more effective here.*

USING A LIQUID STRIPPER

1 *Brush liquid stripper liberally onto the painted surface using an old brush.*

2 *As soon as the paint surface begins to blister, start scraping off the paint. Deposit the scrapings in a metal container as you remove them. Apply more stripper if necessary to remove* *earlier layers of paint.*

USING A PASTE STRIPPER

1 *Spread paste stripper thickly onto intricately-moulded surfaces and leave to penetrate thoroughly.*

2 *After leaving the stripper to penetrate for the recommended time, use a scraper to start peeling it away from the wood. Follow the maker's instructions about neutralizing the* *surface afterwards.*

able to use this on hardwoods.

Of course, in practice, you will rarely begin work faced with brand new wood. It is far more likely that you will be dealing with wood that has already been painted or varnished, and the big question here is: should you strip the old finish off, or decorate over the top of it? The answer is that it all depends on the condition of the existing finish. In general, if it looks reasonable, and shows no overall signs of peeling, flaking, or blistering it can be left, though stripping may still be desirable if, for example, the paint film has built up to such a thickness over the years that doors no longer close properly.

If stripping isn't necessary, preparing the surface for redecoration is quite simple. Wash it down with warm water and detergent (or you could use traditional sugar soap), then give it a light sanding to provide a key for the new finish. In this instance it is best to use wet and dry abrasive, and to use it wet. It gives a faster, more even cut than glasspaper and is less likely to clog.

Don't worry if, on closer examination, small areas of old paintwork prove to be unsound. Simply scrape or sand off the loose material, lightly feathering the edges of the surrounding paintwork, then smooth out the resulting hollows with filler, or, if they are sufficiently shallow, by retouching them with a few extra coats of new paint. Such minor defects are more of a problem where varnish is involved, particularly if the old varnish is tinted. In theory, you could scrape off the damaged areas, and retouch them before revarnishing the surface as a whole, but in practice, you will find it extremely difficult to obtain an 'invisible' repair, and would be advised to strip the old finish completely and start from scratch.

So how do you strip off old paint and varnish? Starting with paint, there are two basic approaches: you can burn it off, or you can remove it using a chemical paint stripper.

Where you intend to repaint, the former is best — it's quicker, cheaper, and a lot less work. You need a blowlamp (preferably a modern gas-operated model), a flat scraper for dealing with flat areas, and a combination shavehook for fiddly bits. All you do is play the flame lightly and evenly over the surface of the paint until you see it start to bubble. You then take the flame away, and scrape off the softened paint with the shavehook or scraper. And that's it!

There are, however, a few points to watch. If you find another layer of paint beneath the one you have stripped you can repeat the softening process to remove it, but take care when using the flame to soften isolated patches of stubborn paint or pockets of paint trapped in mouldings, or you will scorch the surrounding bare wood. Any paint you cannot easily remove with the blowlamp can be sanded off later. Always remember to keep safety firmly in mind: keep children, pets, and similar distractions out of the room in which you are working, and be careful where you point the flame when not directing it on to the paintwork. Wear thick gloves as protection against burns from the very hot, softened paint, and sweep up what you scrape off at regular intervals before it builds up to the point where it presents a

1 *Dead knots eventually shrink and fall out of the wood, leaving a rounded hole — especially at edges. Use a proprietary wood stopper to fill them (match the wood colour if the surface is to be varnished); cellulose fillers may crack and drop out.*

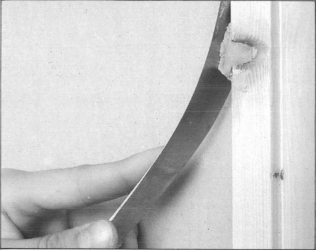

2 *Use a flexible filling knife to force the stopper into the knothole. On a corner such as this, work first from one face of the wood, then from the other, to leave a neat repair. Ideally the stopper should be left just proud of the surface.*

3 *When the stopper has dried hard, sand it down flush with the surrounding surface using fine-grade abrasive wrapped round a sanding block. Treat any sound knots by applying a coat of shellac knotting compound to stop resin bleeding through and spoiling the finish.*

BLEACHING STAINS

1 *To change the colour of stained wood, apply a special wood bleach to the surface using a sponge or brush. Wear gloves to protect your hands. Leave the bleach in contact with the wood as recommended by the manufacturer.*

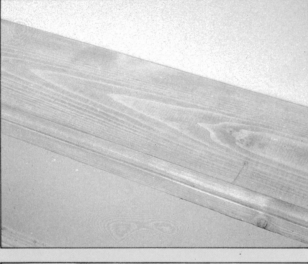

2 *When the bleach has worked, rinse the surface thoroughly to remove all traces of the liquid. If any areas have been bleached unevenly, apply more bleach until the overall colour is uniform.*

3 *Fresh stain can then be applied to the surface with a brush or cloth pad. It's a good idea to dilute the first coat; a second coat can easily be applied if the depth of colour achieved is not sufficient after one application.*

fire hazard — although it shouldn't happen, fragments of paint can catch light, and could start a fire if they fell into a pile of old paint peelings. Finally, always turn the blowlamp off when you are not using it, and follow the manufacturer's instructions to the letter if you have to change a gas cartridge. Follow their advice on the disposal of old cartridges, too.

Stick to the rules, and you will soon find that you can operate the blowlamp to strip paint quickly, efficiently, and in complete safety. But the tool does bother some people, so you might consider using an electric hot air stripper instead. It's a bit like a high powered hair dryer. The technique for using it is exactly the same for a blowlamp, except that there is considerably less risk of scorching the woodwork and virtually no chance at all of the paint catching light. If you are careful, you could, therefore, use a hot air stripper to strip paint prior to varnishing. However, the more usual method of stripping paint in this situation is to employ a chemical stripper.

For large areas, a traditional liquid stripper is best. Those neutralized with water are more convenient than the sort neutralized using white spirit. Decant a little of the thick liquid into an old saucer or something similar, and then, using an old paint brush, apply it thickly to the surface using a stippling action. The paint may start to bubble immediately but leave the stripper to work for at least fifteen minutes (longer if the paint film is very thick) before scraping off softened paint with a scraper or shavehook. If any paint remains, repeat the process until you are left with bare wood, then wash the surface down with plenty of clean water (or white spirit). You'll probably find that some paint will remain in the crevices of moulding. This can be scrubbed out with wire wool dipped in stripper, but for this sort of fiddly work it is far easier to use a different type of stripper.

This comes as a powder that you mix with water to form a thick paste. This is then spread on to the paintwork with a filling knife, and left to work. It's slower than liquid stripper, taking an hour or two (longer for thick paint layers) to do the job, but at the end of that time the paste poultice should come away fairly easily taking the paint with it. Any that remains is usually a sludge that will come off if washed down with plenty of water. You have to wash the surface anyway to neutralize any stripper left in the wood. This type of stripper will, of course, work on straightforward surfaces, too. However, it works out too expensive to be viable for anything more than small jobs.

Whichever chemical stripper you use, take care and always follow the manufacturer's safety instructions to the letter. With the latter type, take care not to inhale the powder when mixing, and don't let it get on your skin or in your eyes. Wear rubber gloves, too, when applying and removing the paste. You also need rubber gloves when using a liquid stripper. It really is very strong stuff and will react with skin, synthetic fabrics, and plastics as well as paint, so avoid splashes, wear sensible protective clothing (with long sleeves), and protect vulnerable floorings with

REPAIRING WOODWORM AND ROT DAMAGE

1 & 2 *One of the quickest ways of repairing small areas of rotten wood — on doors and windows for example — is to use a proprietary rot repair system. First cut away the rotten wood cleanly with a knife or chisel; then brush on special wood hardener to stabilize the surrounding woodwork.*

3 & 4 *Build up the cut-away areas using the special resin-based wood filler, applying it with a filling knife and building the repair up in stages. Finish the patch slightly proud of the surrounding surface and leave it to harden thoroughly. Then sand off the excess filler to leave a smooth, almost invisible repair.*

5 & 6 *To discourage fresh outbreaks of wood rot from occurring in vulnerable areas such as these, drill a series of small holes in the wood on either side of the repaired area and insert small pellets of wood preservative, hiding the holes with more filler. These gradually release the preservative into the wood.*

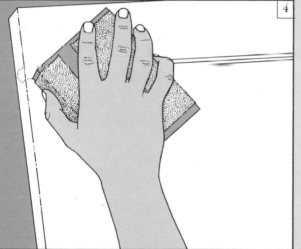

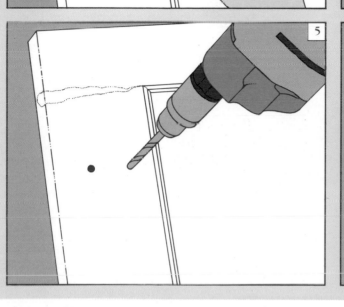

At the beginning of the job, the sheer amount of preparatory work necessary can look extremely daunting. However, the end result always makes thorough preparation worth the effort.

newspaper. If you do get any on your skin, wash it off quickly with plenty of water. You should also ensure ample ventilation, and turn off anything that will heat the fumes. Smoking is particularly dangerous. The fumes aren't explosive — they just turn into a poisonous gas when heated.

And what about stripping varnish? A chemical paint stripper is the best bet, and the only option if you intend to revarnish. But a lot depends on the type of varnish used. Some respond to a fairly mild stripper, others need something far stronger.

Once you have stripped off the old finish, prepare the surface in the same way as new wood. The only complication likely is where the wood has been stained. If you want to varnish but don't like the stain, either restain the wood with a darker shade (bearing in mind that the combination of tones can produce unpredictable results) or bleach out the stain using a proprietary wood lightener.

Preparing Floors

Different floorings differ very little in their needs as far as preparation is concerned. You have to try to ensure that the surface on which they are laid is clean, dry, sound, and reasonably flat. The last is especially important, because a bumpy floor will not only make the new flooring look bad, but also tends to make it wear unevenly, so that its appearance deteriorates with use far more rapidly than is normal. Because levelling directly affects what you do about the rest of the preparation, it's best to make it the first job, and how you set about it depends on whether the floor is made up of floorboards or solid concrete.

In the case of a timber floor, start by attending to any boards in particularly bad condition. There is rarely any need to replace a board entirely as cutting out and replacing a damaged section is sufficient. To do this, lever up board at one end (with tongued and grooved boards, you must saw through the tongues at each side first), and using a couple of stout old chisels or something similar, work along freeing it from the joists until you have lifted a little more than the obviously damaged portion. Now, saw through the board immediately above a suitably placed joist so that when you let it fall back into place, only half of the joist is covered. The exposed half can then be used to support the replacement board which can be screwed or nailed in place — use special flooring brads if you decide to nail.

While you are lifting floorboards, take the opportunity to inspect for signs of wood rot and insect attack in both the boards themselves and the supporting joists. A mirror and a torch will help you make a thorough visual check, and it is also worth prodding suspect timbers with a screwdriver to test their soundness. If you find any suspect timbers or fungal growth, call in a specialist contractor to assess the situation and make the necessary repairs.

Having ensured that the floor is structurally sound, refix any loose floorboards — screws are better than nails here, particularly if the boards are slightly warped — and assess how uneven the floor is as a whole. If things aren't too bad,

LIFTING CARPETS

To lift a fitted carpet, raise one corner and pull it steadily away from the gripper strip. Then prise up the strips all round the room unless carpet will be re-laid.

LIFTING SHEET VINYL

Peel up sheet vinyl that has been stuck to the floor. Then use a hot-air stripper to soften the old adhesive so it can be scraped off the floor surface.

LIFTING WOOD MOSAICS

Use a claw hammer or similar lever to claw up wood mosaic blocks. Then play a blowlamp flame over the old bitumen adhesive to soften it so you can scrape it away with an old broad-bladed chisel or similar tool.

LIFTING CERAMIC TILES

Use a small cold chisel and a hammer to crack and break up old ceramic floor tiles. Then prise them up one by one and chisel away the adhesive bed underneath them as much as possible.

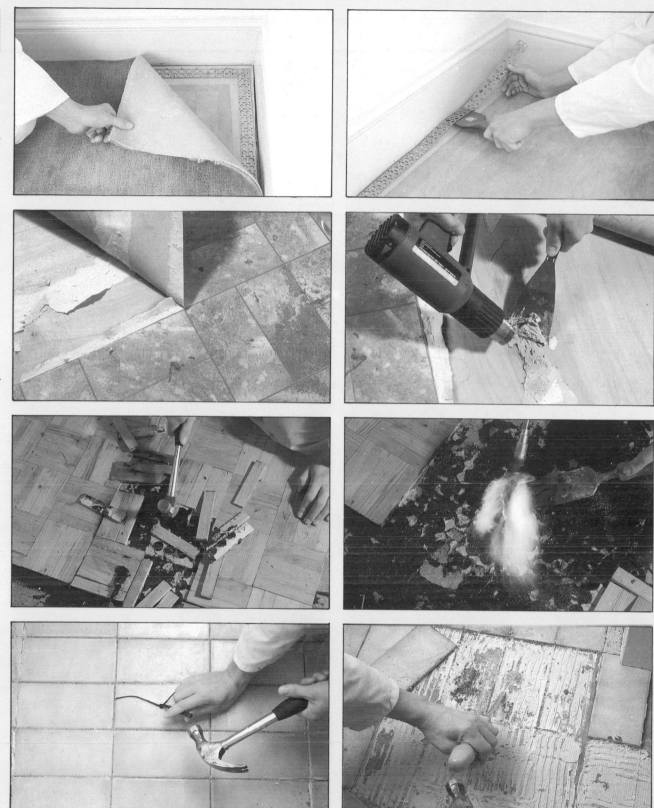

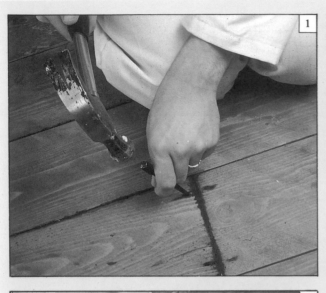

FIXING LOOSE BOARDS

1 & 2 *Before laying a new floorcovering, punch in the heads of any nails protruding above the surface of the boards. If any boards are warped and nails won't hold them, drive in screws instead.*

3 & 4 *To replace a damaged board, check whether it is tongued and grooved by pushing a knife down the crack. If it is, saw through the tongues with a flooring saw. Then prise up the boards at one end using two bolsters or floorboard chisels.*

5 & 6 *If the board passes under a partition wall, cut through it above the centre of the last joist using the curved section of a floorboard saw (or a circular saw if you have one). Then cut the new board to length and nail it into place.*

PATCHING SOLID FLOORS

1 & 2 *Use a cold chisel or brick bolster to chop away crumbling concrete from around holes and cracks in a concrete floor. Then moisten the concrete with water to cut down on the suction and prevent the fresh mortar from drying too quickly.*

3 & 4 *To improve the adhesion of the repair (and to bind together the concrete surface if it is dusty), brush on a diluted solution of PVA building adhesive and leave it to dry. Then mix up a small quantity of ready-mix mortar, adding some PVA adhesive to the mix.*

5 & 6 *Trowel the mortar firmly into the hole, pressing it down to ensure that all voids are filled. Finish off by trowelling the surface smooth and level with the surrounding concrete, and leave it to harden for at least three days before allowing traffic over it.*

it should be all right to carpet over provided you use an underlay. However, other types of flooring — sheet vinyl, and the various tiled finishes — tend to be less tolerant, and so unless the floor is in immaculate condition, it is best to smooth it off by covering it with a layer of hardboard.

Buy this as full sized 2440 x 1220mm (8 x 4ft) sheets and saw it into manageable pieces 1220mm (4ft) square. Brush or spray a liberal, but not excessive, amount of water into the rough side of each sheet, then leave the sheets stacked back to back in the room in which they will be used for at least a couple of days; preferably longer. This conditioning process ensures that when laid, the hardboard will neither absorb moisture from the air and buckle, nor dry out and curl up, so it is important to heat the room normally throughout. To actually lay the hardboard, start putting down a row of sheets along the longest, straightest wall in the room, cutting the last in the row to fit as necessary. Use the off-cut to start the next row. This not only cuts down on waste, but also helps ensure that the joins between individual sheets are staggered brick fashion — vital if the hardboard is to be strong enough to smooth out major undulations in the floor. Fix each sheet into place as you go, starting in the centre and working outwards, using 25mm (1in) annular nails (also known as screw nails). These should be roughly 300mm (12in) apart across the surface of the board, and about 150mm (6in) apart around the edges. Don't worry about cutting in round chimney breasts and so on. Small gaps can be filled later using odd scraps of hardboard.

Solid floors are a little easier to level. Again start by putting right major defects such as deep cracks and holes. Clean them up using a club hammer and cold chisel, aiming to slightly undercut the surrounding material in order to provide a key for the repair. Sweep out any dust using a wet brush and paint the damaged area with a PVA building adhesive. Once this has become tacky, mix up some mortar (for such small repairs it's convenient to buy this dry mixed in small bags) adding PVA to the mixing water according to the manufacturer's instructions. Press the wet mortar into the crack or hole with a trowel, smooth it off level with the surrounding floor, and leave it to set.

Whether or not the floor needs further levelling depends on the flooring you intend to use. Carpeting and quarry tiles bedded in mortar will accommodate a fair amount of roughness, but sheet vinyls, and tiles laid on thin beds of adhesive need an almost completely smooth surface. To obtain this, use a self-smoothing flooring compound. Sold as a powder, you mix it with water, following the manufacturer's instructions, to produce a sort of runny plaster. Pour this on to the floor and roughly smooth it out with a steel float, aiming for an even layer no more than 3mm ($\frac{1}{8}$in) thick, then leave it to set. It will settle out of its own accord to leave a perfectly smooth finish, and if a 3mm ($\frac{1}{8}$in) layer isn't thick enough to cover the ridges in the floor, just apply a second coat as soon as the first is really hard.

Having levelled the floor, whether it is solid or timber, you can be sure it is also sufficiently sound and clean to

SANDING FLOORS

1 *Strip old finishes from floorboards with a power sander — either a belt type for small areas, or else a full-size floor sander. Fit the abrasive belt to the machine.*

2 *Start with a coarse abrasive, and sand at an angle of 45° to the direction of the boards to remove the damaged and discoloured surface of the wood. Fit new belts as they become worn.*

3 *Change to a medium-grade abrasive belt, and sand the surface once again, this time working parallel with the board direction to remove scratch marks left by the initial sanding.*

4 *Finish the job by using a fine abrasive, again working parallel with the board direcion. You will need a small belt sander to reach the edges of the floor if you have used a large floor sander for the bulk of the work.*

receive the new flooring – though it is a good idea to give it a final run over with a broom or vacuum cleaner. But what if you are dealing with a floor that already has some sort of flooring? In most cases it is best to lift it and prepare the bare floor as described above. The main exceptions are permanently-fixed floorings such as old quarry tiles, lino tiles, and so on. So long as they are in sufficiently good condition to provide the new flooring with a sound base, they can be left. Re-stick loose lino tiles. Remove loose or damaged quarry tiles with a cold chisel and club hammer, then fill the resulting hole with mortar, before finally levelling off the entire floor with a self-smoothing flooring compound.

However, if you are covering up old quarry tiles, take care. It is highly likely that rising damp is present, and even if this isn't evident at the moment (quarry tiles usually let the moisture evaporate as fast as it rises through the floor) it could build up into a significant problem once the new flooring is down, destroying any adhesive and possibly the flooring itself. In fact, rising damp is a possibility in any concrete ground floor, so it is always worth testing for it (ideally in winter). The simplest way to do this is to stand a tumbler upside down on the floor, bedding the rim in a ring of putty to form an air-tight seal. If after two or three days, condensation appears *inside* the glass, rising damp is present.

The textbook cure is to dig up the floor, removing at least the top 50mm (2in) or so, and continuing down to a level below that of the damp-proof course in the wall. The floor is then smoothed off with fresh concrete so that a damp-proof membrane can be laid – usually heavy gauge polythene sheets taped together. Having been carried up the wall beyond the level of the dpc, the membrane is finally covered with a 50mm (2in) thick mortar screed. Quite a job, and one most people would prefer to leave to a professional. But it really is the only way to guarantee a cure. Alternatives, such as brushing a couple of coats of bitumen emulsion out over the surface of the concrete, and then covering up with the self-smoothing flooring compound used for levelling floors will, it's true, provide sufficient damp-proofing to protect the new flooring. However, there is a risk that the build-up of moisture beneath the bitumen will simply transfer the dampness to the wall. If you really can't face having the floor dug up, you would be well advised to stick with quarry tiles or some other flooring/adhesive system that doesn't mind getting wet.

Of course, you need not necessarily cover wooden floors. Bare boards, suitably polished, are a very attractive, durable flooring in their own right. If they haven't been polished before, though, you must be prepared for a fair amount of preparation work, because the entire floor must first be sanded smooth.

Start with the normal preparation for wooden floors – repairing damaged boards, and refixing loose ones – then, using a hammer and nail punch, knock every single nail head well below the surface of the boards. You should now turn your attention to any gaps between the floorboards.

To improve the look of the finished floor and prevent draughts, these must be filled. This is simplest using papier maché. Tear newspaper into small squares, soak it in water for about a week, then knead it into a mush, strain off the excess water, and mix with wallpaper paste (one containing a fungicide) to produce a smooth dough that can be pressed into the gaps and neatly smoothed off. The trouble is that papier maché obviously doesn't look like wood when varnished, although the effect can be quite attractive provided the gaps are relatively small and reasonably even. The alternative is to fill the gap with slivers of real timber, carefully planed to fit tightly in between the boards. Drive these slivers firmly into place – protect the edges with scrap wood if you are using a hammer rather than a mallet – leaving them just proud of the surface, then plane off the excess timber.

Of course, you may find that, even after all this careful preparation, the existing boards are not really in a fit state to be sanded and sealed – on an old floor it is quite likely that they are patchily stained and badly dented. In this case, you have two options. The first is to lift every single board and relay it with what was the underside on top, closing up the gaps between boards in the process. The trouble with that is that the underside of the floor may be in little better condition. The second option is to abandon the idea of using the existing boards altogether, and to cover them with a superimposed wooden floor. Normally made from a superior sort of plywood with a thick hardwood veneer, you can choose between parquet effect tiles, or floorboard-like planks. Both are usually tongued-and-grooved for easy fixing, and need the same sort of preparation as a tiled flooring.

Assuming the floor is fit for sanding, you will have to hire two types of floor sander. The first, looking rather like a lawnmower, is a powerful electric belt sander, and is used to tackle the bulk of the floor. The second, is a heavy duty disc sander, and is needed to smooth those areas the main sander cannot reach. Hire a face mask at the same time to keep the dust out of your lungs. Everything you need can be got from a good tool hire shop, who will also sell you the necessary abrasive paper and give you instruction in the tools' use. However, basically what you do is this.

Fit the main sander with a coarse abrasive, and work it diagonally back and forth over any warped boards until they are flush with the rest of the floor. Now, position the sander in a corner of the room pointing in the same direction as the floorboards' grain (ideally next to a long, straight wall), switch on and let it carry you forward, sanding the band of floor next to the wall as it goes. When you have reached the far side of the room, without switching off, pull the sander back over the same strip to its starting point. You will find dragging the sander backwards hard work, but the entire process, and in particular the change of direction at the far wall, must be carried out as smoothly as possible. If the sander is allowed to linger in one spot, it will gouge into the floor and leave a dip that will prove almost impossible to remove. Continue sanding the strip in this way until it is as smooth as you can get it.

You can now switch off, move the sander along a little, and tackle the next strip of floor in the same way. Carry on like this, with each strip slightly overlapping its predecessor, until you have smoothed as much of the floor as you can reach with the main sander. Now, change the paper on the sander to a medium-grade abrasive, go back to the beginning, and sand the whole floor over again. Finish off by sanding the entire floor for the third time using a fine-grade abrasive. To complete the sanding, smooth the edges and corners of the floor left untouched by the main sander. Working through coarse, medium, and fine grades of abrasive as before, simply stroke the disc sander over the surface of the wood, keeping the abrasive as far as possible in line with the timber grain. Any corners that the disc sander cannot work into must be sanded by hand.

All that remains is to clean up before working a priming coat of varnish diluted with white spirit into the wood with a lint-free cloth. The sanding will have produced a lot of dust, so a vacuum cleaner is best for the job. Go over the floor two or three times, allowing sufficient time to elapse between cleaning sessions for any dust to settle.

Preparing details

As well as preparing the obvious parts of the room — the floors, walls, ceilings, and woodwork — there are usually quite a few odds and ends that need attention before you can decorate and many of them may be metal.

In many ways, preparing metal for painting is no different to preparing wood. Faced with bare metal, you simply wash the surface to remove any dirt (and use white spirit to remove grease), then rub it down thoroughly using dry wet-and-dry abrasive paper. You do need to be rather more thorough here, though. The idea is not only to provide a key for the new paintwork, but also to remove any surface rust and other deposits that might stop the new paint adhering.

Once the metal is as bright as new, the final job is to prime it. Do this as soon as you have finished rubbing down — many metals tarnish very quickly – and do use the right primer. For iron and steel, a zinc chromate primer is best indoors, unless the metal has been galvanized, in which case you should use a calcium plumbate primer. Zinc chromate is also the primer to use on aluminium — though anodized aluminium doesn't really need painting. In fact, by painting aluminium you actually make work for yourself in the future, because, although the aluminium won't need any maintenance, other than the occasional wash, the paint film will have to be replaced at regular intervals in the usual way. Brass and copper do not need priming at all. You can apply the top coats of paint directly to the shiny bare metal.

And if the metal has already been painted? As with painted wood, if the existing paint film is in generally sound condition you can merely rub it down with wet, wet-and-dry abrasive, wash off any dirt and grease, then apply new finishing coats directly on top of the old. If, however, it proves necessary to strip off the old finish, use a chemical paint stripper. The heat of a blowlamp (or hot air stripper)

1 *Old decorative plasterwork such as cornices and ceiling centres are often so clogged up with distemper that much of the detail is lost. Spray water onto the surface to soften the old paint.*

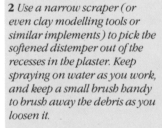

2 *Use a narrow scraper (or even clay modelling tools or similar implements) to pick the softened distemper out of the recesses in the plaster. Keep spraying on water as you work, and keep a small brush handy to brush away the debris as you loosen it.*

3 *Use a hard interior filler or plaster of Paris to patch small parts of the moulding that are cracked or missing. Build up the repair in stages, allowing each layer to dry fully before adding more filler and shaping the repair to match its surroundings.*

could cause some metal items to twist and buckle, and with metal window frames, there is the additional risk of the heat being transferred to the glass, causing that to crack.

There is another important difference between the preparation of metal and that of wood. Metal — or, more specifically, iron and steel — can rust. And quite apart from the fact that rust will ruin your new decorations, if left unchecked it will continue consuming sound metal until nothing else remains. If you find any trace of rust — and bear in mind that it may be concealed beneath blisters in the paintwork — you must deal with it before continuing with the rest of the preparation. Provided it is not so advanced as to warrant the replacement of the affected metalwork, this isn't too difficult.

Start by removing as much loose rust and flaking paint as possible with a stiff wire brush. You can buy wire brush drill attachments for the purpose, but for such small jobs it's not generally worth it. At the same time, cut away any rusty metal that is so obviously weak as to be useless, then carefully rub down the entire area with dry wet-and-dry abrasive and/or wire wool. When you have finished, you should be left with clean, bright metal without any trace of rust at all, and this must now be treated with a proprietary rust inhibitor. That done, you can set about repairing the damage, and in most situations you will find that a car body repair kit contains everything you need. In fact, all of the materials needed to deal with rust tend to be most readily available from car accessory shops. With the damage taken care of, finish off by treating the exposed metal and filler with the appropriate primer. As with sound metal, it is vital you prime as soon as possible — before rust reappears on the surface.

Ornate plasterwork is another detail that will need careful preparation. The general principles involved are the same as for plain plaster walls, but the very intricacy of some plaster detailing poses special problems. To begin with, although it is perfectly possible to merely wash down the surface and repaint (indeed, it's the easiest option), there comes a point when the paint layer on the moulding is so thick that it completely masks the finer details of the ornament. In this situation, you may feel it is worth going to the trouble of stripping back to bare plaster before repainting, but that is easier said than done. You will certainly have to use a chemical paint stripper, but which?

Both the liquid and paste varieties have their advantages and disadvantages in this situation. The paste type, for example, should prove easiest in terms of removing paint from the intricacies of the moulding without the need to resort to a scraper, but it can work out expensive over a large area, and if you allow the stuff to dry out to the point where you have to use a scraper to remove it, there is a chance that you will get plaster and stripper poultice confused — they look similar. A liquid stripper, on the other hand, will be cheaper, but isn't very good at removing old paint from tiny crevices unless you scrub it out with wire wool dipped in the chemical. If the plaster is at all fragile, it could be damaged in the process. The choice is therefore

PREPARING METALWORK

1 *To prepare metalwork for redecoration, start by washing the surface down thoroughly and then sand it over with fine-grade silicon carbide (wet-and-dry) abrasive paper to remove any surface roughness and provide a good key for subsequent coats of primer, undercoat and topcoat.*

2 *If the surface is rusty or pitted in places, use a wire brush to remove the deposits and leave a bright metallic surface. A cup or wheel-pattern wire brush fitted in an electric drill will be quicker than hand-brushing if large areas have to be tackled.*

3 *Alternatively, rust can be removed with a proprietary rust remover. This is brushed onto the metal surface and usually left to dry, by which time it has converted the rust into a hard, inert surface that needs no further preparation before primer and paint coats are applied. Follow the manufacturer's instructions carefully, and take care to avoid splashing the chemical on your hands or in your eyes.*

REPLACING GLASS

1 & 2 *The simplest way of removing a cracked pane of glass to to stick adhesive tape over it and break it with a hammer. Wear gloves for protection as you lift out the broken pieces.*

3 & 4 *Use an old chisel or a glazier's hacking knife to remove the old putty from the rebate. Prime any bare wood you expose, then thumb in a layer of bedding putty all the way round the rebate.*

5 & 6 *Offer up the replacement pane to the bottom edge of the rebate, align it carefully and then press it into place. Use firm hand pressure at the edges of the pane, not in the centre.*

7 & 8 *Secure the pane with glazing sprigs along each edge, then thumb in the facing putty all the way round. Smooth it off neatly with a putty knife, forming neat mitres at the corners.*

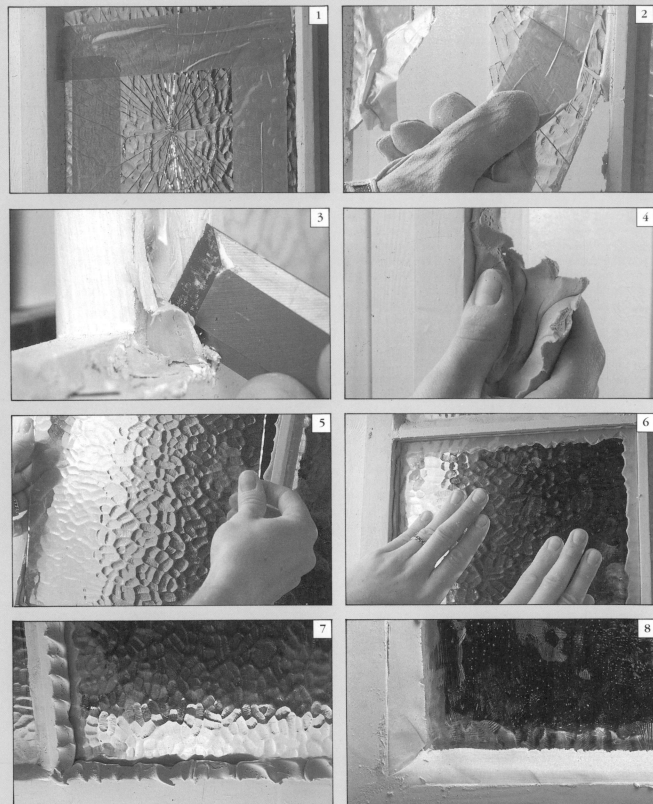

largely a matter of personal preference, but whichever you choose, you will have to work very carefully, and you can expect the job to take a considerable period of time.

Repairing ornate plasterwork can also be a problem. Minor dents, holes and cracks can be tackled using interior filler in the same way as those in a flat wall. Chipped and missing decoration is another matter. Interior filler is again the thing to use, but shaping it in order to replace lost moulding takes time, patience, and not a little skill. You will almost certainly be able to manage small repairs of this sort — few visitors will inspect the results close enough to notice mistakes — but where the moulding is in generally poor condition, complete replacement is a better option.

What you replace old moulding with depends largely on how much you are prepared to pay, and on how keen you are to retain the original design. If the existing moulding is so attractive that you are determined to keep it at all costs, investigate as many firms specializing in reproduction period plasterwork as possible to see if any have your particular moulding (or something so like it as to make no difference) in stock. Failing that, you may be able to find a local specialist willing to produce lengths of replacement moulding from casts taken of the original — but that is expensive. If a plaster replacement is out of your price range, look at glass fibre as an alternative. Most are faithful reproductions of original period mouldings, but are rather cheaper and a lot easier to put up — they usually snap on to clips fixed to the wall. At the very bottom of the price range, come mouldings in expanded polystyrene. These tend to come in a smaller range of simpler designs (including plain modern ones), and should be left unpainted for the same reasons that you shouldn't paint polystyrene ceiling tiles. However, they are better than nothing in a room proportioned to have some sort of cornice, and putting them up is simply a matter of gluing them in place with a special adhesive. Both glass fibre and polystyrene covings and cornices, incidentally, are widely available with ready mitred corner sections to make installation easier still.

If you are planning to completely revamp the room, you may have decided to alter the fireplace and surround, and since this is a fairly major job it should be taken care of before tackling anything else. You may, for example, wish to block off a fireplace that you no longer use, or open up one previously closed up in order to put in an open fire. Or you may simply wish to change the existing fire surround for something more to your taste.

Changing an existing surround is usually the easiest of the three. To remove the old surround, hack away the plaster at each side using a club hammer and bolster chisel, and you should find one or more pairs of lugs through which the surround is fixed to the wall with screws or nails. If these won't come away easily, chop through them with the cold chisel. You can now lever the fire surround from the wall with a crowbar, garden spade, or something equally robust, and cart it away. But do get some able-bodied help for this stage of the operation — fire surrounds can be very heavy. The superimposed hearth in front of the fireplace

REPAIRING STAINED GLASS

1 *Remove the damaged panel and lay it flat on a board. Then cut through the outer section of the lead came with a sharp knife.*

2 *Continue cutting through sections of 'came' until you can separate the damaged section from the rest of the panel. You may need to cut the came from both sides.*

3 *Scrape out the old putty and any splinters of broken glass bedded in it using an old knife. Then brush out the cames with a fine wire brush.*

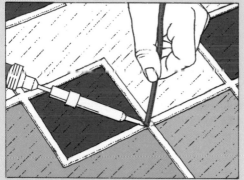

4 *Fit the new piece of glass in position, and reassemble the panel sections carefully. Then apply flex to the joints and solder them together.*

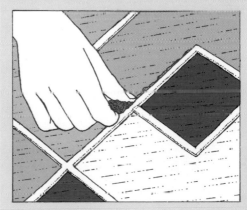

5 *Use your thumb to press putty into the cames all round the new piece of glass, and trim off any excess with an old knife. Then repeat on the underside.*

6 *Finish off by pressing the came back flat with knife strokes. Then polish up the came surfaces by running the wire brush over them.*

should also lever up relatively easily, leaving the opening ready for whatever new surround you have in mind. There are quite a few to choose from including models made from stone, brick, decorative concrete blocks, wood, and even cast iron. They are most widely available from specialist firms as kits, and come complete with detailed installation instructions.

The old surround and hearth must also be removed if you intend to block up the fireplace. Once they are out of the way, clean up the resulting opening, and block it off with a small brick or concrete block wall — you may have to break up and shovel out the old fireback to make room for this. Be sure to build an air-brick into this wall a few inches above the floor; without this to provide ventilation, condensation is likely to form within the disused flue, leading to a nasty outbreak of damp. Finally, plaster over the new masonry and surrounding area to leave a smooth, flat surface flush with the surrounding wall. You can do this yourself using a DIY plastering system. After decorating, neaten the airbrick opening by fitting a metal or plastic grille if desired.

Re-opening a fireplace is a little more complicated, although, basically, you just hack off the plaster, knock down the brickwork sealing it off, and have the chimney swept. But whether or not that leaves you with a usable fireplace depends on a great many other factors – whether the old fireback was removed, the condition of the flue lining, the state of the chimney stack, and so on. Unless you are absolutely sure that everything is in good working order, it is generally best to seek expert advice. Any good supplier of fires and fire surrounds should be able to help.

Finally, don't forget any glass in the room — glass in windows, doors, partitions, and so on. Any broken panes should be replaced before the new decorations go up. Unlike the replacement of external panes, replacing an interior pane of glass is very straightforward. In most cases, the old pane will be simply set into a bed of putty or flexible mastic (probably a silicone based mastic similar to that used to seal gaps around baths), and held in position by lengths of quadrant wooden beading, mitred at the corners and fixed in place with small panel pins. To replace the pane, start by smashing it with a hammer, and pick out as much of the broken glass as possible by hand, wearing gloves for protection. It's a good idea to lay strips of masking tape over the pane before you set to with the hammer: the tape will bind the shards together so they don't scatter all over the floor. Any small pieces that remain embedded in the putty can be extracted with pliers.

Next, carefully lever off the wooden beading using an old blunt chisel or something similar. Scrape out the remains of the old putty, and clean up both the beading and the rebate in which the glass sat with glasspaper, before protecting the exposed timber with a coat of primer. While this is drying, measure up the opening for the new glass. Take two or three readings in different positions to allow for the fact that the frame may be out of true, and working to the smallest height and width, deduct 3mm ($\frac{1}{8}$in) from each dimension to find the size of the replacement pane. Have this cut at the shop where you buy it. The supplier should also be able to advise you on the thickness and type of glass you need. If the original pane used an obscured glass, you might like to choose something more in keeping with the new decor as a replacement. In any case, if the pane is in a door, or some other position where there is a risk of someone accidentally bumping into it or falling through it, choose some form of safety glass — wired glass if you want an obscured pane; toughened glass if you want a clear one. The latter may have to be ordered specially in the size you want.

Having got the glass home, start by running a thick bed of mastic around the rebate. Like caulking, suitable mastic is widely available in cartridges from which you can extrude it using a specially designed gun. Offer the glass up to the opening, centring it within the rebate, and press it into place around the edges using the palms of your hands. Any excess mastic that oozes out can be wiped off with a wet cloth. Run a second bead of mastic around the perimeter of the opening on the face of the glass, ready to receive the beading — you can use the original beading if it is in good condition. Press this on to the mastic, then settle it down into the rebate, and fix it in place with at least two panel pins per side. Again, use a wet cloth to wipe off any mastic that oozes out, and finish by punching the pin heads fractionally below the surface of the wood, so you can hide them beneath filler or stopping ready for painting.

THE COMPLETE PAINTER

PAINTING WITH A BRUSH *202*

PREPARING TO PAINT *203* ♦ PAINTING WOODWORK *204* ♦ PAINTING WALLS *205*
STAINING/VARNISHING WOOD *207* ♦ CLEANING AND STORING BRUSHES *208*

PAINTING WITH A ROLLER *210*

LOADING A ROLLER *211* ♦ PAINTING A WALL *212* ♦ APPLYING GLOSS PAINT *212*
USING SPECIAL ROLLERS *213* ♦ CLEANING AND STORING ROLLERS *213*

PAINTING WITH A PAD *214*

LOADING A PAD *215* ♦ APPLYING PAINT *216* ♦ CLEANING AND STORING PADS *216*

SPECIAL TECHNIQUES *221*

APPLYING TEXTURED PAINT *221* ♦ SPONGING *223* ♦ PAINTING A MURAL *225*
STENCILLING *226* ♦ COMBING *228*

Fifty years ago, applying any sort of paint – and gloss in particular – was a real craft. Paints in those days were simply so thin that you had to know what you were doing in order to achieve even coverage and avoid such faults as brushmarks, sags and runs. Today, things are different. Some modern paints are so designed that a child could obtain a near perfect finish. You don't even have to use a brush anymore. You can roll the paint on, spread it on with a pad, or use a spray gun, if you wish. But some of the traditional skills are worth knowing. They make the paint go farther. And they enable you to achieve good results using the cheaper, more traditional varieties of paint and varnish.

Painting with a brush

The brush is, of course, the traditional tool for applying paint, and in many ways, it remains the most versatile. You will need a selection to do the job properly. For gloss painting, varnishing, and other small scale work, use what's called a varnish brush – the ordinary flat paint brush. These come in a range of sizes, but a 50mm (2in) model is probably the best general purpose tool, while a 25mm (1in) one will enable you to cope with a certain amount of intricate work. For painting walls, a larger, coarser brush is used – called, not surprisingly, a wall brush. These too come in a range of sizes, and when choosing you should bear in mind that, although a large brush will allow you to cover the wall more quickly than a small one, when loaded with paint it may prove too heavy to use for long periods, thus losing its advantage in speed. A 100mm (4in) brush is a good compromise.

A brush's quality is also important. Avoid the very cheapest types with short, coarse synthetic filament bristles. They don't give good results. Some authorities suggest that you should buy the best you can afford, but that too is a mistake. The very best brushes are designed for the professional, who demands tools that can not only cope with the more traditional 'trade paints', but will also last for years. The needs of the amateur are less demanding, and a middle-of-the-range brush (top-of-the-range in terms of DIY brushes) with long, thick bristles that taper to a wedge when the brush is charged, should be adequate. In all probability, if you were to buy a professional-quality brush, you would be too old to use it by the time you had even 'run it in'.

Good brushes do need a certain amount of 'running in' to produce the best results. It is certainly not a good idea to put a brand new brush straight on to gloss work – the bristles won't have the necessary suppleness and shape. Break them in on primers and undercoats first. New brushes should also be thoroughly washed out in warm, soapy water before use, to soften the bristles and remove any that may be loose. Whether the brush is old or new, before

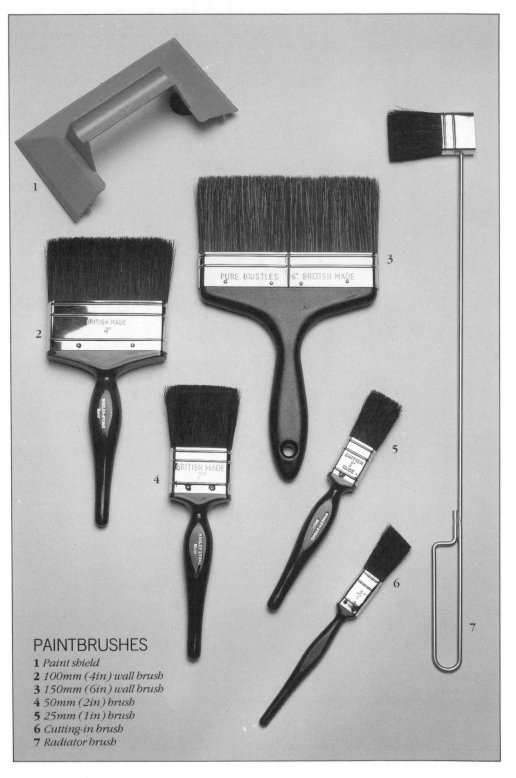

PAINTBRUSHES

1 *Paint shield*
2 *100mm (4in) wall brush*
3 *150mm (6in) wall brush*
4 *50mm (2in) brush*
5 *25mm (1in) brush*
6 *Cutting-in brush*
7 *Radiator brush*

using it, flirt the bristles through your fingers, and then strop them across the palm of your hand. This removes any remaining loose bristles, and gets rid of dust.

Paint, too, has its own starting ritual. Always wipe over the top of the tin to remove any dust before opening it. Lever off the lid with something that won't damage it and make it difficult to replace. If you are re-opening a partly used tin, don't let chips of dried paint fall in, and carefully cut out and remove any skin that has formed. And always give the paint a good stir to make sure the pigment and binder are uniformly mixed. This applies even to non-drip paints which may tell you not to stir them on the tin. Just let the paint stand undisturbed for an hour or so to regain its non-drip qualities.

Finally, it is well worth decanting the paint into a paint kettle — a sort of shallow metal or plastic bucket — rather than dipping your brush straight into the tin. These are not only lighter and easier to carry around, but also the decanting process allows you to strain the paint to remove any minute bits of debris it may contain. Just pour the paint into the kettle through cheesecloth or nylon. In addition, any dust that gets into the paint from your brush will contaminate only that batch — not the whole tin.

Now for the painting itself. With resin-based paint, the idea is to build up a cohesive film of primer (where appropriate) and undercoat, followed by two or more coats of finish (usually gloss). Traditionally, the undercoat's job is to obliterate the original surface colour, thus ensuring that the colour of the finishing coats will be both uniform and true to the colour chart. It also helps to smooth off the surface, and provide a matt finish to which the finishing coats can stick. What's more, it works out cheaper than applying sufficient top coats to achieve the same effect.

In reality, however, undercoat is not always strictly necessary. Where there is no great colour contrast between the surface and new paint, you can expect the top coat alone to produce a good finish and a true colour after one or two coats (depending on its thickness and quality). And as for the business of needing a matt finish for the top coats to stick, there is some evidence to suggest that, on the contrary, modern resin-based paints stick better to a glossier surface.

Whatever you decide, the basic technique for applying the runnier, more traditional paints (and varnishes) is the same. Dip the brush into the paint until about half the length of its bristles are immersed, then withdraw it and scrape off the surplus paint on the side of the paint kettle. This avoids drips and runs. Next, holding the brush by its metal ferrule in much the same way as you would hold a pen, work the brush lightly up and down, applying the paint to the surface in long strokes, following the direction of the grain if you are working on wood. Your aim at this stage is not to cover the surface completely, but to produce a series of parallel stripes a little apart — a process called 'laying on'.

When the brush starts to run dry, you can move on to the next step — 'brushing out'. This simply means working the

PREPARING TO PAINT

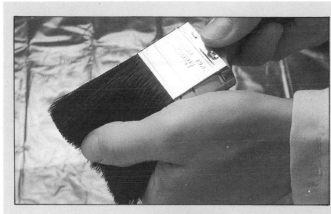

1 *Before using a new paintbrush, 'flirt' the bristles with your fingers and strop it across the palm of your hand to remove any loose bristles and dust which could spoil the finish of your paintwork.*

2 *Dust off the top of the tin before opening it to stop bits falling in the paint. Then lever off the lid carefully with an old screwdriver or similar tool; be careful not to distort it.*

3 *If a skin has formed over the paint, cut all round the edge with a knife and lift it out. Pick out any bits of dry paint you can see, then stir the paint thoroughly (even if it's a non-drip paint).*

4 *Strain the paint from the tin into a paint kettle through a fine sieve to remove any bits remaining in the paint. A kettle is easier to handle than a large tin, and any leftovers at the end of the job can be strained back into the tin again.*

PAINTING WOODWORK

1 & 2 *Dip the brush into the paint to a depth of no more than half the bristle length, then scrape off excess paint by drawing the bristles across a piece of string or wire fixed across the kettle.*

3 & 4 *On surfaces such as doors, apply paint to fiddly bits such as mouldings first. Then paint in the panels, brushing first with the grain and then across it to get good, even coverage. Finish off the area with further light brush strokes parallel with the direction of the grain.*

5 & 6 *Tackle other areas in the same way, first applying the paint in parallel strips, then blending them together with brush strokes at right angles to the first ones. Again, finish off each area with light brush strokes parallel with the direction of the wood grain.*

brush at right angles to the stripes to spread the paint into a thin, even layer that covers the surface completely. That done, lightly work the brush over the surface, once again following the direction of the wood grain, to eliminate any obvious brush marks and leave a perfect finish. Having completed one section as described above, recharge the brush and move on to the next, if possible, arranging for the sections to overlap slightly while the paint is still wet, and blend them together while brushing out and finishing off. This prevents the formation of a 'dry line' which might be visible when all the paint has dried.

The technique for non-drip paint is slightly different. The more you work it, the runnier and more difficult to handle it becomes. So, simply dip the brush in to about half the length of the bristles, and, without scraping off the excess, apply it following the direction of any wood grain, aiming for a fairly thick, even coating that completely covers the surface. The paint will then flow out of its own accord to produce a smooth, even finish. You certainly won't be left with brush marks.

With both types of paint, though, you must be careful when working up to an edge. Always work the brush out over an edge. Drag it back, and you could scrape off enough paint to form a ridge of paint or, worse, a run. Working up to a surface that is not to be painted also needs care. It's called 'cutting in', and is generally easiest with a fairly small, preferably worn brush. Charge the brush a little more fully than normal, and position the bristles on the surface a little away from the desired edge of the paint work. Now, draw the brush along parallel to the edge, applying just enough pressure to splay the bristles out until they just reach the surface you don't want painted. After a little practice you will find that by keeping your hand steady and the pressure constant, you can achieve a remarkably straight line with considerable accuracy.

Having successfully applied one complete coat of paint to the surface, allow it to dry completely before applying any subsequent coats that might be required. Once it is hard, it is advisable to rub it down lightly with fine wet-and-dry paper before repainting. This has nothing to do with reducing the thickness of the paint, as some people imagine: it's purpose is partly to provide a key for the next coat, but mainly to flatten off any 'nibs' of paint that have formed around dust particles. In fact, dust is one of the painter's greatest enemies, so do all you can to avoid getting it in the paint. Never work in a dusty atmosphere, and, before applying any paint, give the surface a final sweep using either an old, clean paint brush, or a special, slightly sticky cloth called a tack rag. After rubbing down between coats, wipe off the paint dust with a damp cloth — one moistened with white spirit is best.

Having mastered the above techniques, you can be confident of achieving a good finish on almost any reasonably plain, straightforward surfaces. Unfortunately, few surfaces in real rooms are straightforward. Most present some sort of problem.

Take doors as an example. With a flush door, you should

PAINTING WALLS

1 *The technique for brush-painting walls with emulsion paint is similar to painting woodwork; the main difference is that you use a larger brush — 75 or 100mm (3 or 4 in) wide instead of 25 to 50mm (1 to 2 in). The first stage is to load up the brush as described opposite, and to apply the paint in a series of vertical bands on the wall surface.*

2 *The next step is to brush out the strips applied in stage 1 with horizontal brush strokes, to ensure that the paint covers the wall surface completely and is applied evenly. Don't reload the brush; work with the paint you have already applied.*

3 *Finish off the area with a series of light vertical brush strokes, in the same manner as laying off the paint along the grain when painting wood. Then load up the brush and repeat the process on the next area of wall, working all the time from the wet edge of the paint outwards.*

Painting doors and windows
Starting from the top, paint edges of opening surfaces first, to allow for drying. Paint sills and baseboards last, to avoid picking up dirt from them.

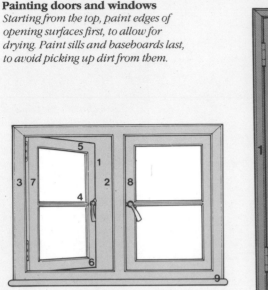

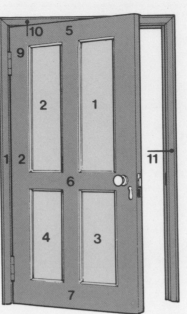

Painting sliding sash windows *Paint the top and bottom edges of the outer sash window with the same type and colour of paint as the outside of the window. Use the same paint and colour as on the inside of the window for the top and bottom edges of the inner sash.*

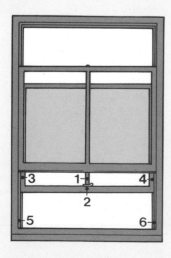

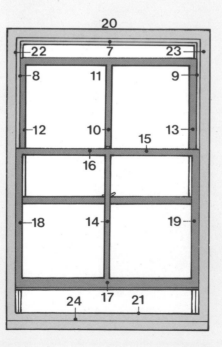

be able to avoid dry lines if you mentally divide the door horizontally into thirds, then divide each third in half vertically to find the sections you should aim to cover with a brushload. With the surface of the door taken care of, you can then tackle the leading or hinge edge, whichever is appropriate. The rule here, incidentally, is that you paint whichever edge is visible from the room when the door is opened in the same colour as the visible door face.

However, there are a couple of practical snags to be overcome. First, if you decided not to lift the flooring before redecorating, you may get paint on it when you come to cut in along the bottom edge of the door. Where carpeting is concerned, you may also get a certain amount of fluff on the new paintwork. If possible, lift the corner of the flooring while you are painting the door, and, in the case of a carpet, leave it folded back until the paint has dried. If for some reason you can't do this, slide newspaper under the door and paint carefully.

There is also the problem of getting in and out of the room while the paint is still wet as, for the best results, you have to remove all door furniture, including the handle. The best solution is to wedge the door open, and keep it open until the paint has dried. It is also well worth jamming a piece of scrap timber into the hole left by the door handle, so that you can use it as a door knob until the door furniture can be replaced. The only trouble with all this is that it allows pets and small children to come and go as they please. And while adults can just about be trusted to understand the meaning of a 'wet paint' sign — even if they insist on touching the paintwork just to make sure — pets and small children are not to be trusted at all in this situation. So, keep an eye on things, or, better still, try to schedule your decorating so that doors can be left to dry unmolested overnight.

More complex pieces of joinery such as panelled doors and windows present even more of a challenge. Since it is almost impossible to paint them without a dry line forming somewhere, you have to use the piece's component parts to disguise the fact, and that means painting the different parts of the door, or whatever, in a special order.

On a panelled door, tackle the panels, together with any associated mouldings, first. Next, paint the rails (the horizontal timbers), starting with the one at the top and working down. Finish off by painting the uprights — the stiles. The only theoretical difficulty here is in deciding where rails end and stiles begin. The answer is to let the wood grain act as your guide. The border line is where the grain changes direction at the joints.

And windows? Ordinary fixed and hinged casement windows are best treated in the same way as a panelled door. Treat each pane of glass as a panel that you don't have to paint. When cutting in around a window pane, though, it is advisable to allow the paint to stray fractionally on to the glass to form a border just under 3mm ($\frac{1}{8}$in) or so wide. This will stop condensation getting under the adjacent paint film and lifting it. Any other paint that strays on to the glass should either be wiped off immediately with a rag dipped in

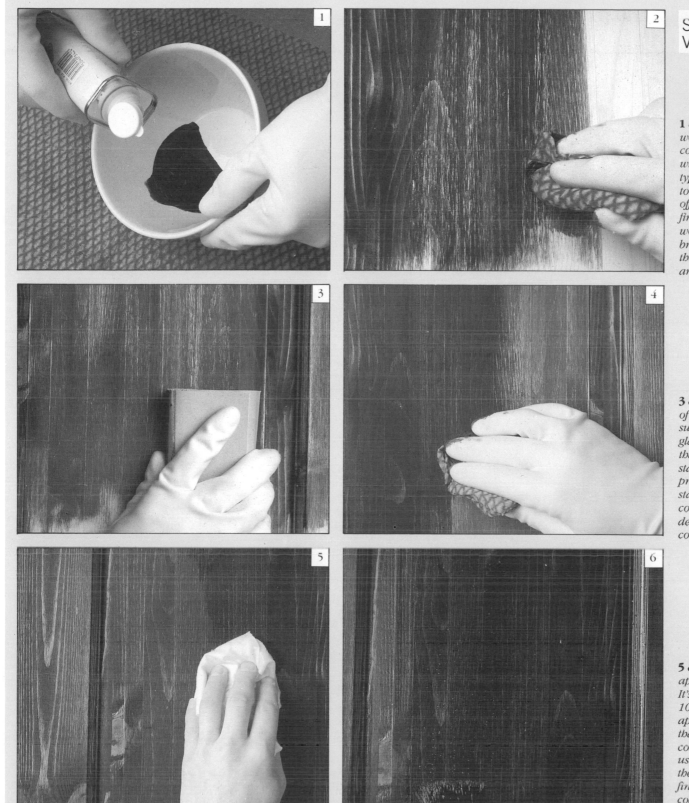

STAINING/ VARNISHING WOOD

1 & 2 *Start by decanting the wood stain into a small container. Dilute it or mix it with other stains of the same type if required. It's a good idea to wear gloves to keep the stain off your hands. Then apply the first coat with a cloth pad, working along the grain in broad stripes. Don't overlap these, or they will show as dark areas.*

3 & 4 *When the first application of stain has dried fully, sand the surface lightly with fine-grade glasspaper to remove any fibres that have been raised by the stain (this is a particular problem with water-based stains). Then apply a second coat of stain to the surface to deepen colour and ensure even coverage.*

5 & 6 *When the stain has dried, apply the first coat of varnish. It's best to thin this with about 10 per cent white spirit and to apply it with a cloth pad rather than a brush. Then subsequent coats can be applied in the usual way with a brush. Sand the surface down lightly with a fine-grade abrasive between coats to remove dust specks and to ensure good adhesion.*

CLEANING AND STORING BRUSHES

1 *When you have finished painting, brush out as much paint as possible on to sheets of lining paper or newspaper.*

2 *Next, rinse the brush in the appropriate solvent — white spirit, paraffin or a proprietary brush cleaner for solvent-based paints and varnishes, water for emulsion paints.*

3 *Wash the brush carefully in warm, soapy water to remove the last traces of paint (and of white spirit, if you used it earlier). Rinse the brush thoroughly in clean water.*

4 *Wrap the brush in some absorbent paper held in place with a rubber band, and leave to dry. This ensures that the bristles retain their shape, and also keeps the brush clean while it is being stored.*

white spirit, or else scraped off when dry using a razor blade.

You may prefer to make doubly sure that your cutting in around the glass will be accurate. One way of doing this is to use a paint shield — a flat piece of plastic, metal, or stiff card which you hold against the glass with one hand while cutting in with the paint brush in the other. As you might imagine, it is a technique that requires some practice. A simpler alternative is to run masking tape around the glass. This will help neaten the border of paint run on to the glass, and can also be used to secure sheets of newspaper over the glass as a whole. In fact, it is not a bad idea to do this in any case: as well as providing additional insurance against drips of paint, the newspaper will give you some privacy while the windows are without curtains.

Sliding sash windows are trickier still, the snag being that the outer sash is always partially masked by the inner, preventing you from painting it in one go. But there is a solution. Start by partially opening both the inner and outer sashes to leave them roughly in the middle of the window opening with 200-300mm (8-12in) of the outer sash showing. Paint this section of the outer sash, together with the exposed window frame at top and bottom, then pull the inner sash almost completely down, and push the outer sash up far enough to expose that part of it which has yet to be painted. Finish painting the outer sash now, then tackle the inner sash and the rest of the frame in the usual way.

Even skirting boards, architraves and the like can pose problems. If the flooring is still in place you will have the same trouble cutting in along the bottom edge as with a door. Again, the best solution is to peel back the flooring until you have finished painting. If this isn't possible, protect the flooring as far as you can with newspaper or polythene sheeting and masking tape. Masking tape can also be used to stop gloss paint straying on to the surface of the wall. If you intend to paint the walls with emulsion, such mistakes will tend to show. Just be careful not to tear any paper you may have left on the wall when you come to peel the masking tape off.

And what about painting metal? In the case of something like a metal window frame, you can treat it in exactly the same way as woodwork, though, unless you have been thorough over the preparation you may have problems with adhesion. You should also beware of condensation on the surface you are about to paint. Try to work on a warm, dry day to minimize the risk, and, as an extra precaution, wipe over the surface with a dry, lint free cloth.

Condensation is even more likely if you are painting cold radiators and pipework. Equally, though, you shouldn't paint them when they are hot, nor should you allow them to become hot until the paint has completely dried — yet another good reason for tackling this particular job in summer. In addition, choose the paint with care. Any resin based paint is perfectly suitable for pipes and radiators — water-based emulsions are not. Incidentally, if you want to retain the natural look of brass and copper, use a clear lacquer or transparent paint.

Lastly, bear in mind the practical difficulties of painting central heating equipment. If possible, having drained down the system, loosen the union nuts connecting the radiator to the pipework, and tilt them away from the wall so you can paint the back and the wall more easily. Alternatively, use a special radiator brush — a bit like a small, long-handled dustpan brush. When you come to tackle the pipework, work the brush along the pipes rather than around them to stop paint building up on the far sides.

After all that, you will no doubt be relieved to know that painting the walls themselves with a brush is a great deal simpler. All you do is charge the wall brush fairly heavily — that doesn't mean dipping it in deeper; it means scraping off less on the side of the paint kettle — and work it up and down and from side to side to produce a sort of ragged star shape. In fact, the more you work the brush in different directions, the less chance there is of small holes and bumps in the surface leaving unpainted 'shadows'. Keep spreading out the 'star' until the brush starts to run dry, then recharge it and begin another star just to one side of the first, and gradually extend this until the two have merged together. Continue in this way until the entire surface has been covered, switching to a smaller brush where necessary to cut in neatly around the edges.

There are just two final skills you need to acquire concerning painting with a brush, and they are the arts of cleaning brushes properly and storing them in such a way that they are still in good condition when you next decide to decorate. First, cleaning. Always clean your brushes thoroughly when you have finished using them, unless you really are only taking a 'five minute break' in which case you can keep them in a workable condition by wrapping them in polythene secured with an elastic band. Don't allow them to stand in jars of white spirit (or water if using emulsion) until you can resume work or get round to cleaning them. This not only distorts the bristles (and if left long enough the distortion will be permanent), but also leaves the brush so charged with whatever they were standing in that the paint you apply for the first half hour or so will be over-thinned.

To clean them, start by working them back and forth across plenty of clean newspaper to remove the bulk of the paint they contain, then dunk them in the appropriate solvent (water for emulsions; white spirit for resin-based paints) to remove the rest, working it out of the bristles with your fingers and taking special care to remove any that has worked up to where the bristles join the handle. Several changes of solvent may be needed before the brush is really clean. The next step is to wash the brush out in warm soapy water, again using your fingers to clean right to the base of the bristles. This not only flushes out any white spirit, but also helps soften the bristles, thus keeping the brush supple. Finally, dry the bristles off with a clean cloth.

If you won't be needing the brush again for some time, now is the time to think about storage. Carefully shape the bristles into the ideal wedge shape, then wrap them in clean paper — kitchen roll or toilet tissue is ideal — to help them hold their shape, keeping this in place with an elastic band. They are now ready to be put away in a drawer or cupboard until the next time they are needed. Wherever you store them, make sure it is free from damp, and lay them flat so that the bristles cannot be bent out of shape during the storage period.

Painting with a roller

Whether you are painting walls or ceilings, using a roller will certainly speed things up considerably. However, if you want to be sure of getting a really first-class finish, it is important that you use the right equipment for the job.

The first essential is, of course, the roller itself. Choose a fairly sturdy one with a stout metal frame and a comfortable handle, and make sure that it not only holds the roller sleeve firmly, but also that changing sleeves is straightforward. After all, the sleeve is really the most important part of the tool. It's the sleeve that actually puts the paint on the surface. It is therefore well worth spending some time deciding on the best sleeve to use in a particular situation. There are several types to choose from.

Foam plastic ones are cheapest but do tend to be rather messy in use. Applying too much pressure delivers too much paint to the surface, so avoiding drips and splashes can be difficult. However, on a smooth or lightly textured surface, they do produce quite a reasonable looking finish. For a really fine finish, though, go for a roller with a definite pile — mohair, sheepskin, or synthetic fibre. Mohair sleeves have a very short, fine pile, and will not only give good results with emulsion on smooth or lightly textured surfaces, but also can be used to apply a resin-based paint such as gloss or eggshell. Some synthetic pile sleeves approach this sort of quality, but others, with their longer, coarser fibres, are best reserved for use on textured surfaces. In fact, if you work on the principle that smooth surfaces need smooth sleeves, and rougher surfaces need sleeves with a correspondingly longer pile, you won't go far wrong. From that you can see that sheepskin rollers are for very highly textured surfaces indeed. On a smooth surface, such a long pile tends to produce a rather rough-looking finish.

You will also need a roller tray — the roller's equivalent of a paint kettle. These are made from either metal or plastic, and you will find the latter far easier to clean. Metal trays, however, do have their advantages. They tend to last longer, and many are fitted with hooks allowing you to fit them to the treads of a step ladder, which is obviously handy if you are working on a ceiling or high wall.

Finally, you will need some sort of paint brush. The one thing rollers are not at all good at is cutting in accurately around the edges of the area you want to paint. That's the brush's job.

In addition to this basic tool kit, there are a few special rollers you may find useful. The first is simply an ordinary roller with a very long handle, and is designed to allow you to paint ceilings and high walls without having to set up access equipment. In practice, you will probably find them rather unwieldy, and this, coupled with the fact that you are

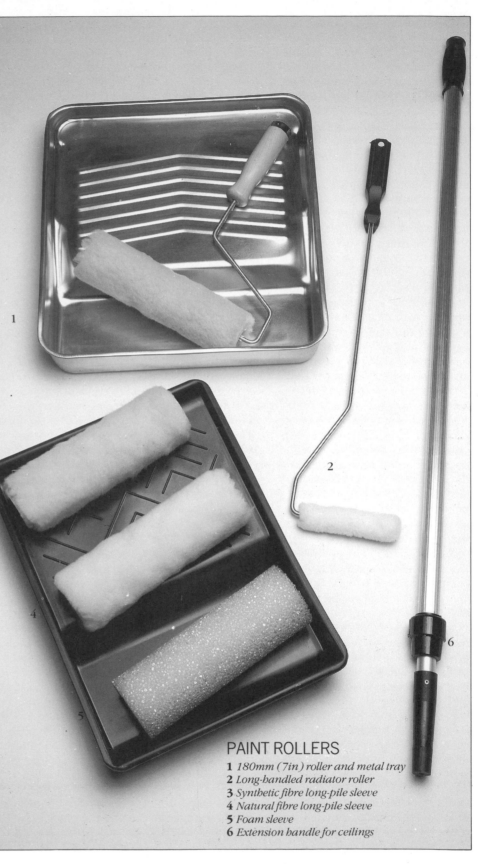

PAINT ROLLERS

1 *180mm (7in) roller and metal tray*
2 *Long-handled radiator roller*
3 *Synthetic fibre long-pile sleeve*
4 *Natural fibre long-pile sleeve*
5 *Foam sleeve*
6 *Extension handle for ceilings*

really too far away from the work to see clearly what you are doing, makes it difficult to obtain a really good finish. More useful is the radiator roller — a small, slim-line roller with a long handle designed to paint behind radiators in the same way as a radiator brush. The third and final type will also come in handy for painting the central heating system. It's called a pipe roller and has two or more small rollers fitted on to a single, flexible shaft so that it can hug the contours of the pipe along which it is run.

As for the technique of actually using a roller, the first step is to pour some paint into the roller tray. Not too much: put just enough into the deep end for the paint level to come a little way up the tray's ramp. And don't forget all the general points about getting paint ready for use mentioned earlier in the section on painting with a brush. They still apply.

You are now ready to charge the roller with paint. Simply run it down into the paint at the deep end of the tray, then run it back and forth over the tray's corrugated ramp a few times to remove the excess before offering the roller up to the wall, ceiling, or whatever. With emulsion paint (don't use a non-drip type with a roller), all you do now is run the roller back and forth in all directions to produce the same sort of ragged star as you would with a wall brush. Here again, when the roller starts to run dry, recharge it, begin another 'star' a little way along, and gradually extend this until it merges with the first 'star', totally covering the surface in between in the process.

There's no need to be too fussy about where one area begins and another ends. It is far more important to obtain an even coverage over the entire surface. You will soon get the hang of it and build up speed, but don't get carried away. It is a mistake to work a roller too quickly. If you do, especially with one that is fully loaded with paint, it will start to spray in much the same way as a car tyre running over a very wet road, and you could end up spattering paint over things best left unpainted.

You should also try to avoid allowing the edges of the area you have painted to dry out before you have had a chance to blend them into the paint film as a whole. With a good quality modern emulsion, such 'dry lines' don't matter so much on the first coat, but where they occur on the final coat of paint they will be noticeable in certain lights. This shouldn't prove too difficult while painting the bulk of the surface, but around the edges where you have to put the roller aside so you can cut in neatly with a brush, it can cause problems. The trick is to put up with the inconvenience of constantly changing tools and to carry out the rolling and cutting in side by side, rather than rolling a large area and going back to brush in over those bits you have missed.

Applying a resin-based paint with a roller is a little more complicated. Matt and semi matt finishes such as eggshell can be treated in the same way as emulsion. Again, don't use a non-drip variety. Gloss is quite another matter. Although a roller will produce a very even coverage, it tends not to leave quite as good a finish as a brush, the main reason

LOADING A ROLLER

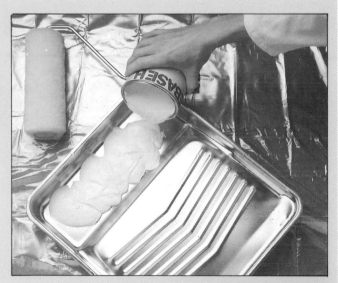

1 You need a roller tray if you are going to decorate with a paint roller. This has a well at one end to act as a paint reservoir, and a ribbed slope that is used to load the roller evenly. Stir your paint thoroughly, then pour some into the well.

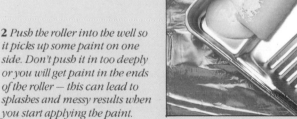

2 Push the roller into the well so it picks up some paint on one side. Don't push it in too deeply or you will get paint in the ends of the roller — this can lead to splashes and messy results when you start applying the paint.

3 Having picked up the paint on the roller, you simply roll it gently up and down the slope of the tray to disperse the paint evenly throughout the roller pile. Don't press too hard or you will squeeze out too much paint and have to reload more frequently. Excess paint runs back down the slope into the well.

PAINTING A WALL

1 & 2 *Start applying the paint by running the roller up and down the wall. Put on several strips side by side; when the roller seems to be running dry, run it over the stripes with a series of horizontal and angled passes to ensure complete coverage and an even distribution of paint.*

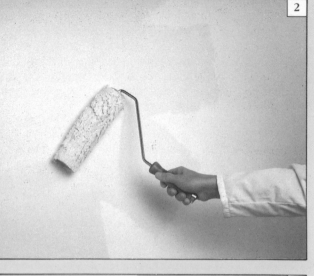

3 & 4 *The one drawback with paint rollers is that you can't decorate right into corners or up to obstructions such a door and window frames. As you near a corner or other obstruction, finish off with vertical passes about 25mm (1 in) away from it. Then touch in the remaining area with a paintbrush.*

APPLYING GLOSS PAINT

1 & 2 *You can also apply solvent-based paints using a paint roller; sleeves with a natural pile are better than those made from synthetic materials. Load the roller as described on the previous page, then apply the paint first along the grain direction, then across it. Finish off with a light pass parallel with the grain.*

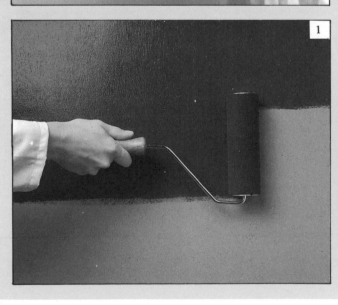

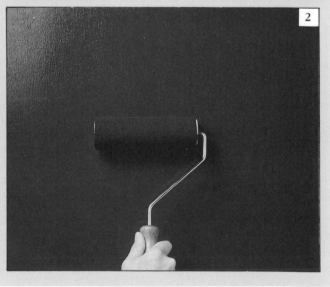

USING SPECIAL ROLLERS

1 & 2 *If you prefer not perch on steps or trestles to paint your ceilings, you can use an extension handle to increase the reach of the roller and work from ground level instead. Use it just like a hand-held roller, first applying paint in stripes and then rolling it out with transverse passes.*

3 *For painting walls behind radiators, a slim roller with a long wire handle is ideal. Pipe rollers are available too.*

CLEANING AND STORING ROLLERS

1 *When you have finished decorating, squeeze out as much paint from the sleeve as possible by running it backwards and forwards over a sheet of absorbent paper.*

2 & 3 *Rinse out the sleeve thoroughly under a tap if you have been using emulsion paint. Use white spirit, paraffin or proprietary brush cleaner to remove solvent-based paints, and then wash the sleeve in warm, soapy water to remove all traces of the solvent. Allow the sleeve to dry in the open air, away from the direct heat source, then wrap it in clean paper or store it in a polythene bag.*

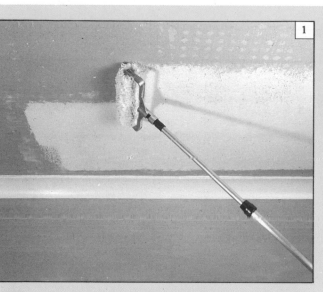

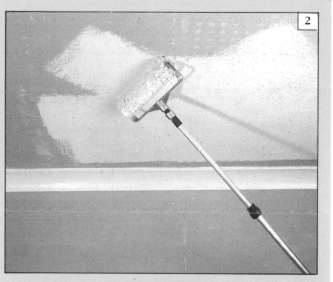

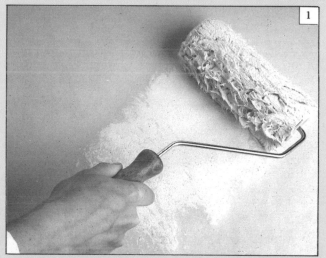

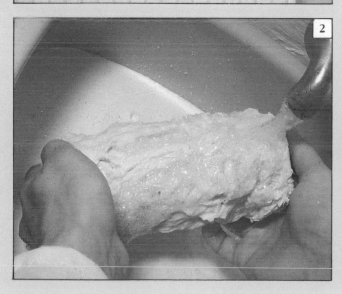

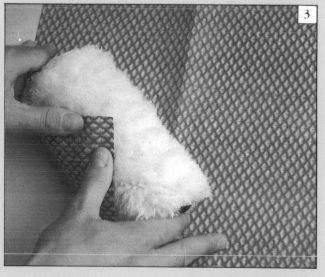

being that a roller simply doesn't put enough paint on the surface to produce that mirror- like deep shine. One possible answer is to simply overload the roller and apply less pressure when you roll it on. However, drips, runs, sags, spraying, and similar problems are then almost certain to mar the finish in any case. A better option is to use the roller simply as a means of getting the paint on to the surface. Once on, you can then lay the paint off with light, smooth strokes using a brush.

Obviously this is somewhat fiddly and time consuming, since you can only tackle the area in relatively small patches — otherwise the paint will have started to harden before you can brush it out. But it does have one very worthwhile incidental advantage. It allows you to apply the paint using cheap foam rollers, rather than the more expensive mohair ones normally recommended for the job. In fact, these are so cheap you can often afford to throw them away when you've finished — something you will appreciate when you realise how difficult and messy it is to clean resin-based paints out of roller sleeves. Incidentally, the slightly mottled finish produced by foam rollers and resin-based paint isn't all that unattractive — particularly when eggshell is used. You might even decide to keep it instead of brushing it out.

Having taken care of the painting, as always, clean up your tools and equipment. Start by running the roller back and forth over wads of clean newspaper to remove as much of the paint it contains as possible, then turn your attention to the roller tray. Pour back into the tin any paint left over, then wash it out thoroughly using the appropriate solvent — water for emulsions; white spirit for resin-based paints. If you have been applying a resin-based paint, leave some white spirit in the tray when you've finished. You can then run the roller through it, squeezing out the excess just as you would when painting, to give the roller sleeve a preliminary clean. That done, finish cleaning out the tray, remove the sleeve from the roller, and complete the cleaning of both sleeve and roller frame separately. Rinse in soapy water if you have been using white spirit and dry off before storing away for the next decorating session. As with brushes, it is a good idea to wrap sleeves in kitchen towel or something similar — it helps keeps them free of dust.

Painting with a pad

Another alternative to applying paint with a brush that you might like to try is to use a paint pad. These normally consist of a square or rectangular piece of natural or synthetic short-pile material similar to that used for mohair roller sleeves, with a foam plastic backing and mounted in a plastic or metal holder. They are available in a range of sizes — normally from around 65 × 50mm (2½ × 2in) for tackling small surfaces, up to about about 230 x 100mm (9 x 4in) for large areas such as walls — and can be used to apply both emulsions and resin-based paint. Although they are available separately, it is more common to find them sold as 'kits', which is possibly a good thing if you are just starting off, but not so convenient if you want a particular replace-

PAINT PADS
1 *Standard wall pad (minus handle)*
2 *Large wall pad*
3 *Crevice pad*
4 *Cutting-in pad*
5 *Small pad*

ment (though the manufacturers should be able to help here).

The technique for using them is quite straightforward. Begin by decanting the paint into a special tray, having first stirred, strained and prepared it in the usual way (see above). The sort of tray used is similar in principle to that employed with a roller, but different in design. The part that holds the paint reservoir is usually both deeper and narrower, and, instead of having a ramp, the better models come fitted with a grooved plastic roller which can be used to remove excess paint from the pad, and even out the distribution of paint across it. You now just dip the pad lightly into the paint, aiming to load only its pile — in other words, don't just dunk it in so the whole tool is covered in paint. Lightly run it back and forth over the roller a few times until excess paint ceases to come off, then draw the loaded pad gently across the surface you wish to paint, reloading it as necessary when it starts to run dry.

For the best results on a smooth surface such as woodwork or metalwork, cover the area in a series of roughly parallel, barely overlapping strips. On less dependable surfaces such as walls and ceilings, work the pad in as many different directions as possible to prevent lumps and dips leaving unpainted shadows.

You should find that the pad allows you to achieve a far more even coverage than a brush. In fact, in this respect, you can expect results comparable with those achieved using a roller — you will just find the tool easier to control. However, it is not quite as versatile as a paint brush. It tends not to cope well with textured surfaces, and coping with fiddly bits, as well as accurate cutting-in, can also prove difficult. These last two problems, though, can be eased by using special purpose paint pads. There are, for example, special edging pads designed for cutting into internal angles — they have a set of small wheels in their edges which guide the pad by running over the surface you don't want to paint. Similarly, there are very small pads mounted on more manipulable handles designed for tackling awkward corners and more complicated sections.

Cleaning paint pads and their associated equipment can also be rather tricky, particularly if you have been applying a resin-based paint. In this case, it is best to adopt the same strategy as when cleaning a roller. Run the pads over wads of newspaper to remove the bulk of the excess paint, then clean out the pad's tray, fill it with a little white spirit, and use it and its roller (if it has one) to continue the cleaning process. Finally, dismantle the paint pad and treat the various components and accessories separately to ensure that they are really clean. Using disposable pads is, on the whole a better option. If you have been using an emulsion paint, of course, the whole cleaning process is far simpler — merely run everything under a tap until it comes clean. Even so, you may find it difficult to completely clean out the pads themselves, a great deal here depending on how long the pad has been in use (and therefore the amount of ingrained dry paint you have to cope with). Again, it is well worth considering using disposable pads.

LOADING A PAD

1 *Most paint pads come in kits containing several differentsized pads and a special tray with a ribbed roller which you use to load the pads with paint. Start by pouring some stirred and strained paint into the reservoir at one end of the paint tray.*

2 *Hold the pad level and dip its pile carefully into the paint reservoir. Don't dip it in too deeply, or you will get paint on the body of the tool and make a mess when you try to paint with it. Take special care with large wall pads — since they nearly fill the reservoir it's easy to push paint up onto the back of the pad as you load it up.*

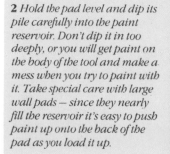

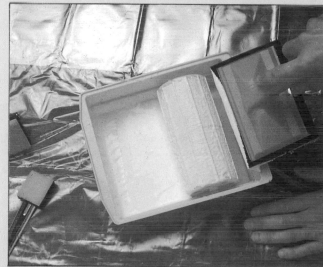

3 *Lift the pad out of the reservoir and run it lightly back and forwards over the ribbed roller to distribute the paint evenly throughout the pile, and to squeeze out excess paint. This then runs back into the reservoir again. Wipe paint off the roller with absorbent paper from time to time to stop it drying and spoiling the pick-up of paint by the pad.*

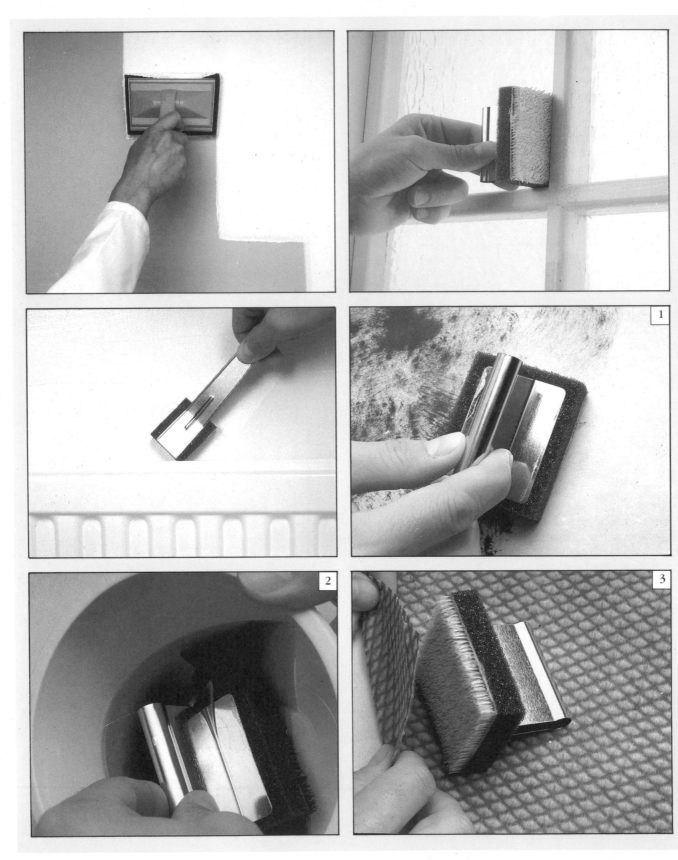

APPLYING PAINT

1 & 2 *If you are applying emulsion paint using a large pad, simply draw it down the wall surface in a series of parallel stripes. Then run the pad over the surface in horizontal and transverse bands to ensure even coverage. Use the smaller pads in the kit for painting awkward areas such a glazing bars.*

3 *Use a long-handled crevice pad for painting hard-to-reach areas such as behind radiators.*

CLEANING AND STORING PADS

1 *When you have finished decorating, press out as much paint as possible from the pad by running it backwards and forwards on some absorbent paper.*

2 & 3 *Next, remove the rest of the paint by rinsing the pad in the appropriate solvent — water for emulsion paints, white spirit, paraffin or proprietary brush cleaner for solvent-based paints. Finally, allow the pile to dry in the open air before wrapping it up and putting it away.*

Spray painting

If brushes, rollers and paint pads don't appeal, why not try a radically different approach to applying paint — spraying it on? It's far quicker, and, with a little practice, you will find you are able to produce a finish far superior (certainly where gloss paint is concerned) to that achieved using any other painting technique.

In terms of tools and equipment, there are two main options. The first is to buy the paint in aerosol form. Although not especially cheap, you will find this an economical method of dealing with most small items such as pieces of furniture and so on, and it does have the additional advantages of being both cleaner (there's no messing about thinning the paint and loading it into the spray gun) and more convenient. The only major snag is that you are limited by what the paint manufacturers choose to sell in this form — generally a fairly basic range of best selling colours in gloss.

The alternative to is hire a full-size spray gun and compressor — the better models are really too expensive to consider buying unless you intend to do a great deal of this sort of work; more than you would find in the average house. But even this is not an especially cheap undertaking, and so you really need to make sure that there is enough work to justify it. Painting the walls and ceiling of a single room probably won't meet this criterion unless the room is very large. Painting a number of rooms or the outside walls of your home almost certainly will, especially if speed is essential — you might, for example, want to give the whole house a quick face lift having just moved in, or smarten it up just before you sell it.

If you do decide to hire spraying equipment, though, there are a few points to bear in mind. First, decide on the type of paint you want to use and let the hire shop advise you on the sort of equipment you need to apply it. So long as you are using ordinary interior resin-based paints and emulsions, you shouldn't have any problems finding suitable equipment. Secondly, decide whether or not you need to work high above the floor. If you do, make sure the equipment comes with a long enough hose between the compressor (which puts the paint under pressure) and the spray gun (which is the bit you hold to actually apply the paint). This will allow you to carry out virtually the entire job from a simple step ladder and/or extension ladder. The alternative is to work from some form of scaffolding arrangement strong enough to raise the compressor to within reach of the work. Finally, make sure you receive adequate instruction on how to operate the equipment — how to set it up, how much (if any) you have to thin the paint, and so on. If you damage the equipment through misuse, you will lose your deposit. Similarly, make sure you know how to clean the equipment before returning it to the shop — they will charge you if they have to clean it themselves.

As for how you set about actually spraying on the paint, the basic technique is broadly the same no matter what equipment you use. Begin by masking off everything in the

SPRAY GUN EQUIPMENT

1 *Spray gun*
2 *Extension nozzle*
3 *Goggles*
4 *Face mask*
5 *Viscosity cup*
6 *Aerosol paint*
7 *Masking tape*
8 *Gloves*

PREPARATION

1 & 2 *Lay dust sheets over floors in the area to be painted. Then pour some paint into the reservoir (after thinning it if required) and screw the reservoir to the body of the gun. Finally, attach the appropriate nozzle for the paint being sprayed.*

3 & 4 *Protect surfaces such as skirting boards by taping strips of paper or polythene along them with masking tape. Use a similar method to mask off windows. Make sure the tape edge is straight, so that a neat finish is left when it is removed.*

5 & 6 *Smear petroleum jelly over small, awkwardly-shaped fittings such as radiator valves to protect them. The jelly is simply wiped off when painting is complete.*

It is best to spray-paint small objects out of doors.

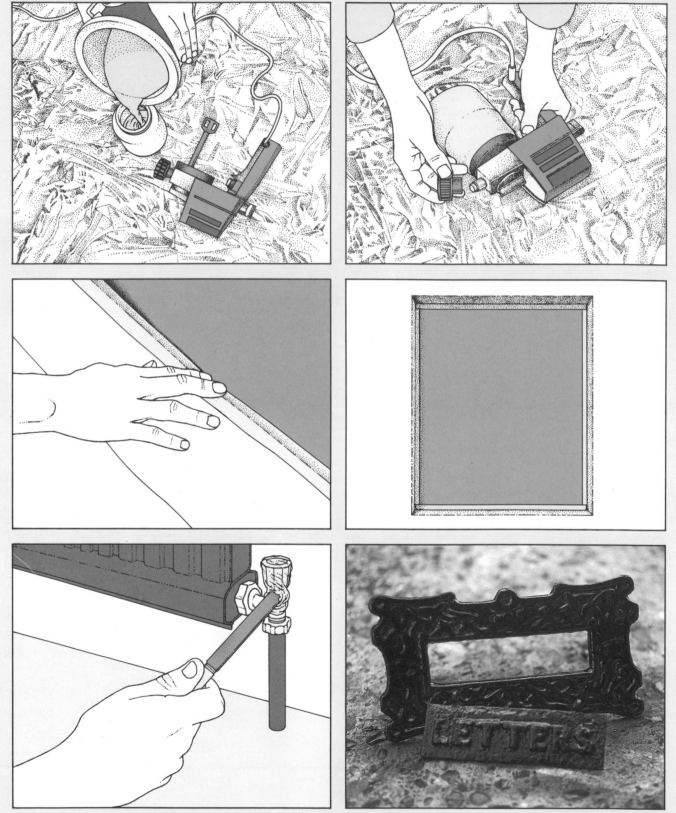

SPRAY PAINTING

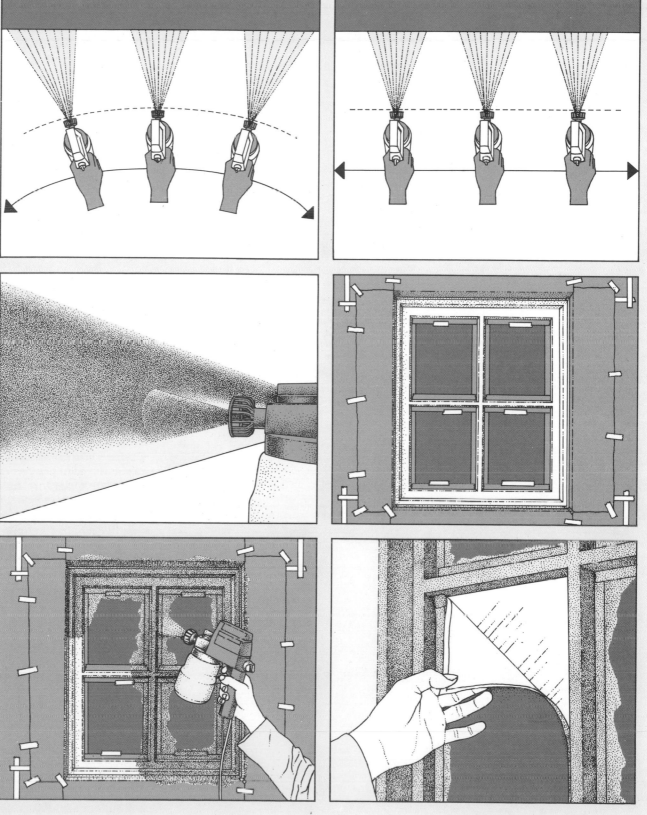

1 & 2 *It's tempting to use the gun by swinging your arm from side to side, but this method applies more paint at the centre point than at the edges of each pass. Instead, move your hand parallel with the surface you're painting.*

3 & 4 *As you work, overlap successive passes slightly to avoid patchy coverage. Apply two thin coats rather than one thick one. When spraying woodwork, spend time masking off other surfaces that are not to be painted.*

5 & 6 *Spray the exposed surfaces with steady passes of the gun, again applying two thin coats rather than one thick one to avoid runs. Peel off the masking when the paint surface is touch-dry.*

CLEANING A GUN

1 *When you have finished decorating, decant any remaining paint from the container back into the original tin. Then squeeze the trigger to expel as much paint as possible.*

2 *When no more paint emerges from the nozzle, dismantle the gun ready for cleaning. Follow the manufacturer's recommendations here — how much dismantling is needed varies from gun to gun. Make sure that you have unplugged the equipment from the mains before you go any further.*

3 *Clean all the components of the gun thoroughly in the appropriate solvent — water for emulsion; white spirit, paraffin or a proprietary solvent for gloss and eggshell; special thinners for cellulose paint. Rinse each component in clean solvent, then reassemble the gun and run some clean solvent through it to complete the cleaning process.*

vicinity that you don't want painted using a combination of masking tape and newspaper or polythene sheeting — there is no way to cut in accurately with a spray gun. This is incredibly time-consuming, but you must take the trouble to do the job properly, particularly where the various areas are to be painted using different kinds of paint. If, for example, you allow resin paint to stray on to walls that you intend to emulsion later, you may find that the emulsion won't cover the error. Be especially careful when masking off areas you have only just painted. You might, for instance, have painted the ceiling, and wish to mask it in order to spray the walls a different colour. The main thing is to allow the new paintwork to dry out for as long as possible before masking. In addition, be sure to use proper masking tape (not ordinary sticky tape), and remove it as soon as possible after you have finished. This not only produces a cleaner line as it tears through the slightly tacky overlying paint film, but also reduces the risk of it lifting paint off the masked area.

Alternatively, if you are really in a hurry and are prepared to take risks, there is a way to avoid masking. Simply spray as close as you dare to the surface you don't want painted — and the best modern spray guns are sufficiently accurate to allow you to go fairly close — then tackle the final cutting-in with a brush.

Incidentally, don't bother about masking off really fiddly items of hardware. If you cannot remove them before spraying, rub them over with a little petroleum jelly. This stops the paint sticking sufficiently for you to wipe or scrape it off once it is touch-dry.

With the masking out of the way, begin spraying. Starting at the top in one corner, hold the spray nozzle about 300mm (12in) from the surface and push the button. As soon as the paint begins to cover, move the spray gun along at a steady speed to paint a broad, evenly covered stripe. That done, without switching off, spray down a little, then back across the surface to form a second stripe which slightly overlaps the first. Continue in this way until the entire surface has been evenly covered.

Just how fast or slow you work is largely a matter of judgement. The trick is to work slow enough to ensure good coverage, yet not so slow that the paint film gets thick enough to run or sag. Having found the right working speed, keep going as steadily as you can to ensure that the coverage is not only adequate, but also even. It is also important to hold the spray gun at a constant distance from the work along the entire length of each stripe. If you simply hold out your arm and swing it back and forth, the spray nozzle will be closer to the work when spraying the area immediately in front of you than it will be at the ends of the stripes, and this will also result in uneven coverage.

If you have problems in this respect, try turning off the spray gun at the end of each stripe, and work faster rather than slower. You can always apply a second or third coat to achieve the necessary complete coverage and colour density. The drawback with this approach is that, each time you stop and start, you increase the risk of the spray gun 'spluttering' — the resulting uneven coverage obviously defeating the object of the exercise.

With a compressor and spray gun set-up, the answer is to clean out the nozzle at regular intervals following the manufacturer's instructions. Taking care to thin the paint correctly and to mix the resulting mixture to a really smooth consistency will also help. In any case, at the start of each spraying session, it is always worth testing the spray on a wad of newspaper or something similar before directing it at the surface you want to paint. This both helps clear the nozzle, and lets you know that everything is working properly.

The problem of spluttering is more difficult to overcome when using an aerosol. Really all you can do is regularly wipe off around the nozzle with a cloth dipped in white spirit (or cellulose thinners if you are using car retouching spray on metal) and replace the dust cap when the aerosol is not in use. If the jet should start to clog, try inverting the can and spraying on to a wad of newspaper for a few seconds to clear it. Never poke out the nozzle's hole with a pin. You could enlarge or deform it, and thus make matters worse.

Finally, as well as taking good care of the spraying equipment, take good care of yourself. Make sure the room in which you are working is well ventilated — though it should be free from strong draughts that could cause the spray to drift. If spraying resin-based or cellulose paints, keep well away from naked flames. And do wear suitable protective clothing. Goggles and a face mask are certainly to be strongly recommended whatever you are doing. If you are carrying out a lot of spraying in a confined space, they are essential.

Special techniques

By now you should have a fairly good idea of how to set about simply changing the colour of a surface using ordinary interior paints. But there are a few special painting techniques worth knowing about for those situations where you need a finish that's that little bit different.

First, there is the application of a texturing compound or textured paint. The majority of those used for low-to-medium relief finishes are simply applied to the surface with an ordinary wall brush — a fairly wide one is best. Aim to cover an area of about 1sq m (1sq yd) at a time with an even film of the required thickness. This might be 2 or 3mm (⅛in) in the case of a texturing compound; the thickness of a rather heavy coat of paint in the case of a textured paint. This, in itself, leaves the surface with a sort of textured effect, but there is a whole host of far more exciting finishes that can be achieved using this sort of product, and to produce them, you need to go back and get to work on the rather plain surface left by the brush.

One of the simplest texturing techniques is to merely run a foam paint roller over the surface. Wrapping coarse string around the roller produces a rather stronger variation on the theme. Sponged finishes are also worth considering. Just dab an ordinary sponge over the surface to pull the

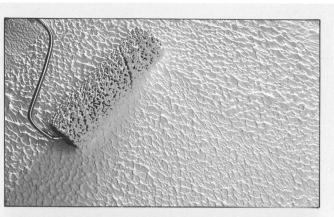

1 *One of the simplest ways of texturing paints of this sort is to run a special texturing roller over the surface. A wide range of different effects can be achieved in this way.*

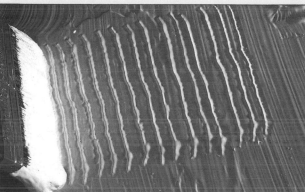

2 *A wall brush used in a tapping motion will produce overlapping ridges ideal for covering up less-than-perfect wall and ceiling surfaces.*

3 *Another simple effect to achieve is a series of random waves, created by drawing a serrated scraper across the still-wet paint film. Each pass should slightly overlap the previous one.*

4 *By using a wide serrated scraper in a circular motion pivoting around one end, perfect grooved circles can be made, either overlapping or evenly spaced*

SPONGING

1 When you're using more than one colour, apply the darkest one first and space the dabs of colour fairly widely to give a sense of depth. Use a genuine marine sponge if possible, rather than a synthetic one, to give the most interesting texture.

2 Add the second slightly lighter colour, spacing the colour dabs more closely together this time. Test the effect first on scrap paper each time, to ensure that you have not taken up too much paint on the sponge.

3 Apply the third, lightest, colour in the same way to fill in the design. Wash the sponge regularly in water or white spirit (according to the type of paint being used), wringing it out thoroughly every time so you don't dilute the paint.

4 Finish off by using a clean sponge to soften the overall effect. Again, rinse the sponge from time to time.

5 You can apply the technique to virtually any surface. Here it has been used to disguise the lines of an old radiator.

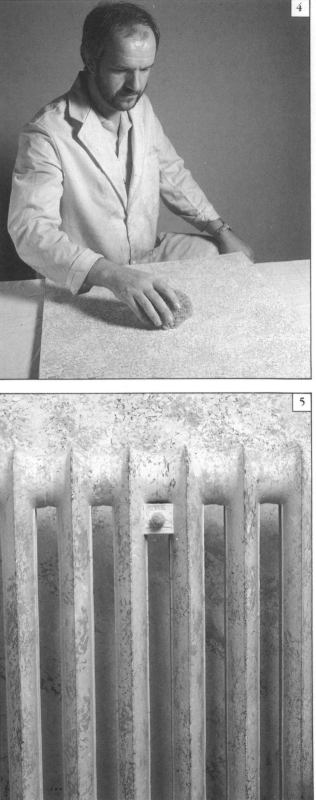

compound out and so produce a random stippled effect. For a more pronounced stipple, try wrapping the sponge in polythene. Give it a twist as you pull it away and you can produce very attractive stippled swirls. Alternatively, use a sponge to drag the compound out into swirls with a wider radius, overlapping arcs that look rather like reptilian scales, zig-zags, or any other pattern that takes your fancy. If you would prefer a more clean-cut finish, use serrated scrapers or metal combs to score out designs. From specialist shops, you can buy a wide variety of such scrapers and combs specially designed for the job in a choice of shapes and sizes, but there is no reason why you cannot obtain equally successful results using improvised equipment — ordinary hair combs, coarse brushes, bits of scrap plastic and metal filed to give a serrated edge, and so on.

Use your imagination, and experiment with the texturing compound on a piece of scrap hardboard or something similar before getting to work on the wall or ceiling. Just avoid creating anything too exotic unless you are absolutely sure that you can live with it for evermore. Remember, texturing compounds are extremely difficult to remove.

Painting murals is something else you might like to try your hand at. You don't have to be another Michelangelo to achieve acceptable results. If you have doubts about your artistic talents, you could limit yourself to creating simple geometric designs — something as basic as a painted stripe at dado or picture rail height can be surprisingly effective — or you could crib from pictures found in magazines.

You don't need much in the way of equipment. A selection of ordinary decorators' paint brushes will cope with most basic designs, but you will need a few smaller 'artists' paint brushes to tackle fine detail. As for paint, any interior emulsion or resin-based paint can be used, though emulsion is generally the best bet for beginners. Don't buy any most basic designs, but you will need a few smaller artist's plus small cans of the primary colours (red, yellow, and blue) will go a long way. Remember, you can mix emulsion quite easily to produce a wide variety of intermediate colours and shades. Paint left over from previous bouts of decorating can also be put to good use, as can the small pots of paint now widely sold as colour samplers — though these can prove expensive. Look out, too, for special dyes purpose made for tinting emulsion. At a pinch, you could even mix in a little children's powder paint, though results cannot be guaranteed.

There are just a few points to bear in mind when mixing paint. Firstly, work out as accurately as you can how much of a given colour you need (allowing for the fact that several coats may be needed to achieve good coverage) and mix it in one batch. If you run out, you will find it almost impossible to achieve exactly the same shade a second time. Next, make sure you mix the paint really thoroughly so as to avoid streaks and other more subtle colour variations throughout the batch. Finally, try the paint out on the wall, allow it to dry, then check that it is exactly the colour you want — the colour of the paint in a mixing bucket isn't a good guide to the finished result. Make sure, too, that you check all the colours in the same light — either daylight or artificial light — or the results of your matching will be unpredictable.

To make a start, prepare the wall in the normal way and paint it completely in a suitable background colour. Ideally, go for a moderately light colour that occupies a lot of space in the finished mural. Failing that, choose a neutral grey or something similar. Once that's dry, you can begin creating the mural in earnest. If you are using your own design, and are confident of your ability, sketch it on to the wall in charcoal to begin with. Any mistakes can then easily be rubbed out with a cloth. Once you are satisfied, go over the lines in soft pencil, felt tipped pen, or diluted paint applied with a small artist's brush. Wash off any excess charcoal dust before continuing.

If you are less sure of being able to draw directly on to the wall, make a preliminary sketch on paper (working to scale) and transfer the design onto the wall in the same way as you would one you had decided to copy from an existing picture. There are two ways in which this can be done. The first is to draw a grid in paint or pencil on the wall, then draw a similar grid, accurately scaled down, on the picture you want to copy. You should then find it relatively easy to transfer the design by hand, a little at a time — the smaller the squares on the grid, the easier it will be. The alternative is to photograph the design in order to get a slide that you can project on to the surface using an ordinary slide projector. You can then merely trace off the relevant features.

Geometric designs are, naturally, rather easier to achieve, and can be safely constructed directly on the wall. For straight lines, either use a long, straight timber batten as a rule, or a chalked line. The latter method is particularly useful for marking out a grid on the wall if you are using that method to transfer a design. Simply rub chalk into a length of soft string (or use a purpose-made chalk line which automatically chalks the string as you pull it from its reel), stretch it along the intended line and snap it against the surface like a bowstring — the result is a neat chalk line.

For circles, either draw round a plate, cup, or something similar, or, if you need a larger circle, make up a 'string and pencil compass'. Push a drawing pin into the wall where the centre of the circle is to be, and tie a piece of string to it. Tie the other end of the string to a pencil so that the length of the string equals the radius of the circle, then start drawing, keeping the string absolutely taut. Pins and string can also be employed to draw ellipses. Stick two pins into the wall this time — the farther they are apart the flatter the ellipse — to anchor an oversize loop of string. Using a pencil, pull out one side of the loop to create a string triangle, then draw the pencil right round both pins keeping the constantly changing string triangle as taut as possible.

One tip: if your design involves repeating the same motif over and over again, draw it on card, cut out the shape, then using this as a template, trace round it on to the wall.

Once the design is on the wall, it is simply a matter of getting to work with paint and brushes to colour in the outline. If you need really precise divisions of colour between

PAINTING A MURAL

1 & 2 *Select a design you want to reproduce, and draw a squared grid over it. Then work out how many times you want to enlarge it, and draw a similar but larger grid on the wall using pencil or charcoal. Use a spirit level to ensure that the grid lines are truly horizontal and vertical.*

3 & 4 *Stick your original up on the wall, and refer to it as you sketch in the outline of the design square by square. Then mix up each colour in turn in a shallow dish, and brush it onto the appropriate areas of the mural.*

5 & 6 *When you have completed the painting, outline the design with fine black lines using an artist's paintbrush or a felt-tipped pen. Allow the paint to dry thoroughly, then wipe off the grid lines and seal the surface with a coat of varnish.*

areas, use masking tape to define each area, paint it in, then peel off the tape when the paint is just tacky.

Of course, a simpler way to paint a pattern on a surface is to use a stencil. You can make up one of your own if you wish, carefully cutting it out of thin card using a very sharp knife. Or you can buy stencils ready made from good craft shops, decorating shops, and department stores — though availability does depend rather a lot on the current fashionability of the technique.

Using the stencil is quite simple. All you need is some masking tape, and a fairly small brush with short, stiff bristles — a purpose made stencil brush is obviously best, but an old, worn paint-brush that fits the description will do. As when painting a mural, no special paint is needed. Use ordinary interior emulsion or resin-based paint, bearing in mind what was said earlier concerning colours. Hold the stencil against the surface or the wall or whatever, and tape it securely in place using the masking tape. Next, load the

brush, aiming to leave little more than a film of paint standing on the very ends of the bristles. You will find this ideal a lot easier to achieve if you pour a very small amount of paint into a shallow dish, rather than a paint kettle — a dish so shallow and containing so little paint that it is physically impossible to dip the brush in too far.

All you do now is apply the paint to the surface through the stencil, working the brush in a series of light stabbing strokes until you have achieved just the right degree of coverage. This is important if you want a really crisp finish. If you don't work the brush absolutely vertically, or if you apply too much paint, there is every chance that paint will find its way under the stencil and blur the outline.

When you have finished, allow the paint to become tacky, then peel off both masking tape and stencil in one clean movement. As when using masking tape on its own, if you remove the stencil too soon, paint may run out beyond the desired outline. Remove it too late, and in tearing the hard-

There is no limit to the results you can achieve with applied decorations. In this kitchen **above left** *a clever 'trompe l'oeil' effect has been used on the cupboard doors to echo the natural stone wall cladding above.*

With murals, simple effects often work best, as with this cleverly painted window **top** *thronged with colourful birds.*

Even a simple splash of colour combined with a striking motif **above** *can bring a room alive, especially where strongly contrasting colours are used.*

STENCILLING

1 & 2 *First, prepare your stencil board, using special stencilling paper. Then stick it firmly in position on the surface you're decorating using masking tape. Apply the paint with a flat-ended stencilling brush, holding it vertically by the ferrule.*

3 & 4 *If the paint shows any signs of getting underneath the edges of the stencil, hold it down while you work with a broad filling knife or similar implement. When the paint is touch-dry, position a stencil with a complementary pattern so you can apply the second colour. Check the alignment carefully before you start.*

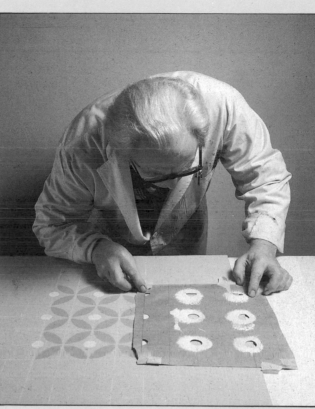

5 & 6 *Peel the stencil away from the paint by lifting it vertically so you don't smudge the paint edges. Wipe off any excess paint before you reposition the stencil to continue the next section of the design. Note here the half-circles cut in the sheet as an aid to accurate alignment.*

7 & 8 *Once stencilling is complete, you can touch up any small defects in the pattern using a small artist's paintbrush. A range of simple stencils can be used to build up quite complex overall designs.*

COMBING

1 *Use a soft, long-bristled brush to lay on the base coat, allowing the bristles to form parallel 'trim-lines' in the paint film.*

2 *Draw a rubber-toothed comb over the paint to straighten the lines.*

3 *Create a kinked herringbone effect with a stiff fine-toothed comb.*

4 *Repeat the effect at right angles to give the surface a woven effect.*

5 *Make short, curved passes with a rubber comb to create a fish-scale pattern.*

6 *The overall effect closely resembles the three-dimensional effect often used with textured wall and ceiling finishes.*

ened paint film, it could pull off paint from within the area of the stencil's design. You therefore need to work fairly quickly if you are using different colours for different parts of the design. To avoid mistakes, either carefully block off with masking tape the holes that do not apply to the colour you are using, or remove the stencil completely when you have finished one colour and wait for the paint to dry before carefully repositioning it and applying the next.

There is one last group of techniques you may like to try out. They are based on the idea of modifying the surface film of paint once it has been brushed onto the wall, either before it has dried or by adding further colour over the top. The step-by-step photographs show how the various methods work, and what sort of effects can be achieved using them.

Having painted the surface in a suitable background colour, take a different coloured paint and mix it with a little of the treacly substance that gives the technique its name — scumble — to form a fairly runny glaze. You now, brush this on over the painted background, and then wipe it off again with a clean, lint-free cloth, manipulating the cloth as you go to leave just enough of the scumble layer behind to produce the desired effect. For the crisper lines required for woodgraining, combs and sharp points are used to remove the scumble layer. This, of course, is where the skill comes in. It's all too easy to end up with nothing more than a mess. But persevere. For more complex effects, repeat the process with further layers of scumbling in different colours, allowing each to dry thoroughly before applying the next.

If desired, the basic scumbled finish can be used as a base for more extrovert random finish techniques — flicking paint on to the surface with a heavily loaded brush, for example, to produce a spatter effect. Again, with such techniques you need to put in a fair amount of practice before you achieve anything like control over them. And you also need a good eye and sufficient self-restraint to know when enough is enough.

THE COMPLETE PAPERHANGER

BASIC TECHNIQUES FOR WALLS *230*
CUTTING AND PASTING *231* ♦ BASIC PAPERHANGING *232*

HANGING CONVENIENCE WALLCOVERINGS *234*
HANGING READY-PASTED PAPERS *235*

TACKLING AWKWARD AREAS *236*
PAPERING ROUND OBSTACLES *236* ♦ TURNING CORNERS *237*
PAPERING ROUND DOORS AND WINDOWS *238*

PAPERING STAIRWELLS *241*

PAPERING A CEILING *242*
PASTING AND FOLDING *243* ♦ HANGING CEILING PAPER *243*
PAPERING ROUND CEILING OBSTACLES *244*

HANGING LINING PAPER *245*
HANGING RELIEF DECORATIONS *246*
HANGING UNBACKED FABRICS *247*

HANGING FABRICS *248*
FRIEZES AND BORDERS *249*

Paperhanging has, for a long time, had something of a reputation for being one of the more difficult ways to decorate a wall. Certainly it takes a little care to produce good results. But difficult? So long as you start by setting yourself a fairly straightforward stretch of wall to gain confidence, and build up gradually to the more complicated bits of papering, then given the right equipment plus modern pastes and wallcoverings, you will be surprised at just how easy it is — once you know how.

Basic techniques for walls

Your very first job is to decide where to start — where to hang the very first length of paper, or 'drop', as it is called. In years gone by, this was quite a complicated business. The drops overlapped, and it was therefore important to paper in such a way that these overlaps weren't too obvious; the usual practice being to start above and below the room's main window and to work out in both directions around the room. Today, virtually all papers are made so that drops merely butt up against each other. Where you start is therefore up to you, and although there is still something to be said for starting above a main window, or somewhere equally awkward such as in the centre of a chimney breast, this really applies only if you are using a paper with a very large, prominent motif. For the rest, you would do better to start in a corner of the room and tackle a long, uncomplicated wall to get your hand in.

Having chosen a starting place, measure out from the corner and, with the aid of a plumbline, draw a vertical line on the wall to indicate the edge of the first length of paper. This should be about 25mm (1in) less than the paper's width out from the corner of the room. Don't rely on the walls, door frame, or anything else to judge whether the first drop is truly vertical. They are usually out of true, and if you start crooked, things will become progressively more difficult as you paper round the room. You can now use the vertical line as a guide to measure the height of the wall, and therefore the length of paper needed for each drop.

Now cut the first few drops from the roll ready for pasting. It's best to do this on a pasting table — these are not expensive, and really do make paperhanging much easier. Transfer the measured height of the wall on to the paper with a tape measure, add about 100mm (4in) to allow for trimming at top and bottom, and cut across using a pair of long-bladed paperhanger's scissors — another specialist tool well worth buying. To make sure you hang the paper with the pattern the right way up, write 'TOP' on the back of the drop at the appropriate end. To cut subsequent drops to length, use this first one as a guide. Lay it face up on the pasting table, pull more paper from the roll and adjust the latter's position until the patterns match exactly, then

WALLPAPER QUANTITY GUIDE

IMPERIAL

| Distance round walls (incl. doors/ windows) | Number of rolls needed | | | | | | |
| | Height in feet from skirting | | | | | | |
	7 — 7½	7½ — 8	8 — 8½	8½ — 9	9 — 9½	9½ — 10	10 — 10½
30	4	5	5	5	6	6	6
34	5	5	5	5	6	6	7
38	5	6	6	6	7	7	8
42	6	6	7	7	7	8	8
46	6	7	7	7	8	8	9
50	7	7	8	8	9	9	10
54	7	8	9	9	9	10	10
58	8	8	9	9	10	10	11
62	8	9	10	10	10	11	12
66	9	9	10	10	11	12	13
70	9	10	11	11	12	12	13
74	10	10	12	12	12	13	14
78	10	11	12	12	13	14	15
82	11	11	13	13	14	14	16
86	12	12	14	14	14	15	16
90	12	13	14	14	15	16	17
94	13	13	15	15	15	16	18
98	13	14	15	15	16	17	19

METRIC

| Distance round walls (incl. doors/ windows) | Number of rolls needed | | | | | | |
| | Height in metres from skirting | | | | | | |
	2 — 2.2	2.2 — 2.5	2.5 — 2.7	2.7 — 3	3 — 3.2	3.2 — 3.5	3.5 — 3.7	3.7 — 4
10	5	5	6	6	7	7	8	8
11	5	6	7	7	8	8	9	9
12	6	6	7	8	8	9	9	10
13	6	7	8	8	9	10	10	10
14	7	7	8	9	10	10	11	11
15	7	8	9	9	10	11	12	12
16	8	8	9	10	11	11	12	13
17	8	9	10	10	11	12	13	14
18	9	9	10	11	12	13	14	15
19	9	10	11	12	13	14	15	16
20	9	10	11	12	13	14	15	16
21	10	11	12	13	14	15	16	17
22	10	11	13	14	15	16	17	18
23	11	12	13	14	15	17	18	19
24	11	12	14	15	17	17	18	20
25	12	13	14	15	17	18	19	20
26	12	13	15	16	17	19	20	21
27	13	14	15	17	18	19	21	22
28	13	14	16	17	19	20	21	23
29	13	15	16	18	19	21	22	24
30	14	15	17	18	20	21	23	24

CUT & PASTE

1 & 2 *Unless you are using a ready-mixed tub paste, your first task is to mix up a quantity of powder paste sufficient for the number of rolls you intend to hang. Follow the manufacturer's instructions, mixing the paste carefully to avoid lumps. Then measure out your first length, adding an allowance for trimming.*

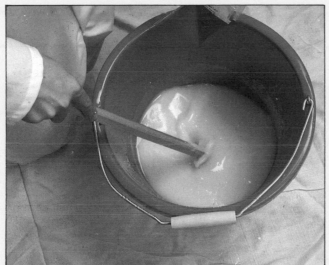
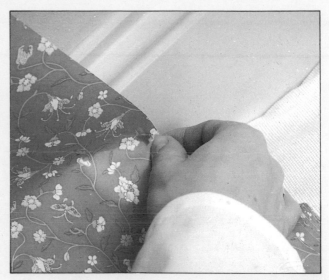

3 & 4 *Fold the paper carefully in line with your length mark, making sure the edges of the paper are parallel to guarantee a square edge to the cut. Then fold the paper out flat on the pasting table and cut carefully along the marked line with your paperhanger's shears.*

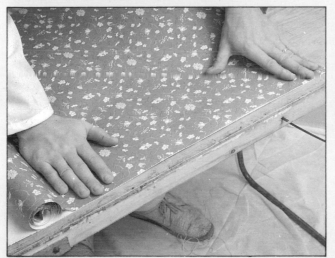
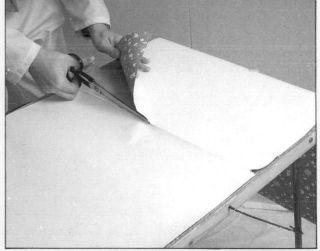

5 & 6 *Brush the paste on to the back of the length generously, making sure you don't miss any parts. As you brush out towards the edges, align the paper with the table edge so that you don't get paste on the table itself (and then on to the face of the wallpaper itself). When you've covered the area on the pasting table, fold over the end pasted side innermost so you can tackle the rest of the length.*

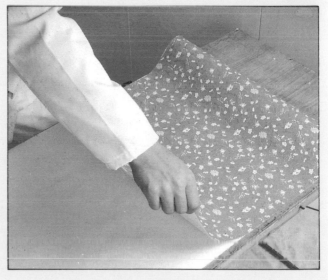

BASIC PAPERHANGING

1 & 2 *Measure along the wall from a corner a distance just greater than the width of the wallpaper, and suspend a plumbline at that point. You can make pencil marks on the wall and join them up with a straightedge, or simply work with the plumbline left in position. Then measure the length of the first 'drop', paste it and offer it up.*

3 & 4 *When you have positioned the top of the length, slide it across until its right-hand edge is perfectly aligned with the plumbline. Then use your paperhanger's brush to smooth the length into place. Work from the centre out towards the edges.*

5 & 6 *At the top of the length, use the brush again to tap the paper firmly into the angle between wall and ceiling (or, as here, at picture rail level). Draw the back of the shears along the angle to form a clearly marked crease along the angle, ready for trimming.*

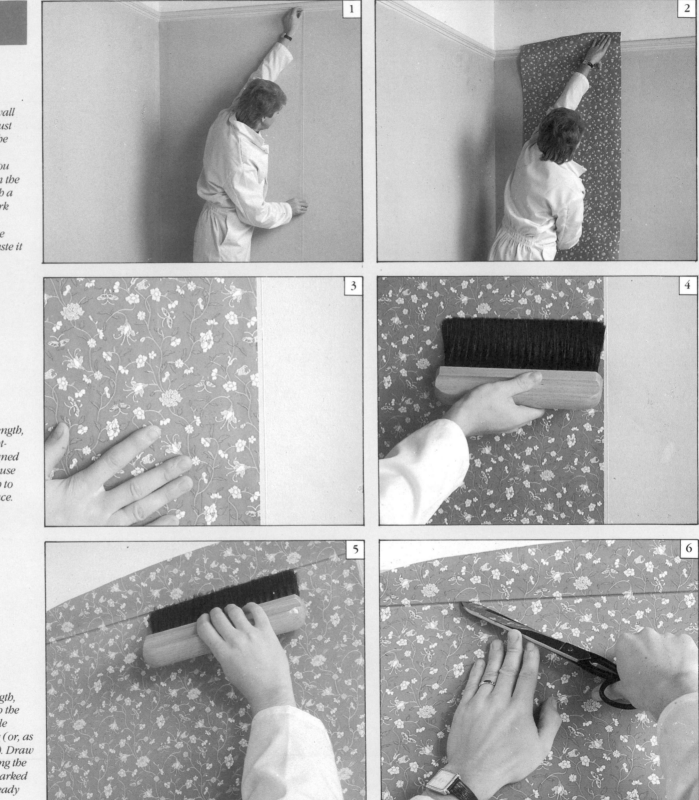

7 & 8 *Peel the top end of the length away from the wall so you can cut along the creased line with the shears, following the profile of the angle precisely. Then brush it back into position on the wall. Repeat the brushing-in process at skirting-board level.*

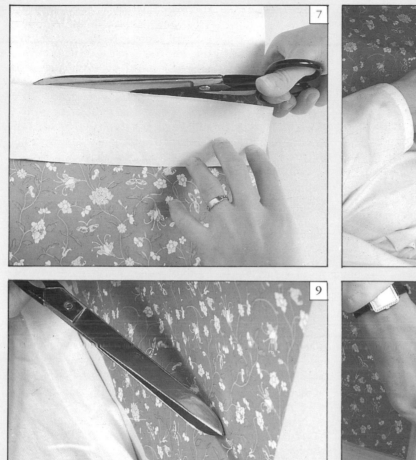

9 & 10 *Once again, use the back of the shears to mark the profile of the angle between wall and skirting board on the paper. Then peel the bottom of the length away from the wall, trim off the excess paper and brush it carefully into place.*

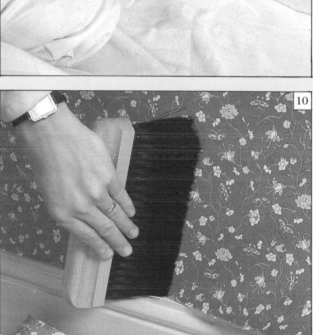

11 & 12 *Cut and paste the second length, take it to the wall and offer it up at the top, aligning it roughly wib the edge of the first length. Then slide it carefully into its exact position to form a perfect butt join. Brush the length into place as before, trimming the excess at top and bottom. Repeat the process for subsequent lengths.*

cut it to size; again marking the appropriate end with the word 'TOP'. This makes it easier to achieve an accurate pattern match when the paper is on the wall.

In most cases, you will find that the pattern either runs straight across the two lengths, or else matches if you stagger them slightly (this is known as a drop pattern). But watch for wallcoverings bearing the instructions 'reverse alternate lengths'. This means every other drop is hung upside down, so remember to turn the paper round on the pasting table to obtain the correct pattern match before cutting.

The next job is to paste the first length. Lay it face down on the pasting table and apply an even, liberal coat of paste with a paste brush, taking care not to miss even the smallest patch, and not to get paste on the patterned side of the paper. There are a few tips that will help here. Start by placing the loaded paste brush in the middle of the paper and paste out towards the edges. To paste right up to an edge, adjust the position of the paper so that the edge you are pasting overhangs the table top by about 25mm (1in), and work the paste brush out across it. Never draw the brush back across the edge or paste will be scraped off on to the patterned side of the paper. And do try not to get paste on the surface of the pasting table.

Make sure, too, that you use the right sort of paste. Ordinary paste is fine for light/medium weight papers, but heavyweights, most vinyls and washables, and embossed wallcoverings need a heavy-duty paste. In the case of vinyl and washable wallcoverings — and papers you intend to paint — make sure the paste contains a fungicide. It is also important to mix the paste correctly (unless, of course, you have bought it ready-mixed). You will find full instructions on the pack, but basically, you slowly pour the contents of the packet into a bucket containing a measured amount of cold water, stirring in the paste granules as you go. Give the mix a final, really thorough stir, then leave to stand and thicken for about 15 minutes. It is now ready to use. Tie a length of string between the lugs that take the bucket's handle, to provide a handy brush rest and to allow you to scrape excess paste from the brush.

Having pasted the top half of the paper, take hold of the edge marked 'TOP', and loosely fold it over so you can move the paper along and paste the rest of its length. That done, simply fold the bottom of the paper up towards the edge of the first fold. The only complication is that, where you are pasting a very long drop, you won't be able to paste and fold the bottom section in one go like this. Instead, you must tackle it in sections, pasting as much as you can get on the pasting table at a time, and then folding it concertina fashion under the top fold so you can bring on the next section and paste that. Aim to end up with a neat concertina of paper that can be easily supported over one arm.

When you have finished pasting the first length, put it to one side, and paste a few more in exactly the same way. This is not only a more efficient way to make use of your labour, but also gives the paste a chance to soak in and soften the paper. However, you must judge this softening time quite carefully. It should be long enough to make the paper supple, yet not so long that it becomes soggy and tears at the least provocation. By trial and error, you should be able to work out a rhythmic cycle of pasting and hanging drops in batches such that, by the time you have finished pasting the last drop in the batch, the first is ready to hang. In addition, subsequent drops in the batch should reach the optimum degree of suppleness just as you finish hanging the preceding length, though in practice, this isn't always possible — the soaking time for thin paper may be less than the time needed to hang a drop; that for thick paper may be much longer.

To hang the first piece of paper, carry it draped over your forearm to where it is needed, open out the top fold, and offer it up to the wall, lining up its edge with the vertical guideline drawn earlier, and allowing a trimming allowance at the top of approximately 50mm (2in) — this enables you to obtain a neat fit even if the ceiling or picture rail is out of true. Hold the drop in place by brushing the top half on to the wall using a paperhanging brush, then open out the bottom fold, and brush out the remainder. The important thing here is to avoid trapping bubbles of air under the paper. Always brush down from the top and out towards the edges.

You can now trim the drop to fit. Run the back of your scissors over the paper, pushing it well into the angle between the wall and ceiling, picture rail, skirting board or whatever, to leave a neat crease. Carefully peel back the trim allowance, together with a little of the paper on the wall, cut along the crease line — it's better to cut off a fraction too little than a fraction too much — and finally brush the trimmed drop back into place. Again, be sure to brush out towards the edges of the paper to avoid trapping air. Neaten the trimmed edges by stabbing at them with the bristles of the brush to push them right into the angle defining the edge of the papered area.

Subsequent drops are hung in exactly the same way, having positioned them to obtain an exact pattern match. You will find this easiest if you brush the top half of the drop into place a little to one side of where it should actually go. If you have pasted the paper properly and sized the wall, you should now be able to slide the paper over to butt up against the edge of the preceding drop, then slide it up or down as required to match the pattern. Use the palms of your hands to manoeuvre the paper — there is then less risk of tearing it.

Hanging convenience wallcoverings

As you will have gathered from the above — although it may sound complicated — hanging ordinary wallpaper isn't really that difficult. And hanging some of the most modern 'convenience' wallcoverings is even easier.

There are the ready-pasted vinyls, for example. With these, instead of laboriously pasting individual lengths, you simply soak them in water for a minute or so to activate the paste coating on the backing paper. Many come with a cardboard trough for the purpose (or you can buy more robust

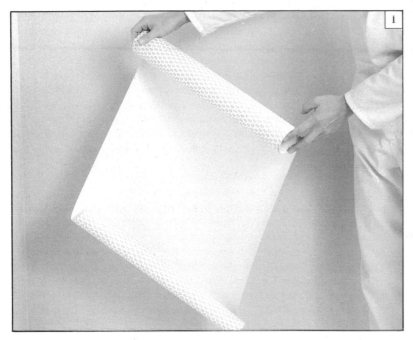

HANGING READY-PASTED PAPERS

1 *Measure the length of paper required for the drop, then roll it up with the bottom of the length innermost.*

2 *Immerse the roll in the soaking trough, which should be positioned at the foot of the wall below the hanging position. Use cold water, and do not exceed the manufacturer's* recommended soaking time.

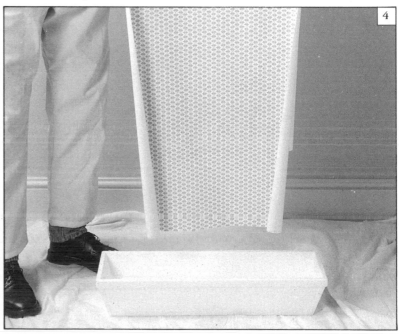

3 *When the soaking time is up, grasp the end of the length and draw it up out of the trough towards the top of the wall. Water will run down the length and back into the trough.*

4 *When most of the water has run off the length, position the top at ceiling level and use a paperhanger's brush (or a sponge with vinyls and* washables) to press it into place. Trim as before.

PAPERING ROUND OBSTACLES

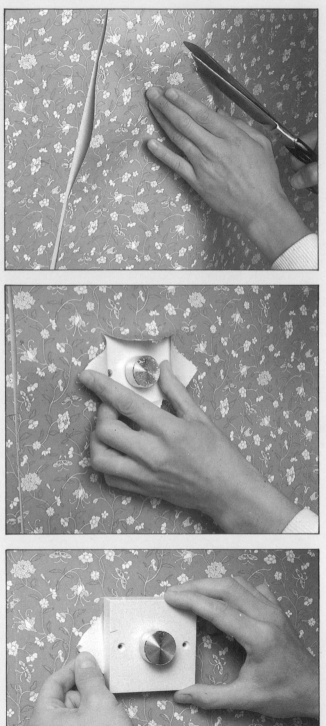

1 *Where the drop hangs over a light switch, power point or similar small obstacle, feel for the centre point of the faceplate and make four short cuts at right angles to each other, radiating outwards from that point, with your paperhanging shears or a smaller pair of scissors.*

2 *Fold back the four tongues formed by the cuts. Then you can either brush them into the angle between the faceplate and the wall and trim them off along the marked line, or tuck them behind the faceplate — see below.*

3 *The neatest effect is achieved by snipping off about two-thirds of each triangular tongue and tucking the remainder behind the faceplate of the switch or power point. If this is being done, it is essential that the current to the circuit is switched off at the mains before the faceplate is unscrewed.*

metal and plastic troughs), but, in practice, it is best to use these solely to carry the drops to where they are needed. You can then speed up the work by having a number of drops in the process of soaking, say, in the bath. To hang the paper, just take hold of the top edge, offer it up to the wall — it will simply unroll from the trough — and smooth it into place with a moist sponge. The only snag is that, when dealing with especially tricky parts of the room, you may find that the paste dries out and refuses to stick. The answer is to have a bucket of conventional paste standing by so you can brush a little fresh paste on to the appropriate sections as required.

Getting the wallcovering to stick where drops have to overlap – at a corner, for example – can also be a problem. Since paste doesn't produce a particularly strong bond, stick down the overlaps as a separate operation using a clear, rubber-based household adhesive such as Copydex.

Another 'convenience' wallcovering that is much easier to hang than ordinary types is Novamura. This contains no paper; it's made from foamed polyethylene (polythene) and is stuck to the wall with a specially-formulated ready-mixed adhesive. The two major points of difference here are that you brush the adhesive onto the wall, not the wall-covering, and that, because the material is so light, you can work with the complete roll rather than separate lengths. You simply let the roll lie on the floor below the position of the next drop, draw it up into position (not forgetting the trim allowance), smooth it into place with a damp sponge and trim off the excess at skirting board level before returning to the top edge and trimming there too.

Tackling awkard areas

Once you have mastered the basic techniques for papering plain, flat walls, you can set about tackling the trickier parts of the room.

Light switches and similar wall-mounted fittings are among the first obstacles you will have to get round. The trick is to brush the paper down as far as the switch, and let the rest of the drop hang loosely over it. You then feel through the paper for the switch, poke your scissors through at what you judge to be the middle, and then make a snip out towards each of the switch's corners — or, in the case of a round fitting, several snips to form a circular star of cuts. The idea is to allow the switch to poke through the cuts as you now brush the rest of the drop into place. The triangles of waste paper left around the outline of the switch can now be trimmed off in the usual way. Simply score with the back of your scissors and then cut along the crease. For a really neat finish, loosen the retaining screws in the switch's faceplate just enough to allow the trimmed edges of the paper to be poked underneath with the paper-hanging brush. However, if you do tamper with the faceplate, play safe and turn off the electricity supply at the mains first.

Corners are another common problem. You simply cannot count on the room's walls being sufficiently true to paper straight round them. The answer is to trim the width

TURNING CORNERS

1 & 2 *Measure the distance from the edge of the last complete drop to the corner. Add about 25mm (1 in) to this measurement and cut a strip of paper to match it.*

3 & 4 *Paste and hang the narrow strip in the usual way, butting its right-hand edge against the length already hung and brushing the other edge into the angle so it just turns onto the other wall. Then mark a plumbed line on the wall just less than the width of the rest of the strip from the corner.*

5 & 6 *Paste the off-cut part of the length and hang it to the plumbed line, brushing the overlap well into the angle for a perfect finish. At an external corner, again cut the length concerned so about 25mm (1 in) will turn onto the adjacent wall face.*

7 & 8 *Hang the rest of the strip so that it overlaps the turned edge by a few millimetres, and brush it into position. If you are hanging a washable or vinyl wallcovering, use a special vinyl overlap adhesive to ensure that the overlapping part is well stuck down.*

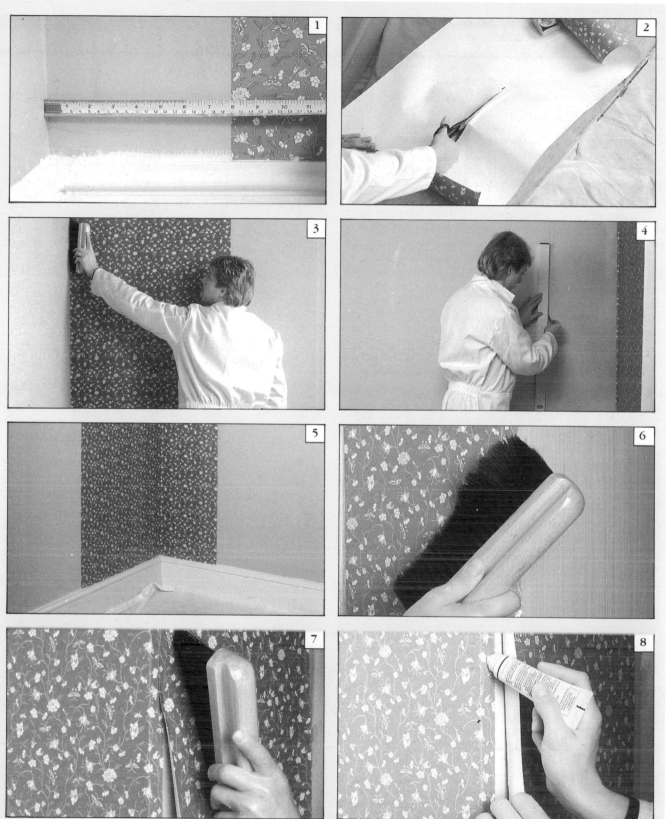

of the drop so that it turns the corner by only about 25mm (1in). The next drop — the one around the corner — is then hung absolutely vertically (strike a guide line with the aid of a plumb line in the same way as when you first started papering) so that it covers as much of this overlap as possible. The only snag is that this method makes it quite difficult to achieve a good pattern match at the corner. Using the off-cut from the first drop to start on the second wall can sometimes help — though, in this case, it needs to be fairly wide, and you must trim the first drop to width very carefully indeed to leave the off-cut with a clean, straight edge — but really the fault lies with the walls, rather than the method. You simply have to aim for the best pattern match you can in the circumstances.

And doors? These are usually one of the simplest obstacles to paper round. As usual, brush the top of the drop on to the wall, and let the rest hang down over the door surround. Almost invariably, part of the drop will lie above the surround, and part over the flat wall at the side of the door, so, with a paperhanging brush, push the loose paper well into the angle formed by the top of the door surround's architrave, crease along it with the back of your scissors, and cut along the crease as far as the architrave's corner. Finish brushing the paper above the door into place, then hinge back the flap created by the freeing cut you have just made, and brush the rest of the drop on to the wall. Run the back of your scissors down the angle formed between the architrave and the wall at the side of the door, then, finally, use the resulting crease to accurately trim off the flap of excess paper. The drop should now fit snugly round the door surround, and the remainder of the wall above the door can then be covered with a number of short drops in the usual way.

The same technique can be adapted to paper round flush windows. Simply make additional freeing cuts so you can fit the bottom of the drop around the window sill and turn it on to the wall beneath the sill where it can be brushed into place. Then, in addition to hanging short drops to cover the wall above the window frame, all you need do is hang similarly short drops to cover the wall below. The only trouble with this very simple approach is that where the window acts as a visual focal point for the room, and where you are using a paper with a fairly prominent motif, the result can look rather lop-sided. It is better to hang a drop centrally above the window to centre the motif, and to work outwards from there to paper the rest of the wall. Any discrepancy in pattern match between this wall and the plain walls you have already papered can generally be 'lost' or corrected at the corners.

Starting with a central drop in this way is, in any case, essential if you wish to paper neatly around a window set back in a reveal — one of the most difficult papering jobs you are ever likely to meet. Begin by measuring the width of the reveal on the wall above the window to find its exact middle, and mark this with a pencil. From this centre point, you must now measure out towards the end of the reveal in units equal to the paper's width, marking the edge of each

PAPERING ROUND DOORS AND WINDOWS

1 *When papering across a window or door reveal, hang the length as shown so it overlaps the opening. Ideally the part overlapping the opening should be wide enough to reach to the back of the reveal when the release cuts are made.*

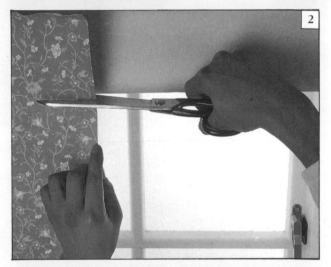

2 *Mark the trimming cut at ceiling or picture rail level, and make the first release cut level with the top edge of the reveal. Make a similar release cut further down the length, level with the window sill.*

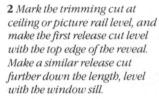

3 *Brush the central 'tongue' back onto the side wall of the reveal, crease its rear edge with the shears where it butts up against the window frame and trim off any excess material before brushing the tongue back into place. If it doesn't reach the frame, cut and hang a narrow strip of paper to fill the gap.*

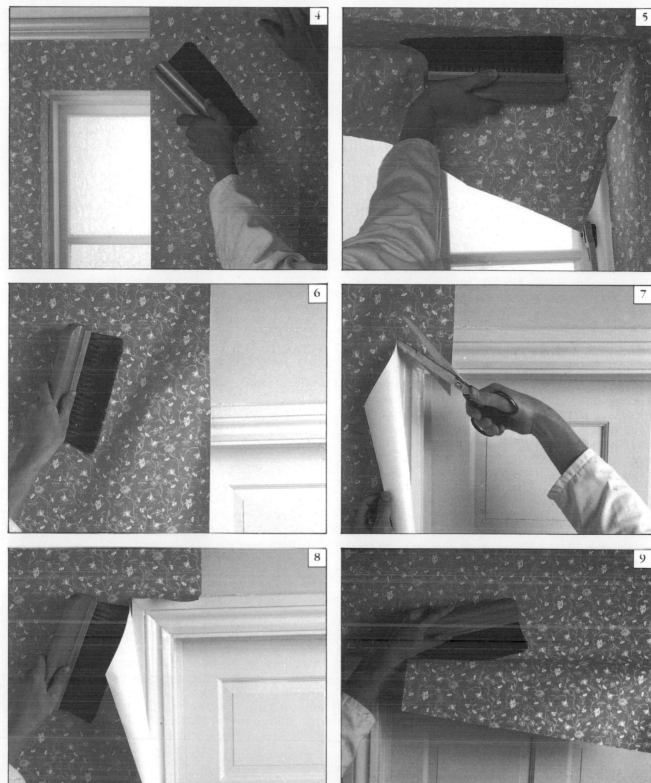

4 & 5 *Hang the next length over the reveal in the same way. With a reveal wider than this a short length may be needed above the centre of the window before the next full-length drop is hung. The underside of the reveal head is then papered with short lengths that overlap on to the wall above the opening.*

6 & 7 *At a doorway with a projecting architrave, brush the edge of the length over the corner of the door frame, and mark where this comes on the paper. Then make a cut with your shears at an angle of 45° from the edge of the paper up to the mark.*

8 & 9 *Brush the freed sections of paper into the angles between the wall surface and the edge of the architrave, and mark and trim them in the usual way. Then hang a short length of paper on the wall above the door opening before hanging another full-length drop at its far side.*

imaginary drop as you go — a spare roll of paper makes a convenient gauge for this. The question you must now ask yourself is whether, with the drops arranged in this fashion, it is possible to turn those at each side of the window round on to the reveal in order to cover it. If the answer is no, with the aid of a plumb line, strike a vertical guide line to indicate the edge of the first drop to be hung above the window, half the width of the paper to the right or left of the reveal's centre point. If the answer is yes, strike the guide line through the centre point.

Working to this line, you can now paper the wall above the window reveal with short drops. Provided the reveal isn't too badly out of square, these can in fact be turned into the reveal to cover the soffit (the reveal's 'ceiling') as well. However, if the reveal is badly askew (or if you are using a pattern that highlights the slightest inaccuracy), merely turn these drops about 25mm (1in) on to the soffit, and paper the soffit separately with drops hung at right angles to the window frame.

The next step is to tackle the drops at each side of the reveal. Brush these into place at the top of the wall and let the rest of the drop hang loosely over the reveal in the same way as when papering round a door. You must now make two freeing cuts in the paper hanging over the window in order to produce a flap that can be turned on to the reveal. The first should be about 12mm ($\frac{1}{2}$in) below the level of the soffit; the second exactly level with the top of the window sill. Brush this flap into place, then make further freeing cuts as necessary to allow the rest of the drop to be fitted around the window sill and brushed out on to the wall beneath. The reveal should now be completely papered (unless very deep, in which case additional thin drops may be needed to extend the side flaps to cover its sides), save for the very ends of the soffit.

To cover these, make a vertical freeing cut in line with the side of the reveal, up through the strip of unstuck paper produced by making the side flap's top freeing cut 12mm ($\frac{1}{2}$in) below soffit level. This strip can then be turned on to the soffit and stuck down — as is common when tackling complicated papering jobs, you will probably have to apply a little fresh paste here to make it stick. Now, cover the remaining bare soffit with a small patch of paper, cut to turn down on to the sides of the reveal by about 12mm ($\frac{1}{2}$in). Peel back the paper already covering the side of the reveal at these points, to allow these small turns to be tucked away neatly out of sight.

To complete the job, cover the wall beneath the window sill with short drops of paper hung in the normal way. Here, though, you should start with drops butted against the full length drops at each side of the window, and work in towards the centre.

Another situation where it is advisable to begin papering with a central drop is where you are using a paper with a bold motif on a chimney breast. It can look very odd if the design isn't exactly centred, and since a chimney breast is often the main focal point of the room, any inaccuracy here can have an effect on the look of the room as a whole. As with the window reveal, you should start by measuring up to find the exact centre of the breast, and step out from this point in 'paper-width' units to find out where the joins between drops fall in relation to the chimney breast's external corners. The aim this time, though, is for as much as possible of the drops turning these corners to lie on the chimney breast's face, yet still allowing a reasonable amount to turn on to the breast's sides. Accordingly, you must decide whether to hang a drop in the centre of the chimney breast's face — that is, hung to a vertical guide line half a paper-width to the right or left of the centre point — or to start with two drops hung on each side of a vertical line drawn through the centre point itself.

Once you have made that decision, paper the face of the chimney breast in the normal way, allowing the outer drops to turn on to the side walls by about 25mm (1in). Next, paper the side walls, covering the overlaps in the process, and turning about 25mm (1in) on to the walls of the alcoves. As usual when turning a corner, these drops should be hung to a vertical guide line, but, if the chimney breast is very shallow, there may not be room. In this case, use a plumb-line to check directly that the front edges of the drops are exactly vertical. Finally, paper the alcoves — yet again hanging the drops there to a vertical guide line so that they overlap the paper turning off the chimney breast's side walls. It sounds straightforward, and so it is if the fireplace in the chimney breast has been blocked off. But what if you are faced with papering around a complicated fire surround?

This can be a very fiddly job, but it's not difficult. Basically, all you do is brush the paper down flat on the wall as far as you can (probably level with the top mantelshelf), then make a freeing cut in the same way as when papering round a door in order to allow you to brush out a little more of the drop. If the fire surround widens out beyond this point, simply repeat the procedure. Brush down as far as you can, make a freeing cut, then brush down the rest of the drop until you meet another obstacle. If the surround narrows — say, where it cuts in beneath a long shelf — merely brush the flap created by the previous freeing cut into the gap, and, starting at the top, carefully trim to fit the side of the fireplace.

Where 'cut-backs' of this sort are fairly large, take them into account when working out where to hang the first drop on the chimney breast, making sure that the arrangement of drops you settle on produces a sufficiently large flap when the freeing cuts are made to fill the 'cut-back' without the need to resort to using odd-looking strips in order to cover the wall there. It is more likely, however, that your problem will be having to cope with too much excess paper. This can make it very difficult to make freeing cuts accurately. The way round the problem is to cut off the bulk of the waste before any freeing cuts are made. So long as you are careful not to remove too much at this stage, you will find trimming the paper exactly to fit much easier and much less messy. This applies when tackling any obstacle — not just fireplaces.

Papering stairwells

Although most stairwells contain lots of large, flat walls, papering them — indeed decorating them at all — can still be a real problem. How do you reach to the very top of the well? You cannot simply stand a ladder on the stairs. Clearly, some more effective means of access must be found.

The traditional method is to improvise using a combination of scaffold boards, a step ladder, a single section ladder, and a 'hop up' — essentially a small, portable staircase with two steps, which you can either buy, or make yourself from chipboard or natural timber. The idea is to arrange the hop up, ladder, and steps so that they can support the scaffold boards at the required working height. However, the arrangement does have to be carefully thought out, moving it to tackle another section of stairwell is a major operation (you usually have to dismantle everything and start again from scratch in the new location), and there is the question of safety.

You must certainly make sure that all the components of the set-up are securely joined with ropes and G-cramps to make sure that nothing slips out of place. Similarly, you must make sure that the feet of ladders (and steps where they are being used closed as a mini-ladder) are securely anchored, either by using the stairs themselves to resist any tendency to slip, or timber battens screwed temporarily to the floor. Even then, walking about on a couple of scaffold boards at the top of a stairwell is not everyone's idea of fun.

You might therefore prefer a simpler alternative. One possibility is a combination ladder — a step ladder that can be opened out to form a straight ladder if desired. The more complex models also convert into a sort of scaffold arrangement, and in many cases can be set up quite safely on the stairs. Perhaps a better bet though, is to hire an indoor scaffold tower — many allow you to extend the legs on one side so they will stand on a flight of stairs. This arrangement is, admittedly, slightly inconvenient in that it allows you to tackle only a relatively small section of wall at any time, and moving the tower along to tackle the next section is only slightly less arduous than dismantling and moving the traditional, make-shift arrangement mentioned earlier. But, if you follow the manufacturer's recommendations covering assembly and moving, it should be completely safe. The fact that you can construct a tower with a safety rail around the working platform is an added bonus if you are not very good with heights.

But reaching the heights of a stairwell isn't the only problem you are likely to encounter. The fact that you are dealing, for the most part, with very long drops of paper can also prove a burden. They are difficult to paste, difficult to handle, and difficult to hang unless you are careful not to let the paper stretch unevenly as you brush it into place — by the time you have reached the bottom of the drop, it may have stretched to the point where the pattern no longer matches that on the preceding length.

As far as the pasting is concerned, there isn't a great deal you can do to make life easier. Just be especially careful to

Access equipment for papering stairwells

On a straight flight, set a ladder on the stairs sloping in the opposite direction and pad its stiles **right**. *Use a step-ladder to support the other end of the scaffold board at a suitable height. Remember to tie the board to the ladder and steps for safety.*

Where there is a quarter-landing, use steps and a hop-up or stout timber box to support a second board at right angles to the first **left**. *Nail the batten to the landing floor to secure the steps safely, and either tie the planks together where they overlap or drill holes through them and drop coach bolts in to lock the boards together.*

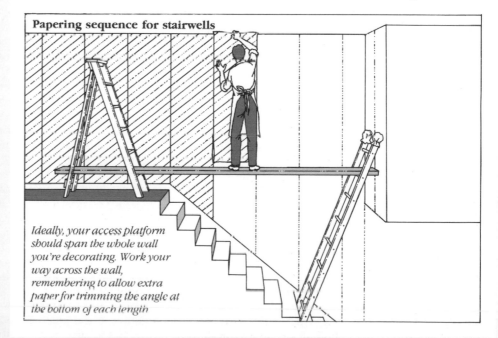

Papering sequence for stairwells

Ideally, your access platform should span the whole wall you're decorating. Work your way across the wall, remembering to allow extra paper for trimming the angle at the bottom of each length

fold the drop into a neat, manageable concertina, and try to avoid allowing the paper to soak for too long — soggy paper is more likely to stretch unevenly. The handling you can make a lot easier by getting a helper to support the bulk of the drop while you concentrate on hanging it. Having an assistant to take care of the pasting is, in any case, a good idea. It will save you a lot of climbing up and down, and allows you to store the drops waiting to be hung safely out of the way. Working single-handed, the alternatives are either to take an entire batch of drops with you up on to the scaffold (in which case you risk treading on them), or to put them to one side and then fetch each drop as you need it (which entails even more climbing up and down).

And what about the actual hanging technique? As already mentioned, the main thing to avoid is uneven stretching, so do try to brush each drop into place in a uniform manner, without varying the pressure of the paperhanging brush. However, it must be said that some papers, notably the thinner ones, are especially prone to stretching, so avoid using these in stairwells unless you have to. The only other thing to watch is the trimming. This is carried out in exactly the same way as when papering any other wall, but do remember that you obviously need a far larger trim allowance at the bottom of each drop to accommodate the slope of the stairs.

Papering a ceiling

Mention papering a ceiling, and most people immediately conjure up visions of chaotic slapstick comedy routines in which gravity triumphs over paste and paper. But in reality, it's a relatively simple task. After all, how many other surfaces in your home can you think of that are so uncomplicated? Of course, the fact that you do have gravity working against you has to be taken into account, and handling the sort of long lengths of paper generally needed for the job creates a certain amount of difficulty in itself. However, don't be put off. With a little know how and organization, all of the problems you are likely to encounter are easily overcome. There are really two keys to success.

The first is good preparation. In order to disprove the old adage 'what goes up must come down' it is obviously vital to do all you can to ensure that the paper sticks properly. And it won't stick properly on a surface that has not been adequately and correctly prepared. Sizing — that is sealing the surface with a coat of dilute wallpaper paste — is also essential. This not only helps improve adhesion, but also makes it a good deal easier to manoeuvre lengths of paper into place without stretching and tearing them.

The second is arranging good access. In this case, however, good access is not simply a question of coming up with a way to reach the ceiling comfortably and in safety — though, obviously, neither factor can be ignored. Step ladders and access towers are not much help here. While they would enable you to brush the start of each length into place without much difficulty, what happens then? The answer is that you have to climb down, move the steps or

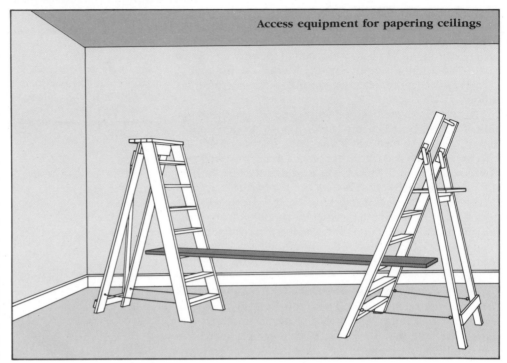

Access equipment for papering ceilings

When papering a ceiling, you need to be able to move freely across the room as you position each length of paper. The best method is to use two step-ladders with a scaffold board set between them.

tower along, and climb back up before you can continue work. The chances are that at some stage during that process, your neat concertina of pasted paper would unravel into a tangled mess, and it is virtually certain that the weight of unhung paper would simply pull down the section already in place. What you need, therefore, is some sort of access equipment that allows you to walk from one side of the room to the other, brushing a length of paper into place on the ceiling as you go.

There is only one piece of equipment that fits the bill — long scaffold boards supported at each end by step ladders, decorator's trestles, access towers, or a combination of any two of these. The necessary boards can be hired quite easily from a good tool hire shop, together with the necessary supporting steps, trestles, or whatever. For safety's sake, though, do hire a pair of boards, and set them up side by side to form a reasonably wide catwalk. And don't be tempted to improvise by using ordinary planks instead of purpose-made scaffold boards — they won't be strong enough.

Having sorted out the access equipment, you can turn your attention to actually hanging the paper, and the first question you have to answer is: where should you start? The traditional advice is to start with a drop hung parallel to the wall containing the room's main window, and to work out from there across the room. However, as with the comparable advice on where to start papering walls, this way of doing things was originally devised to help make the overlapping joins between old-fashioned ceiling papers less obvious. Since virtually all modern papers simply butt together at the joints, it consequently no longer applies. You can start against any wall you choose. Pick one adjacent

PASTING AND FOLDING

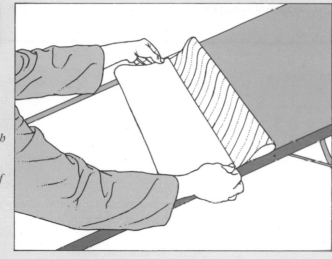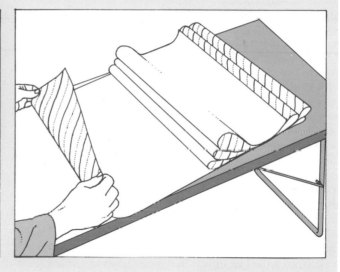

1 & 2 *Because of the length of paper needed to cover the width of a room, you have to paste and fold ceiling paper differently. Paste the first part of the length, then fold a short section over on itself. Continue to paste and fold in this way until you have created a series of concertina-like folds.*

HANGING CEILING PAPER

1 & 2 *Use a string line pinned across the ceiling to mark a guide line on its surface. This should be just less than the paper's width from the edge of the room, to allow the long edge to be trimmed precisely to fit. Unfold the concertinas and brush the first length into place against the line.*

3 & 4 *Crease the ends of the length (and the long side edge of the first and last lengths hung) into the angle between ceiling and coving, then peel them back and trim off the excess. Hang subsequent lengths in the same way, with neat butt joins between lengths.*

to a nice long, uninterrupted stretch of totally flat ceiling. You will find, though, that the old timers were right in one sense — ceiling paper does somehow look better if hung parallel to the wall containing the room's largest window.

You must now draw a line on the ceiling parallel to the wall to indicate where the edge of the first drop is to go. This should be about 50mm (2in) less than the width of the paper from the wall to allow a reasonable trimming allowance to turn down on to the wall. To draw the line, you could simply mark the appropriate measurement at various points across the ceiling and joint up these points using a long, straight batten as a ruler. However, that's not very accurate — the wall may not be straight. A better method is to use a chalked line. You can buy these from good decorating shops. The line comes on a reel designed to chalk the string as it is pulled out. Alternative, just take a length of soft string and rub a dark coloured chalk into the fibres. Mark the line's position on the ceiling at opposite ends of the wall, stretch the line tightly between these two points, then snap it against the ceiling like a bowstring to leave a dead straight chalked line.

Using this line as a guide, cut the first few drops to length, allowing an extra 100mm (4in) or so at each end for trimming. Paste them in the usual way, folding each drop into a neat concertina, then when they have soaked for the required time, carry the first drop to where it is needed, open out the top fold, and offer it up to the ceiling — you will find this a lot easier if you support the concertina on a spare roll of paper or something similar. Position its edge against the guide line, remembering to allow the trim allowance at the ends to turn down on to the wall, then brush the first section in place just as you would if you were brushing it on to a wall, at the same time poking the trim allowance at the side well into the angle between wall and ceiling using the tip of your paperhanging brush.

Once a little less than a metre of paper has been brushed into place, it should stay there, allowing you to open out a little more of the concertina and brush the next section into position. Continue in this way, aiming to unfold and brush the paper into place in one smooth movement as you walk the length of the scaffold board, until the entire drop is in position. You can now trim the paper to fit along the side and end wall. This is done in the usual way by running the back of your scissors along the angle between wall and ceiling to leave a score line to which you can cut, but take care when peeling back the paper for the final cut not to peel back so much that the entire drop starts to come away. Make sure, too, when brushing the paper back into place after trimming, that it really does stick. If you find the paste has dried out, brush on a little fresh paste to achieve a really strong bond.

With the first drop in place, you now simply move your access equipment along as necessary to hang the second and subsequent drops, butting each one tightly against its predecessor to achieve a good pattern match, just as you would if you were papering a wall. On most ceilings, there are just two problems you are likely to encounter. To begin

PAPERING ROUND CEILING OBSTACLES

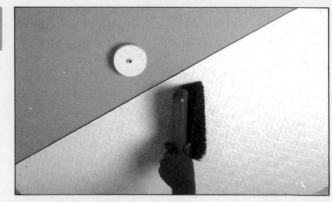

1 *If you have pendant light fittings, turn off the power and remove the pendant before you start decorating. Hang the length of paper adjacent to the ceiling rose in the usual way; then hang the length that will lie over it.*

2 *Brush the paper over the rose position so you can mark its centre point. Then use your shears or a smaller pair of scissors to make a series of short cuts out from the centre point to just beyond the perimeter of the rose itself.*

3 *Crease the tongues neatly against the edge of the rose, and trim them off with scissors or a sharp knife. Alternatively, unscrew the rose cover and tuck the trimmed ends of the tongues behind it for a neat finish.*

SLOPING CEILINGS

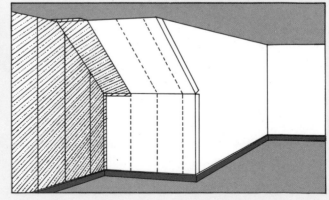

Where a sloping ceiling is being decorated with the same paper as a wall, it's easier to hang separate pieces on the sloping and vertical surfaces. Allow a generous turn onto adjacent surfaces to avoid gaps.

with you will probably have to paper round a pendant light at some point. This is done in more or less the same way you would paper round a light switch. Brush the paper up to the ceiling rose, hold the next section of paper loosely over the rose — you will have to hold the light flex out of the way while you do this — then push the scissors through at the point you judge to be the rose's centre, and make a star-shaped series of freeing cuts out towards the ceiling rose's circumference. You then drop the light flex and bulb holder through the resulting hole, brush that section of the paper firmly on to the ceiling and trim off the little triangles of waste paper around the rose's rim. As with light switches, for a really neat finish, you can loosen the screws holding the rose to the ceiling just enough to push the trimmed edges of the paper underneath. These fixing screws are located on the terminal plate beneath the rose's screw-on cover, though, so do turn off the electricity at the mains before removing the cover, and don't turn it back on again until the cover has been screwed back in place.

The second thing you may have trouble with is hanging the very last drop. If this is too narrow, the weight of waste paper turning down the wall tends to pull it away before you can trim it accurately to size. The solution is to cut the paper approximately to width before attempting to hang it — allow about 50mm (2in) extra to turn down on to the wall. Even then, a very narrow strip of paper can be tricky. It is therefore a good idea to work out how wide this final drop will be before you start papering. You can then adjust its size by moving the starting guide line closer to the wall, increasing the side trim allowance on the first drop by the amount you want to increase the width of the last. Again, if this trim allowance proves unmanageably large, trim off the bulk of it before brushing the first drop into place.

Hanging lining paper

People often wonder how professionals manage to achieve such a smooth, even finish using paint and wallcoverings. Part of their answer is obviously that constant practice gives them rather more skill than the average amateur. However, that aside, much of their success is actually due to the fact that they will line the wall prior to decorating if it shows the slightest imperfection, where an amateur might not bother.

That's an example you should follow. Lining paper isn't that expensive, nor is it particularly difficult to hang. If you are planning to paint over the lining paper, put it up in exactly the same way as ordinary paper. Where you wish to paper over it, however, it is much better to cross-line — that is, to hang the paper horizontally instead of vertically. There are two main reasons for this. Hung vertically, there is a risk that the joins between lengths will match up with those between the drops of the finishing paper. That would leave a weakness in the finish and the paper could peel off. More importantly, with the lining and top paper running in opposite directions, the layer as a whole tends to do a better job of smoothing out imperfections in the surface. Hanging both papers in the same direction can sometimes

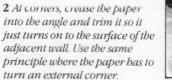

1 *Lining paper is hung horizontally on wall surfaces, starting at the top of the wall. Paste it and fold it into concertinas as for ceiling paper, then brush the paper onto the wall parallel with the top edge.*

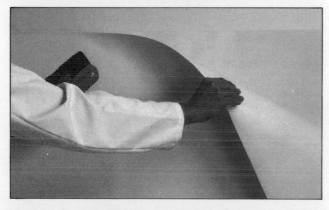

2 *At corners, crease the paper into the angle and trim it so it just turns on to the surface of the adjacent wall. Use the same principle where the paper has to turn an external corner.*

3 *Hang subsequent lengths in the same way, butting the top edge of each length up against the bottom edge of the previous one. Take care not to let the edges overlap, since this would show through the final wallcovering; if anything, it's preferable to leave a slight gap between the lengths.*

4 *Finish off the wall by cutting and hanging a narrow strip at skirting board level. This will have to be creased into the angle between wall and skirting board before being trimmed all the way along.*

highlight lumps and bumps instead of concealing them. There is just one other method of lining a surface. It's called double lining, and is generally reserved for walls and ceilings so rough that a single layer of lining paper will not produce a smooth base for the finishing paper. All it involves is hanging one layer of lining paper vertically, and then cross-lining over the top.

Hanging paper horizontally for cross-lining is obviously not as simple as hanging relatively short vertical drops, but it is not nearly as difficult as you might imagine. The trick is in the way the paper is folded when pasted. Fold it concertina fashion in the same way as any other long drop, but make smaller folds than you might otherwise — small enough to allow you to hold the entire concertina in one hand. Starting at the top right-hand side of the wall (or top left if you are left-handed), pull off a couple of folds from the concertina, press the end of the paper on to the wall until it holds, then smooth it into place properly with a paperhanger's brush.

Once the end is securely in place, you can merely walk the length of the wall, unravelling the concertina and brushing the paper into place as you go, in much the same way as when papering a ceiling. There is no need, incidentally, to strike a guide line for the first drop unless you want to be really particular. Remember, the lining paper won't show when the wall is finished. Equally, you need not worry too much about accurate trimming, nor about achieving really neat butt joins between lengths. However, don't be too slap-dash. Major imperfections in the lining paper layer will show through the covering layer of paper.

The only other thing to consider when lining is the choice of lining paper. You will find several different types in a good decorating store. Some are thick; some are thin. Some have a beautifully smooth finish; others use a somewhat rougher paper. As a general rule, the smoother quality papers are made to receive a painted finish. Beneath a finishing layer of wallcovering, the roughness of the cheaper paper's doesn't show. Choosing the correct thickness of paper, on the other hand, is rather more a matter of judgement. The rougher the surface of the wall or ceiling, the thicker the paper needs to be if it is to smooth out the imperfections.

Hanging relief decorations

For the most part, hanging a relief wallcovering is no different to hanging any other kind of wallcovering. The basic techniques of pasting, hanging, and trimming still apply. However, for the very best results, there are a few additional points to bear in mind.

To begin with, watch the soaking times of pasted drops waiting to be hung. Embossed wallcoverings tend to be a good deal thicker than the average plain wallcovering, and it therefore takes a lot longer for the paste to soak in and make them supple. At the same time, bear in mind that they will also soak up a good deal more paste in the process, so be sure to apply a slightly thicker coat than you would normally during the initial pasting. This helps stop the paste drying out while the paper is soaking. Even so, drying out may still be a problem around the edges of each drop, so keep a bucket of paste handy when hanging the drops. You can brush a little extra paste on to any sections of the wallcovering that need it — or brush paste on to the appropriate bit of wall if that's more convenient. Working on a surface that has been thoroughly sized will also help alleviate the problem. And while we are on the subject of pasting, you really do paste the whole of the drop. Work it right into the indentations formed by the embossing. Take care, too, when folding the drop. The thicker wallcoverings will still be fairly stiff at this stage, and if you try to force them into too tight a fold, they could bend, leaving a crease mark across the embossed surface.

The relief pattern of the thinner embossed wallcoverings is even more vulnerable once the paper has become supple. Take care when brushing the drop on to the wall or ceiling that you aren't too heavy handed or you could 'iron out' sections of the relief. Similarly, try not to slip when using the back of your scissor to crease the line to which the wallcovering will be trimmed. Such accidental creases remain far more obvious in a relief decoration than in an ordinary wallcovering. At the same time, don't be too gentle. The wallcovering must be stuck firmly in place, and you must be able to see guide creases to which you want to cut.

With embossed wallcoverings, it is also even more important than usual to obtain a really exact pattern match, and really tight butt joints between drops. Inaccuracies in either department are not only rather more obvious than with an ordinary wallcovering, but also rather more permanent, since the heavier embossed wallcoverings designed to be painted over (those in the Anaglypta family, for example) are not the sort of thing you want to strip off each time you redecorate. Nor should you need to. They are designed to be semi-permanent wallcoverings. Just try to make sure they are semi-permanent monuments to your paperhanging skill, not semi-permanent catalogues of your mistakes.

There is just one other important difference between hanging embossed wallcoverings and hanging flat ones. With the latter, when turning a corner, papering into a window reveal, or something similar, you can safely afford to overlap adjacent drops in order to compensate for variations in the squareness of the walls. Apart from the occasional mis-match in the pattern, such overlapping joints hardly notice, and if they do look too bulky for your taste, you can always flatten them out with a wooden or plastic seam roller. Not so with an embossed wallcovering: given the thickness of the pattern, any overlap between drops will be very noticeable indeed, and not particularly attractive. A seam roller won't help either. That would only flatten out the design.

How then do you avoid overlaps? Let's suppose that you have just papered round a corner and are ready to hang the first drop on the adjacent wall. What you must do is straighten up the edge of the drop turning the corner so that the next drop can be butted up against its edge. Remember that this second drop must be hung absolutely vertical, so the

HANGING UNBACKED FABRICS

1 & 2 *Measure and cut each drop in turn, allowing for trimming top and bottom, and then roll the fabric right side in and bottom end first on to a cardboard tube. Apply ready-mixed tub paste to the wall surface.*

3 & 4 *Align the top edge of the fabric with the plumbline and let the tube unroll down the wall surface, then use a hard felt roller to press the fabric gently into the adhesive. Don't press too hard or you will stretch it.*

5 & 6 *Hang subsequent lengths with a slight overlap, rolling the material firmly into place. Then use a straightedge and a very sharp handyman's knife to cut off the excess fabric at ceiling and skirting board level.*

7 & 8 *Where adjacent lengths overlap, position a straightedge over the centre line and cut through both layers of fabric from top to bottom of the seam. Pull away the offcut of the upper layer of material, then lift its edge and peel away the strip underneath. Finally roll the seam for a perfect finish.*

edge of the first drop must be trued up with a sharp knife (guide the blade using a long, straight batten to ensure a straight cut), or a pair of scissors. Check where the cut should be made using a plumb-line, and, if you are using a knife, make sure it is absolutely razor sharp. A slightly blunt blade will merely tear the wet paper and leave a ragged edge.

The big snag with this method is, of course, that success depends almost entirely on your ability to cut a clean, straight line, so you may prefer to try a variation on the technique where this is less important. What you do is allow the two drops to overlap temporarily, and then use a knife (again guided along a batten) to cut a vertical line through the double thickness of paper. If you then remove the waste from both drops (you have to peel back the overlying drop to do this), you should find that they now butt together perfectly. Only try this on a wallcovering that will be painted over, though. The temporary overlap usually leaves a paste stain on the surface of the first drop.

Hanging fabrics

Another type of specialist wallcovering you might wish to hang is fabric. Hessian, grasscloth, and silk are widely available paper-backed, and hanging these isn't so very different from hanging ordinary wallpaper.

Apply a liberal coat of paste to each drop in the usual way, taking extra care not to get paste on the fabric-covered face, then allow to soak for around four minutes to allow the paper backing to soften. Do follow the manufacturer's recommendations on the sort of paste you use. Traditional starch-based and modern ready-mixed pastes are generally preferred. When you come to hang the drops, smooth them on to the wall with a foam or felt-covered roller rather than a brush, and trim at top and bottom using a very sharp knife and a straightedge in preference to scissors — using the normal method of trimming wallpaper, any crease you manage to get in this sort of wallcovering is usually too vague to be of much use for accurate trimming. And what about overlapping drops? As with embossed wallcoverings, overlaps will be very obvious so avoid them in exactly the same way. Once again, takes great care not to get paste on the surface of the fabric. It will leave a prominent, messy-looking stain. If you do have an accident, wipe off the paste immediately with a damp cloth, then wipe over the area a second time using a cloth moistened with a little methylated spirit.

Fabric wallcoverings that don't have a paper backing are another possibility — the most common is hessian. To hang these, although the basic principles of paperhanging still apply, the details of the technique are a little different.

The first and most obvious difference is that you paste the wall, not the wallcovering. As with paper-backed fabric wallcoverings, starch paste or ready-mixed paste is normally used for the job, but do follow the manufacturer's recommendations over the choice of adhesive.

There are other important differences that relate to hanging this sort of wallcovering. Always use a soft roller to smooth the fabric on to the wall; never a paperhanging brush. And do take care not to stretch the fabric unevenly with the roller in such a way that the cloth's weave becomes crooked. In addition, you will not be able simply to butt adjacent drops together — the edges of the fabric are often frayed, making it impossible to obtain a neat join. Instead, allow each drop to overlap its predecessor by about 12mm ($\frac{1}{2}$in). You can then obtain a good join by cutting through the double thickness of fabric using a sharp knife and straightedge, peeling away the waste fabric from both drops, and then smoothing the newly cut edges back on to the wall — this will almost certainly need another application of paste to make the edges stick. Complete the join by running over it with a seam roller.

The same techniques are used to avoid overlapping joins at corners, but here there are a couple of additional points to bear in mind. Firstly, when turning external corners, be sure to carry round a fairly wide strip of fabric on to the second wall — 50 to 75mm (2 to 3in) at least. Hessian in particular is quite likely to fray at the edges, and where the edge is close to a join, fraying is not only more likely, but also far more obvious. Secondly, when tackling internal corners, bear in mind that the fabric may shrink and pull out of the angle as it dries. To avoid this, make a neat butt joint along the line where the two walls meet, rather than allowing a single drop to turn the corner.

Incidentally, if you want to paint over plain hessian — and the effect is both unusual and not unattractive — do make sure you allow adequate time for the paste to dry. Anything over 48 hours is usually safe. Apply the paint, either emulsion or a resin-based paint, using a long piled roller to work the paint right into the fabric's weave.

Another pasted-on fabric wallcovering you may wish to hang is paper-backed felt. This is treated in more or less the same way as unbacked hessian, except that having rolled joins smooth, you can use a fine wire brush (a suede brush will do) to disguise them almost totally by teasing fibres from each drop to cover the line between it and its neighbour. There is, unfortunately, one major snag. Unlike hessian, paper-backed felt is normally very wide, and very heavy. In fact, so awkward is it to handle that even with a helper you will probably have trouble. But there is a way round the problem. Cut each drop approximately to length, roll it up, with the paper backing facing outwards, around a long, stout timber batten, and support this in front of the wall you wish to cover on a pair of step ladders or decorator's trestles. You can then paste that section of wall and smooth the felt into place, starting at the bottom. You should find that, as you work upwards, the felt unrolls itself off the batten, allowing you to concentrate on hanging it rather than on supporting its weight.

Finally, it is possible to decorate walls with other types of fabric. In fact, you can use almost any fabric you wish — though furnishing fabrics obviously wear better. And that is just as well if you are looking for a really bright, patterned finish, for the majority of purpose-made fabric wallcoverings either come in plain, rather muted colours, or else are incredibly expensive — so expensive it's probably not worth taking the risk of hanging them yourself. How is it done? There are two main options.

The first is to paste it into place in much the same way as unbacked hessian, using a thick ready-mixed wallpaper adhesive. The only major difference is that where the fabric has a pattern you must obviously try to achieve as good a match as possible between adjacent drops. This generally proves far more difficult than matching patterns on a wallpaper — it's so easy to stretch the fabric unevenly as you roll it out on to the wall. And there's no easy solution to the problem. You simply have to work as carefully as you can. What's more, fabrics not specifically made for the job are far more likely to shrink drastically as the paste dries out. Applying the bare minimum of paste to the wall will help, and this is worth doing in any case to avoid the risk of paste soaking through the fabric and staining its surface. But some shrinkage will almost certainly occur even then, so you must allow for this when hanging. The best way to do that, is to hang the fabric without trimming it — not even at the overlapping joins between drops. If you then allow plenty of time for the paste to dry, by which time the fabric will have shrunk as much as it is going to, you can trim with absolute confidence, tackling the entire room in one go.

The second fixing option is to staple the fabric in place using a heavy-duty staple gun. This is generally a good deal safer than pasting, and makes it a lot easier to obtain an accurate pattern match. What's more, there is nothing to stop you using the staples to hold the fabric in pleats, ruches, and so on, if you wish for a really luxurious effect. Don't fix the fabric directly on to the wall, though. Staple it to thin 25mm x 6mm (1 x ⅟₄in) timber battens.

Starting in one corner of the room, cut the first drop of fabric about 50mm (2in) longer than the height of the wall. Staple one edge to the edge of a batten cut to match the wall's height exactly (centre the 50mm/2in trim allowance); then, having tucked the trim allowance over the ends, fix the batten in place by nailing through its face into the wall (or staple if your staple gun is up to the job). If you now pull the fabric over the batten's face, none of the fixings will show. To secure the other edge of the fabric, fix a second batten to the wall at the appropriate distance from the first, pull the fabric taut, and staple to the batten's edge.

If you now repeat the whole process for the second and subsequent drops, you will find that the first batten of each drop effectively conceals the final fixings of the drop before. That is, until you reach the far end of the wall. Here, you have no choice but to staple the fabric to the batten's face. Do this as close to the edge as possible. In this way, if you are continuing around the corner, the first drop on the adjacent wall will cover the staples. If not, you can cover them with a strip of decorative beading or something similar, pinned in place. To make this cover-up less obvious, it's a good idea to frame each wall with the same beading.

Friezes and borders

Although decorative friezes and borders are no longer as popular as was once the case, they are by no means old fash-

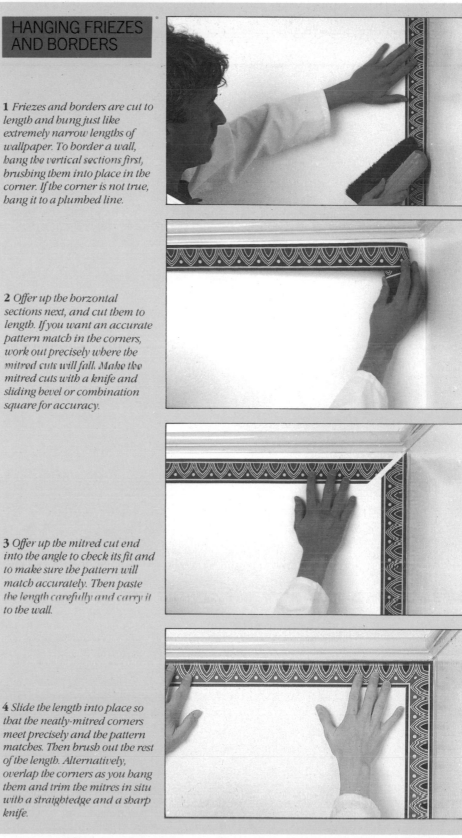

HANGING FRIEZES AND BORDERS

1 *Friezes and borders are cut to length and hung just like extremely narrow lengths of wallpaper. To border a wall, hang the vertical sections first, brushing them into place in the corner. If the corner is not true, hang it to a plumbed line.*

2 *Offer up the horizontal sections next, and cut them to length. If you want an accurate pattern match in the corners, work out precisely where the mitred cuts will fall. Make the mitred cuts with a knife and sliding bevel or combination square for accuracy.*

3 *Offer up the mitred cut end into the angle to check its fit and to make sure the pattern will match accurately. Then paste the length carefully and carry it to the wall.*

4 *Slide the length into place so that the neatly-mitred corners meet precisely and the pattern matches. Then brush out the rest of the length. Alternatively, overlap the corners as you hang them and trim the mitres in situ with a straightedge and a sharp knife.*

A small pattern can be used on both walls and ceilings to dramatic effect **left,** especially if the colours are chosen to complement those of the furnishings.

A tiny, repetitive motif on the wallpaper can echo a larger design on furnishing fabrics **above.** A slim frieze frames each wall to perfection.

Wallcoverings can be used to create contrast too. Here an alcove **above right** has been papered to add interest to the room.

Strong vertical stripes combined with a light-coloured ceiling **right** help to give an illusion of height in a low-ceilinged room.

ioned. On the contrary, they can still do a very useful job in any decorating scheme, helping to break up large areas and highlight architectural features by simply forming dados and 'picture rails', or more complex effects such as forming a frame around an entire wall.

In principle, putting them up is no different to putting up an ordinary wallcovering. Just cut them approximately to length, paste them, allow them to soak for a while, then brush them into place, and finally trim off any excess. There are, however, a few additional tips worth knowing.

If you are hanging them horizontally, make sure they are truly horizontal. Hang them to a guide line drawn lightly in pencil with the aid of a spirit-level and a long, straight batten — rested on top of the spirit-level, the batten effectively increases the length of the spirit level. Similarly, if you want a vertical border hang it to a guide line drawn with the aid of a plumb-line.

If you are laying the frieze or border on top of some other wallcovering — the one covering the bulk of the wall or ceiling — don't apply any more paste than is needed to ensure that it sticks. If you do, it could ooze out as you brush the frieze or border into place and leave a nasty stain.

Finally, if you want to create a frame using a paper border, do mitre the corners — it looks so much neater. This isn't as difficult as it may sound. At each corner, allow the borders to overlap (don't paste the ends), then cut through the double thickness of paper with a sharp knife following a straightedge held to draw an imaginary line between the frame's internal and external corners. Remove the waste paper from both layers, then finish off by brushing a little paste on to the unpasted sections of each border and smooth them into place.

*This gloomy and uninviting hall and staircase **above, right** has been transformed by the use of a bright, lightly patterned wallpaper and gleaming white paintwork. Small details such as the carpet runner and the table cloth add highlights of colour.*

252

THE COMPLETE TILER

BASIC TECHNIQUES   *254*

MARKING UP *255* ♦ FIXING TILES *256* ♦ CUTTING TILES *257*
GROUTING TILES *258*

TILING TRICKY AREAS   *259*

TILING CORNERS AND EDGES *259* ♦ TILING WINDOW REVEALS *260*
TILING ROUND OBSTACLES *261*

APPLYING MOSAICS   *262*

LAYING MOSAICS *263*

CORK TILING   *262*

FIXING CORK TILES *264*

TILING CEILINGS   *266*

FIXING POLYSTYRENE CEILING TILES *267*
FIXING TILES TO BATTENS *270*

Tiles of one sort or another have been used to decorate homes since the days of the Romans. And when you think about it, it's easy to see just why they have remained so popular for so long. Quite apart from the hardwearing, easy-clean qualities of ceramic tiling, tiles in general provide one of the quickest, simplest cover-ups for walls and ceilings there is.

Basic techniques

Let's start by looking at ceramic tiling. The simplest way to get a feel for the job is to tackle a straightforward tiled area such as a splashback behind a bath or basin.

Having prepared the surface thoroughly, the first step is to tackle what's know as the 'setting out' – that is, working out the approximate position of every tile on the wall; the aim being to come up with an arrangement that is both symmetrical, and that avoids the need for unsightly, awkward-to-cut tiles around the edges and other obstacles. This sounds fairly tedious, and so beginners often rush through it in their eagerness to get a few tiles on to the wall. But it really is worth taking the time and trouble to do the job properly. Get the setting out right, and you will save yourself a great deal of trouble in the long run. It makes putting up the tiles so much easier, and you get a better looking end result.

Start by drawing a horizontal pencil line on the wall to indicate the position of the bottom edge of the bottom row of tiles. Use a spirit-level and a long timber batten here to ensure that this line really is straight and absolutely horizontal, then carefully measure it and make a mark at a point exactly half way along its length. This represents the mid-point of the tiled area – the point at which you will begin tiling, and from which you will work out towards the edges of the tiled area in order that all the tiles and joints are arranged symmetrically. You must now check that starting at this point will leave cut tiles of a reasonable width around the edges of the tiled area, so step off along the line in units equal to one whole tile plus the width of a grout line, and indicate the position of each grout line on the wall. If you find that cut tiles less than about 25mm (1in) wide are needed at the edges, move the starting point half a tile width to the left or right and try again.

Now, obviously, if you do all this by carefully measuring to find each point, even using a tile as a gauge, it will take some time, and inaccuracies are likely to creep into your calculations. It's therefore better to use something called a gauge rod. You can make this yourself. Arrange a number of tiles in a row on the floor, taking care to leave the correct spacing for grout between each one. Then lay a long, straight timber batten next to the row, and mark the positions of the tile edges on its edge to form a handy 'ruler'

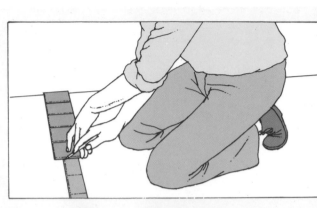

1 *Begin by laying out a row of tiles (plus spacers if necessary) on the floor, and mark the tile spacings on a long, straight timber batten to make a tile gauge.*

2 *Use this to work out where cut tiles will fall, in both vertical and horizontal rows. Don't be afraid to adjust your starting point to avoid very narrow cut pieces at the end of rows.*

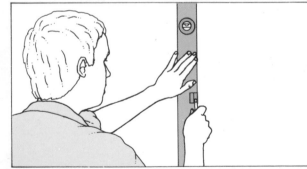

3 *When you have found a satisfactory arrangement, draw a vertical line through the centre point of the area to be tiled. Use a spirit-level to ensure that it is truly vertical.*

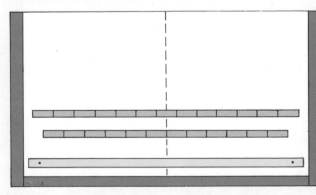

4 *Fix a horizontal batten across the bottom of the area to be tiled, with its top edge in line with the bottom edge of the lowest row of whole tiles. Note the effect of fixing the first tile across or at one side of the centre line.*

graduated in tile-plus-grout-line units.

Once you are satisfied with the arrangement of the vertical joints between tiles, use either a plumb-line, or a spirit-level that allows you to check verticals as well as horizontals — the latter is more convenient — to strike a vertical line through the point you have selected as the best place to start. Then, working up from the horizontal line representing the bottom of the tiled area, work out the positions of the horizontal joins, again using the gauge rod. As when checking the vertical tile positions, if you find that any cut tiles needed at the top are less than about 25mm (1in) wide, adjust the position of the starting point — this time moving it up half the width of a tile — and restrike the horizontal line. One tip: whenever you have to make an adjustment during the setting out, scribble out those marks that no longer apply so that they cannot confuse you when you are ready to move on to the next stage — fixing the tiles on to the wall.

Begin tiling at the intersection of the vertical and horizontal guide lines. Apply a thin coat of tiling adhesive to the wall using a notched plastic spreader (often provided with the adhesive), aiming to cover an area equivalent to about half a dozen whole tiles — you can increase this as you become more proficient. If you have done this properly, you should be left with the bare wall more or less showing between the ridges of adhesive left by the spreader's notches. You now simply take the first tile, and press it on to the wall, lining its edges up with the vertical and horizontal guide line. That done, take a second tile, position this on the horizontal line, and press it into place next to the first tile. Continue adding tiles in this way, spreading on more adhesive as required, until you have a row of whole tiles running the length of the horizontal guide line (don't worry about the cut tiles at this stage). Repeat to produce a row along

TILE QUANTITY CHART				
Area to be tiled (sq m)	Number of tiles needed			
	10×10	15×15	10×20	30×30
1	100	44	50	12
2	200	87	100	23
3	300	130	150	34
4	400	174	200	45
5	500	217	250	56
6	600	260	300	67
7	700	303	350	78
8	800	347	400	89
9	900	390	450	100

MARKING UP

1 *Always start tiling by marking a true horizontal line on the wall, in line with the bottom edge of the lowest row of whole tiles. This is especially important if you are tiling a whole room, to ensure each row is at the same level when you get back to your starting point. Don't rely on skirtings being level.*

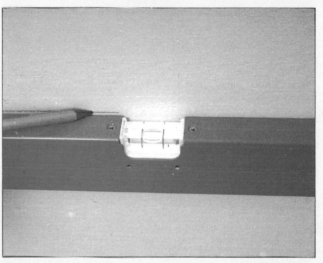

2 *Measure the width of the tiled area, and halve the answer. Then measure this distance along your horizontal line from one edge of the area and mark the exact midpoint. Use your spirit level (or a plumbline) to draw a truly vertical line through this point.*

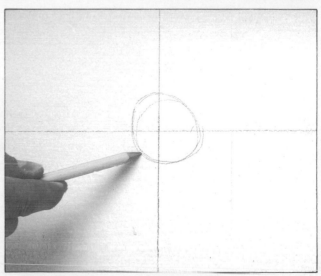

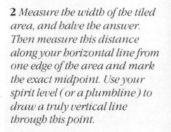

3 *Identify the point where the lines cross as the midpoint of the tiled area by circling the intersection. You can then use your tiling gauge to check whether cut pieces of sensible width will be left at each edge of the area. If they are, the first tiles will be fixed in the angle between the lines; if not, the vertical line is moved half a tile width along the horizontal line.*

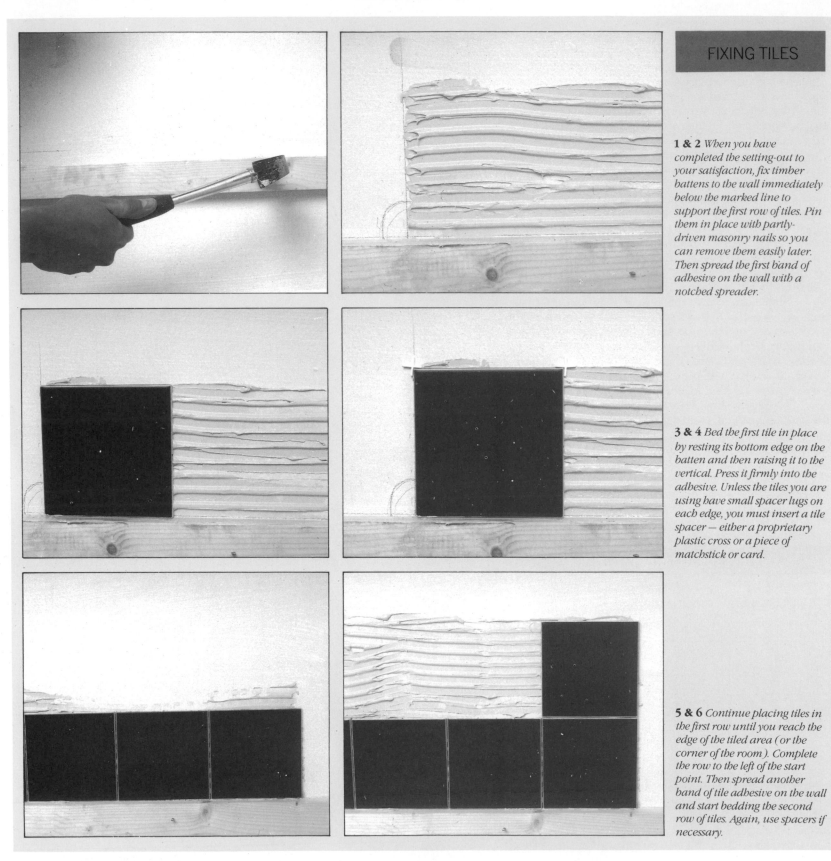

FIXING TILES

1 & 2 *When you have completed the setting-out to your satisfaction, fix timber battens to the wall immediately below the marked line to support the first row of tiles. Pin them in place with partly-driven masonry nails so you can remove them easily later. Then spread the first band of adhesive on the wall with a notched spreader.*

3 & 4 *Bed the first tile in place by resting its bottom edge on the batten and then raising it to the vertical. Press it firmly into the adhesive. Unless the tiles you are using have small spacer lugs on each edge, you must insert a tile spacer — either a proprietary plastic cross or a piece of matchstick or card.*

5 & 6 *Continue placing tiles in the first row until you reach the edge of the tiled area (or the corner of the room). Complete the row to the left of the start point. Then spread another band of tile adhesive on the wall and start bedding the second row of tiles. Again, use spacers if necessary.*

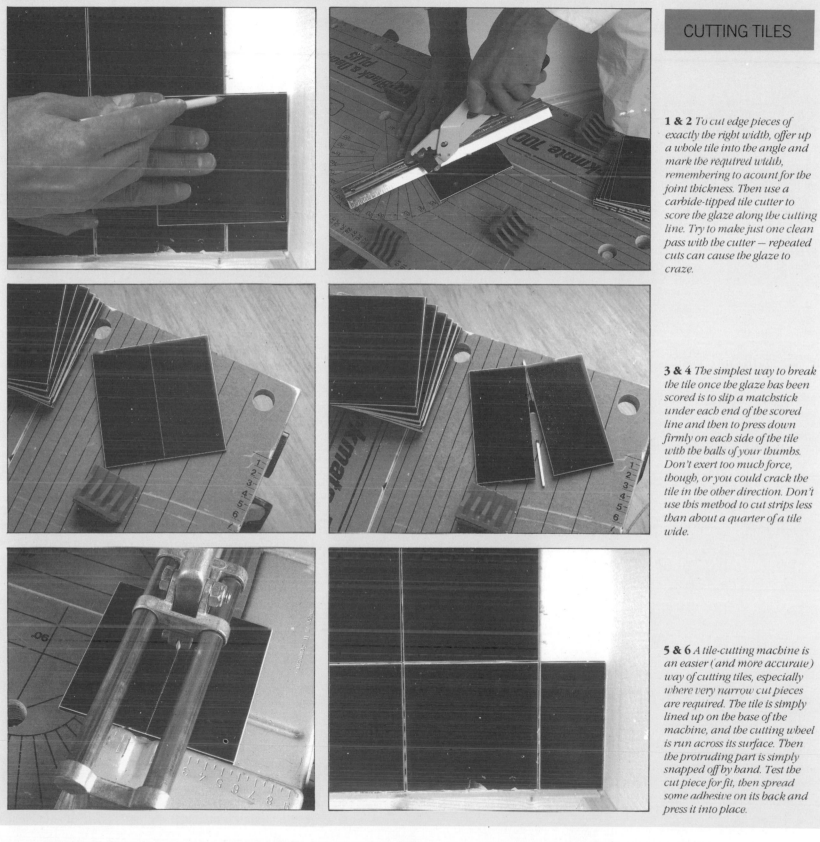

1 & 2 *To cut edge pieces of exactly the right width, offer up a whole tile into the angle and mark the required width, remembering to acount for the joint thickness. Then use a carbide-tipped tile cutter to score the glaze along the cutting line. Try to make just one clean pass with the cutter — repeated cuts can cause the glaze to craze.*

3 & 4 *The simplest way to break the tile once the glaze has been scored is to slip a matchstick under each end of the scored line and then to press down firmly on each side of the tile with the balls of your thumbs. Don't exert too much force, though, or you could crack the tile in the other direction. Don't use this method to cut strips less than about a quarter of a tile wide.*

5 & 6 *A tile-cutting machine is an easier (and more accurate) way of cutting tiles, especially where very narrow cut pieces are required. The tile is simply lined up on the base of the machine, and the cutting wheel is run across its surface. Then the protruding part is simply snapped off by hand. Test the cut piece for fit, then spread some adhesive on its back and press it into place.*

GROUTING TILES

1 *When the tile adhesive has set, mix up some grout (or buy ready-mixed grout) and use a flexible squeegee to press it into the joint lines between the tiles, tackling a small area at a time. Scrape excess grout off the faces of the tiles as you work to minimize the amount of cleaning-up that will be needed later.*

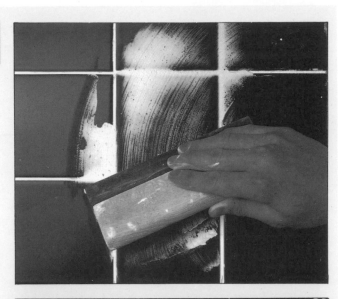

2 *Remove excess grout from the joints by drawing a rounded object such as a piece of dowel along each joint line in turn. Don't use your fingers for this; grout is surprisingly abrasive, and will soon cause very sore fingertips.*

3 *Leave the grout to dry for the time recommended by the manufacturer. Then polish the surface of the tiles with a clean, dry cloth to remove surplus grout from the faces of the tiles and leave the tiled area looking fresh and sparkling. Here, special plastic tile-edging strips have been used to create a neat finish round the edges of the window reveal — see opposite.*

the vertical guide lines, then fill in as much of the remaining tiled area as you can using whole tiles.

There are just two points to watch. Unless the bottom row of tiles is supported by, say, the bath, basin, or whatever, it may slip. You should therefore provide it with temporary support, where necessary, by nailing a timber batten to the wall with its top edge just level with the horizontal starting line. This can be removed once the adhesive has set. Secondly, as you press tiles on to the wall, make sure they are correctly spaced to leave an even grout line 2-3mm ($\frac{1}{8}$in) wide. With many modern tiles, you can achieve this simply by butting each tile hard up against its neighbour. The tile's edges either have built-in spacing lugs, or else slope to leave exactly the right gap for grouting automatically. You may come across a few tiles with plain, square edges, however, and with these it is up to you to ensure the correct spacing. The simplest way to do this is to space the tiles out by inserting matchsticks or special plastic spacers.

Now you can fill in round the edges with cut tiles. These are put up in exactly the same way as whole tiles, except that you may find it easier to spread adhesive on to the tile back, rather than on to a narrow strip of wall. The big question, of course, is: how do you cut a ceramic tile? This is another of those jobs that beginners dread. But try it. The first tile you cut will show you just how easy it really is. Naturally you may have a few accidents (usually once your new found skill has tempted you to over-confidence), but even professional tilers break the occasional tile.

The first step is to measure up to find the width of the cut tile. Take two readings for this — one at the top of the space to be filled, and another at the bottom. This allows for the fact that whatever it is you are tiling up to may be out of square. Transfer both measurements on to the face of the tile (making sure you get them the right way round) then, with the tile laid on a flat surface, lay a straightedge between these two points to indicate the line of the cut. All you do now is run a tile cutter along the line with sufficient pressure to cut through the glaze, carrying the cut down both edges of the tile to score through any glaze there. Don't try to cut right through the tile. And don't worry if you have to run over the line a few times. The important thing is to finish with a clean score line that goes right through the glaze along its entire length. Now for the moment of truth. Place the tile face up on a table so that the table's edge lies immediately underneath the line scored in the tile's glaze. Hold the tile firmly on the table top with one hand, press down on the overhang with the other, and the tile should snap cleanly in two along the line. And that's it.

It's all a question of confidence. If you feel happier about it, you don't have to snap the tile over a table edge. You can snap it over a pencil or a couple of matchsticks. Alternatively, you will find a variety of tile cutting tools that will take care of the snapping as well as the scoring stages of the job — some are also designed to help with the transfer of measurements on to the tile's face.

Once all the cut tiles are in position, allow the adhesive to set completely — leaving it overnight is usually sufficient —

then finish off by filling in the gaps between tiles with grout. Mix this up according to the manufacturer's instructions to a thick, creamy consistency (or buy it ready-mixed) and apply it to the tile joints with a plastic spreader (often provided with the grout). Don't worry about getting grout on the face of the tiles. Just make sure you push it right into the gaps. Once you have covered about 1sq m/1 sq yd (by that time the grout should have started to harden) go back and smooth off the surface of the grout joins by running down them with a wet dowel, pencil or even your finger. If you do use your finger, though, wear rubber gloves to protect your skin from the cement most grouts contain.

Having treated the entire surface in this way, leave the grout to harden for 12 to 24 hours (see the instructions on the pack), and then wash down with plenty of clean water to remove the surplus grout still clinging to the surface of the tiles. Repeat the washing process as necessary until the water comes off clean, then allow to dry. As the surface dries, watch for a fine 'bloom' of grout residue to appear on the surface of the tiles. This is quite normal and can be polished off when completely dry using a soft cloth. Don't try to wash it off as each time you leave the tiling to dry it will reappear.

Tiling tricky areas

Many real life tiling situations are, of course, a little more complicated than the simple splashback described above. Tiling a whole room, for example, can prove very awkward indeed. But it's rare to find a tiling problem that cannot be overcome. The key to success in this sort of situation is to be found in the setting out. You simply have to take as much time and trouble as necessary to make sure you get it absolutely right before putting a single tile on to the wall.

The principles of setting out mentioned above still apply.

You must aim for symmetry and avoid the need for awkward, unsightly, narrow cut tiles. And to these two basic tenets you can add a third — aim for an arrangement that makes tiling around obstacles such as taps, light switches, windows, and so on, as simple as possible. So, assuming you are tiling a whole room, where should you start?

The best bet is usually the room's main window. Creating a symmetrical arrangement about this not only makes for easy tiling, but also, because that window is a natural focal point within the room, helps give the tiled effect as a whole a more balanced look. With the aid of a plumb-line or spirit-level, draw a vertical line on the wall above and below the window to indicate half the window's width, then, using a gauge rod, step out from this line along the window's top and bottom edges to see how the vertical tile joints will fall in relation to the window's sides.

Ideally, unless you are lucky enough to have a window that is an exact number of whole tiles wide, the corners of

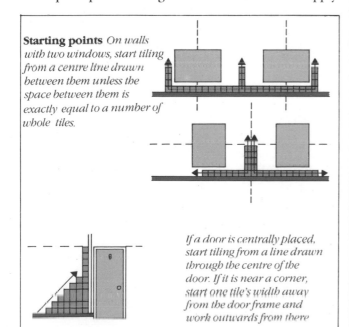

Starting points *On walls with two windows, start tiling from a centre line drawn between them unless the space between them is exactly equal to a number of whole tiles.*

If a door is centrally placed, start tiling from a line drawn through the centre of the door. If it is near a corner, start one tile's width away from the door frame and work outwards from there

TILING CORNERS AND EDGES

1 *Where tiling continues on the next wall, begin each row with the offcut from the end of the preceding row. Leave a small gap between the edge of the cut piece and the wall to allow the joint to be grouted later; if the pieces are butted tightly together, any slight movement in the wall could cause the tiles to crack.*

2 *To finish off external corners neatly when using universal tiles, you can bed special plastic edging strips in the adhesive and butt the edges of the last row of tiles up to them. Similar strips are available for edging areas that are tiled only for part of their height or width — splashbacks, for example.*

the window (or its reveal) should come roughly half way along a whole tile, though, in practice, any split that leaves more than about 25mm (1in) of a whole tile extending beyond the width of the window or reveal is acceptable. You see, this dimension is also the width of the cut tiles needed to fill in along the sides of the window, and quite apart from the fact that strips narrower than 25mm (1in) are difficult to cut, you must allow for the fact the an L-shaped tile may well be needed at the corners. The less tile you have to remove to produce the L-shape, the easier it will be to end up with a cut tile that is both strong and attractive. If you find that you are left with tiles that over-run by less than 25mm (1in), move the vertical starting line half a tile width to the right or left, and try again.

Having sorted out where the vertical columns of tiles are to go, turn your attention to the horizontal rows. You will find this easier if you strike a second, temporary vertical guide line a little to one side of the window or reveal. Mark a point on the line about 50mm (2in) above the floor or skirting board that defines the lower edge of the tiled area, to represent the bottom edge of the bottom row of tiles. Why not start the bottom row off along the skirting board or floor? The reason is that there is no guarantee that such fixtures are absolutely straight and level. You could, there-fore, end up with crooked tiling, or with some very awkward cutting to make a horizontal row of tiles fit in around any dips and bumps. From this starting point, now use the gauge rod to work out the positions of the tile rows in relation to the top and bottom of the window or reveal, then continue up to the ceiling and check the width of any cut tiles needed to fill in there.

Where the top and bottom of the window are concerned, bear in mind the points mentioned in connection with its width. Don't worry too much about achieving perfect symmetry, though. Any arrangement that is approximately symmetrical is usually good enough, so try to visualize how the finished tiling will look and make up your own mind as to whether or not it looks reasonable. At the ceiling, the ideal is to end up with a row of cut tiles of about the same depth as the cut tiles filling in along the bottom of the wall, though again small deviations from perfect symmetry are generally acceptable so long as the end result looks right. Whatever you do, avoid finishing at the ceiling with a row of whole tiles. Ceilings are no more likely to be straight and level than floors and skirting boards.

Having said all that, you will be very lucky indeed if you arrive at the perfect arrangement at the first attempt. Indeed, even after several tries, each time starting with the bottom row of tiles in a slightly different position, there is no guarantee that you will be able to satisfy all of the condi-tions outlined. In such cases, you simply have to use your own judgement, settling on the arrangement that comes closest to the ideal.

To complete the setting out around the window, finally work out the positions of the tiles that will line any reveal, starting with one set so that its edge is flush with the faces of the tiles covering the main wall. As usual, you should avoid

TILING WINDOW REVEALS

1 *When tiling up to and within a window reveal, fix the tiles on the facing wall first. If you are using edging strips, bed these in the adhesive before fixing the last row of tiles. Then tile the sill, beginning with a row of whole tiles butting up to the angle trim.*

2 *When all the whole tiles have been laid across the sill, cut and fit narrow pieces to fill the gap between the whole tiles and the window frame. As with internal corners, leave a slight gap between the cut pieces and the frame to allow for any movement that might occur in the future.*

3 *Tile the sides of the reveal in a similar manner, fixing whole tiles first and then adding cut pieces as required. If edge trim is not being used, simply position the whole tiles so that they overlap the edges of those on the face of the wall. Finish off the reveal by tiling the underside of the reveal head; you may need to support the tiles by propping an offcut of timber across them until the adhesive sets.*

the need for narrow cut tiles as you fill in the window side of the reveal. In this case, though, you cannot adjust the starting position to correct errors. Instead, be prepared to cut the first line of tiles down in depth, in order to increase the depth of those running back to the window frame.

There is, unfortunately, one major snag with this arrangement. It allows you to see the edges of the tiles lining the reveal. If those edges are unglazed, let alone unglazed and studded with spacing lugs, the result is obviously not going to be very attractive. So, is there an alternative? After all, the same problem will occur when tiling around any external corner.

The traditional solution to this problem was to use a special kind of tile, called an RE tile. Unlike the field tiles used to cover the bulk of the surface (which had square cut, unglazed edges), RE tiles had one edge not only glazed, but also slightly rounded to give the corner (or the edge of an isolated tiled area) a smoothly contoured finish. There were REX tiles too — tiles with two rounded, glazed edges designed to produce a neat corner. The snag is that RE and REX tiles are now rare. In fact, virtually the only tiles now made using this three tile system are a few of the thicker, more traditional types of ceramic floor tile — quarry tiles, and the like. On walls, their job has largely been taken over by the continental two-tile system, comprising field tiles and edging tiles (the latter basically just field tiles with one or more edges glazed), and by the more recently introduced universal tiles — tiles with four sloping edges glazed, the edge slope providing automatic spacing.

There is, however, another possibility, and that is to use special quadrant tiles — essentially the ceramic equivalent of timber quadrant beading. These come in straight lengths, plus mitred pairs for internal and external corners, but the choice of colours is limited, and you may therefore experience some difficulty in finding quadrant tiles that match the tiles chosen for the rest of the wall. In this case, consider choosing quadrants in a strongly contrasting colour, rather than settling for a near miss. There is one other thing to remember if you do decide to use quadrant tiles. Be sure to allow for them when working out the sizes and positions of cut tiles leading up to the corner.

Having worked out the optimum tiling arrangement for the area around the window, restrike the starting horizontal guide line at the foot of the wall and extend it right round the room. If it runs past any noticeable changes in the level of the floor or ceiling, use your gauge rod to see how these changes relate to the positions of the horizontal rows at that point. If you discover a potential problem — for example, if extra narrow cut tiles become necessary — decide whether or not it is worth starting all over again with a slightly adjusted starting point beneath the window.

Similarly, if the line runs past (or up against) an obstacle mounted on the wall — a bath, for example — work out how the tile rows will fit round it. Again, if such obstacles pose severe problems, you may decide it is worth adjusting the starting point at the window to make things easier. Incidentally, where such obstacles prevent you continuing

TILING ROUND OBSTACLES

1 When you have to fit tiles round obstacles such as light switches, or where L-shaped pieces of tile are required at the corners of window openings, the easiest way of ensuring an accurate, crack-free cut is to use a special tile saw — rather like a coping saw for woodwork. Grip the tile securely in a vice and cut steadily along the marked line.

2 Test each cut piece carefully for fit round the obstacle, and trim it slightly if necessary using a tile file or similar abrasive. Then butter some adhesive on to its rear face and press it into position. Check that it sits flush with its neighbours, then grout the joints neatly to complete the job. If the faceplate screws are long enough, you can release them and set the tile edges behind the faceplate.

the guide line along the foot of the wall, strike a vertical guide line, measure up this in whole tile-plus-grout units to a point above the obstacle, then restart the horizontal guide line from there. Reverse the procedure to return the guide line to the foot of the wall once you are past the obstacle.

The final stage of the setting out procedure for complete rooms is to work out how the vertical columns of tiles fit in with the room's corners and any other obstacles. Starting at the vertical guide line beneath the window, merely use the gauge rod to step off tile widths along the horizontal guide line. As usual, the aim is to come up with an arrangement that avoids the need for awkward fitting and narrow cut tiles. Here, however, if you encounter a problem on any wall other than the one containing the window, there is usually no need to go right back to the beginning and try a slightly different starting point. Instead, for the purpose of setting out tile columns, you can treat each wall as a separate entity, adjusting the column's positions as necessary to achieve an easy-to-tile, reasonably symmetrical arrangement.

Whatever you do, take care at the corners of the room. If the finished wall is to look right, it is important to maintain some visual continuity between the tiling on the two adjacent walls. In theory, the best way to do this is to use the off-cuts from the tiles on one wall to begin tiling on the next — this having the added advantage of saving work as well as saving tiles. However, it is not always such a good idea in practice. If the walls are out of square, the off-cuts may need some delicate trimming before they fit. What's more, the use of off-cuts in this way may not give the best column arrangement on the second wall. Once again, you will have to use your own judgement. Make use of off-cuts to fill in by all means, but not to the detriment of the tiling as a whole.

Now that you know, more or less, the position of every tile in the room, you can move on to the actual tiling. This is carried out in just the same way as when tiling a small splashback. However, you will need to know how to cut more complex tile shapes. Let's start with the L-shapes needed around windows, doors, and similar obstacles. Mark out the line along which the cut is to be made in pencil, then score along it with a tile cutter, as usual remembering to score through any glaze on the tile edges to ensure a clean break. You now take a pair of carpenter's pincers and nibble away the waste material a little at the time. You will find it easier to nibble away the waste area of tile if you cross-hatch it first using your tile cutter. When you have removed as much as you can safely with the pliers — there is a risk of snapping the tile in two — neaten the cut edges with a file.

The same technique can be adapted to cut more complex shapes in the edges of tiles. Alternatively, consider using a special saw. The most widely available type is a bit like a fretsaw, fitted with a specially hardened blade similar to an *Abrafile*. But what about cutting round something like a pipe that passes through the middle of a tile? The trick is to cut the tile neatly in two along a line running through the centre of the desired hole, then to cut the outline of half the hole in each half of the tile using the technique described above. Once the tile has been stuck in place on the wall, the join between the halves of the tile will hardly show.

Applying mosaics

Mosaics have to be among the oldest of all forms of interior decoration, but to produce one these days, you don't have to mess about chipping bits of marble exactly to fit, or set each piece in by hand, laboriously building up the finished design fragment by fragment. Instead, you can buy modern ceramic mosaics. These are made up, not of stone, but of a series of small glazed ceramic tiles. The really clever thing about them is that you don't have to assemble the surface bit by bit. The tiny tiles come already arranged in the correct order, temporarily stuck in place on a backing sheet of fabric or covered with a facing sheet of paper.

Creating a perfect mosaic-covered surface is therefore almost as easy as hanging wallpaper. Measure up the area you wish to cover, taking two or three readings in different places for both the length and breadth just in case it is out of square. Now, working to the smallest reading for each dimension, cut the mosaic sheet to size with a pair of scissors, following the gaps between the rows of tiles — leave the sheet fractionally undersize if necessary, rather than make it too large.

If the resulting trimmed sheet is too large to be handled comfortably, cut it up into sections and lay each one separately. In this case, though, do take care to leave the correct gap between the tiny tiles at the edges of the sections when you come to reassemble the mosaic on the surface. With the sections still stuck to their backing sheets, you can usually judge this by eye, taking the spacings between tiles in the centre of each sheet as a guide. And if the mosaic has to fit round an obstruction such as a tap? Just lay the sheet in its final position on the surface, and snip out as many whole fragments as necessary to obtain the best possible fit.

The next step is to apply a layer of the recommended adhesive to the surface with a serrated spreader (often provided), covering an area the same size as the trimmed mosaic sheet. Now, just lay the sheet in place (paper-facing uppermost, fabric down) aiming to centre it on the area it is to cover, and smooth it over with a soft cloth or soft paint roller to bed each of the small tiles in place. Once the adhesive has set, carefully peel back away the backing paper (you may need to soak it first) and begin filling in any wide gaps around the edges with cut tiles.

This has the potential for being a rather fiddly chore, but fortunately, since minor inaccuracies tend not to show, you don't have to be too particular. Just nibble away at the tiles — taken from an off-cut of the main sheet — using a pair of carpenter's pincers until they fit. You may find this easier if you grip the tile you are working on in a pair of pliers. Constantly check the fit of each piece as you work, and when you are satisfied, coat the back with a little adhesive and pop it into place.

Once you have completed the mosaic, all that remains is to grout the joins between tiles — grout can also be used to fill gaps around the edges that proved too small to fill with tiles. Don't bother to treat each join individually as you would with full-size ceramic tiles. Apply the grout thickly over the entire surface, scraping off the bulk of the excess and working the grout right down into the gaps with the spreader as you go. Similarly, don't attempt to neaten individual joins. When the grout has hardened sufficiently, just wipe over the surface with a damp sponge or cloth. That done, all that remains is to wait until the grout has hardened completely, and then wash and polish the surface down in the usual way.

Cork tiling

Cork tiles are also worth considering as a finish for walls. As well as being attractive, and thick enough to cover up minor imperfections in the surface, they can help to deaden echoes within the room (useful if the room has a hard floor-

LAYING MOSAICS

1 & 2 *Fabric-backed mosaics are bonded to a net backing for ease of handling, but are laid in the same way as other ceramic tiles. Start by marking setting-out lines on the surface to be tiled. Then spread an area of adhesive slightly larger than the sheet, and bed it in place. Press it down firmly into the adhesive for a good bond.*

3 & 4 *Cut through the mesh backing with scissors to remove unwanted areas of the mosaic at the edges of the tiled area. Small cut pieces of mosaic will fill any gaps that are left. With obstacles such as a shower waste outlet, lay the sheet over it and then snip away whole pieces of mosaic as required.*

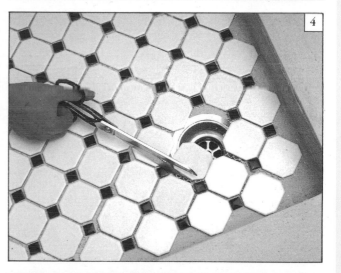

5 & 6 *Cut small pieces of mosaic to fit gaps at edges and round obstacles by nibbling away the unwanted portions with pincers or special tile nibblers. Then stick each cut piece in position with a blob of adhesive. When all the mosaics are in place, grout the whole area as for ordinary tiling, and polish the surface with a cloth.*

FIXING CORK TILES

1 & 2 *When fixing cork tiles to a wall surface, start by marking out a true horizontal line across the wall. Then find the midpoint and draw a vertical line here to indicate your starting point. Move it half a tile width to one side if the layout requires very narrow strips at the edge of the tiled area. Then apply adhesive to the wall.*

3 & 4 *Spread a thin layer of adhesive on the back of each tile using the notched spreader supplied. Then press the first tile into place on the wall, lining it up carefully with the vertical and horizontal guidelines. Make sure that it is well stuck by pressing it all over with the palms of your hands.*

5 & 6 *At the edges of the tiled area, mark the width of the gap on a whole tile and cut it down to size with scissors or a sharp craft knife. Test its fit, then spread adhesive on its rear face and press it into position. Where you are tiling round an external corner, fit a corner trim of wood, metal or plastic to protect the crumbly edges of the tiles from damage.*

covering), and warm up the surface. However, don't choose them solely because you want to improve the wall's sound and/or thermal insulation. They are not nearly thick enough to stop unwanted noise entering the room, nor for that matter are they usually thick enough to prevent heat escaping.

You should also think twice about using this type of wall-covering as a cure for condensation. Although it should provide sufficient insulation to warm the wall to the point where condensation will no longer form on the surface, this cannot be guaranteed. You could just end up with soggy cork tiles, instead of damp wallpaper. In addition, there is a chance that this sort of treatment for condensation could make matters worse elsewhere, unless you also take steps to tackle the root cause of the problem — high humidity levels — by improving your home's heating and ventilation.

How do you put them up? As when using ceramic tiles, start with some setting out. Let's suppose you are tiling a single wall as a special feature of the decor. Strike a vertical guide line exactly half way along the wall using either a plumb-line or a spirit-level that will test verticals. Now with the aid of a spirit-level, strike a horizontal guide line through this exactly half way along its length — in other words, exactly half way up the wall. If you now start tiling with four tiles set around the intersection of these two lines, you will finish with the perfectly symmetrical arrangement you need.

But don't start tiling just yet. First check on the sizes of any cut tiles needed to fill in at the top, bottom, and sides of the wall. Simply step off along both the horizontal and vertical guide lines in whole tile widths marking the positions of the joins between tiles as you go. You can use a spare tile as a gauge for this. Cork tiles simply butt together, so there is no need to bother with a gauge rod to ensure an even grouting allowance. If you find that the cut tiles needed are too narrow to be cut easily — treat 25-50mm (1-2in) as a practical minimum — move the appropriate guide line by the width of half a whole tile. To correct for narrow tiles at the top and bottom, move the horizontal guide line up or down. To correct for narrow tiles at the sides, move the vertical guide line to the left or right.

Now you can start tiling, starting with the four tiles that cluster around the intersection of the horizontal and vertical guide lines. Simply spread a thin coat of contact adhesive on to the wall with a smooth plastic spreader, aiming to cover an area equivalent to about four whole tiles at a time, then apply a similarly thin coat to the back of each tile, and allow the adhesive on both tile and wall to become almost touch dry. Offer the tile up to the wall, with its edge just touching the surface so you can check its position, then 'hinge' it down flat against the surface and smooth into place with a soft clean cloth. If you are using very thin, flexible tiles, begin smoothing in the centre and work out towards the edges to avoid trapping bubbles of air.

Although obviously slightly inaccurate, this method of positioning the tile with only its edge touching the surface

is necessary. Most contact adhesives grip hard the moment the two layers of adhesive come together. Even if you go for a contact adhesive that claims to allow some adjustment after the surfaces are brought together, you will find that the amount of adjustment possible tends to be rather small.

There is one other point to consider when choosing the adhesive. Most conventional contacts use petroleum-based solvent, and therefore give off fairly heady and highly inflammable fumes as they dry out. So, if you decide to use this type, make sure the room is really well ventilated, and don't allow naked lights to come anywhere near. Certain mixtures of solvent fumes and air are more than inflammable — they can explode. If you cannot meet these safety requirements for any reason, be sure to choose one of the more modern water-based contact adhesives. You may, in any case, find using these more comfortable, because with these the 'fumes' are nothing more than water vapour.

Once the first four tiles are in place, continue tiling out along the four arms of the cross formed by the guide line, butting each tile tight against its neighbour, until you reach the point where cut tiles are needed to fill in around the edges of the wall. You should now go back and cover the rest of the wall as far as you can using whole tiles. This may sound a slightly strange way to set about things, but you should find it appreciably quicker than simply working outwards for the four centre tiles in a more or less *ad hoc* fashion.

With all the whole tiles in place, turn your attention to filling in the gaps around the edges with cut tiles. As with ceramic tiling, measure the width of each cut tile at both sides to allow for the fact that the wall may be out of square and transfer these measurements, the right way round, on to the face of the tile with a pencil. Finally, join up with a pencil line to indicate the line of the cut. As for actually cutting the tile, so long as the tile is not too thick, a pair of strong scissors will do the job. However, some cork tiles are rather crumbly, and so you will probably find that a sharp craft knife leaves a far neater edge. Simply place the tile on a flat surface — a sheet of scrap hardboard is ideal, because it doesn't matter if it gets scratched as the knife breaks through — lay a metal straightedge along the line of the cut, and run the knife along its edge two or three times until you are through. The cut tile can then be stuck in place on the wall in the normal way.

To complete the tiling, vacuum the surface of the wall to remove any dirt and dust clinging to the tiles and inspect it closely for gaps, and chipped edges. This is not to suggest that your workmanship is at fault. Some tiles crumble so easily it's very difficult to put them up without doing a certain amount of damage, and this, coupled with the fact that few cork tiles are absolutely square, makes a few defects of this sort almost inevitable. Often effective repairs can be made merely by breaking chips of cork from waste off-cuts and glueing them into place with a little PVA woodworking adhesive — any that oozes out should be wiped off immediately with a damp cloth. Very narrow gaps, unfortunately, don't respond easily to this treatment. Really all you can do is camouflage them with a little paint.

All that remains is to seal the surface. Unless you have bought ready-sealed tiles, the cork needs some protection against airborne moisture and dirt. A polyurethane varnish is perhaps the best choice for the job as it also helps strengthen the cork against physical damage. It's up to you whether you use one with a gloss, matt, or satin finish, but you will need at least two or three coats to obtain a satisfactory result. Dilute the first coat with a little white spirit according to the manufacturer's instructions and lightly rub this into the cork with a soft, lint-free cloth, taking care not to damage the tiles in the process. This should effectively seal the surface ready for the finishing coats, which you apply unthinned using an ordinary paint brush. For the best results, allow each coat to dry thoroughly before applying the next. On smooth cork tiles, it is also worth lightly rubbing down the surface between coats using fine grade wire wool, glasspaper, or silicon carbide abrasive used dry. In this case, wipe over with a damp cloth to remove dust, and leave to dry off before continuing.

Tiling ceilings

Just as tiles offer a speedy and effective cover-up for less than perfect walls, so too can they be used to give a ceiling that's in poor condition an attractive decorative finish. There are two types of tile commonly used for the purpose – expanded polystyrene tiles, and tongued-and-grooved fibre tiles. Both are put up in an entirely different way, so let's take them one at a time, starting with the procedure for those in polystyrene.

Start with the setting out. This is carried out in broadly the same way as for cork wall tiling. Measure up the room and, using a chalked line, strike guide lines on the ceiling between the mid-points of opposite walls. They will cross

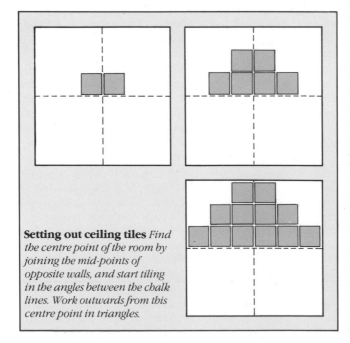

Setting out ceiling tiles *Find the centre point of the room by joining the mid-points of opposite walls, and start tiling in the angles between the chalk lines. Work outwards from this centre point in triangles.*

in the exact centre of the room, and this is where you should begin tiling, with four tiles set in the angles between the chalk guide lines, in order to give the tiled ceiling an attractive looking symmetry. There is, however, one possible exception to this rule, and that is where a pendant light forms the dominant feature of the ceiling. In this case, decide whether the ceiling might not look better with a group of tiles clustered around the ceiling rose. If you think it does, work out as accurately as you can where the edges of these tiles will fall and restrike the guide lines accordingly – in line with the outer edges of two of these tiles, so that you don't have to start the tiling with the fiddly job of cutting tiles to shape.

As usual, though, before putting up a single tile, check that the cut tiles needed around the edge of the room are a reasonable size – anything over 25mm (1in) is about right – by stepping off whole tile widths along the guide lines. Where there are chimney breasts to be fitted round, and alcoves and window bays to be tiled into, check what will happen to the tiles there. Reposition the starting guide lines as necessary until you have achieved a satisfactory arrangement – one that gives a reasonable constant border of adequately wide cut tiles around the walls, and one that avoids awkward cutting in around chimney breasts and other external angles.

There is one last check to make, and that is to ensure that the final guide lines look right. If the room is badly out of square, tiles laid to guide lines that are correct according to the text book can sometimes look rather odd, and in such circumstances it is usually worth cheating a little, restriking the lines in a compromise position that fits in better with the shape of the room. Just make sure that the guide lines end up crossing each other at right-angles.

You can now start putting up the tiles, following the same order of work as described for cork tiling a wall. Begin with the tiles at the intersection of the two guide lines, then lay a row of tiles along each guide line, fill in between the arms of this tiled cross as far as possible using whole tiles, then finish off by filling in around the edges of the room with cut tiles tailored to fit. You'll find actually cutting very easy indeed. Just use a sharp knife and a straightedge in the same way as when cutting cork tiles. But do take care not to mark the tiles as you press them into place – they are quite soft. Don't use your hands for this job. Instead, make up a flat pressing board from scrap plywood with a block of softwood for a handle. If you must use your hands, at least protect the tile you are fixing by covering it with a spare tile to spread the load. It is also worth making sure your hands are clean before handling the tiles – they get dirty easily and finger marks are not easily washed off.

There are just a few final points to watch concerning the long-term safety of the ceiling. Always buy good quality tiles – ones containing a fire retardant. Always use an adhesive specially designed for use with polystyrene tiles, and follow the maker's recommendations on using it – the usual recommendation these days is to set the tiles in a continuous bed of adhesive rather than with a blob of adhesive in

FIXING POLYSTYRENE CEILING TILES

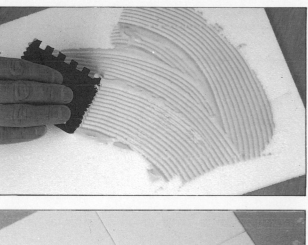

1 *When you have completed the setting-out and know where tiling will start on the ceiling, spread special polystyrene adhesive all over the back of each tile; don't rely on just a blob at each corner of the tile.*

2 *Start fixing the tiles against your guidelines, working from the centre of the room out towards the walls. Where there is a central ceiling rose, trim the corners of the tiles to fit round it.*

3 *Press each tile into place carefully, aligning it with its neighbours. Beware of denting the tiles with your fingers; it's better to use an offcut of hardboard or something similar to press them into position.*

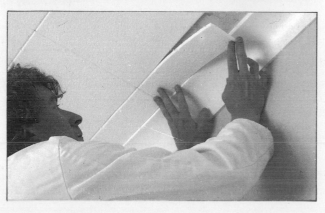

4 *At the perimeter of the ceiling, measure and cut narrow strips to fit the gap. Test the fit dry first, then spread adhesive on the back and press the strip into place carefully.*

each corner as was once common practice. Finally, never paint polystyrene tiles. If you do and there is a fire in the room, the paint film will counteract the safety effects of the two previous precautions. It really is very dangerous.

And what about tongued-and-grooved fibre tiles? There are two main differences between using these and putting up any other kind of tile. The first is that they are not stuck in place. They are fixed to slim timber battens. Secondly, you should begin fixing them in one corner of the room, rather than in the centre of the ceiling.

You still need to set the tiles out properly though. Strike chalk guide lines in the usual way to determine the size and position of the ceiling's cut tile border, then use panel pins to fix a 50 x 12mm (2 x ½in) softwood batten parallel to a wall adjoining the corner at which you intend to begin tiling. Use sawn softwood battens, incidentally — their rough finish will be covered by the tiles, and they are cheaper. But how do you decide which wall to place the batten against? Obviously it is preferable not to choose one containing obstacles such as chimney breasts and alcoves, but there is another consideration. The timber battens must be run at right-angles to the ceiling joists so that their fixing pins can be driven securely into the joists' timber, rather than into the ceiling's plasterboard or lath and plaster skin — they won't grip otherwise.

You must therefore take the time to locate the exact position of each joist, and having found them, it's a good idea to mark the lines of their centres on the ceiling's surface with a chalk line. Locating the joists in an upstairs room where you have access to the loft is easiest. Once in the loft you can poke through the ceiling with a bradawl or something similar to indicate the position of each side of any given joist. There is no need to mark every joist in this way. Once you know the spacing between a pair of joists and the direction in which they run, you can measure to find the line of the remainder on the ceiling below — they are generally parallel and evenly spaced. And if you cannot gain direct access to the joists? All you can do is drill a series of test holes up through the ceiling until you strike wood.

Once the first tiling batten is in position, fix a second along the line of the joints between the cut tile border and the first row of whole tiles. You now continue adding battens across the ceiling with their centres one whole tile apart. Measure the first gap using an actual tile. For the rest, you will find spacing quicker if you make up a gauge from scrap softwood. Simply recess the ends of this with a saw so that the distance between the recesses is equal to the distance between battens. By running the gauge along between battens you can also check that they are parallel to each other.

Having completed the battening, cut a tile to fit the corner of the cut tile border, and secure this to the first and second battens using either small panel pins or a heavy-duty stapler — the latter is quicker and allows you to work one-handed. Those that form the fixing to the second batten should be driven through the top lip of the tile's grooved edge. Now, work out from this corner tile along

This unusual bathroom **left** makes excellent use of the water resistance of ceramic tiles. They have been used to tile the custom-built bath and shower area, and the same tiles have been taken up the walls to shoulder height as a splashback. Note that the size of the bath has been gauged to avoid the need for cut tiles.

Tiles provide the perfect decoration for this combined bath and basin surround **above** and their use on the walls above give the whole room a unified look. Again, careful planning has avoided unnecessary tile cutting.

Floor-to-ceiling tiling is the perfect answer for a modern style washing area such as this **right**. The pale overall colour is brightened by the unusual use of surface-mounted conduits for the light and power supplies.

FIXING CEILING TILES TO BATTENS

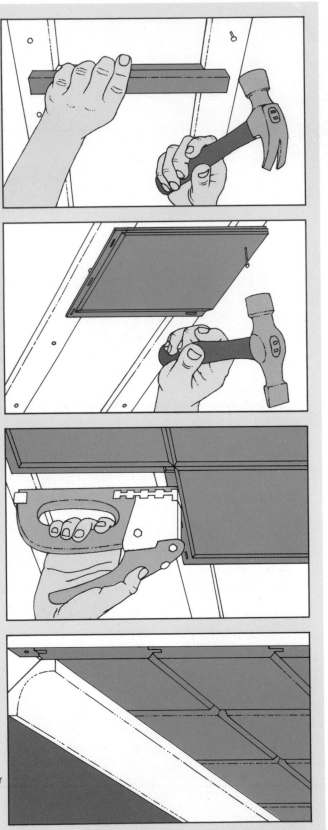

1 *Start by nailing slim timber battens to the ceiling surface at right angles to the joists. Use a timber spacer to ensure that the battens are truly parallel and the right distance apart.*

2 *Begin tiling at one edge of the room, pinning through the face of the tile into the perimeter batten. Punch the pin head just below the surface and disguise it with filler.*

3 *Continue tiling by locating the groove of each tile over the exposed tongue of the previous one, and stapling through its tongue into the batten beneath. A staple gun is essential, as it leaves the other hand free to position the tile.*

4 *Either fill the last row with small pieces of cut tile, or disguise the edges of the tiles by fixing a decorative cornice right round the room. Lightweight types can be fixed in place with adhesive.*

both adjacent walls, fixing the remaining cut tiles in place in the same way, again with their tongued edges pointing in towards the centre of the room.

With these two rows in place, it's a relatively simple matter to tile outwards from the corner, using whole tiles. Simply slot their tongues into the grooves of the preceding tile, and secure their tongued edges to a batten with pins or staples. The only likely hitch will come when you reach a pendant light fitting. The rose will have to be removed and remounted on the surface of the tiles. This can wait until the tiling is complete, but for now, turn off the power at the mains, remove the ceiling rose, and draw the cables that come out of the ceiling through a hole cut in the tile at that point just before you fix it in place. Once all the whole tiles have been put up, finish off the ceiling by fixing cut tiles along the two remaining sides of the room, securing them to battens run along the ceiling next to the walls. You will probably have to cut these slightly undersize in order to locate their tongued edges in the grooves of the adjacent whole tiles, but this gap can be easily concealed beneath a decorative coving. It is, in any case, a good idea to use coving to neaten all the edges of the ceiling. It will cover up any accidental gaps between cut tiles and wall, as well as concealing the exposed heads of the pins used to fix the cut tiles to the wall battens.

THE COMPLETE
PANELLER

CLADDING WALLS   272
FIXING BATTENS 273

CLADDING CEILINGS   273
FIXING CLADDING 274 ♦ COPING WITH OBSTACLES AND CORNERS 275
FINISHING TOUCHES 276 ♦ FIXING WALLBOARDS 277

When it comes to finding a way to both decorate and cover up a wall or ceiling that's in really poor condition, panelling is hard to beat. It's not a particularly cheap treatment and to do it properly does involve a fair amount of hard work, but then, unlike so many other forms of decoration, you can view it as a more or less permanent addition to your home – a genuine improvement. And it is undeniably attractive.

There are basically two types of material you can use for the job. For genuine timber cladding, tongued and grooved softwood matchboarding is the usual choice. Widely available from good timber yards and DIY stores it allows you a number of subtle variations on the basic theme. For example, you can alter the look of the cladding by staining it, or by putting it up in an unusual way — perhaps diagonally to form chevrons. Even the type of varnish you choose to seal it, whether gloss, matt or satin finish, can have a surprisingly great effect.

This is, unfortunately, one of the most expensive forms of cladding, but even if your budget won't stretch to it, you can still achieve the same sort of look using the second cladding option — wallboards. These are basically sheets of tough plywood or hardboard printed or veneered to look like a genuine article. The surface is usually embossed to create the illusion of tongued and grooved joints between planks, but you are not restricted solely to a matchboarding finish: wallboards are also available with tile effects, as well as in plain colours for where you want a really chic lacquered look.

Whichever you choose, you will find that although putting it up takes time, it's not very difficult. Let's look at how you would set about creating a single clad feature wall.

Cladding walls

Although wallboards will cover-up a good many faults, they won't tolerate dampness, so do make sure that the wall you intend to clad is free from penetrating and rising damp. As an additional precaution, line an *exterior* wall with heavy-gauge polyethylene (polythene) sheeting. This can be taped into place (the cladding will provide a more permanent fixing) provided adjacent sheets overlap by at least 150mm (6in). To complete the final preparation, remove all skirting boards and picture rails, plus door and window architraves, from the relevant wall.

If you are putting up genuine matchboarding, you must cover the wall with a framework of softwood battens to provide suitable fixing points for the cladding — 50 x 25mm (2 x 1in) sawn softwood is adequate. For vertical cladding, fix one batten at the top of the wall and one at the bottom, then add further intermediate battens at roughly 600mm (24in) centres. For horizontal cladding, fix the bat-

tens vertically — one at each end of the wall; then at approximately 600mm (24in) centres in between.

Use a spirit-level/plumb-line to make sure the battens are truly horizontal/vertical, and check that the faces of the battens represent a reasonably flat surface to which the cladding can be fixed. Any inaccuracies in the wall can simply be corrected by inserting packing pieces of scrap plywood behind the battens before fixing them in place. For speed, secure the battens to masonry walls using masonry nails; on stud partition walls use ordinary wood nails, but do make sure you drive these into the wall's timber framework, not just into the plasterboard skin. The framework's vertical studs are generally spaced about 600mm (24in) apart and can be located by drilling test holes through the plasterboard with a drill and a small diameter twist bit. Tapping the wall gives a good indication of where to start drilling — it sounds less hollow over a stud (a vertical baulk of timber to which plasterboard is nailed).

With all the battens in place, begin putting up the cladding. Start at one edge of the wall and position the first board with its grooved edge facing into the corner, securing this edge to the battens by driving small panel pins at an angle through one lip of the groove. Fix the tongued edge to the battens by driving in further pins just where the tongue emerges from the body of the board. Again drive these at an angle so that they emerge obliquely through the underside of the board's body. This is called 'secret nailing' and allows you to secure the second board merely by sliding its groove over the first board's tongue. The tongued edge of this second board is now pinned to the battens using the same secret nailing technique. If you find secret nailing difficult, special clips are available which allow you to secure the tongued edges of the boarding without it.

Continue in this way until you come to the very last board; it almost certainly won't fit, so plane its tongued edge down until it does, then remove just enough extra to allow its groove to be located over the neighbouring board's tongue. Finally, secure the remaining free edge — the one you planed — with pins driven into the battens through the face of the board. Their exposed heads, together with any gaps around the cladding due to inaccurate cutting or variations in the line of adjacent walls, can be covered with decorative wooden moulding. Similar defects at the top of the wall can be covered by ceiling coving, while those at the bottom will be hidden when you replace the skirting board.

Once you know how to clad a single wall, it is but a small step to apply the technique to a room as a whole. In fact, the only real difference is that you need to know how to get round obstacles such as doors and windows, and how to turn internal and external corners. The methods described

1 *The first stage in cladding a wall with tongued-and-grooved timber is to fix a network of supporting battens to the wall surface. Begin by fixing horizontal battens at floor and ceiling level; then add a batten at each edge of the wall. Remove skirting boards and architraves if they're fitted.*

2 *Add further intermediate battens at roughly 600mm (24in) centres to provide extra support for the cladding. Here the boards will be fixed vertically, so horizontal battens are used. An offcut of timber helps to ensure even spacing.*

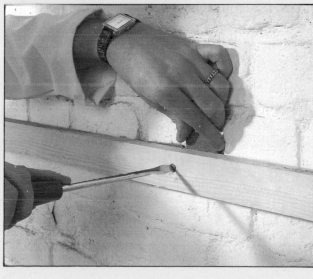

3 *To get a true finished surface to the cladding on an uneven wall, the battens may have to be packed out. Test them with a straightedge; where hollows are found, release the screws and insert packing pieces of hardboard or thick card before tightening up the fixing screws again.*

below are for vertical matchboarding, but if your cladding is horizontal, you should have no difficult whatsoever in adapting them to suit.

Let's start with external corners. Having butt-jointed the battens at that point to provide adequate support, clad up to the corner as far as the last board, then begin cladding the adjacent wall in the usual way. You can now finish off the cladding on the first wall, planing the tongued edge of its final board flush with the cladding around the corner. Fix this free edge by pinning through the board's face into the tongued edge of the first board on the second wall. Much the same technique is used for internal corners. Here though, it is simply a matter of planing down the tongued edge of the last board on the first wall until it fits into the gap left once the first board on the adjacent wall has been fixed in place.

Doors and windows can be a little trickier. The simplest way to clad round them is to surround them completely with battens, then clad round these in the same way as an external corner to leave a neat finish. Alternatively, with a door, you can widen the door lining to leave it flush with the clad surface, and neaten the join by covering it with architrave. In this case, the door must obviously be re-hung. There is another option, too, for windows set into a reveal. If the window frame is thick enough, you can turn the cladding into the reveal and rely on the frame to conceal the final edge — a decorative beading should help. Lastly, don't forget about light switches. It's best to resite these, together with their mounting boxes, so that they finish flush with the surface of the cladding, but to do this, the cladding will need extra support, so frame the old switch position with battens.

And what about wallboards? Like matchboarding, these can be simply pinned in place on battens. But there is an easier alternative, and that is to stick them in place directly to the wall using a special gap-filling panel adhesive. The adhesive comes in cartridges from which it is extruded with a special gun in the same way as mastic and caulking. All you do is apply it to the wall in stripes (though do check the manufacturer's instructions), and press the cut-to-size board firmly into place.

This method does, however, pre-suppose that the walls are in reasonably good condition. If they are not, consider getting the best of both worlds by combining the two techniques — glueing the wallboards to battening. The battens help accommodate any defects in the wall, and the adhesive gives you an invisible fixing.

Cladding ceilings

The exact method used to clad a ceiling tends to depend not so much on what type of cladding you intend to use, as on why you want to clad the ceiling in the first place. If it is simply a question of giving the surface a tongued and grooved look, then you can proceed in the same way as when cladding a wall — pin the cladding in place; don't rely on adhesive. There are only three important differences. First, you will have to remount any ceiling roses on the sur-

FIXING CLADDING

1 & 2 *Cut the first board to be fitted to length, and offer its tongued edge up to the side wall so you can see how uneven this is. If there are gaps here and there, it's best to scribe the wall profile on to the board with a pencil and a small block of wood, and to saw along the line with a jigsaw or padsaw to ensure a perfect fit.*

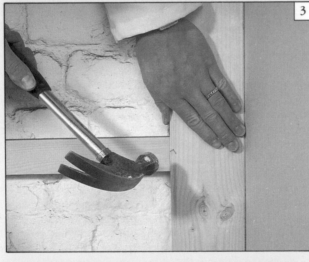

3 & 4 *Offer the scribed board up into the corner, checking that it is tightly butted against the other wall, and drive pins through the tongue into the battens to hold it in place. Then slide the groove of the second board over the tongue of the first, and tap it home using a cladding offcut to protect the tongue. Pin as before.*

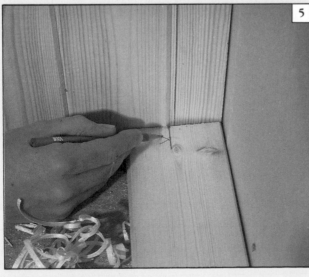

5 & 6 *When the last whole plank has been pinned in place, mark the width of the narrow strip needed to complete the cladding. If the wall surface is uneven, scribe and saw its long edge first. Then offer the strip up and fix it in place by driving pins through the face of the board into the battens. Punch in the nail heads.*

face of the cladding. This is done in much the same way as when repositioning a lightswitch on a wall. Second, there is no need to worry too much about concealing gaps and exposed nail heads around the perimeter of the clad area — framing the ceiling with a decorative wooden moulding used in the same way as ordinary coving gives excellent results. And finally, you must make sure that the supporting timber battens are nailed to the ceiling joists for the same reason that, when cladding a stud partition wall, you must make the fixings into the wall's supporting studs — the plasterboard or lath-and-plaster skin doesn't provide a strong enough anchorage.

If, on the other hand, your reason for choosing cladding as a finish is that you want to physically lower the ceiling level in order to alter the proportions of the room, then a slightly different approach is required. The fact is that the thickness of ordinary battens and cladding are unlikely to make a great deal of difference. Instead, you must construct what's known as a suspended ceiling — more accurately, a false ceiling set well below the level of the original. In this case, although the method of applying the cladding remains the same, the system of battening required is rather more complex — mainly because it needs to be a good deal stronger in order to carry the weight of the cladding all on its own.

You should therefore start by deciding on the new ceiling height and by drawing a line right round the walls of the room at the appropriate level, less the thickness of the cladding, with the aid of a spirit-level and a long, straight timber batten. This line can now be used as a guide to positioning the ceiling's main supports — lengths of 75 x 50mm (3 x 2in) sawn softwood screwed to the walls. Known as wallplates, these must be very firmly fixed indeed. This means that, as usual, if you are dealing with a stud partition you must make the fixings into the the wall's supporting timber studs. If you are fixing to a masonry wall, the use of good quality wallplugs should give sufficient strength.

You see, the wallplates' job is to carry the weight of the new joists used to support the ceiling's cladding. Also made from 75 x 50mm (3 x 2in) softwood, these should be spaced at roughly 400mm (16in) centres and fixed to the wallplates on opposite walls using simple halving joints. You must therefore work out the best arrangement for the suspended ceiling's structural timber work at an early stage in order to notch the wallplates ready to receive the joists, before any of the timbers are fixed in place.

There is another reason for carefully planning the job before you start work. Joists of this size have a tendency to sag under their own weight and the weight of the cladding. If they are made to span a distance of more than about 2m (80in), this sag can be significant, so, on most ceilings, additional support must be provided. This additional support comes in the form of vertical timbers called hangers — hence the name, suspended ceiling. Fixed between the new timberwork and the original ceiling, they simply transfer some of the load to the latter's heavier supporting joists.

No complicated joints are needed here. The hangers can

COPING WITH OBSTACLES AND CORNERS

1 *Where the cladding will be fixed round obstacles such as light switches and power points, fix short lengths of batten to the wall to support the cladding. If you have flush-mounted fittings, they must be repositioned so the edge of the mounting box is flush with the cladding.*

2 *Mark the size of cut-out needed in each length of cladding surrounding the obstacle, then make the cut-outs with a jigsaw or coping saw. Pin each piece in place to the battens, then reconnect the faceplate and attach it to the box before restoring the power supply.*

3 *At external corners, fix a complete strip to the second face of the wall with its edge flush with the surface of the battens on the first face (A). Then saw or plane down the tongued edge of another strip (B) and pin it in place so it overlaps the edge of strip (A).*

4 *At internal corners, use a similar technique. Fit the whole strip (A) to the second wall first, then cut a strip down to width to complete the first wall (B). Pin it in place through its face.*

FINISHING TOUCHES

1 *Either fit completely new skirting boards across the newly-clad wall, or else re-fix original cladding that was removed earlier.*

2 *If the edges of the cladding look a little ragged, you can improve their appearance by pinning slim quadrant or scotia beading all the way round. Punch in the heads of the fixing nails ready for filling.*

3 *Use wood stopping in a colour that matches the cladding to fill any visible nail holes. Press it in with a filling knife, leave to harden, then sand smooth for an almost invisible repair.*

4 *Finish off the cladding by giving it three coats of clear polyurethane varnish. Apply the first with a cloth pad, after thinning the varnish with about 10 per cent white spirit. Then brush on the next two coats, making sure that the joints are well treated. Sand lightly between coats.*

merely be screwed on to the sides of the new ceiling joists. There is, however, a choice of methods when it comes to fixing the hangers to the original ceiling joists, and you must decide which is most convenient in the circumstances. If you can gain access to the void above the original ceiling, the simplest method is to just poke the hangers through the old ceiling's skin and screw them directly to the sides of the original joists. The success of this method, though, obviously depends on the old and new joist being in just the right place. You could try deliberately arranging things so that the new timbers are in just the right position, but, in practice, this approach tends to be harder work than adopting the alternative fixing technique.

This is simply to fix the hangers to yet another timber — one on the underside of the old ceiling, held in place by stout screws driven through the ceiling's skin into the joists above. The obvious snag with this method is that you have to locate the exact positions of the old ceiling's joists, but as we have already seen elsewhere in this book, that's not difficult. Just drill a series of test holes through the ceiling with an electric drill and a small diameter bit until you bore into the timber of a joist. A more real problem is that, where the new joists run at right angles to the originals, you are unlikely to find an original joist in exactly the right position — that is along the line of the joist hangers. There are ways to obtain a secure fixing for the joist hangers' support timber in spite of this (involving yet more timberwork above or below the ceiling's skin), but it is generally simpler to make the fixing to the old joist closest to the optimum position. This shouldn't weaken the structure too much, but if you are worried, build in an additional set of hangers to bring the unsupported joist span within acceptable limits.

There is just one final point to bear in mind. It concerns the fixing of the cladding itself. Instead of using a pin hammer and panel pins, it is well worth considering using a heavy-duty staple gun to fix the matchboarding or wallboards in place. There are plenty of models capable of firing the necessary extra long staples through wood, and if you don't think it worth buying one just for this job, you shouldn't have too much difficulty in hiring a suitable tool.

Of course, all that timberwork does put up the cost of your new ceiling, but at least the result is every bit as permanent as the original. What's more, with the structural timberwork in place, you are actually not restricted merely to cladding the ceiling. You can build a genuinely new ceiling by covering the joists with sheets of plasterboard.

Starting in one corner of the room, put up as many whole sheets as you can — standard sheets of plasterboard measure 2440 x 1220mm (8 x 4ft) so you will need help — fixing it to the new joists with plasterboard nails. Complete the 'row' with a cut sheet, then use the off-cut from this to begin a second row, the idea being to stagger the joins between sheets as far as possible. Completely cover the ceiling in this way then neaten the joints between boards using joint filler, joint tape and joint finish — this is a good deal easier if you use taper-edged plasterboard. Basically, all you do is fill the depression created by the taper where two

FIXING WALLBOARDS

1 & 2 *Wallboards need support at the edges and at intervals in between. Fix battens to the wall surface at spacings to suit the board dimensions, and back out any low spots. Then measure the floor-to-ceiling height, cut the first board to length and offer it up to the battens.*

3 & 4 *Line the board up with the centre of the vertical batten and drive in the fixing pins. Use more pins to secure the board to the intermediate supporting battens. Where only part of a board is needed to finish off the wall, the quickest way of cutting it to size is with a power jigsaw.*

5 & 6 *Complete the cladding by offering up the cut-to-size section and pinning it to the battens. Finish off the area if necessary by pinning beading round the perimeter.*

If the wall surface is flat and true, the panels can be fixed in place with special panel adhesive instead of being pinned to battens. Simply apply the adhesive to the wall and press the panel into position.

boards meet, bed the tape into the filler while it is still wet, then, when the filler has set, cover with a layer of joint finish, feathering this out across the adjacent boards with a damp sponge. When that has set, apply a second coat of finishing compound to further neaten the joint, then apply a slurry of joint finish over the entire ceiling to leave the surface completely smooth. Full details on how to do the job,

together with advice on the specialist tools you need can be found on the filler and finish compound's pack, or ask the plasterboard's manufacturer for their advice.

The new ceiling can now be decorated using the same sort of finish as you would use on any other ceiling — just be sure to prime it with all-surface primer if you intend to apply a resin-based paint.

Squares and rectangles of varnished plywood have been used to create an unusual panelled effect in this bedroom. The same material has been used to face the built-in units.

THE COMPLETE
FLOORER

TILING FLOORS   *280*

LAYING HARDBOARD *281* ♦ LAYING WHOLE TILES *282* ♦ LAYING QUARRY TILES *283*
LAYING BORDER TILES *284* ♦ GROUTING *285* ♦ SEALING QUARRY TILES *286*
COPING WITH THRESHOLDS *286*

LAYING RESILIENT VINYLS   *287*

LAYING RESILIENT VINYL *288* ♦ COPING WITH INTERNAL CORNERS *289*
COPING WITH EXTERNAL CORNERS *289* ♦ USING TEMPLATES *290*
SEAMS AND THRESHOLDS *291*

People expect a great deal of the floorcoverings in their home. After all, a flooring is expected to be attractive, yet hardwearing; comfortable, yet easy to keep clean. That's asking a lot of a single material, so it's not really surprising that most floorings on the market are better in respect of some of these qualities than in others. Choosing a flooring for a particular room is therefore largely a matter of choosing 'horses for courses'. In the kitchen, for example, it's more important to have a durable, easy-to-clean floor than it is to have one that is comfortable. That's why 'hard' floorings such as tiles and sheet vinyls are usually preferred to carpet. In a bedroom, on the other hand, comfort is everything, since bedroom floors are not usually subjected to heavy soiling or heavy traffic. And that's why most people go for carpet rather than a spartan, 'practical' floorcovering.

You can apply the same sort of logic to choosing the flooring for every room in the house, and so long as you strike the right balance in rooms, such as the lounge, where you need a flooring that is both durable and comfortable, your new flooring should prove a very worthwhile investment — assuming, that is, you lay it correctly.

Tiling floors

Tiling is perhaps the easiest way to get a new floor, and, thanks to the wide variety of flooring tiles now available, it's a technique you can apply to almost any room in the house. There are cork tiles, wooden tiles, carpet tiles, vinyl tiles, glazed ceramic tiles, unglazed ceramic tiles, and many more besides. Obviously, each of these is laid in a slightly different way. But all floor tiling has one thing in common — the setting out.

This is carried out in the same way as on a ceiling. Measure up and use a chalked line to strike guide lines between opposite walls so that they cross exactly in the centre of the room. It's best to ignore ancillary features such as window bays or chimney breast alcoves when doing this. Since the object of the exercise is to give the tiling a symmetrical appearance, what you are really after is the centre of the bulk of the tiled area. For the same reason, if you are tiling the floor of a room that has some sort of fitting occupying most of one wall — say, a bath, or a line of built-in wardrobes — you should treat the fitting as if it was a wall, and adjust the position of the relevant guide line accordingly.

Now, step out from the centre of this cross in whole tile units (or whole tile plus grout line units as measured with a gauge rod if you are using ceramic tiles), and see what happens around the edges of the room. Ideally, the cut tiles needed to fill in here should all be of a reasonable width — certainly no less than 25mm (1in), and preferably a lot more. If they are not, move the relevant guide line along by half the width of a tile and try again. As a final check that the floor tiles will be both easy to lay, and attractively set out, work out how any awkward corners and obstacles fit within the tile arrangement. Further adjustments in the positioning of the starting guide lines may be necessary to avoid over-awkward cutting in.

And what about actually laying the tiles? Vinyl tiles are simplest. You merely coat the floor with contact adhesive using a notched spreader, aiming to cover roughly a square metre at a time, and then press each tile into place, smoothing it over finally with a soft cloth. As always, begin with four tiles set into the angles at the centre of the cross where the chalk guide lines intersect. Next lay as many whole tiles as you can along each arm of the cross, then cover the remainder of the floor as far as possible with more whole tiles before filling in the gaps left around the edges of the room with cut tiles individually tailored to fit.

Now there is a little dodge you may find useful. It saves you having to measure up for each cut tile — and no matter how careful you are, when transferring measurements there is always the chance of a mistake. What you do is lay the tile you wish to cut exactly on top of the whole tile that comes before the gap you want to fill. If you now place a spare whole tile on top of that, this time positioning it with one edge butted tight against the skirting board, (or whatever else it is you are tiling up to) you will find that exposed portion of the tile you wish to cut is exactly the right size to fill the gap. So, start by drawing a line on the tile to be cut using the edge of the uppermost tile as a straightedge. Place the tile to be cut on a sheet of scrap hardboard or something similar to protect the new flooring, then lay a metal straightedge along the guide line and cut along the line using a sharp knife.

The same trick, with slight modifications, also enables you to mark out tiles due to be fitted into an internal angle, or around an external angle. In the former case, position the tile to be cut over the whole tile nearest to the angle, then mark it first with the uppermost gauge tile butted against one wall, then again with the gauge tile butted against the second wall. This transfers not only the size of the cut tile, but also the angles of the wall just in case these are out of square. Similarly, for an external corner, mark the cut tile to fit against one wall just as if there were no corner there at all. That done, move the cut tile around the corner (without rotating it), and mark it to fit against the wall there, again just if the corner did not exist. These two sets of guide lines now perfectly describe the outline of an L-shaped cut tile that will fit the corner like a glove.

Awkwardly shaped obstacles such WCs are more difficult to cut round. The simplest way to mark out the cut tile is with a template. Take a tile-sized sheet of paper, and posi-

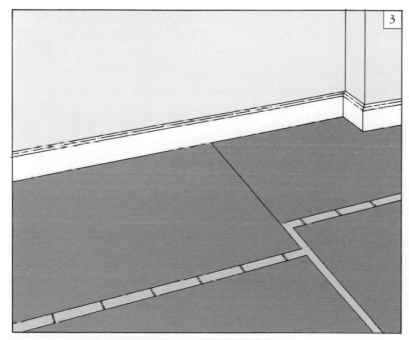

1 *Hardboard forms the perfect underlay for many floorcoverings, masking uneven boards and the gaps between them.*

2 *Lay manageable sections — say 1220mm (4ft) squares — in a row along one edge of the room. Make cut-outs where necessary to allow the sheets to fit round obstacles.*

3 *Try to stagger the joins between rows as you lay the boards. Butt them tightly together and pin them to the subfloor at 150mm (6in) intervals all over.*

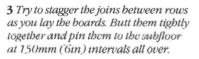

SETTING OUT

Find the centre point of the room by joining the mid-points of opposite walls with string lines. Start by fixing the first tile in the angle formed by the lines.

LAYING WHOLE TILES

1 *Mark out the floor to give a centre point. Then spread some adhesive in the angle betwen the guidelines.*

2 *Lay the first tile in the angle, offering it up to the lines and lowering it into place. Bed it down with firm hand pressure, and check its alignment again.*

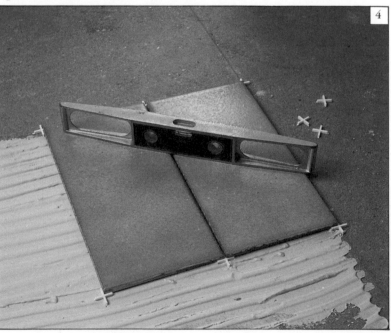

3 *Position the next tile alongside the first one, aligning it and bedding it into the adhesive as before. Use spacers to ensure an even gap between the tiles.*

4 *As you work, use a spirit level to keep checking that the tiles are level in both directions and that they are lying absolutely flush with their neighbours.*

LAYING QUARRY TILES

1 *Quarry tiles are laid in a mortar bed. Set out battens to form bays big enough to take, say, nine tiles.*

2 *Check that the battens are level using your spirit level, adding packing if necessary where the floor dips, and nail them in place. Then spread mortar in the bay.*

3 *Bed each tile securely in the mortar bed using firm hand pressure, and check regularly with a spirit level or straightedge to ensure that tiles are level with the battens and each other.*

4 *When you have completed one bay, lift and reposition the battens to form the next one. Note that the edge of the first bay forms one side of the second bay.*

LAYING BORDER TILES

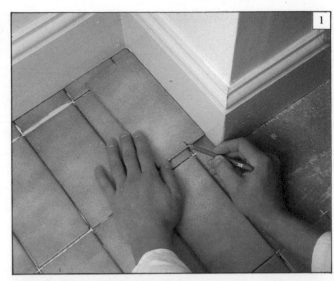

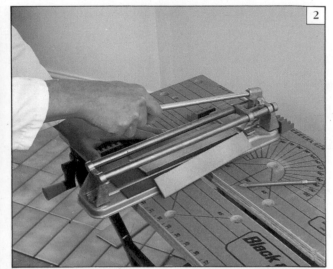

1 & 2 Mark the width of the border pieces at each point on a whole tile butted up against the skirting. Then cut the tile with a tile-cutting machine rather than a hand tile-cutter.

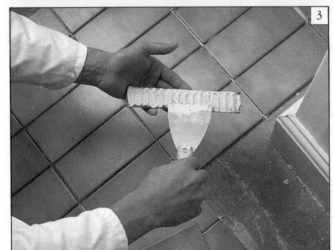

3 & 4 Test the cut piece for fit, then butter some tile adhesive on to its rear face and bed it in position. Fit spacers if necessary to maintain the grouting gap, and check that the border piece is level with its neighbours.

5 & 6 At external corners, an L-shaped cut tile will be needed. Mark the position of the cut on one edge of the tile first, then on the other edge, and remove the waste with a tile saw or by nibbling it away carefully with pincers.

tion it just as you would the tile you wish to cut. Obviously it won't go in, so make a few freeing cuts to fit it neatly round the obstacle, folding back the waste and creasing it around the obstacle's outline in much the same way as you would if hanging wallpaper. If you now carefully cut around this crease, you will be left with a piece of paper exactly the same size and shape as the cut tile required.

As for cork and wooden tiles, these are laid in exactly the same way, but do remember to finish off the floor by protecting the surface with a tough polyurethane varnish. This is even more important here than on cork wall tiling. In fact, the more coats you apply the better. You will certainly need to brush on at least three, in addition to the initial thinned sealing coat rubbed in with a cloth. Take special care to avoid getting dust in the finish, though. Before applying any of the coats, wipe the floor over with a damp cloth, allow to dry, then vacuum up any dust that has resettled.

And carpet tiles? The main difference with these is that the majority do not need to be stuck down. Their backing, aided by their weight and the restraint imposed by the neighbouring tiles, is normally sufficient to keep them in place. It is, however, worth sticking down cut tiles plus a row of whole tiles around the perimeter of the room. Use double-sided sticky tape for this, putting it down in 'tramlines' so that it grips the edges of the carpet tiles. There is just one other thing to watch. With carpet tiles, it is best to measure up to find the size of each cut tile. If you use the gauge tile trick, you will find that the carpet pile allows sufficient movement in the tile 'sandwich' for inaccuracies to creep in. In addition, be sure to do the marking out on the back of the tile in pencil (not felt-tipped pen because of the risk of getting it on the pile), and take care when cutting the tile, not to shave off the pile next to the cut edge. You may find this easier to avoid if you cut the tiles with scissors.

Finally, there are ceramic tiles. Putting down glazed versions is really no different to tiling a wall, except that you are likely to have more trouble in cutting tiles to fit. Most floor tiles are too thick to be snapped in two. Instead, having scored through the glaze in the usual way, tap along the line with a hammer and a cold chisel, gradually working round and round the tile until it breaks. Unglazed ceramic tiles — quarry tiles — are quite another matter. These are set, not in adhesive, but in a thick mortar bed. Temporarily fix timber battens around the walls of the room along a line corresponding to the outer edge of the whole tiles there, then divide off a strip of the room (about four tiles wide) with another batten. Hold the battens in place with blobs of mortar spaced about 600mm (2ft) apart. Use battens equal in thickness to the mortar bed plus the thickness of a tile. Check that these battens are absolutely level, using a spirit level, and pack out beneath them with scrap timber or card as necessary until they are. Now put down about a square metre (sq yd) of the mortar bed within this battened-off bay, set in the tiles, and use the upper edges of the battens as a guide to levelling them.

Continue in this way until the entire bay has been tiled, then remove the batten nearest the centre of the floor and

1 *When all the tiles have been placed and levelled, use a squeegee or sponge to force the grout into the gaps between them. Scrape off excess grout as you work.*

2 *Then use a piece of dowel or some similar implement to neaten all the grout lines. Don't scrape out too much grout, or you will leave dust-gathering depressions.*

3 *Finally, wash off the grout stains from the surface of the tiles with a damp cloth. Work diagonally rather than along the grout lines to avoid disturbing the grout.*

4 *Grout quarry tiles with a 'runny' mortar mix. When it has set, point the gaps with a stub of dowelling and wipe clean with a damp rag.*

SEALING QUARRY TILES

1 & 2 *Ordinary quarry tiles need sealing to make them stain — and waterproof. Use a clear floor sealer for this, and apply the first coat with a cloth pad. Then roughen the surface with abrasive paper to ensure a good bond between coats.*

3 *Finally, brush on a second (and possibly a third) coat.*

COPING WITH THRESHOLDS

1 *You can protect the tile edging at doorways by nailing down a proprietary threshold strip. Do this before laying the tiles, so you can butt them neatly up against the edge of the strip as you work.*

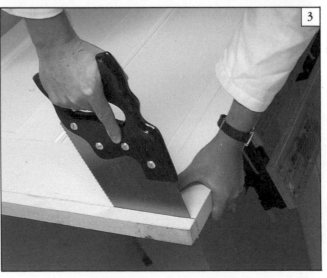

2 & 3 *An alternative to the metal threshold strip is to shape a piece of hardwood and secure this to the floor against the edge of the tiled area. Finish it with three coats of clear varnish.*

Remember that a tiled floor is relatively thick, so you will have to saw off some wood from the bottom of doors to the tiled room. Remove the doors before you start tiling.

The natural colour and surface texture of quarry tiles provide the perfect floorcovering for this conservatory. A frost-proof type has been selected, so the same tile could be laid as a surround to the outdoor pool beyond.

move it along to create a new bay ready for tiling. When you have covered as much of the floor as possible with whole tiles, remove the edging battens, and fill in the gaps with cut tiles. Grout the gaps between quarry tiles with a 'runny' mortar mix. When the grouting has set firm, but not hard, point the gaps with a stub of dowelling and wipe off excess mortar with a damp rag.

Laying sheet vinyls

While laying a sheet vinyl flooring is, in theory, both quicker and easier than laying tiles, a lot depends on the room — its size, its shape, and on the number of obstacles it contains. It is therefore well worth running through the job in your head before you buy the flooring, to identify the likely problems, and work out how best to overcome them.

In this respect, the main thing to consider is the need for joins between adjacent lengths. In general, they are best avoided. They complicate the job of laying, they don't look particularly attractive, and they introduce an unwanted weakness into what is otherwise a very durable, water-proof, easy-to-clean surface. This is where extra-wide vinyl floorings come in. At 4m (12ft) wide, they make it possible to cover the floors of most small rooms without any joins at all. Even on a larger, long, narrow room you may be able to avoid joins by simply laying the vinyl starting against one of the narrower walls.

In some rooms, though, no matter what you do, at least one join is inevitable, and in this case it is important to plan things so that the join is positioned where it will be least noticeable, and will do least damage. In particular, avoid having joins in heavy traffic areas — around doorways, in the centre of the room, and in the area immediately in front of

LAYING SHEET VINYL

1 *Start laying against the longest straight wall in the room. Butt the end of the roll up against the skirting and check to see whether the long wall undulates.*

2 *If it does, you have to scribe the edge of the sheet so you can trim it to match the profile of the wall. Use a pencil and a block of wood slightly wider than the widest gap, drawing the block along the skirting to mark the cutting line.*

3 *Slide the length away from the skirting board and cut carefully along the scribed line with a sharp handyman's knife. Peel away and discard the offcut strip.*

4 *Slide the vinyl sheet back into position to check the fit, and make any minor trimming adjustments that may still be needed. You can then trim the other end of the length neatly to butt up against the skirting at the other end of the room.*

the family sofa and armchairs. Joins in this sort of position tend to wear very rapidly, and as they wear, there is every chance that they will lift and create a trip hazard. What's more, if someone should trip over the edge of the vinyl, the flooring will chip and/or tear and be completely ruined. If possible, therefore, arrange for joins to fall off to one side of the room, preferably so that they run beneath some large, little-moved piece of furniture that will both help to protect and conceal the vinyl's vulnerable edges.

You are now almost ready to begin laying. There is just one final bit of preparation to be attended to — when you get the vinyl home, loosen the roll as much as you can and leave it in a warm room for 12 to 24 hours. You will then find that, when you come to start laying it, the now warm, 'relaxed' vinyl is a lot easier to handle. In fact, so great is the effect of temperature on the vinyl's flexibility that, in winter, it is well worth thoroughly warming up the room before you start work. This is particularly important at the trimming stage. If the flooring is extremely cold, it has a tendency to crack rather than bend.

Once the vinyl is warm enough, lay the roll down in a corner of the room, and line it up against the wall opposite the one you have chosen as your starting point. Now take a firm grip on the free edge, and start pulling the flooring off the roll by walking back across the room. Having unrolled rather more than you need to cover the floor between the walls, cut the vinyl roughly to length, allowing an extra 50mm (2in) or so trim allowance at each end, and move the remainder of the roll out of the way. You must now straighten up the vinyl, using the walls as a guide, at the same time positioning it so that a 50mm (2in) trim allowance turns up the third wall at that end of the room. If the vinyl is actually large enough to cover the entire floor, then simply centre it as accurately as you can.

The next step is to make enough freeing cuts for the vinyl to be more or less flattened out. At internal corners simply cut off the corner of the vinyl there at an angle of about 45 degrees so that as you settle the vinyl in place, a separate trim allowance turns up the adjacent walls. Deciding on the position of the freeing cut at this stage is of course largely a matter of guesswork, but the important thing is not to cut off too much. It is therefore best to make a few preliminary freeing cuts, testing the fit of each one, and gradually paring the vinyl back to the optimum line.

External corners — say, those of a chimney breast — require a slightly different approach. Here your first priority is to make a freeing cut that will allow you to continue smoothing out the vinyl into the alcove, window bay, or whatever beyond. A straight cut from the edge of the vinyl to the point where it meets the corner will do the trick, and again you must decide where to end the cut by a process of trial and error. However, make sure you angle the cut so that it runs through vinyl you know beyond a shadow of a doubt will be waste — on a chimney breast, that will be the vinyl running up the the breast's face. In this way, as you smooth the vinyl past the corner, a trim allowance will be left to turn up the side wall, thus giving you the opportunity

COPING WITH INTERNAL CORNERS

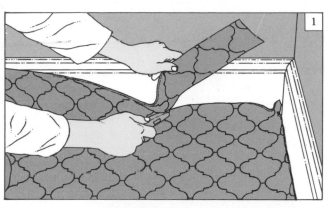

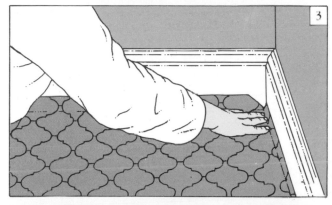

1 & 2 *Start by removing most of the waste material from the edge of the sheet with a sharp knife. Then lift the corner and make a diagonal cut across it.*

3 & 4 *Press the sheet back into the angle so the tongues on each side lie up against the skirting board. Then use a sharp knife held at a 45° angle to trim the tongues and let the sheet lie flat.*

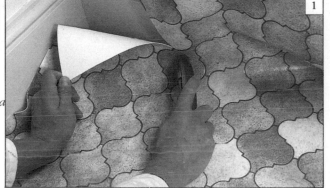

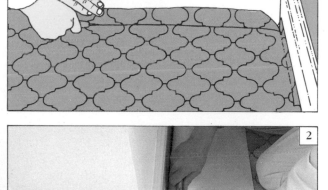

COPING WITH EXTERNAL CORNERS

1 & 2 *At external corners, make a diagonal cut downwards from the edge of the sheet to allow the tongues on each side to lap up the skirting board. Don't cut too far. Then roughly trim away excess material.*

3 & 4 *Extend the diagonal cut slightly if necessary to improve the fit of the corner point, then press the tongues down into the angles and trim them neatly to fit the profile of the skirting boards (as for internal angles).*

USING TEMPLATES

1 *Use a paper template to mark and cut vinyl round awkwardly-shaped obstacles. Cut out the shape roughly and make scissor cuts all round so the tongues can be bent up for accurate marking.*

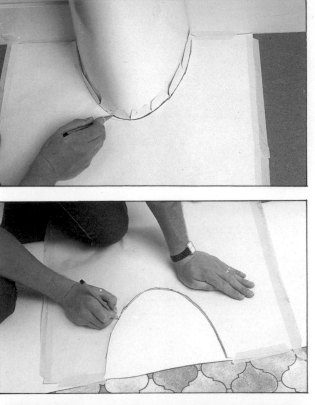

2 *Snip off the tongues along the pencil line. Then tape the template to the vinyl and transfer the outline of the obstacle on to its rear surface (this is easier than working on the pattern side).*

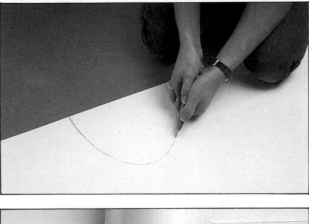

3 *Use a sharp knife to cut carefully round the marked outline. Make sure that the sheet is resting on scrap material or a hardboard underlay, not on sheet vinyl that has already been laid.*

4 *Offer the cut sheet up to the obstacle and make any slight adjustments that may be needed. Then trim the excess material from the wall edge behind it to complete the job.*

to trim within the alcove to achieve a perfect fit no matter how out of square the corner may be. Having made the freeing cut and laid the vinyl flat, you can trim off the bulk of the obvious waste to make the final fitting easier.

Incidentally, don't be daunted by complex shapes such as a hearth, fire surround or chimney breast and alcove combination. Simply make a freeing cut for each external corner as you come to it. As for really complex shapes such as the foot of a WC, at this stage merely make a straight cut from the edge of the vinyl to the point where you judge the front of the pedestal will come, cut out a hole of about the right size in approximately the right place (erring on the side of making it markedly too small). This should allow you to come close enough to laying the vinyl flat around the obstacle for you to make a series of freeing cuts in the vinyl turning up its sides.

You are now in a position to trim the vinyl accurately to fit, and there are two ways in which this can be done. The first applies to the thinner, more flexible vinyls. All you do is push the vinyl into the angle between the floor and the wall, using a block of softwood, so that the edge of the block leaves a sharp crease where the two surfaces meet. You can then simply trim along the crease with a sharp knife, guiding the blade with a straightedge to ensure a neat cut finish. In other words, in essence, it's just a scaled-up version of the technique used to trim wallpaper.

For thicker vinyls, though, you have to use a technique called 'scribing' to mark the line along which you must cut. Assuming a uniform 50mm (2in) trim allowance, lay the vinyl flat on the floor with its edge butted up against the wall. Now, starting in one corner of the room, press a 50mm (2in) wide block of wood against the wall, press a pencil against that, and run the two together down the length of the wall so that the pencil draws a line at a constant 50mm (2in) from the wall's surface. Cut along this line and, when you push the new edge up to the wall, you should find that it fits perfectly, no matter how uneven the line of the wall may be.

Unfortunately, this technique cannot be used to trim round obstacles such as pipes and WCs. What you must do instead is make a paper template. Take a sheet of paper large enough to surround the obstacle while keeping one edge on the edge of the vinyl. In it cut an oversize hole, fit it around the obstacle, and tape it into place making sure the paper still lines up with the vinyl's edge. Next, use your scribing block and pencil to scribe round the obstacle in order to produce an oversize replica of its outline on the paper, then pull both vinyl and paper template clear and lay them out flat on the floor. All you do now is repeat the scribing procedure, this time running the scribing block around the inside of the line drawn on the paper to produce an actual size outline on the vinyl. Cut along this line, and you should be left with the vinyl a perfect fit.

Now what about coping with joins? What you must aim for is a perfect pattern match and a perfect butt joint between lengths, and there is a trick to it. Position the second piece of vinyl so that it overlaps the first, and adjust its

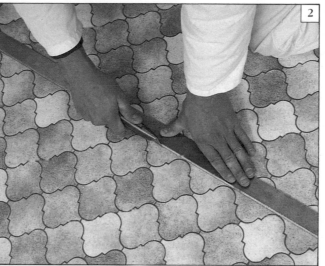

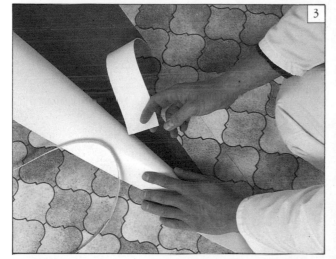

SEAMS AND THRESHOLDS

1 & 2 *To form perfect seams between lengths, overlap the edges slightly and align the pattern carefully. Then lay a steel straightedge along the centre of the overlap and cut cleanly through both layers.*

3 & 4 *Discard the offcut strip from the upper layer; then lift this and peel away the offcut from the layer underneath. Position a strip of double-sided adhesive tape underneath the seam and press the cut edges firmly down on to it.*

5 & 6 *Secure the edges of the lengths by bedding double-sided tape all round the perimeter of the room. Finish off at doorways with special threshold strips, nailed into position.*

position until the patterns match perfectly. Now, with the aid of a straightedge, cut along the line of the intended join, carrying the blade through the double thickness of vinyl. Having removed the waste from both vinyl layers, you should be left with a perfect join.

To complete the floor, all that now remains is to do a little sticking to hold the vinyl firmly in place. Now this isn't absolutely essential — vinyl can be loose-laid — but it is definitely advisable. In the vast majority of cases there is no need to stick it down over the entire floor. Merely fixing a strip about 300mm (12in) wide around the perimeter of each sheet (and especially the edge where it joins another sheet) is generally adequate. So, just peel back the edge of the sheet, spread a layer of flooring adhesive on to the floor with a notched spreader (follow the vinyl manufacturer's recommendations on which adhesive to use), and press the edge into place, smoothing it out with a cloth in the direction of the walls and taking care not to trap bubbles of air.

The exception to this rule is where the vinyl flooring is expected to endure a lot of foot traffic, as in a busy hallway, for example. Here it is best to glue the flooring in place across the entire floor. To do this, fold back the vinyl to leave just over half of the floor exposed, and cover this half with adhesive. Carefully roll the vinyl back into place, smoothing it out as you go so as not to trap any air, then fold back the vinyl on the other half of the floor and repeat the process to stick that down. Finally, working from the centre of the floor out towards the edges, drag something smooth, soft, and heavy over the surface of the vinyl to remove any remaining air bubbles, and at the same time bed it firmly into place. One of the best things to use for this job is a thick plastic refuse bag filled with sand or earth. Place a wad of sacking between it and the floor to avoid scratching the surface. Better still, place the bag inside an old sack — plastic bags have a nasty habit of splitting when you least expect it.

If you do decide to stick the vinyl down, whether just

Ceramic tiles are a popular choice for kitchen floors because they are immensely hard-wearing and easy to keep clean. Note the use of a delicate green wood stain on the cupboard fronts to emphasize the colour of the tiles themselves.

around the edges or across the entire floor — and it will help the flooring wear better — there is just one last point to bear in mind. Once the new flooring has been in normal use for a few days, it will start to spread, and with adhesive holding it in place around the edges, that means it will start to lift off the floor in the centre of each sheet. To prevent this, allow the newly trimmed vinyl to settle in for a week or so before sticking it down. It is also worth checking the fit around the edges of the room at that stage. Although a certain amount of expansion can be accommodated by slipping the edges of the vinyl into the gap between skirting board and floor, in severe cases it may be necessary to retrim the flooring slightly.

With the flooring neatly trimmed and glued in place, just one more job remains. That is to give some protection to raw edge of the vinyl left vulnerable in any doorways. A simple wooden or metal threshold strip is all that is required. Fix it firmly to cover the edge using screws or nails.

Vinyl floor tiles provide a durable and hygienic surface that's ideal for busy traffic areas. Here small black squares at the tile intersections give a cool, formal look to the room.

Laying foam-backed carpet

Carpet laying is one of those jobs where, although you are unlikely to make any really major errors at your first attempt, you will probably find that a really neat, professional finish eludes you. The fact is it requires the sort of skill that only comes with practice. For this reason, if you are not a particularly 'handy' person, or if you are buying a very expensive carpet, it is generally best to leave the job to an expert — though don't put too much faith in the 'free fitting' schemes operated by many carpet suppliers. But where you are getting a relatively inexpensive foam-backed carpet for a room where small flaws are likely to go unnoticed — a bedroom, for example — then you may as well have a go. Who knows, you may turn out to be very good at it.

There are four main ways to tackle the job. You can loose-lay the carpet, tack it in place, use double-sided tape or stretch it and use wood or metal gripper strip (a special type is used for foam-backed carpet) to hold it in place around the edges of the room. Of these, the last is undoubtedly the most popular, so let's see how it's done.

Start by fixing the gripper strip right round the perimeter of the room, nailing it in place (using masonry pins on a concrete floor) with its teeth pointing at the wall. Leave a gap roughly equal to the thickness of the carpet between gripper strip and skirting board. Any cutting to length necessary is easily done with a hacksaw.

The next step is to cover the floor with underlay. This is not strictly necessary with foam-backed carpet, but it is worthwhile. It makes the floor warmer and more comfortable, and, just as important, stops the carpet's foam-backing sticking to the floor in heavy traffic areas. Simply roll the underlay out across the floor, smooth it down, and trim it to fit within the inner edges of the gripper strip. To stop it riding up in use, tape together any joins, and fix it in place at one end with carpet tacks or double sided sticky tape.

Now for the carpet. Having unrolled it, manoeuvre it roughly into position, if possible with the pile direction facing the room's main door and with one machine-finished edge lying along a straight, uninterrupted wall. Now begin fixing it to the gripper strip along this wall, starting in the centre and working out towards the corner, stretching the carpet reasonably taut as you go. That done, pull the carpet taut across the room, and hook it on to the gripper strip along the opposite wall, again starting in the centre and working out towards the corner. To complete this first stage of the fitting, stretch the carpet in the other direction, fixing it first along one side wall, then along the other. You should now check that the carpet is lying perfectly flat and that it has been stretched evenly in all directions. If it is wrong, re-stretch the appropriate sections as necessary, working out from the centre of the room so you can refix the edge on the gripper strip.

This stretching is important. It not only leaves the carpet lying flat, but also helps improve its ability to withstand wear and tear. You will find it easiest to do using a special tool called a knee kicker — widely available from tool hire shops. But take care not to overstretch the carpet, nor to

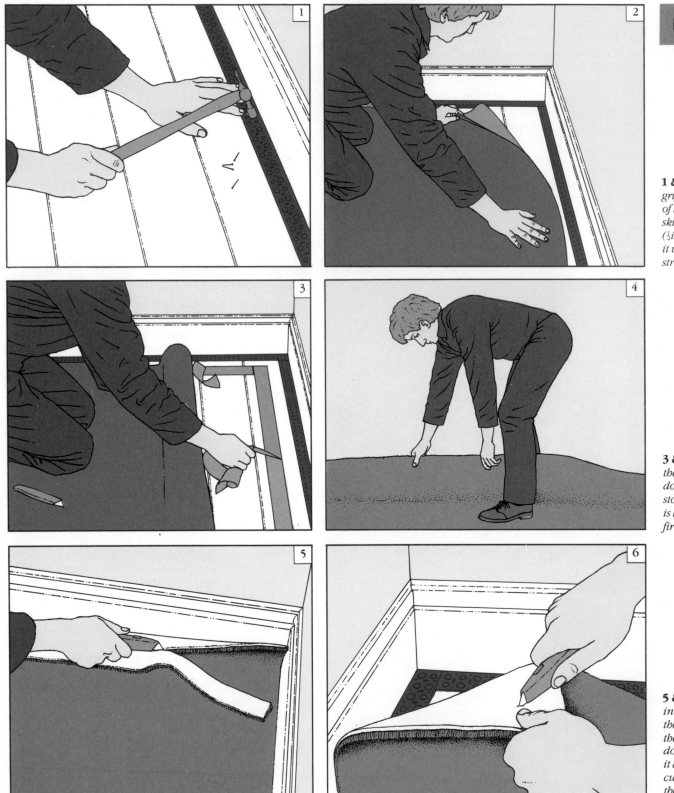

LAYING CARPETS

1 & 2 *Start by fixing carpet gripper strips all round the edge of the room set in from the skirting board by about 6mm (¼in). Then cut the underlay so it will lie within the gripper strips.*

3 & 4 *Secure the underlay to the floor surface with strips of double-sided adhesive tape to stop it creeping while the carpet is laid. Press the underlay down firmly*

5 & 6 *Lay the carpet out roughly in position, and trim off most of the excess material all round the room. Then press the carpet down into internal corners, lift it away and make a diagonal cut across the corner to allow the tongues to lap up against the skirting board.*

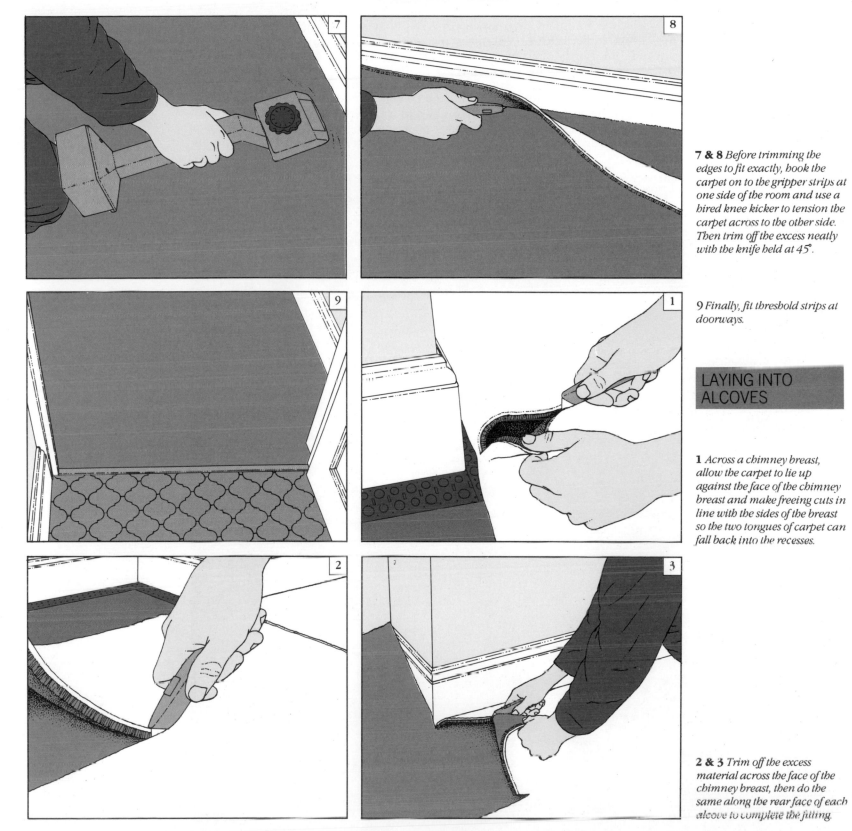

7 & 8 *Before trimming the edges to fit exactly, hook the carpet on to the gripper strips at one side of the room and use a hired knee kicker to tension the carpet across to the other side. Then trim off the excess neatly with the knife held at 45°.*

9 *Finally, fit threshold strips at doorways.*

LAYING INTO ALCOVES

1 *Across a chimney breast, allow the carpet to lie up against the face of the chimney breast and make freeing cuts in line with the sides of the breast so the two tongues of carpet can fall back into the recesses.*

2 & 3 *Trim off the excess material across the face of the chimney breast, then do the same along the rear face of each alcove to complete the fitting.*

stretch it unevenly. That can do more harm than not stretching it at all.

Once you are satisfied with the way the carpet is lying, trim it exactly to size using a sharp knife. Just run the knife blade along the angle between wall and floor, then tuck the trimmed edges neatly out of sight by poking them down in between the skirting board and gripper strip with a bolster chisel or something similar. Finally, trim off the carpet squarely across any doorways, and protect the cut edge with a metal or wooden threshold strip — one with a built-in gripper strip is best.

And what about carpeting around obstacles and awkward corners? The short answer is that you make freeing cuts in just the same way as when laying a sheet vinyl flooring in order to leave the carpet lying flat, then stretch it on to the gripper and trim accurately to fit as described above. The only major problem you are likely to encounter is where the carpet is to be fitted against a rounded or irregular surface — say, with a half-round window bay. You can't buy curved gripper strip. All you can do is cut the gripper strip into short sections, and fix it in place following the curve as closely as possible.

Carpet is by far the most widely used floorcovering in most homes today. The huge range of plain colours and patterns available ensures that you can always find one to suit your colour scheme. Here a neutral colour and a short pile are the perfect foil for the wealth of detail in the decorations and furnishings.

CEILING
IDEAS

INSTALLING AN ILLUMINATED CEILING *299* ♦ PUTTING UP COVING *300*

In some ways, the ceiling is the Cinderella surface of any room. When thinking about different colour schemes and decor ideas for the room as a whole, it's so easy to find yourself considering the ceiling's decoration as an afterthought – something that deserves no more and no less attention than is needed to keep it looking respectable. To some extent that is understandable. After all, when you enter a room, the ceiling is by no means the first thing you look at — if you look at it at all. But that doesn't mean that the way in which it is treated is of no significance. On the contrary, the ceiling can have an enormous effect on the way people react to the living space beneath.

As we have already seen when looking at the basics of colour scheming, there is the ceiling's height to consider. For whatever reason, the fact is most people associate low ceilings with a sense of cosiness, safety, and intimacy, while high ceilings can conjure up images of grandeur, airiness; even of the inhospitable coldness of distance. And that applies whether the height is real in the physical sense, or purely illusory — a product of the way the surface colour affects our brains.

There is the matter of interest, too. Just because the majority of ceilings are flat, featureless expanses of painted or papered plaster doesn't mean that that approach is necessarily best. After all, ornately decorated ceilings have been around for thousands of years, and for good reason. You don't have to live in the Sistine chapel to benefit from a lively and attractive decorative surface above your head. If you are totally honest about such things, then you have to accept that there are rooms in even the most modern home where you spend a fair amount of time staring at the ceiling — bedrooms and bathrooms are the most obvious example.

And don't forget the more subtle tricks the ceiling decoration can play. There is the effect it can have on the room's lighting, not to mention its ability to generally 'set the scene' – try to imagine an 'olde worlde' cottage without oak beams in the ceiling. So, before settling for one of the usual paint, paper, texture or tile options, look at some of the more exciting and unusual alternatives. Most of them are remarkably simple to achieve.

Since we have already mentioned them, let's start with ceiling beams. For a real taste of yesteryear, you'll find a number of firms now producing replica beams in glass fibre. Cast in moulds taken from genuinely ancient timbers, these are almost uncannily realistic — they even have woodworm holes — yet they are not too expensive, and could hardly be easier to install. Being extremely lightweight, in most cases, the larger beams just snap on to special clips screwed to the existing ceiling, while the smaller members are usually glued in place. Some manufacturers even offer advice on how to arrange their products to be both architecturally and historically accurate. Having said that, though, it must be said that no amount of antique woodwork (however genuine) will turn a modern suburban 'semi' into a Tudor cottage. This sort of treatment is therefore best reserved for homes that already have a fair measure of olde worlde character and charm.

But some beamed effects do work in more modern looking homes. It's all a matter of choosing obviously modern looking beams, treating them in a modern way, and arranging for the rest of the room's decor to complete the effect. The simplest of these 'modern' beam treatments is to merely fix a series of parallel softwood battens to the ceiling's surface, screwing or nailing them to the existing ceiling joists — running the beams at right-angles to the joists makes this easier. By varying the size of timber used, and the way in which beams and ceiling are coloured, you can exercise considerable control over the finished effect. Even the type of timber used — whether planed or rough sawn — can make a difference.

Alternatively, consider fixing beams well below the level of the existing ceiling, notching their ends into timber wallplates screwed to opposite walls at the appropriate level. This is essentially the same structure as you would use to support a genuine, clad suspended ceiling, except that you omit to add the cladding. If you paint the ceiling above the beams in a suitably dark colour, the result has just as great an effect on the room's perceived height, yet works out at a fraction of the cost of a full suspended ceiling. As a variation on the idea, consider introducing climbing plants into the arrangement to give it something of the flavour of an outdoor pergola. One tip: support the centres of the beams not with vertical timber hangers, but with lengths of stout galvanised wire twisted around large screw-eyes set into the beams and original ceiling joists. Timber hangers would be visible through the beams and could ruin the effect.

For a pseudo suspended ceiling with an even more outdoor flavour, why not make use of ordinary garden trellis — with or without the addition of suitable indoor climbing plants. This is so light there is really no need to provide it with a supporting timber framework. Instead, merely hang it on lengths of stout wire fixed to the existing ceiling's joists via large screw-eyes. With the trellis painted in a different colour to the ceiling above, the effect can be really very striking.

Remember, too, that there is no need to hang trellis over the entire ceiling area. Experiment with simply hanging a section in the centre of the ceiling to give the surface a split level look. And there is no need to stop at using just a single island of trellis. If you wish, you can dot sections of trellis

FITTING AN ILLUMINATED CEILING

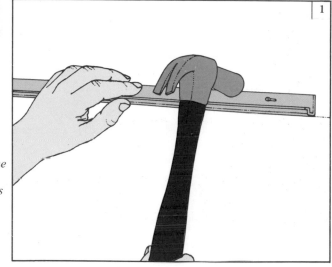

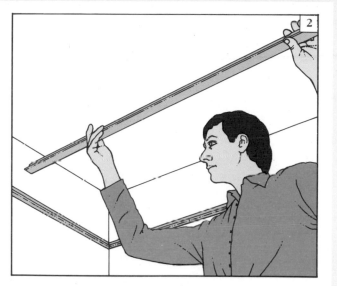

1 & 2 *Decide on the height at which the ceiling is to be fixed, and draw a true horizontal line all round the room at this level. Then nail the perimeter battens to the wall with masonry pins, and position the main cross bearers by resting them on the perimeter battens at the required spacing.*

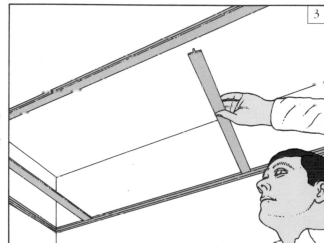

3 & 4 *Next, lay in the short transverse bearers, resting them on the flanges of the main cross bearers — again at the required spacing. With some systems, small clips are used to hold these transverse bearers in position. You can then offer up the whole tiles through the openings in the grid, and drop them into place on the bearer flanges.*

5 & 6 *At the edge of the ceiling, cut narrow filler tiles; you can use scissors on most translucent plastic tiles, but you'll need a sharp knife to cut solid types. Ragged edges will be hidden by the bearer flanges when the pieces are slotted into their final positions.*

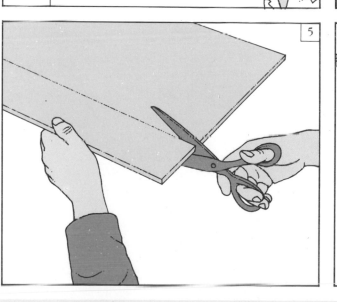

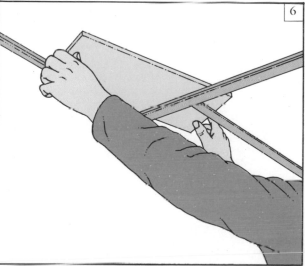

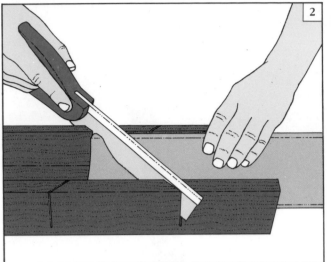

1 & 2 *Before starting to fix coving in place, mark a line on the walls to indicate the position of the coving's lower edge and strip wallpaper from the area above it. Then cut a mitre at one end of the first length to be fixed.*

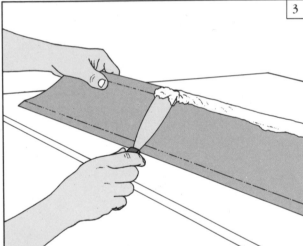

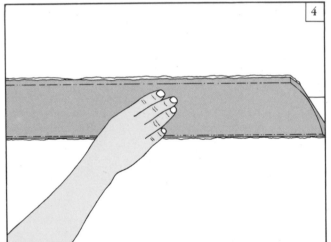

3 & 4 *Butter the coving adhesive onto the rear edges of the length. Then offer the mitred end up to the corner of the room and press it firmly into position. Hold it for a few seconds to allow the adhesive to grip, and if necessary support it with partly-driven masonry pins.*

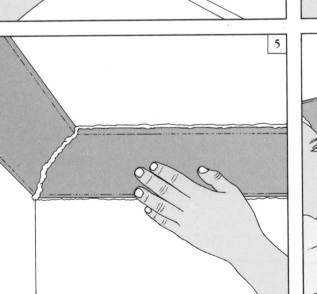

5 & 6 *Complete internal corners by offering up a second length with its mitre cut in the opposite direction. Butter some adhesive onto the mitred end and push the length into position to form a neat join. Add further square-edged lengths as required, and finish off by neatening joins and removing excess adhesive from ceiling and wall surfaces.*

around the room. Come to that, there is no reason why you should limit yourself to using trellis in this way. You can use a solid material such as plasterboard, or tongued and grooved matchboarding if you like. Obviously these heavier materials will need the support of a reasonably substantial timber framework – fixing the panels to stout battens supported entirely by timber hangers screwed to the original ceiling's joists will do in most cases – but the treatment can be made to do more than merely partially alter the ceiling level. Just think of all the possibilities for concealed lighting that it opens up.

There are a number of other variations you might consider, too. For example, having installed the necessary supporting timberwork for a full-scale suspended ceiling you could clad it with timber slats. Bear in mind that they don't have to run in boringly parallel rows. You could clad different areas of the ceiling with battens running in different directions to create a variety of geometric patterns – a basketweave or herringbone design, sequences of concentric mitred squares, concentric diamond patterns, and so on. Even simply running the battens diagonally is worth a try. Carry the diagonal theme a stage further and you could cover the ceiling with dramatic chevrons. And there are dozens of other options.

Another possibility is to fit a different sort of suspended ceiling – what's known as an illuminated ceiling. This consists basically of translucent plastic tiles (available in a variety of colours) supported below the level of the original ceiling on a metal grid (usually aluminium), and the idea is that, by installing fluorescent lighting above this, you illuminate the entire ceiling surface, turning it into a sort of cross between a giant light and a glass roof. If that's a little too much for your taste, then you can tone it down by introducing opaque fibre acoustic tiles into the arrangement. Or you can use opaque tiles throughout, though in this case you may find the result rather too reminiscent of shops, offices and factories.

Whichever type of tile you choose, you will find the system remarkably easy to install. Basically, all you do is screw steel L-shaped bars to the walls at the desired level, and use these to support T-shaped bars spaced a tile width apart which run right across the room – over long runs these may need additional support from vertical hanger bars or wires. The grid is then completed by the addition of shorter T-bars fitted at right angles to the main cross members to create square or rectangular bays ready to receive the tiles. Normally the whole assembly either clips together or else is held in place by its own weight, but different systems vary in detail, so do refer to the normally quite comprehensive instructions supplied by the manufacturer when you buy.

Even simple cornices and covings can make a surprising difference to the look of the ceiling. Available in a variety of styles and materials – wood, plaster, glass fibre, and expanded polystyrene – they are very easy to fix. Timber mouldings are simply pinned in place, while the rest are generally stuck on to the wall with a suitable adhesive. And if you are using mouldings to create a period look, you can

complete the effect with a matching ceiling centre. The majority these days are in expanded polystyrene or glass fibre, and are fixed in exactly the same way as the coving.

Finally, what about using fabric as a ceiling ornament? It's lightness makes it very easy to fix in place, and as well as providing a simple yet effective way of introducing both colour and pattern into the upper reaches of the room, there is no denying that, no matter how inexpensive the fabric you are using, it always gives the room an atmosphere of luxury, if not outright decadence. And of course it's hard to think of a simpler way to lower the ceiling height in order to give the room a more cosy atmosphere; all of which combine to make fabric an excellent choice for bedrooms.

One of the simplest effects to achieve is to take long, fairly narrow strips of light, open weave fabric, and merely drape them across the room in a series of airily billowing parallel stripes, each set slightly apart from its neighbour. If you like, allow the ends of each stripe to hang loosely down the face of the wall. Strips of plain muslin about 450mm (18in) wide are ideal here. If you wish, you can dye them to suit the room's colour scheme. This treatment, incidentally, usually works best in very simply furnished rooms, decorated in light, sunny colours, giving the room something of the feel of an outdoor pavilion.

Alternatively, consider draping shorter lengths of fabric between poles hung from screw eyes driven into the ceiling joists by stout cord. A wider fabric tends to look most effective. Sew deep open hems at each end to receive the poles – decorative curtain poles, lengths of dowel or broomstick, or lengths of bamboo.

Fixing lengths of fabric to the walls at picture rail height or lower and then gathering them all up to a single fixing point in the centre of the ceiling (preferable culminating around a central pendant light) to create a sort of tent, is another popular treatment. It's usually combined with suitable wall hangings, oriental rugs and lots of floor cushions to create sort of Hollywood pastiche of an Arabian harem. But that's up to you.

Do bear in mind that you don't have to carry any of the above treatments across the entire ceiling. Using them over just part of the room can sometimes be equally effective. The ceiling immediately above the bed is an obvious candidate for this sort of partial treatment. For example, you can use either of the first two drape effects to create something of the impression of a four-poster, or you could simply construct the imaginary tent to enclose just the bed.

Whatever you decide, and you can really let your imagination have full rein, there are a few practical points to consider concerning the use of fabric in this sort of situation. First and foremost, think about safety. Since it is not always possible to buy fire-resistant cloth, you should at least make sure that you do all you can to stop a fire starting. In particular, watch the positioning of fabrics in relation to lights. Keep them a safe distance apart. Secondly, although there is nothing to stop you securing fabric to walls and ceilings with a hammer and some tacks, you will undoub-

tedly find a heavy-duty staple gun a lot more convenient. Quite apart from the fact that stapling is quicker and involves less effort, the use of a staple gun will also leave you with one hand free to position the fabric, mould in pleats and tasteful festoons, and so on. Finally, do allow for the fact that fabric drapes are likely to collect quite a lot of dust in a fairly short time. You should therefore at least make sure that the arrangement allows access for cleaning with a vac-uum cleaner. It is also well worth fixing the fabric with a view to being able to take it down again fairly easily — another plus for the staple gun. It will, after all, need wash-ing from time to time, and there is also the possibility that you might tire of its novelty and fancy a change. Having fixed it in a semi-temporary sort of way, you should be able to remove it without disturbing the rest of the room's decorations.

*A heavily-panelled and stained ceiling **above left** contrasts with pale pine-clad walls.*

*A simple tented fabric ceiling **above** brings a light, airy feel to this dining room.*

FINISHING TOUCHES

CURTAINS & UPHOLSTERY   304
BLINDS   306
LIGHTING   308
HARDWARE   312

Having now looked at all the major decorating materials and the various techniques for applying them, it is worth remembering that a room's decor does not end with paint, paper, and flooring. On the contrary, in many cases it's the details that you put into the room after your decorating equipment is packed away that really make the difference between good decor and a room that is merely proficiently decorated.

Curtains & upholstery

Perhaps the most obvious, and important, of these 'details' is the room's furniture, and soft furnishings. In particular, it is vital that they fit in well with the overall colour scheme.

This doesn't necessarily mean you have to buy new furniture each time you redecorate. Some upholstery fabrics go equally well with a variety of colour combinations. All you need do is select the room's colour scheme accordingly. Even if you feel you really must alter the furniture's colour and pattern, there are cheaper ways to set about it. Wooden and metal items, for example, can be repainted, or stripped and then stained and/or varnished. Upholstered furniture, too, can be given a bright new facelift. Merely adding new cushions will some times do the trick, but for a more drastic change consider transforming them with fitted covers in the furnishing fabric of your choice. So long as the furniture isn't too complex in shape, these are surprisingly easy to make up. Basically all you need is a moderate amount of skill with a sewing machine, and a good, specialist book on the subject to show you the ropes.

Existing curtaining can also be given a facelift if you wish. Often, simply having them cleaned and making all necessary repairs to the tape and linings can work wonders. And if they are in reasonably good condition, and you simply want a change of colour, consider dyeing them. Unpick them to remove the lining, and then follow the instructions on the dye's pack. However, do first check that the fabric is suitable. Some synthetics — pleated Tricel, acrylics, and glass fibre, for example — will not take the dye. Think about replacing old linings and curtain tape, too. In the latter case, you can alter the curtains' appearance considerably at the same time by choosing a new tape that gives a slightly different style of pleating. And if you really have to get new curtains? Have a go at making them up yourself. As with loose covers, there is no shortage of literature on the subject, and so long as you are not too ambitious too soon, there is no reason why you shouldn't do an excellent job.

While you are thinking about curtains, don't forget that the curtain track may also benefit from an overhaul. Clean it up, make sure that it works smoothly, and check that any cording is in good condition. Make sure, too, that it is securely fixed to the wall or ceiling. If necessary, refix the

Curtains and other fabric accessories such as bedspreads and cushions add the finishing touches to a room. Here **left** the colours have been chosen to echo those of the wallcovering. The fabric pelmet has been cleverly extended right round the room to draw the eye downwards from a high ceiling.

Upholstery in a neutral colour is in keeping with the light, airy feel of this room **right**. The piping on the cushions picks up the blue of the carpet, while cane and bamboo shelves and accessories suit the style of the room to perfection.

track, drilling fresh holes and using fresh wallplugs to receive the screws.

However, if you have decided to buy new curtains, it is well worth considering buying new curtain track to go with them. You will probably have to in any case if the new curtains are heavier than the old — the existing track may not take the additional weight. There are several different types on the market, made from either plastic or metal, but your choice really depends on just three basic factors. First, there is the track's strength to consider. Heavy curtains need strong track. Second, do you want a cord operated track, or are you happy to draw the curtains by hand. And finally, where the track will show, does it suit the style of the room. Would curtain poles look better? If they would but you have always chosen track because you want cord operation, consider buying a corded track designed to look like a pole. There are now quite a few on the market.

Having chosen the track, make sure you fix it correctly. It must be absolutely level — check this with a spirit-level — and securely anchored to the wall, ceiling, or window frame, as appropriate. For a wall fixing, use screws and wallplugs. If drilling the required number of holes proves too tedious, screw and plug a timber batten to the wall, and then fix the track's brackets to that. For a ceiling fixing, drive woodscrews into the joists. If these don't happen to be in the right place, bridge them on the underside of the ceiling with a timber batten, screw the batten to the joists, then screw the curtain track to the batten. If fitting to the window frame, screw directly into the frame if possible. Failing that — and it may be that the frame timbers are too small to accept the brackets — screw them to a batten fixed to the underside of the window reveal using screws and wallplugs. There is one further point to watch. If you are fixing to a batten laid over masonry, make sure the timber is thick enough to accommodate the full length of the track bracket's screws.

Blinds

Naturally, curtains are far from the only option when it comes to decorating windows. In many cases, blinds are not only better looking, but also considerably more practical. In a kitchen or bathroom, for example, most blinds tend to stand up far better to the humid conditions than any curtaining.

There are, of course, a number of different types of blind to choose from. Roller blinds are generally simplest and cheapest. Available in a wide range of sizes, materials and designs, you should have little difficulty in finding ones suitable for virtually every room in the house. Although the majority are sold made to measure, roller blinds are widely sold in kit form, too, though unless the kit allows you to use your own fabric — with the aid of a stiffening spray — this does rather limit your choice of design.

Venetian blinds are another traditional choice, but give you rather greater control over the amount of light entering the room. You can either tilt the slats, or pull the blind up completely out of the way. It's true that the difficulty of

cleaning the slats places a question mark over their use in the kitchen, but elsewhere in the house they can really help give a room a touch of class. Just look at some of the most modern versions aimed at the domestic market. Made to measure in a good range of really striking colours, they are a far cry from the drab 'office grey' venetian blinds you are probably familiar with.

Alternatively, consider vertical louvre blinds. These are almost, but not quite, venetian blinds hung on their sides — the operating mechanism is, in fact, rather different, and they have rather wider slats, generally made of plastic or fabric. You will find these particularly good for very large glazed areas — patio doors being their real forte. Like venetian blinds, they are normally sold made to measure.

For a slightly more decorative effect, consider roman blinds, or one of the really ornate, frilly festoon blinds. The former are drawn up in straight pleats when you pull the cord to open them; the latter are gathered up in billowing swags. Look out, too, for the many other variations on the pleated blind theme — normally made from translucent paper or plastic. And don't forget about roll-up blinds made from split cane.

Simple accessories and smart pleated blinds give this room a cool, uncluttered air **far left**. *The plants provide living highlights to an otherwise neutral colour scheme.*

An all-white colour scheme **above left**, *extended to include the roller blinds as well, calls for simple furnishings — wicker chairs complement it perfectly.*

Cleverly concealed lighting and a slimline venetian blind add to the air of cool, streamlined efficiency in this modern kitchen **left**.

But whatever you choose, do make sure that you fit it properly. To begin with, make sure that the blind is the right size for the window. If you are buying a made-to-measure blind, make sure you measure up accurately in the manner specified by the blind manufacturer. If you are buying off-the-shelf, make sure that the blind is either exactly the right size, or slightly large and capable of being cut down. And do remember that it is not only the width you have to worry about. The length of the blind is also important.

Having got a blind that fits, fixing it is generally just a matter of screwing brackets to either the window frame itself, or to the underside of the window reveal's soffit — with most blinds you can choose whichever is the more convenient. In both cases, make sure that when the blind is hung on its brackets it will be absolutely horizontal. You can easily check this with a spirit level when working out where to drill the holes that take the fixing screws, but watch out if you have decided on a soffit fixing — the window opening may well be out of true. With most blinds, a slight discrepancy shouldn't matter too much, but if the soffit is badly awry, or if you are hanging a blind that might object to being put up on a slope (with a vertical louvre, for example, gravity could cause the blind to open or close of its own volition) you must take steps to correct the fault.

How you do this mainly depends on how many fixings you need to make in the soffit. If it is just a couple, merely insert packing pieces of thin card beneath one of the brackets as you screw it into place to leave it level with its twin. Where several fixings are required, screw a timber batten to the soffit, packing out behind this as necessary to level it, then screw the blind to the batten. Any unsightly gap between batten and soffit can be concealed with caulking or interior filler.

Once the brackets are securely in place, normally all you do is hook the blind on to them, and check to see that it works properly. However, do read the manufacturer's instructions to find out exactly how the blind should be fitted and if there is anything else you have to do in the way of adjustments to make the thing work properly. For example, roller blinds have to be correctly tensioned to run up and down smoothly.

Lighting

The lighting is another important 'detail', and one that is often sadly neglected. The fact is that, in terms of its effect on the decor, there is a lot more to a good lighting scheme than buying pretty light fittings which fit the style and colour scheme of the room. You have to think about the effect on the room of the light provided by those fittings. Will it be attractive? Will you be able to vary the effect to suit the occasion? Will it be practical? Will it be safe? Finding the answers to these questions requires detailed planning, and although the choice of fittings does come into that planning process, it should come at the very end.

Now obviously, learning to design lighting schemes properly, having regard to all of the many factors that must

Lighting should not only illuminate the room and any task being carried out in it, it should also reflect the style of the room and its furnishings. In this ornate bathroom **right** the brass fittings and glass shades are in perfect harmony with the decorations.

The most unusual feature of this room **far left** is the use of fabric for both the walls and the pleated window blind. The floor-to-ceiling mirrors round the fireplace help lighten what could otherwise be an oppressive colour scheme, while the pale upholstery provides a natural focal point.

be taken into consideration, could take you years. It would certainly take an entire book to explain how to do it. However, follow a few simple guidelines, and combine them with ideas gleaned from books, magazines, other peoples' houses and so on, and there is no reason why you should not come up with a fairly respectable scheme. Build up to it one step at a time.

Start by thinking about background lighting — lighting that lets you see where you are going. Ceiling mounted fittings and ordinary pendant lights are the usual choice here, and very effective they are, too. But, with the possible exception of a workroom, such as a kitchen, and stairwells where your ability to see where you are going is obviously vital to your safety, don't try using them to light the whole room in one go. The result is at best flatly boring; at worst stark, and altogether very unhomely. Instead, keep this sort of background lighting to a fairly low level. Better still, control the relevant lights with dimmer switches so that you can vary the intensity of background light to meet your needs at the time.

Next, think about what you need in the way of purely practical lighting — lighting that lets you see what you are doing. In the bedroom and living room, for example, do you need reading lights, and if so, how many and where? In the kitchen, does the overhead light really illuminate the working surfaces or would some additional lighting help? Is a separate light needed above the dining table? As far as reading lamps are concerned, the most important thing to decide on when choosing the fittings that will do the job is brightness. Ideally, you should arrive at a compromise. You need a light that's bright enough for you to see with absolute clarity, yet not so bright that the reflected glare off the page quickly tires your eyes.

With more general purpose working lights you must also try to avoid positioning the lamps so that shadows are cast across whatever it is you are doing. For this reason, you may find the overhead light in a kitchen rather unsatisfactory as a working light. Standing at the worktops laid out round the room, you tend to have your back to it, and so are constantly working in your own shadow. A better solution might be to provide both general and working light with downlighters — cylindrical lights mounted into or on to the ceiling so that they illuminate only the area immediately beneath them — arranging them in rows directly above the most used worktops. Alternatively, supplement the background lighting with fluorescent or tungsten strip lights mounted on the undersides of the wall cupboards.

You should also think about what is perhaps best described as the lighting position's permanency. For example, above a workbench, do you want a light that pushes out of the way when you have finished the close work and are moving on to something that requires a little more elbow room? In this sort of situation, consider clip-on spotlights and desk lamps. Elsewhere, spotlight and table lamps of all sorts can be pressed into service. It is also worth thinking about the lighting position's permanency in terms of how often you need it. For instance, you may need a bright work-

*Simplicity in colour scheming is often all that is needed in a perfectly proportioned period room. Here a plain fabric wallcovering **right** matches the curtains and complements the rich colour of the polished floorboards.*

*Black and silver colour highlights **left** stand out in stark contrast against white walls and a pale parquet floor.*

*Shelving can be eye-catching too. Here **left** an alcove has been fitted with concealed lighting to show off the ornaments within it, and the shelves have been decorated with the same wallpaper as the rest of the room.*

Pale varnished cork provides the perfect backdrop for an unusual collection of treasures, and the effect is matched by the use of handmade trelliswork in the partition leading to the entrance hall.

and dramatic shadows; lights that break the room up into cosy, well defined areas, and so on. The possibilities are almost endless here, and there is no shortage of hardware on the market designed to create purely decorative lighting effects. There are ordinary wall lights designed to make a contribution to the background lighting. There are wall lights, wall washers, and spotlights that allow you to transform the look of plain walls by flooding them with light. There are uplighters and downlighters, designed respectively to throw a pool of light on to the ceiling and floor. And there are straightforward table lamps and floor lamps which, thanks to the beauty of their shades, can act almost as lit sculptures as well as performing any number of the lighting functions already mentioned.

Having worked out the basic elements of the room's lighting scheme, try to imagine how they will work together in concert, in all the various combinations made possible by turning some lights off while leaving others on. The greater your ability to conduct the lighting like an orchestra in order to transform the mood and appearance of the room, the better. Which, of course, raises the subject of controls. In general, it's a case of the more the merrier. But don't just restrict yourself to straightforward on/off switches. Consider two-way switching arrangements that allow you to control the same lights from two or more different parts of the room or house. Think about dimmer switches that give you the ability to fine tune the parts of your lighting orchestra, increasing its versatility still further. There are also a great many specialized switches that may be of use — remote control switches, and security timer switches, for example.

And what about safety? The most important point is to make sure that if the new lighting scheme involves making any alterations to your home's wiring (and it almost certainly will) they are carried out by a qualified electrician. Secondly, when choosing lights and switches for the bathroom, make sure they are safe, or the electrician simply won't fit them. Basically, if you stick to lights specifically designed for bathrooms, have them permanently wired in (you cannot have plugs and power sockets in bathrooms), and control them using a cord-operated pull switch, you should be alright, though there are obviously a number of more detailed rules in the electrical regulations. And finally, do remember what we said earlier about lighting staircases. To reduce the risk of people tripping, these must be adequately lit, preferably in such a way that the treads of the staircases are made still more obvious by the shadows they cast. Do take care, though, if you are using spotlights or other fittings with exposed bulbs to do the job. If these are positioned where people using the stairs might be dazzled, they could be as dangerous as having no lights at all.

ing light in order to operate the stereo or video recorder, but for most of the time, that light will be sitting around doing nothing. An easily adjustable spotlight could be the answer. When not needed as a working light its versatile beam can be directed elsewhere to play some other role in the lighting scheme.

The next step is to consider lights whose purpose is partly practical and partly decorative. These are lights used to highlight particular objects or collections of objects — lights pinpointing your favourite picture, or illuminating a collection of ornaments on a shelf. In many cases, spotlights are again a good choice for this sort of job, but there are other possibilities. Shelf and cabinet lighting for example, could be provided by small tungsten or fluorescent strip lights partially concealed by being mounted on the undersides of the shelves. Strip lights can also be used to illuminate pictures on the wall, and in fact you will find wall mounted lights specially designed for the purpose.

Finally, taking into account the effect of all of the above types of lighting on the room, think about installing lights that have a purely decorative value — lights that highlight certain features within the room, lights that cast interesting

Hardware
To complete the transformation of your rooms, give some thought to the hardware detailing.

The doors, for example, might well benefit from some new door furniture — door furniture more in keeping with

Bare brick and natural timber **above** *frame this fireplace attractively, allowing the enamelled cast iron stove and brightly polished steel fender to catch the eye.*

The strong colours in the curtains are complemented by the painted spiral staircase **above right**. *The unusual fish mural gives an illusion of descending into deep water.*

the new decor. There is an enormous variety to choose from here with knobs, handles finger plates, escutcheon plates, kick plates, key hole covers, lavatory latches, name plates and much more besides widely available in materials as diverse as gold plate and porcelain — though for those without a bottomless bank account, brass, aluminium, steel and plastic are the normal choices — and in styles ranging from ornate reproduction period pieces to modern fittings so sleek and brightly coloured as to be almost futuristic. Take a wander round a good specialist hardware store to get a taste of what's on offer. Walking into one of the better outlets is like entering an Aladdin's cave for interior designers.

The room's windows can also be improved with new catches and window stays. But don't forget the security aspect when choosing. In the average house a window is to a burglar what the front door is to you, so make sure that all windows on the ground floor, together with any on the upper storeys that can be reached by climbing extensions, drainpipes, and so on, are fitted with good quality window locks of some sort. Lockable stays, cockspur handles, and catches are best for the windows you use most frequently.

Elsewhere less convenient security devices such as dual screws (which literally screw the window to the frame) are more economical.

External doors also need good security. Although the majority can be adequately protected by a reasonable lock and a good bolt at top and bottom, the door by which you normally come and go (the 'front door') needs something more sophisticated — you cannot bolt it shut from the outside. Consider a good cylinder rim lock backed up by a mortise lock and a door chain as the bare minimum.

Door and window furniture isn't the only type of hardware you should be thinking about. In the hall and bathroom, think about adding bright new coat hooks. In the bathroom and kitchen, consider changing the taps to give baths, basins, and sinks a brand new look. Lavatories and bathrooms also give you the opportunity to introduce a great deal more hardware that is not only practical, but also helps add interest to the decor. There are towel rails, toilet roll holders, toothbrush holders, medicine cabinets, shaver sockets, soap dishes and more besides. Again, look round a good specialist hardware store, department store or 'designer' store to see what's on offer.

Page numbers in italics refer to
captions and illustrations.

A

abrasive, silicon carbide 266
accent colours 28, 33
access towers 242
acrylic paints 99
acrylics 304
adhesive
  contact 265
  panel 273
  PVA woodworking 265
  tiling 255
  wallpaper 249
advancing colours 28
aerosol 217
Agas 110, 113, 114
air-brick 200
alcoves
  laing carpets into 167
  papering 240, 251, 290
all-white rooms 24, 27, 28, 48, 56, 91
Allen, Janet 147
Allmilmö 110
aluminium 313
Ambrose Heal Collection 13
American Museum 98
Amsterdam 10, 24, 26, 58
Amtico 12
Anders, Peter 85
answerphones 79
appliqué work 21
Arbor, Caroline 17
Architectural Services 74
architrave 52, 273
archive prints 78-9
Arles 10
armchairs 49
Art Deco motifs 8, 10, 13, 54, 155
Art nouveau motifs 17, 57
Artemide 49
artificial flowers 93
Arts Council 8, 24
Ashley, Laura 16, 37, 39, 41, 45, 53, 120
Ashley, Nick 120
Atelier Martine 93
Auerbach, Frank 33
Austen, Jane 82
Avanti 62
awkward areas 158-63, 236
  basements 158
  halls 160-3
  lofts 160
  stairs 158-60

B

Babcock, Abi 70
backdrop, varnished cork 312
Baker, G.P. & J. M. 37, 39, 43, 45, 82
Baker, Herbert 26
balconies 73
bamboo 301
barbecue grills 116

barbecues 73
Barber, Gill 57
Barratt houses 50-2, 51
Barrow, Jean 13
Barstow, Joan 142
basements 158
basins 136-74, 149-50, 149
  fittings 141
  paintins 144, 144
  repairing 144
  see also sinks
Bates, Ralph 95
Bates, Virginia 95
bath and basin 269
baths 136-46, 147-8
  corner 146, 146
  fittings 141, 141
  repairing 141
  styles 147
  whirlpool 148
bathrooms 137-57
  accessories 150-2
  ceramic tiles 268
  colour 135, 138
  ensuite 151
  heating 157
  lighting 142, 156, 154-7
  one-room living 59
  plumbing 147
  radiators 69
  stencil decoration 155
  towel rails 152, 156
  ventilation 157
  walls 152
  windows 152
battens, timber 249, 252, 254, 258, 267,
    272, 273, 275, 285, 301, 305
  fixing 273
Bauhaus 10
Bazeley, Roger 20
Beaton, Sir Cecil 40
bedrooms 82-109
  children's 97-102, 96-102
  colour 88-97
  fabrics 88-91
  heating 105-6
  high-tech 85, 105
  insulation 106-8
  minimalism in 85, 85
  print bedrooms 90-4
  spare rooms 108, 108
  storage 102-5
  studies in 81
beds 82-109, 87
  furniture 52, 87, 93
  shelving 62
  bunk 98, 98
  children 48, 48
  four-poster 14, 14, 16, 82, 90, 94, 94
    107
  platform 97, 98
  sofa beds 108, 108, 109
  styles of 94
  tester 94
bedside lamps 104
bedsitting rooms 58, 109

bird window 243
black and silver highlights 310
blackboards 97
Blackheath 57
blankets, electric 106, 107
blinds 306-8
  bathrooms 152
  bedrooms 86
  children's rooms 98-100
  festoon 308
  made-to-measure 308
  pleated 306
  roller 306, 308
  roll-up 307
  roman 307
  venetian 102, 306, 307
block, standing 171
blowlamp 184, 187, 188, 196
blue 28, 36
Bl,umert 146
bolster, brick 171
Bonsack 142
books 48, 106, 107, 141, 142
bookshelves 106, 107
border tiles, laying 184
Bowman, Fielding 128
bradawl 267
Bradbury, Norman 95
Brandt, Bill 74
brass 313
bricks, flooring 127
broken tiles, replacing 179
Brown, Alan 142
brush
  artist's 223
  dusting 170
  paperhanging 238, 244
  'running in' 202
  scrubbing 171
  varnish 172
  wire 248, 171
brushes, cleaning and storing 202,
  208, 209
'brushing out' 203
built-in cupboards, bedrooms 102, 103
Bulthaup 122, 125
bunk beds 98, 98
Byrne, Margaret 50-2, 51

C

Campbell, Sarah 13
Canning, John 52, 70, 71, 99
carpets 68
  bathrooms 68
  colour scheme 296
  laying 294, 295
  lifting 191
  stairs 160
  tacks 293
  see also floors
Carrier, Robert 110, 118, 119
Casakit 74
Castle Coole 90, 126
Catskill mountains 16
cavity walls, insulation 67

ceiling
  beams 298
  cladding 275-8
  colour scheme 296
  cornices 14, 50
  ideas 297-303
  obstacles 244, 244
panelled and stained 302
  papering 242-5
  plasterboard 121
  preparing 182-3
  suspended 301
  rose 245
  tented effect 21
  tiling 266-70
ceiling tiles
  polystyrene 199, 267
  setting out 266
central heating equipment 209
Cézanne, Paul 34
Chaimowicz, Marc 10, 24
chairs
  knockdown 55
  living room 49
  Shaker 19
chalked line 244
Chalon 39
charcoal dust 223
Chassay, Tchaik 139
Chawton 82
children, beds 98, 98
children's bedrooms 97-102, 96-100
  floors 96, 97, 101
  lighting 98-100
  murals 101
  play areas 98
  safety 100, 101
  storage 100-2
chimney breasts 194, 240
China 36
chipboard furniture 55
chips, touching in 184
chisel
  bolster 296
  cold 194
chrysanthemum 36
cladding 273, 276
  fixing 274
  timber 272
cleaning
Clendenning, Max 119
climbing extensions 313
coach lamps 13
coat hooks 313
cockspur handles 313
Cole and Son 37, 39, 41
Colefax and Fowler 10, 21, 39, 43, 86,
  153
collages
collections 57, 62
  settings for 53
Collier, Susan 13, 122
Collier Campbell 37, 39, 43, 45, 49, 122
colour 28-45
  accent 28, 33
  advancing 28

all-white rooms 24, 27, 28, 40, 56, 91
archive prints 38-9
bathrooms 136
  in bedrooms 88-97
  characteristics 28
  children's bedrooms 101
  complementing 28
  document 90
  kitchen 119
  living areas 50-2
  neutral 30, 40-2
pale palette 42-3
pastels 19, 30, 31, 32, 91
schemes 307
'that dance' 44-5
warm 68, 68
colour wheel 28, 28
combination ladder 241
combing 228
combs, metal 223
complementary colours 28
computers 74-79
  games 76
  storage 76-77
concertina of paper 234
condensation 285
Conran 37, 62
Conran, Sir Terence, 74
convenience wallcoverings
  hanging 234
cookers 113-5, 113
  hoods 135
  safety 114
Coombes, Roger 74, 77
Copydex 236
corian surfaces 124-7
cork tiles 127
corners 236
  external 289
  internal 289
  turning 246, 237
cornices 14, 50, 301
  stripping and repairing 196
country kitchens 110, 112, 115
coving 275, 301
  ceiling 272
  fitting 300
cracks, fitting 181
Crete 61
cross-lining 245, 246
cupboards,
  bedroom 102-5
  kitchen 122-4, 110-35
curtain
  poles 301, 305
  track 304, 306
  and upholstery 304-6
cushions 55, 68
cut and paste 231
'cut-backs' 240
Czech and Spectre 141

D

dados 252
damp

penetrating 176
rising 176, 195, 272
damp-proof course (dpc) 176, 195
darkrooms, photographic *141*
Darwin, Charles 10
Davey, Dennis *65*
Day, Keith *14*
Design Council 21
Designer's Guild 30, *32, 41, 42, 43, 45*
designs
basketweave 301
diamond patterns 301
geometric 223
herringbone 301
mitred squares 301
photographing 223
transferring 223
desks 81
details, preparing 196-200
Dimbleby, Josceline 122
dimmer switches 73
dining areas 68-73
in kitchens 130-33
lighting 73
dishwashers 135
displaying objects 53, 55, 56, 61
children's bedrooms 100-2
shelves 61-3
Divertimenti *41, 43*
DIY plastering system 200
document colours 90
door
chain 313
furniture 312
doors and windows, papering round
238-9
double lining 173, 246
downlighters 48, 310, 312
drainpipes 313
drapes, beds 94
draughts 67
dressers *122, 125, 133*
dressing rooms *104*, 141
drill, electric *171*
'drop' 230
'drop pattern' 234
Drummond Patricia 148
Dulux *28, 93*
Dunham Massey *90*
Dunne, Michael *134*
d'Urso, Joe *27*, 59
dustsheets 173
duvets 105, *107*
Dux *62*

E

efflorescence 170
Eighteenth Century Company *82, 112*
electric blankets 106, *107*
electric fires 67
electric sockets
colour 50
safety 98, *99, 111*
electronic equipment 74-9
storage of 76-7

Elk, Ger van *10, 26, 139*
Elliott, Jon 85, *85*
Elliott, Ruth 85, *85*
Ellis, Perry 82, *82*
emulsion, bitumen 195
enamel, baths and basins 141, *144*
ensuite bathrooms 151
Erdigg *57*
escutcheon plates 313
Expressionists 33
extractor fans
bathrooms 157
kitchens 130, *130*

F

fabrics
archives prints 38-9
bedroom 88-91, 106-8
colours 30, 33, *33*, 44-5
curtains
drapes 302
grand style 14, 16
hall walls 161
hanging 248-9
living areas 52
modernism 24
neutrals 30, *40-1*
pale palette 42-3
pastel colours *10, 30, 32, 36*
removing 176
wall coverings *88*, 106-8,
walls and blinds *308*
face mask 220
faceplate 236
fans
bathrooms 157
kitchens 130, *130*
Farlow, Peter *14, 106, 141*
felt, paper-backed 278
filters, lighting 50
finishing touches 276, 303-13, *305, 306*
Finton Company *108*
fireplaces 63-66, *64-7*
as focal point *52*, 53
hand-painted *52*, 53
frame *313*
fire retardant 266
fires
electric 67
gas 66-7
open 63-6, *64-7*
fitted cupboards, bedroom 102, *103*
garnet paper 184
float, plasterer's *171*, 173
floorer, the complete 279-96
flooring compound,
self-smoothing 194, 195
floors and flooring
bathrooms *146*, 152-4
brick 127
carpets *see* carpets
children's bedrooms *96, 97, 101*
cork tiles 127
grand style *14*
kitchens 112, 127, *127*, 132
laundry rooms 135

living rooms 52
loft conversions *160*
preparing 190-5
quarry tiles 194, 195
rugs *36*
sanding *194*
stencilled *14, 68, 70, 71, 99*
tiles 127, *127*
utility rooms 175
vinyl *135*, 154
flowers, artificial *93*
flues 63, 65
fluorescent lighting 130, *131, 154*
flush windows 238
foamed polyethylene 236
focal points 53-5, 63, *64*
Foederer, Tom *86*
folding furniture 59
food storage 122, 123-4
four-poster beds 14, *14, 18, 82, 90,
94, 94, 107*
'Four Rooms' exhibition *8, 10, 24*
Fox Linton, Mary *37, 41, 43, 45, 94*
frames, pictures 50-5
friezes and borders *249, 52*
furnishings
bedrooms 86-8
colours 30, *32*, 33
slip covers 55
furniture
bedrooms 86-8
childrens bedrooms 100-2
country 16
folding 59
grand style 14
living areas 55
media rooms 76-7
one-room living, 59
painting *99, 123*
restoring *43*
Rietveld 24
Shaker *18, 19, 82*
stencilling *102, 110*
trompe l'oeil *123*
on wheels 59
wicker *13*
work areas 60-1
futons 13, *82, 85, 85*

G

Gagnère, Olivier *8, 26, 76, 80*
garnet paper 184
gas fires 65-6
gas hobs 66, *68*
gauge rod 254, 255, 267, 269
G-cramps 241
German Expressionists 33
Giacometti, Alberti 23
Giverny 10
Glasgow, Willow tearooms 10
glass
replacing 190
safety 200
stained-glass windows *24*
toughened 200

wired 200
glass fibre 199, 298, 304
glasspaper 197, 200, 206
gloss paint, applying 202, *212*
goggles 221
gold plate 313
Gough, Piers *8, 27, 55, 106*
Graham, Daphne *21, 53, 60, 61, 134,
153*
Grange, Jacques 14, 21
grand style 13-6
Gray, Eileen *10, 13*
Green, Hilary *79, 81*
greens 28
Grey, Hallie 55
Greg, Henrietta *90*
Grey, Henry *135*
Grey, Johny 121
Grigson, Jane 120, *120*
grilles, radiator 68
gripper strip 293, 296
groupings 16
grout 259, 262
grouting 287, *285*
grout line 254
Guild, Tricia 30, 31, *32, 33, 34, 132*
Gujarat 2, *61, 85, 87*

H

Habitat *37, 41, 43*, 123
Hadley, Albert 13
halls 160-3
lighting 162
staircase *252*
hammer
claw *171*
club *171*, 176, 194
pin 176
Hammond, Charles *37, 41*
handle, door 50
hangers 276, 277, 298, 291
hardboard 194, 272
laying *281*
tempered 173
hardware 312-3
Harrison, David 13
Hartford, Conn., *70*
Heal, Ambrose 13
heating
bathrooms 157
bedrooms 105-6
electric fires 67
fireplaces 64-7, *65-8*
gas fires 6-7
insulation 67
living areas 64-68, *64-67*
night-storage heaters 105
radiators 67, 68, 69, 105, *106*
stoves 64, 67
underfloor 68
warm colour schemes 68, *68*
height, illusion of *252*
Herengracht *41*
Herman, Bill *142*

Hicks, David *139*
high tech 22, *22, 26, 73*
bathrooms 157
bedrooms *85, 105*
Hiroshige 34
Hitchcock, Alfred *139*
hobbies room 108
hobs 115-6, *115*
Hockney, David 139
Hodgkins, Howard *8, 33*
holes, treating of 170
home computers 74-9
Hopkins, Michael *76, 85, 85, 105*
Hopkins, Patty *76, 85, 85, 105*
'hop up' 241
hot-air ovens 115
hot water 65
Howell, Georgina 22

I

Ideal Home Exhibition *51, 74*
illuminated ceiling 301
fitting 299
Impressionists 33
India 21, *40, 61*
Indonesia *36*
innes, Jocasta 21, 98
insect attack 299
insulation 265, *67*
bedrooms 106-8
loft conversions *160*
Interlübke 80

J

jacuzzi *145*, 148
Japan *36, 85, 85, 153*
Jayakar, Pupul 40
Jencks, Charles *26*, 85
Jiricna, Eva *8*
John Lewis Partnership *37*
Johnson, Lionel 94
joint finish 278
joists 190, 267, 275, *276*, 301, 305
Jonelle *45*
Jones, Chester *93*
Jones, Owen *38*

K

Kaplichy, Jan *73, 153*
Kaufman
keyhole covers 313
kick plates 313
Kinnarps 77
kitchens 110-35
choosing equipment 113-7
colour 119
country 110, 115, *122*
cupboards 122-41, *110-35*
dining areas *72, 73*
eating in 130-33
floor coverings *112*, 127, *127*, 132
lighting 130, *131*
planning 116-20, *116-7*

radiators *69*
safety 114
shelving *122, 125*
sinks 120-22, *121*
storage 122-4
units 123
utility areas 133-5
ventilation 130, *130*
wallcoverings 125
work surfaces 124-5
kitsch 21-2
Klein *157*
knife
broad filling 170, *171*
craft 265
sharp *171*
stripping *171*
knobs 313
knot holes, filling *189*
Kutch *61*

L

lace 94, *95*
lacquer *36*, 209
Lalanne, Francois 21
lamps
bedside 104
desk 310
floor 312
reading 310
table 312
Lancaster, Nancy 86
Lancelot Furniture *105*
Lane, Shirpa 94
laundry rooms 133-5
lavatories 136, *154*
lavatory latches 313
'laying on' 203
Le Corbusier 27, *85*
le Droff, Richard 66
Lee/Jofa *39*
Le Gates, Yann 74
Leigh, Sue 144
Leith, Prue *116*
Leveson, Caroline *14*
Leveson, Charles *14*
Lewis John 124
Liberty *39, 43*
libraries 48, 73
light boxes 60
lighting 308-12
background 310
bathrooms 154-7, 142, *156*
bedside lamps 104
cabinet 312
children's bedrooms 98-100
clip on 98
concealed *307*
dimmer switches 73
dining areas 73
downlighters 48
filters 48
fluorescent 130, *131*, 154, *301*
halls 162
high-tech interiors 26

kitchen 130, 131
living areas 48-50
low voltage 48, 163
reflections 48-50
shelves 63, 312
spot bulbs 48
spotlights 63, 130, *131*
strip 130, *131*, 154
studies 81
studios 81
track lighting 59, 63, 98
tube batten lights 63
lights
fluorescent strip 310, 312
pendant 310
tungsten strip 310, 312
wall-mounted 312
light switches 236, *245*
lining paper 173
hanging 245, *245*
living areas 48-73
cushions 55
displaying objects 61
flooring 52
focal points 53-5, 63, *64*
furniture 55
heating 63-68, *64-67*
uplighting 48-50
one-room living 55-61
proportions *56*
seating *49*
shelves 61-3
Lloyd Loom chair 49, *91*
locks, children's rooms 101
cylinder rim 313
mortice 313
lofts, conversion *160*
loose boards, fixing *192*
loose covers 304
Los Angeles 27
Louis Quinze 95
Love, Gilly *93*
low voltage lighting 48, 63
Lutyens, Edwin *26*

M

MacCulloch and Wallis *45*
Mackintosh, Charles Rennie 10, *28*
Maclean, William 79
McLuhan, Marshall 74
McNichol, Carol 21, *62*
Magistretti, Vico 16
Manhattan 142, *142*
Mann, Mani 82, *87*
mantelshelfs 53
marbled effects *52, 53, 106*
Margo international *41, 43*
marigold 36
Martex *82*
Marvic Textiles *37, 39, 41*
masking tape 200, 209, 220, 227
mastic, silicone 200
mastic gum *171*
matchboarding 172, 173, 176, 301
mattresses 59, *59*

Maugham, Somerset *17*
Maugham, Syrie 27, *40*
media rooms 74-80
medicine cabinets 313
metal, painting 196, *197*
micro computers 74-81
microwave cookery 115, *115*
minimalism 11, 27, 48, 50
bedrooms 85, *85*
mirrors
bathrooms 139, 150, *139, 146*, 154-6
children's rooms 98
halls 162
lighting *137*
on mantelshelfs 53
Mlinaric, David 13, *57, 90, 126*, 88-100
Mobus + *105*
modernism 22
modular shelving 61
Molenaar, France *149*
Moloney, Karen 59, *59*
Monet, Claude 10
monochrome schemes 28, *28*
Monsoon 82
Montgomery, Stephen 16
mortar
beds 285
mix 287
Morris, William *38*
Morrow, Laurie 55
Mortiz, Ulf *64, 78*
mosaics
applying 262
ceramic 262
laying *263*
Mosiman, Anton 124
motif and colour *225*
mouldings 180, 199, 275, 301
and cornices 14, 50
murals, children's bedrooms *101*
painting 223, *224*
Murphu beds 59, 108
muslin 301

N

nailing, secret 272
nail punch 195
nails
annular 194
masonry 272
plasterboard 276
screw 194
wood 272
nameplates 313
National Consumer Council 65
National Trust 16, *57, 90, 126*
Neff 113, 115, *115*
neutrals 30, *40-2*
New Delhi *40*, 82, *87*
New York 14, 59, 85, *86, 146*
Nice Irma *41, 45*
night storage heaters 105
Norton, Bill *112*
Novamura 172

O

obstacles, papering round 236
obstacles and corners *275*
office areas 77, 79, 80-2,
Ohrbach and Jacobson *146*
oil-based paints 99
old wallpaper
painting over 172
removing 172
Oliver, john 37, *39*
One Off *98, 104*
one-room living 55-61
bath furnishings 59
beds for *109*
furniture
open weave fabric 301
optical illusion 168
oranges 28
orient, inspiration from *12*
Oriental textiles 21
Osborne and Little *37, 41, 153*
ovens 113-5, *113, 131*
overalls *171*
overlaps 246, 248

P

paint
acrylic 99
celluose 221
emulsion 214
grout 176
non-drip 205
oil-based *99*
powder 223
resin based 176
paint, applying *215*
paint brushes
cutting in *202*
50mm *202*
radiator *202*, 209
25mm *202*
wall *202, 221*
paint colour charts
painter, the complete 202-228
painting
architraves 209
central heating radiators 209
doors and windows 205-6, *206*
furniture *99, 123*
kitchen 127
metal window frames 209
pipework 81
rails 206
skirting boards 81
sliding sash windows *206*, 215
stiles 206
walls 212, *205*
with a brush 202-209
with a pad 214-6
with a roller 210-3
woodwork 204
paintings 27, *34, 42, 47, 87*
bathrooms 142, *142*
children's bedrooms 101

hallways 162
inspiration from 10
trompe l'oeil 162, *123*
paint kettle 205, 210, 225
paint pads
cleaning and storing *215*
crevice *215*
cutting-in *216*
disposable 216
edging 216
large wall *216*
loading *217*
small *216*
standard wall *216*
paint rollers
extension handle *210*
felt 248
foam sleeve *212*, 216, 221, 248
mohair 212, 216
natural fibre *212*
180mm and metal tray *212*
radiator *212*, 213
sheepskin 212
synthetic fibre *212*
paint shield *202*, 209
paint strippers
chemical 187, 188, 190, 196, 197
hot air 184
liquid 188, 197, *186*
paste 197
steam 172
paintwork, stripping 185
paneller, the complete 211-7
panelling 180, 272
pantries 123
paper
abrasive 170, *170*
embossed 180
paperhanger, the complete 229-52
papier mâché 195
paste
heavy-duty 234
ready mixed 248
starch based 248
paste brush 234
paste granules 234
pastel colours 10, *30*, 31, *42*
in bedrooms *91*
pasting 230
and folding *43*
table 230, 234
patchwork 95
pattern, on walls and ceilings *251*
Pawlson, John 50, 85
pegboard 81
pendant light 245, 270, 310
petroleum jelly 220
Phipps, Diana 10, 123, *123, 148*
pictures
27, *52*, 53-5, *82*
framing 53-5
grouped *57*
rails 252
trompe l'oeil 162, *123*
Pike, Max 199
pine cladding *142*

pins
masonry 293
panel 267, 276
plasterborad 173, 276, 301
filling joints in 182
plasterwork, ornate 199
plastic 313
play areas, children's bedrooms 98
plumbing, bathrooms 147
plumbline 230, 238, 240, 248, 252, 255, 260
plywood 195, 272
varnished 278
polystyrene, expanded 199
porcelain 142, 313
Portugal 60
Post-Impressionists 34
post-modernism 46-7
Prelle et Cie 126
preparing to paint 203
Prestel 77, 79
primer
all-surface 184, 278
aluminium wood 184
calcium plumbate 196
wood 184
zinc chromate 196
primer-undercoat 184
print bedrooms 90-4
prints 14
hallways 162
proportions, of a room 56
Puck and Hans 64, 78, 128
purples 28
putty 200
PVA building adhesive 194

Q

quadrant beading, timber 200, 261
quarry
laying 285
sealing 286
tiles 287

R

radiators 68, 69, 105, 106
thermostat controls 67
Raj furniture 87
Rajasthan 61, 82
razor blade 209
ready-pasted papers, hanging 235
rebate 200
record players, storage 79-80
Redmile, Antov 21
red 28, 36-7
refrigerators 122, 123
relief decorations, hanging 246-8
relief finishes 221
Renoir, Pierre Auguste 34
restoring furniture 54
retro 95
Rhodes, Zandra 21, 86
Rietveld, Gerrit 24
Riley, Bridget 28

Robertson-Smith, Michael 79
roofs, insulation 67
room dividers: one-room living 59
shelving 62
Roquebrune 10
Rug Shop 21
rugs 36
country style 16
rust 197
inhibitor 197

S

Sackville-West, Vita 16
safety
children's bedrooms 100, 101
in kitchens 114
Sallick, Robert 135
sander
belt 171, 195
floor 197
heavy duty disc 197, 198
orbital 170, 170
Sanderson, Arthur, and Sons 37. 39, 41, 45
sanding drum 184
Sapper, Richard 49
scaffold board 181, 242, 244
scaffold tower 183, 241
Scandinavian furniture 13
scissors, paperhanger's 230
scraper
flat 187
serrated 223
wallpaper 171
screw-eyes 298
screws, dual 313
scribbing 290
scumble 228
seam roller 246, 248
seams 291
seating, living areas 49
Sekers 41, 43
setting out 281
Shaker interiors and furniture 16, 19, 82
shavehook, combination 171, 187
shaver sockets 313
sheet lifting 191
shellac knotting compound 84
shelving 106, 310
bathrooms 150-2
facing strips 63
kitchens 122, 125
lighting 63
living areas 59, 61-3
supports for 62
Sheppard, Peter 14
showers 136, 142, 148, 148
sideboards 54
Signac, Paul 34
silicone exterior sealant 176
sinks, kitchen 120-2, 121
Sissinghurst 16
'Six Views' Collection 13
Skarston scraper 172

Skelzo 20
skirting boards
Skrine, Fiona 102, 155
slats, timber 301, 307
slip covers 55
sloping ceilings, papering 244
Smallbone of Devizes 110, 118
small-scale living 55-9
soap dishes 249
sofa beds 108, 108, 109
soffit 240, 308
solid floors 194
patching 193
solvent, petroleum-based 265
Sony 279
Souleiado 37
soundproofing 81
bedrooms 106
utility areas 135
space, children's bedrooms 100-2
Space Design Group 157
spacer lugs 258, 261
spare rooms 108, 108
spatter effect 228
special rollers, using 212
special tecniques, painting 221-8
spiral staircases 160, 313
spirit level 252, 254, 255, 259, 265, 272, 285, 305, 308
splashback 259
split cane 307
spluttering 221
sponge 171
sponging 223, 222
spotlights 63, 312
children's bedrooms 98
clip-on 310
kitchens 130, 131
spray gun and compressor 217, 221
spray painting 217, 220
application of 219
cleaning a gun 220
preparation 218
spreader, notched 255, 259, 262, 280, 292
stabilizing primer 181
stained ghlass 24
repairing 199
stains, bleaching 188
stair-gates 101
stairs
carpeting 160
open tread 158-60
space under 158-60
spiral 160
stairwells, papering 241-2, 241
staple gun 249, 267, 276, 302, 88
steam stripper 171
steel 313
steel wool 170
Stefanides, John 61
stencil brush 225
stencilling 226, 227
bathrooms 155
furniture 102, 110
wooden floors 14, 68, 70, 71, 99

stencils 225, 228
stereo systems, storage 79-80
stipple 223
stopping compound, ready-mixed 183
storage
bathrooms 148
bedrooms 102-5
children's bedrooms 100-2
computer equipment 76-7
kitchens 122-4
loft conversions, 160
work areas 81
stoves 64, 67, 158
Strangeways, Christopher 21
straw
strip lighting 130, 131
bathrooms 154
stud partition walls 272, 275
studs 272
studies 73, 80-81
in bedrooms 81
in spare rooms 108
studios 80
lighting 81
style 8-27
bathrooms 139-47
country style 16-21
grand 13-6
high-tech 22, 22, 26, 73, 85, 105
inspiration 10-5
kitsch 21-2
minimalism 11, 27, 50, 85, 85
modernism 22
post modernism 26-7
surrealism 21
sugar soap 187
surrealistic style 21
Sutherland, Graham 93
Sutton-Vane, Mark 149
switch
cord-operated pull 312
dimmer 310, 312
on/off 312
remote control 312
security timer 312
two-way 312

T

table cloths 126
tables
bedroom 154
dining 72
kitchen 132, 132, 133
taps 312
Tamesa Fabrics 41, 45
taps, bathrooms 141, 141
telecommunications 79
telephones 79
teletext services 79
television 74, 76, 77-80
in bedrooms 105
storage 79-80
television room 108
templates 280, 290, 290
tented ceilings 21

tester beds 94
textured finishes, removing 117
textures
all white rooms 40
tone and 30
texturing compound 221
texturing the surface 221
Thompson, Jim 94
Thomson 74
three-piece suites 59
thresholds 286, 291
threshold strip 293, 296
Tibet 36
Tihany, Adam 139
tile cutter 258, 262
tiler, the complete 253-270
tiles
basic techniques 254
bathrooms 136, 139, 146, 152-4
carpet 280
ceramic 91, 254, 258, 285, 292
cork 262-5, 280, 285, 264
corners and edges 259
expanded polystyrene 256, 257
fixing 266
floors
grouting 258
kitchen floors 122-4
marking up 55
opaque fibre acoustic 301
quadrant 261
quantity chart 254
quarry 285
ready-sealed 266
REX 263
setting out and centring 254, 254, 259, 280
tongue-and-groove fibre 266, 267
vinyl 280, 293
window reveals 260, 260, 261
tiling, floor-to-ceiling 269
tiling round obstacles 261
Tissunique 39, 43, 45, 57, 90, 126
toilet roll holders 313
toilets 136, 154
tone, texture and 30
tongue-and-groove board 195
tortoiseshelling 52
Toulemonde Bochard 41, 43
towel rails 152, 156, 313
toys, children's bedrooms 96-100
track lighting 59, 63, 98
trellis garden 298
trestle
decorator's 242, 248
painter's 181
Tricel, pleated 304
tricky areas, tiling 259
trimming allowances 234
trompe l'oeil 225
on furniture 123
in halls 162
trowel, pointing 171
tube batten lights 63
tumble driers 133, 134-5
Turkey 19, 60

turntables, storage 79-80
Tye, Alan *96*

U

unbacked fabrics, hanging *247*
undercoat 203
underlay 194, 195
upholstery, slip covers 55
USA, country style 16, *19*
utility areas 133-6
   applicances 134-6
   flooring 136
Utrecht 23

V

Van Gogh, Vincent 10, 53
Vane Percy, Christopher 81
Vario cupboards *125*
varnish
   polyurethane 266, 285
   stripping 190
varnish stains 202
   Velsen, Kroen Van *128*
Venetian blinds, colouring 102
Venice *14*
ventilation, bathrooms 157
   kitchens 130, *130*
Vidal Gore 74
video games 76
videos, storage 79-80
vinyl 292, *12*
   bathrooms 154
   'easy strip' 172
   kitchens *127*
   ready-pasted 234
   sheet 280, 287, *288*
   utility areas 135
Vuillard, Edouard 10, *34, 42,* 90

W

Wadley, Peter *79*
Wagner, Sherle 144
Walker, Maureen *49, 64*
wallboards 272, 273, 276
   fixing *277*
wallcoverings
   Anaglypta 173, 246
   convenience 234
   embossed 234, 246
   fabric *311*
   grasscloth 248
   hessian 248
   washable 234
   woodchip 173
wallpaper, stripping *174*
wallpaper, quantity guide 230
wallpapers 14, 38-45
   grand style 14
   hanging *235*
wallplates 275
wallplugs 275, 305
walls
   bathrooms 152

children's bedrooms 97-8, *101*
cladding 272
colour 28-45
cornices 14, 50
fabric coverings *88,* 106-8
grand style 14, *14*
halls 161
insulation *67*
kitchens 125
masonry 272, 275
pictures 27, *52,* 53-5, *87*
preparing 170-177
trompe l'oeil 162
walls, paperhanging 230-234
   basic techniques 230-234, *232-3*
wall tiles
   ceramic 173
   cork 173
warmth, colour schemes 68, *68*
   furnishings 68
Warner & Sons 40, *41, 43, 45*
washable paper, stripping *175*
washing machines 122, 133, 134
Waterworks 135
West One 144
wet-and-dry paper 205
whirlpool baths 148
white rooms 24, *27, 28, 40, 56, 91*
white spirit 184, 188, 196, 205, 209,
   214, 266
whole tiles, laying *282*
wicker furniture *13*
Williams, Christopher 59, *59*
Willow tearooms, Glasgow 10
window
   bathrooms 152
   blinds 86
   catches 313
   child-proofing 100, *101*
   displays 14
   locks 313
   reveal 240, 246
   seats 158
   stained glass 24
   stays 313
wire, galvanized 298
wire brush 197
wire wool 197, 266
wood
   filler 183
   mosaics *191*
   rot 176, 190
   staining and varnishing *207*
woodgraining 228
woodwork
   preparing for 183-9
   washing and sanding 183
woodworm and rot damage, repairing
   189
word-processors 74-6
work areas 60-1
work surfaces, kitchens 124-5
Wrighton 120, *120, 132*

ACKNOWLEDGEMENTS

Interviews with decorators, designers and architects are the cornerstone of this book so my list of acknowledgements begins with a thank-you to Judy Brittain, editor of the 'Living' pages in British 'Vogue' who commissioned me in the first place to collect information from many sources for her pages. Among the many designers who contributed their working plans and ideas to this book, I would like to thank in particular Susan Collier and Sarah Campbell — their great sense of style can be seen in their textile designs on the front cover, and throughout the book; Tricia Guild of Designer's Guild for her inspiration on colour; David Hersey, the theatrical lighting expert for Broadway and West End musicals, whose patient explantions of the principles and practicalities of lighting in the home clarified a complex subject. My special thanks to the art editor of Quarto, Nick Clark, for making the book beautyful as well aspractical; to editors Emma Johnson and Lucinda Montefiore for shaping the book into its present readable form; to Catherine Carpeter for editing the American edition; to Keith Bernstein for picture research; and to team-mates from the 'Brides and Setting Up Home' magazine days; Christine Knox who collected the fabric swatches from many sources, and Anne Holker who helped to compile capitons and the directory of suppliers, working at speed with good humour and professionalism. Pictures from many sources are credited elsewhere but I would like to single out for my thanks those publicity officers and public relatins officers who helped to produce working drawings and photographs for this book: Sheila Fitzjohns, Juliette Hellman and David Farquhar, Fiona Wiley of Tina Caprez Associates, and Barbara Lovelt of Paul Winner Marketing Communications. I would also like to thank the following photographers who were particularly helpful: Christine Hanscomb, Karen Bussolini, John Vaughan, Michael Dunne, John Wyand, Michael Boys and Ken Kirkwood.

PICTURE CREDITS

Key: (tr) — top right (bl) — bottom left; (t) — top; (m) — middle; (r) — right; (t) — bottom; (l) — left; EWA — Elizabeth Whiting & Associates

p8 Arts council of great Britain; p9 Christine Hanscomb; p10 Arts council of Great Britain; p11 John Vaughan; p12 Amtico; p13 Christine Hanscomb; p14 Chrstine Hanscomb (tl), Settocento (tr); p15 John Wyland; p16 EWA; p17 Christine Hanscomb; p18 Karen Bussolini; p19 Walter Rawlings; p20 Mark Ross; p21 EWA; p22 Ken Kirkwood; p23 John Vaughan; p24 John Vaughan; p25 John Vaughan; p26 John Vaughan; p27 John Vaughan; p28 Rowney; p29 Dulux; p30 EWA; p31 John Vaughan; p32 Michael Boys; p33 Michael Boys; p34 Musée de Grenoble/photo Ifot, Grenhole; p35 Trustees of the British Museum, London (tl), Tate Gallery, London (tr), National Museum of Wales, Cardiff (bl); p48 Christine Hansbom; p49 Options: Syndication International Ltd; p50 Options: Syndication International Ltd; p51 Barratts, Margaret Byrne; p52 EWA (l), Karen Bussolini (tr, br); p53 EWA; p54 EWA (t), Stirling Roncraft (b); p55 EWA; p56 EWA, p57 Tissunique (t), EWA (b); p58 John Vaughan; p59 Steve Shipman; p60 John Wyland; p61 John Wyland; p62 EWA; p63 Dux Design; p64 EWA (tl, tr, bl), Options, Syndication International Ltd (br); p65 John Vaughan; p66/7 © Karen Bussolini, 1981. Reprinted by permission of House Beautiful's home Remodeling, © 1982 by the Hearest Corporation; p68 EWA; p69 EWA; p70 Karen Bussolini; p71 Karen Bussolini; p72 Christine Hanscomb; p73 John Vaughan (1) Ken Kirkwood; p74 AKai (UK) Ltd; p75 La Maison Marie Claire; p76 EWA; p77 John Heseltine; p78 John Vaughan; p79 Sony (tl), EWA (tr); p80 Ken Kirkwood (tl, m); p81 Chris Drake (tr); p82 Martex; p83 Karen Bussolini; p84 Ken Kirkwood; p85 EWA; p86 Mark Ross; p87 EWA (t), James Mortimer (b); p89 Christine Hanscomb, Collier Campbell Fabrics (t & br); p90 Tissunique; p91 Martex (t), Dulux (bl), EWA (br); p92 Options, Syndication International Ltd; p93 EWA (r), Dulux (tl); p95 EWA; p96 Ken Kirkwood; p97 EWA; p98 One Off Ltd, London; p99 Karen Bussolini; p100 EWA; p101 EWA; p102 John Vaughan; p103 Fiona Skrine; p104 One Off Ltd, London; p105 Finnemore & Field (UK); p106 EWA (1), Christine Hanscomb (r); EWA; p108 Denis Groves Ltd (UK); p109 EWA; p110 Smallbone of Devizes (UK); p111 Almilmo; p112 Karen Bussolini; p113 Neff (UK) Ltd; p114 EWA (tl), Neff (UK) (tr); p115 Smallbone of Devizes (UK); p119 EWA (t), John Vaughan (b); p120 Wrighton Kitchens; p121 EWA (tr & tl), Neff (UK) Ltd (b); p122 Michael Dunne (1) Bulthaup Kitchens (r); p123 EWA; p124 Bulthaup (t), Ken Kirkwood (bl), EWA (br); p125 Bulthaup; p126 Tissunique; p128 John Vaughan (t), © Karen Bussolini, 1981. Reprinted by permission of House Beautiful's Home Remodelling, © 1982 by The Hearst Corporation; p129 Karen Bussolini (m), John Vaughan (t); p130 EWA (m); p131 Bulthaup (r); p132 Wrighton Kitchens (l), Michael Boys (m); p133 John Wyand; p134 EWA; p135 EWA, p136 EWA; p137 John Vaughan; p139 Mark Ross (tl), John Vaughan (tr); p140 EWA; p141 John Wyand; p142 Ken Kirkwood; p143 Karen Bussolini; p144 EWA; p145 EWA; p146 Mark Ross; p147 EWA; p149 John Vaughan; p151 EWA, Michael Dunne (m); p153 Ken Kirkwood; p155 Fiona Skrine; p156 Zehnder Radiators; p157 Mark Ross (t), EWA (b); p158 EWA; p159 EWA; p160 Ken Kirkwood; p161 EWA; p162 EWA; p163 Ken Kirkwood; EWA p190 T Leighton (t & b); p225 M Dunne, M Nicholson (tr), M Nicholson (b); p250 Dennis Stone; p251 C Helm (tl), Eigenhuis (tr), T Street Porter (b); p252 S Powell (l & r); p259 T Street Porter (b); p278 M Dunne; p287 G Chowanetz; p292 C Helm; p293 J Tubby; p296 J Tubby; p302 M Nicholson (l), C Helm (r); p304 m Nicholson; p305 T Leighton; p306 M Nicholson; p307 S Colby (t), C Helm (b); p308 M Dunne; p309 S Powell; p310 M Nicholson (t), C Helm (b); p311 J Bouchier; p312 EWA; p315 J Tubby (l), m Nicholson (r). From p181-313, all photographs by Rose Jones, unless otherwise indicated.